MW01627443

SS Panzergrenadier

Other works by Hans Schmidt

Books:
Jailed in 'democratic' Germany (in English)
End Times/End Games (in English)
Endzeiten/Endspiele (in German)
Deutschlands Zweite Stunde Null (in German)

Brochures: (all in English)
German Hegemony in Europe
Das Deutsche Reich und die USA
Will the United States lose Germany to Russia

Newsletters:
Ganpac Brief (in English, monthly since 1983)
Amerika-Brief (in German, monthly, 1988-1991)
USA-Bericht (in German, monthly, since 1992)

plus articles and esssays in both languages

SS Panzergrenadier

A true story of World War II

by Hans Schmidt

First Edition

Copyright © 2001, Hans Schmidt

Published in the United States by Hans Schmidt.

All rights reserved. No part of this publication may be reproduced or transmitted in any form or by any means, electronic or mechanical, including photocopy, recording or any information storage and retrieval system, without permission in writing from the author/publisher. Short excerpts for book reviews are excepted from these restrictions.

Requests for permission to make copies of any part of the work should be mailed to:

Publisher:
Hans Schmidt Publications
P.O.Box 11124
Pensacola, Fl 32524
Fax 850-478-4993

Schmidt, Hans 1927 -
SS-Panzergrenadier, *a true story of World War II*

ISBN No. 0-9669047-4-5

1. Schmidt, Hans, 1927 -
2. Soldiers - Germany - Biography
3. Germany - History - 20th Century
4. Military history - Elite units
5. World War, 1939-1945 - German Armed Forces - Waffen-SS
6. Germany - National Socialism
7. Personal Narratives, German

First Edition

Printed in the USA

We thank the following for permission to quote excerpts:

Colonel Trevor N. Dupuy, from his book "Hitler's Last Gamble", HarperCollins Publishers, New York, 1994
Robin Lumsden, from his book "SS, Himmler's Black Order, 1923-45" Sutton Publishing, Stroud, Gloucestershire, England, 1997
General Michael Reynolds, from his book "Steel Inferno", Sarpeton Press, New York, 1997

Other highly recommended books concerning this subject matter:

"Battle of the Bulge, then and now" by Jan Paul Pallud,
After the Battle magazine, England, 1984
"Hitler's Ardennes Offensive" ed. by Danny S. Parker,
Greenhill Books, London, 1997
"Hitler's Last Gamble" by Trevor N. Dupuy,
Harper Collins, New York, 1994
"SS - Himmler's Black Order 1923-45", by Robin Lumsden,
Sutton, England, 1997
"Steel Inferno" by Michael Reynolds,
Sarpedon, New York, 1997
"Uniforms of the SS" (6 volumes) by Andrew Mollo,
Windrow & Greene, England, 1992
"Waffen-SS" by Keith Simpson,
Gallery, New York, 1990
"Waffen-SS Soldier 1940-1945" by Bruce Quarrie & Jeffrey Burn,
Osprey, England, 1993
"Weapons and Fighting Tactics of the Waffen-SS", by Drs. S. & R.Hart,
MBI, Osceola, 1999
"Wenn alle Brüder schweigen" a large book of illustrations,
MUNIN-Verlag, Germany, 1973
Der Freiwillige, the monthly magazine of the German
Waffen-SS veterans, MUNIN, Germany
Siegrunen magazine and books, Richard Landwehr,
P.O.Box 6718, Brookings, OR 97415
"Other Losses" by James Bacque, Stoddard, Toronto, 1989
"Surrender of the Dachau Concentration Camp"
by John H. Linden, 1997

Dedicated to the brave soldiers

from many countries who

during World War II

fought with the Waffen-SS

in the defense of Europe,

the cradle of Western

Civilization.

Their sacrifice was not in vain.

Contents

Prologue

My situation could not possibly have been worse. It seemed I had but two choices: Quick death by an American bullet right between the eyes, or there was the somewhat slimmer chance of dying a slow death by freezing. Even while the incessant shooting by the enemy riflemen was still going on, I could not help noticing the horribly cold water from melting snow creeping up on me from the ground, seeping through all the clothes I was wearing, eventually encasing, with all its wetness, that part of my body which I was forced to press into the ditch so that none of the Americans would notice me.

Then and there I was certain that this was going to be the worst day of my life, should I survive this ordeal. Unfortunately, the great possibility of dying through a well-aimed American bullet did not prevent, for the first hour or so of my ordeal, a deadly fear overcoming me, a fear that was exacerbated by the realization that I could not survive as motionless as I had to be for the few hours until dark, without succumbing to hypothermia.

Then I heard it: One shot after another hit the dying boy lying less than a hundred feet in front of me, the blood from the resulting wounds coloring the snow around him red. Almost every time the young soldier was hit, probably when one of his bones was shattered or when a bullet grazed his head, he let out a weak, plaintive cry. It sounded like the helpless yelp of a young dog being kicked by cruel boys. In quieter minutes, when there was a momentary lull in the artillery barrages of friend and foe, one could hear the boy sobbing. But the enemy showed no mercy: Some of the GIs obviously wanted him dead, and used this human being as a target for their shooting skills.

For the rest of my life I never understood how American soldiers could so cold-bloodedly fire at that unarmed, wounded boy soldier who was at first running, then lying crying in the deep snow so close to their positions. This happened hours after our one-sided skirmish, and long after I had seen GIs come unhesitatingly out of their fox holes and search for "souvenirs" among the many German dead a good stone's throw in front and to the side of me. The guys from across the Atlantic were in no danger, and in my opinion their shooting now was, war or no war, pure, callous murder. For myself I can only say that I never could have done what I witnessed on this ice-cold afternoon of the 12th of January 1945 in the Ardennes forest. Only a few days earlier, while I was in charge of a forward machine gun emplacement, we saw a Jeep occupied by three American soldiers driving nonchalantly along a narrow field road through the snow-covered landscape, totally oblivious to the fact that they were within easy shooting distance of the German infantry. They had obviously lost their bearings. As my machine gunner lifted the MG-42 to "finish off" both the Jeep and its occupants, I merely gave him the sign not to shoot. Since the Americans had not seen us there was no reason to expose our position to them and others, and I did not believe that the outcome of the war would hinge on killing three enemy soldiers who were at this moment no danger to us. A similar situation developed months later, in April of 1945, on the Eastern front while we were fighting the Russians in our last battles of the war.

Since my dying comrade was closer to the Americans than to me, they must have heard his last plaintive call, *"Heinz, Heinz, so helf mir doch."* - - "Heinz, Heinz, why don't help me?" - - while another, and this time the last, round of bullets tore into his body. But his buddy Heinz never came. He too was probably lying dead somewhere nearby on these frozen fields, one of the many victims of our failed mission. Finally, the dying boy lifted his helmetless head once more, and then he was lying as still as the hundred or two hundred other German soldiers who had earlier in the day lost their lives in the meadow.

The dead and I had been part of an ill-fated attempt to regain an important crossroads not far from Bastogne in Eastern Belgium during the now famous "Battle of the Bulge". That I had not been hit in the furious American fusillade that surprised us on our way to the crossroads will forever remain a puzzle to me, for my few comrades in front of me, and all those from our squad following single file, had been killed right away. From my vantage point I could see many of their lifeless bodies lying grotesquely where they had fallen.

For me, the worst of it all was that I was forced to lie absolutely still for what seemed an eternity. Any movement at all could cost my life. For an hour or so after we ran into the ambush, the Americans had made a sport out of shooting at anybody and anything that moved, and there were times when bullets hit the ground so close to me that I thought I was the target. Perhaps it was the tree line directly behind me, and the fact that a small clump of weeds shielded my face, that had made me somewhat invisible to the enemy soldiers. And, although I was in a shallow ditch, possibly a hole from a tree felled long ago, I was located on slightly higher ground than the killing fields.

As the American soldiers were shooting at the young soldier, I felt like just getting up from my hiding place, walking over to the GIs and asking them whether they were crazy or worse. But without a Red Cross flag this would have been pure suicide. A half century later, discovering which enemy unit had been on the opposite site, it is likely that even the Red Cross emblem wouldn't have saved me from being killed had I attempted to rescue my young comrade. These Americans belonged to the same unit that was mentioned on page 119 of famed U.S. General James M. Gavin's book "On to Berlin," where he describes a D-Day incident that would most certainly have been called a war crime had the shooters been German soldiers:

"It was anticipated that the newly arrived U.S. 90th Division would pass through our bridgehead that night and launch an attack against German positions in the morning. Fresh from the boats, just at dusk they marched from Ste.-Mere-Eglise toward the causeway, getting more apprehensive with each kilometer. The

signs of battle - - the dead, knocked out vehicles, and scattered equipment - - were everywhere. As they made the last turn approaching the causeway, a column of German prisoners unfortunately emerged from the stone buildings on the other side and started across the causeway. The 90th opened up with everything they had. But their jitteryness soon disappeared, and they went on to relieve Captain Rae and the small band of parachute troops who had accomplished so much that day."

(Considering the circumstances we can assume that these German soldiers were unarmed and had their hands up as a sign of surrender. And having no weapons, they most certainly did not fire back. The way the incident is described, we must assume that the German POWs were already under American guard. Furthermore it is interesting to note that the otherwise meticulous General Gavin left it up to the imagination of the reader to guess how many German POWs were literally executed in this massacre. I doubt that there was ever an inquiry: The alleged *Malmedy Massacre* of American soldiers ascribed to my division was months away.)

I had been lying in that icy ditch but 10 km east of the heart of Bastogne for several hours, when this German boy soldier, judging from his appearance perhaps seventeen years old, came running out of a line of hedge rows to the right of me that was largely beyond my view, dragging his obviously wounded left foot in the deep snow. But instead of trying to reach German lines that were somewhere far, perhaps a mile or more, to the rear of us, or lifting his arms in surrender and going over to the Americans, he ran in his panic exactly parallel to the front, about equidistant from where I was lying, and the American lines, resulting in his horrible death.

While the boy was being killed, I had, for five or ten minutes at least, forgotten my own predicament. But as the hours passed I noticed the icy cold of the wet snow atop which I was lying finally creating an excruciating numbness on the underside and in the extremities of my body. Eventually there were moments when I just wanted to go to sleep, and forget about this insane war, the Americans, the snow, the hunger and the stupid shooting around me.

Once, just when I almost felt warm and cozy in that white bed of ice crystals, - - the onset of hypothermia? - - I was suddenly awakened by a new sound of incoming shells: Having been trained on these heavy guns I knew that the rounds were from a battery of German 155mm (s.I.G.33) howitzers, each of whose grenades weighed almost a hundred pounds. As was normal, the first rounds of the German artillery were somewhat short of the enemy positions, the next four shells went over the target, and the third barrage of rounds following immediately was supposed to explode right in the center of the enemy positions. Alas, this did not happen: all the German grenades fell right between the bodies of my dead comrades, and, in succeeding barrages, even much too close to me. In addition of having to fear of being killed by the Americans, or slowly freezing to death, I now had to worry about being torn to shreds by exploding shells of German origin.

I assume the German battery did not have a forward observer but aimed at the target from predetermined markers in the area, like the tower of a church, a stand of high trees, or the roof of a farm house. This can easily lead to errors in the desired distance, and in this case it led to the shells exploding but 30 to 100 feet in front of the enemy line. Guessing that the Americans would be somewhat distracted by the shelling, I used the opportunity of an incoming barrage to slowly glide back in the ditch for a few yards behind some of the thicker trees framing the large open field. I could still observe the enemy soldiers but now there was less chance of being seen by them. I left my damaged rifle where I had first dived to the ground when the shooting began, but I took the two hand grenades I had carried on my person with me, and placed them next to me, the strings to the fuses ready to be pulled in a second, if necessary. Alas, I had not used them when the Americans were looking for souvenirs: the GIs were just out of my throwing range, and I had not used them when they killed the boy, for the same reason. Still, the grenades gave me the slight feeling of again being master over my own fate. Surveying, from my new vantage point, a possible way back and out of sight of the Americans, it was quite clear that retreat was impossible as long as daylight lasted. Many more dead German soldiers were lying behind me than in front, namely in the open expanse between the enemy and myself.

Having amble time to do so, I watched the incoming howitzer shells exploding at the bottom of the meadow, and then I tried, by looking at the deep craters and which way the black earth had been thrown, to estimate the trajectory at which the shells had burst into the ground and from which direction they probably came. As a result, I guessed the distance between the cannons and my position to be about 4,000 meters, and that the battery of four guns was located due north of the Bohey/Doncols crossing that had been our target earlier in the day.‡

As the hours went by, and while I was waiting for the promising envelope of darkness, my thoughts went to my family, to all of whom I did not know where they were now, or even if they were still alive: to my mother and four siblings who had been evacuated for the second time in the war from the Saarland about a month earlier because the enemy had come within sight of our house; to my father who was stationed as an occupation soldier somewhere in Norway; and to my older "Navy" brother Richard from whom I had last heard months ago when Greece was still in German hands, and the German *Kriegsmarine* was guarding the Mediterranean.

I was thinking, "how did I get into this predicament of being close to losing my life at the young age of seventeen years and eight months?" Not having anything else to do, except keeping an eye on

---

‡ A quarter century after this incident, in the winter of 1970, I had a chance to visit the Bastogne area for the first time since the war. Showing my father, who accompanied me, where I had almost lost my life, I pointed to a good map of the area which I had procured, and told him that the likely position of the German 150mm howitzers had been at or near the village of Niederwampach, four kilometers due north. To discover whether my assumptions were right, we drove to this remote farm village with the intention of asking an older person who remembered the war whether he or she recalled any heavy German artillery pieces having been firing from that area.

Once we had arrived in Niederwampach we did not have to ask anybody: next to a farm house, probably still near the position from where it was last fired, we discovered one of these heavy guns, a German s.I.G.33, with obvious signs of 25 years of total neglect and of having been used that long as a childrens' plaything. During a visit 10 years later, one of the wooden wheels was broken, and some of the metal shields of the gun had rusted away. An old farmer told us that the Americans captured the village on January 13th, 1945, and that it was then when the guns fired their last rounds.

Now this particular cannon has finally found its permanent place in history: The good citizens of Niederwampach erected a concrete pedestal at the entrance of their village and placed the repaired howitzer on it. There it stands now to commemorate the battles that took place so long ago, in the unforgettable winter of 1944/45, and for me and my descendants it will forever be one of the heavy cannons that was one of the four shooting "at me."

the Americans, I even tried to figure out the additional days but by then I was so numb that I was unable do it.

In Memoriam

A sculpture by Paul Bronisch. Exhibited in 1941 at an art exhibition in Munich. As with so many "Nazi" art objects it is likely that this sculpture was destroyed by Allied soldiers after the "Liberation".

Chapter 1

I was only twelve years old when World War II began on September 1, 1939. At the time few Germans believed that the justified incursion of the *Wehrmacht* into Poland (certainly more justified than were similar American military incursions into Mexico in 1916, and into Panama and Grenada in the 1980s) would turn into a World War lasting almost six years. How well I remember that following fateful Sunday, September 3, 1939, when, already evacuated from our home located near the *Westwall* zone (the German fortifications along the border with France), I went to my great-grandmother, *Oma Busse*, and asked her what it meant when two nations were in a "*Kriegszustand*" (state of war), for that is what I had then just heard on the radio would henceforth exist between the empires of Great Britain and France on one hand, and the German Reich on the other.

"*Kriegszustand* means war, and a horrible time to come," *Oma Busse* answered. None of us would then ever have dreamt that toward the end of this war I would not only be a combat soldier but would also lie in the snow, slowly freezing to death, not very far from where *Oma Busse* was still living, just having celebrated her 90th birthday. She would eventually die in 1954, two weeks shy of her 100th birthday because the attention of the news media had been too much for her to handle.

For Germany, World War II officially lasted from September 1, 1939, when the German campaign against Poland began, to May 8, 1945, when the *Wehrmacht* capitulated unconditionally. Without question there is some truth to the argument that World Wars I and II together were really one Thirty Years' War, the second one in a millennium in the continuing battle for hegemony over Europe. The first Thirty Years' War lasted from 1618 to 1648, the second from 1914 to 1945, but this argument will really only be settled by history long after we are all gone.

There was not a day during this time when I did not follow the course of events, having begun to read the daily newspapers by the time I was ten, a couple of years before the war, when the Spanish Civil War had dominated both the world's headlines and my attention.

By 1943 World War II had taken a decidedly bad turn for Germany when the remnants of the Sixth Army had been forced to capitulate at Stalingrad at the end of January. Of the 250,000 men encircled in this city on the Volga river, 2,000 kilometers from Germany, 90,000 survivors went into Russian captivity after some of the fiercest hand-to-hand fighting of the war, and of those but 5,000 or 6,000 ever saw Germany again. When the spring thaws in and around Stalingrad permitted the burial of the corpses of fallen soldiers that had given their lives for their countries, 125,000 dead German soldiers and perhaps ten times as many soldiers of the Red Army needed to be buried.

While 1942 had been a relatively normal year for us in spite of one major British air raid on my home town of Saarbrücken that destroyed much of the inner city, including the beautiful new opera house but none of the surrounding steel mills and the many other plants producing war materiel, 1943 brought one great defeat after another. Soon after the survivors of the 6th Army had surrendered at Stalingrad, the remnants of the Afrika Korps experienced a similar fate in Tunis in May of that year, and in the following September Italy switched sides, leaving the fighting on the Italian peninsula mostly to German troops. In July of 1943, in the Kursk salient of the Eastern front, the greatest tank battle in history had taken place, with the Wehrmacht having been unable to reach its objective. In the second half of 1943 the American Eighth Air Force had joined the British Royal Air Force in attacking targets inside Germany, with one large German city after another being gutted, and many famous edifices of a thousand years of German culture being destroyed. The year 1943 was also the time when the German U-Boats incurred their greatest losses, with the best of the U-Boat commanders losing their lives in the cold waters of the Atlantic. They had found their match in the radar-equipped ships and planes of the Western allies.

In April of 1943 I had turned sixteen years of age. At the time I was employed in Saarbrücken, the capital of the German province of Saarland near the French-German border. I was in my second year as a business apprentice at the *Kohlenhandelsgesellschaft "Westmark"*, the privately owned coal trading corporation - - a part of a larger, super-capitalist monopoly - - that had official wartime control over the distribution of coal in the entire Saar, Palatinate and Lorraine region, then part of the German Reich. The work itself was boring and, in a way, hard for a teenager who hated to sit for hours in front of a typewriter, sending out delivery orders, or entering endless numbers into a ledger. But there was a war going on in which most of the men normally performing these tasks were in the Armed Forces, or elsewhere in the service of the government. Instead, old World War I veterans, young housewives, and boy and girl apprentices between the ages of 14 to 18 years of age, such as myself, kept things running. We did amazingly well, I must admit. Besides doing regular work we also had to attend special classes pertaining to our profession, and on every second weekend it was my duty to keep watch in our office buildings in case the British RAF dropped incendiary bombs that could be doused before doing too much damage.

Richard, my older brother, had completed his duty in the Labor Service (*Reichsarbeitsdienst* or RAD) between November of 1942 and February 1943, almost immediately thereafter joining the Navy (*Kriegsmarine*) as a volunteer. With him being but a year and a half older than myself, this meant that from the fall 1943 on I had to seriously contemplate which branch of the services I was going to join. One thing was clear, especially after the disaster at Stalingrad where an inordinately large number of regular Army infantrymen from the Saarland had been lost: I had no intention of letting myself be drafted and becoming an infantry soldier on the Eastern front.

By volunteering, I had a much better chance to be assigned to units in more exotic places like in the Mediterranean theater of operations, in France or even in Denmark or Czechoslovakia, where the food was supposed to be still plentiful. Throughout the war I did miss good bread, butter, honey, and especially fine desserts with lots of whipping cream.

If in the fall of 1943 someone had asked me which branch of the services I really wanted to join, I would have said the *Luftwaffe* (Air Force). Due to the fact that Richard had already joined the Navy, and considering the never-ending sibling rivalry between the two of us, this part of the German armed services was eliminated from the start. But often having seen huge flying armadas of the Allies, frequently consisting of hundreds of four-engine bombers, making their way at great heights resolutely and seemingly untouchable above the Saarland toward the East, into the Reich, I had the sincere wish to become a fighter pilot and to assist our flying aces, such as Adolf Galland, Hermann Graf, Hajo Herrmann, Walter Nowotny, "Bubi" Hartmann and others, in shooting down the "Lancasters", the "B-17s" and the "B-24s" of the British and the Americans. Alas, after inquiring at the *Luftwaffe* recruiting office it became clear that all I could hope for in the German Air Force was being assigned to an anti-aircraft unit. I simply did not have the educational prerequisites to become a pilot.

Even a good friend of mine who had been a member of the *Flieger*-HJ (the branch of the Hitler Youth closely connected with the Air Force) and who had earned his wings as a glider pilot, was never accepted to the *Luftwaffe* pilot program because he did not have the "*Abitur*", the stringent German high school diploma. Adolf Galland, the fighter ace who became the commanding General of the German fighter pilots at the end of the war, lamented this stupid policy in his book "The First and the Last".

Up to about a year before the end of the war, the Waffen-SS was the only branch of the German Armed Forces whose losses at the front could not be made good through induction of draftees. Theoretically at least the Waffen-SS was an all-volunteer army, and some of the high-ranking Generals of the regular army were anxious to keep it that way; they obviously feared the competition. The result was that SS efforts to get the cream of the crop of potential volunteers were finely tuned, and special attempts were made to discover boys with leadership qualities in the cadres of the Hitler Youth. Surviving recruitment posters of the Waffen-SS still show the efforts that were made to dig into the Hitler Youth reservoir of future manpower. To the best of my (later) knowledge, the Waffen-SS did not have a barracks or training grounds in the entire Saarland. Most were located in the center of Germany, in Bavaria and Austria, and also in occupied areas such as in the protectorate of Bohemia and Moravia, former Czechoslovakia, and in Holland. This meant that I had little contact with this service before I joined it.

The only SS soldiers I had ever had some direct contact with before donning the uniform with the SS runes on the collar patch and the German national emblem (the eagle with outstretched wings holding a wreath with the swastika in the circle) on the left upper arm of the tunic, were the two Jähne brothers, Kurt and Heinz, both exemplary Hitler Youth leaders from our town; Kurt Thiel, a distant cousin and neighbor, and one of the apprentices of our company who had joined just when I started at the firm. All four of them would eventually give their lives for Germany.

Even in the fourth year of the war, the occasional Waffen-SS soldiers on furlough in Saarbrücken left, as a rule, a better impression than the infantrymen home from service on the Eastern front. The Waffen-SS fellows walked more erect, their uniforms were better fitting and in better shape, and there is no doubt that the awareness of belonging to an elite unit contributed to the proud bearing of the young soldiers who wore the names of their famous divisions like *Das Reich, Totenkopf, Wiking, Adolf Hitler, Hitlerjugend,* and others, on their sleeve cuffs.

I do not recall when I first went to an SS recruiting office to inquire about joining. It might have been in the summer of 1943, shortly after a small group of us, all minor Hitler Youth leaders, had been invited by the regular army to attend a weekend retreat (actually a ploy to get us to volunteer) at the Army-Panzergrenadiers at Landau in the Palatinate. I found it all very interesting and we all were touched by the cleanliness of the relatively new barracks, and the good food we received. The officers we dealt with, all highly decorated men, also left us with a good impression. Furthermore, there is no question that we admired the new weapons shown to us, such as the MG-42, the new assault rifle, night-vision goggles and hand-held anti-tank rocket launchers. We were told that much more new weaponry was in the offing. What I didn't like was the asinine barracks drill I was able to observe from the distance. On the very weekend of our retreat, a group of new draftees had arrived at this training facility, and some overzealous drill instructors made the most of it. The new arrivals seemingly had all their uniforms and boots just thrown at them without regard to their sizes, and the spectacle before us had the quality of an Italian comedy as the poor fellows hobbled in their ill-fitting outfits from one place to another, constantly being harassed by screaming asses, namely the most obnoxious drill instructors (DIs) one can imagine. I knew from the

Waffen-SS soldiers of my home town that in this branch of the German services Hitler's orders of "no stupid barracks drill and no mean-spirited DI harassment" had been (generally) followed. But obviously the Army drill instructors still stuck to their old ways. This experience eliminated the regular Army once and for all from my considerations, and soon thereafter I visited the Waffen-SS recruiting office in Saarbrücken to garner information.

In November of 1943, the Hitler Youth allocated a few places for a fortnight of semi-military exercises at a *Wehrertüchtigungslager* (in short, "WE-Lager": "military training and fitness camp") to the HJ-units in our area. As a minor Hitler Youth leader I was in position to name those boys who could participate, and I did not forget to place myself on the roster. The WE-Lager system had been instituted in the middle of the war in order to provide teenage boys with some of the necessary military skills that did not involve the use of weapons. While the overall organization of these camps was in the hands of the Reich offices of the Hitler Youth located in Berlin, all the instructors were officers and non-coms of the four armed services who due to injuries or other reasons could no longer do combat duty. Here I must mention that the WE-Lager system of that time can in no way be compared with the so-called "Boot camps" or even military schools available to American youths of the present. Here and now it seems endemic that the grown-ups in charge of such institutions should, in many cases anyway, not be entrusted with young people. The many horror stories we read about are, unfortunately, all too true.

My boss at the *Kohlenhandelsgesellschaft* was not very happy when I told him that I would be absent for about half a month. Particularly since he had to continue paying my meager salary while I was away. The fact is, he couldn't do anything about it. But I enjoyed my stay at the WE-Lager near Bergzabern in the Palatinate. The instructions we received there focused largely on how soldiers ought to behave in the field. For instance, how to dig proper fox holes, how to camouflage, and how to find our way with a compass. But most important for me was the fact that the food rations we received was good and plentiful.

At the Bergzabern WE-Lager I also had my first contact in the war with officers and non-coms of Austrian extraction. I found them much more likable and easygoing than *Reichsdeutsche* (Reich Germans) but no less German in their outlook. The truth is that of all the Germans from the many tribes that constitute the German people, to this day I regard the South Tyroleans, men from part of our people cut off from greater Germany by the post-World War I treaty (really a dictate!) of St. Germain, to be not only the all-round best soldiers but also the best Germans in spite of the fact that according to the papers they carried they were Italian citizens.

An inordinately large number of volunteers of Austrian, Bavarian, and other German tribal background coming from Southern Germany and Southeast Europe served in the Waffen-SS. I therefore maintain that this elite corps that began in the late twenties as a paramilitary unit more or less based upon the ideals of the much more strict Prussian military code of honor, eventually turned into a symbiosis of the two main lines of Germandom, namely of Prussia and Austria. This undoubtedly accounted for the fact that the Waffen-SS spirit was much more free and tolerant than was the German military as a whole. One British expert on the subject even ventured the idea that by war's end the Waffen-SS had become the most 'democratic' outfit among the German armed forces.

When I finally went to a Waffen-SS recruiting office to enlist, I was told that due to my age I needed written permission from both of my parents, and that really nothing could be done until I had a draft board classification. Due to the length of the war, and as a result of the increasing air activities of the enemy, it was no fun anymore to remain in formerly quite livable Saarbrücken. Except for some artificially sweetened tea, and also artificially-made clear beef broth, and probably low-alcohol beer, by then nothing could be bought in stores or eateries without ration coupons.

The Saarland is a small German province of about one million people living on roughly 1,000 square miles of land. Meaning, it is much overpopulated. The soil is poor, and not conducive to profitable, large-scale farming. A large part of the food consumed in the Saar area has always been imported from German agricultural states or from neighboring Lorraine and Palatinate provinces. This fact, plus the result of the first evacuation lasting from 1939 to 1940 that had emptied the warehouses, resulted in the Saarlanders from the start of the war having to sacrifice on food essentials. Still, the people didn't complain and continued, along with the Ruhr and the Upper Silesian industrial areas, to provide the basis for the German industrial war potential. Taking the shortages in stride and remembering better times are not the

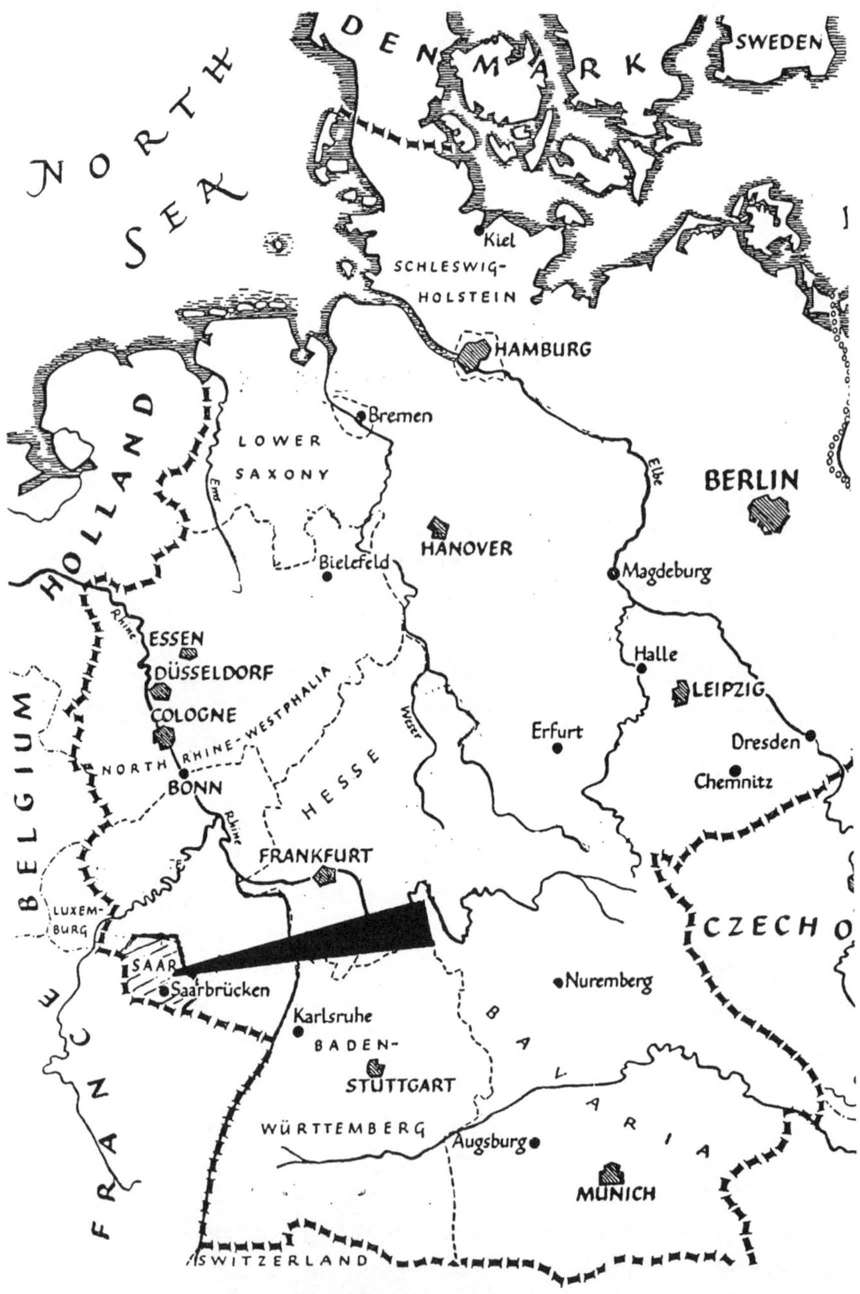

Note little Saarland in the lower left corner of Germany. Population one million. The Saarland is only twice the size of Eglin AFB in Florida. Saarbrücken, the capital, is about 600 kilometers from Berlin but only 400 km from Paris if one uses the autobahn.

same thing. It sometimes happened that on a tram to Saarbrücken one neighbor would ask the other good naturely whether he was traveling to the inner city to visit the "1-2-3" (an 'American'-style "automat" restaurant similar to Horn & Haddards in New York) or whether he was going to have a piece of *Marzipan Torte* at the famous Schlosscafe. - - - Both of these places were, unfortunately, by then dismal looking ruins.

(An allegorical story about Berlin in 1945, fitting to the above: An American occupation officer takes a ride in a street car filled with Germans. He listens to their stories. Then, somewhat surprised, he says to an older German next to him that he is shocked by what he is hearing:

"Sir, I thought the Germans were a people of culture, but all I am hearing is talk about food and other necessities of life that are now missing. However, if one rides in a subway of New York and listens to the people there, one can always hear them speak of things pertaining to culture. What do you have to say about that?"

"Well, Herr Offizier, there is really an easy explanation for this phenomenon: People always like to speak of the things they do not have!")

The fall weather in late November 1943 was quite miserable; and the city was partially destroyed, dark (due to the blackout), cold and dirty. The concussion bombs that had been dropped onto the main business district of the city had not only created many ruins but had also left a choking veneer of cement dust that seemed to penetrate into every corner and lie on every cornice. In addition, from the doused fires of the incendiary bombs the obnoxious stench of burnt houses permeated most buildings. For young people like us there was nothing to do anymore except perform war-related duties such as being air raid wardens in our office building on alternate weekends, or to assist, with the *Feuerwehr-Hitler Jugend*, the fire engines after the enemy planes had dropped their bombs.

After Stalingrad all "unnecessary" businesses had been shut down, and that included places where one could dance. Those movie theaters that had not been reduced to rubble, like the famous UFA-Theater in Saarbrücken, or had been confiscated by the government to serve as sleeping quarters for the huge number of all sorts of foreign workers assigned to our war industry often showed films that were both outdated and uninteresting. Volunteering for one of the services was the only way to get away from these miserable conditions.

Within weeks after I had come back from the WE-Lager, all the boys born in 1927 were ordered to appear at the local draft board, there receive their classifications. This was accompanied by a thorough medical examination. Due to my heart murmur, the legacy of scarlet fever in 1938, when I was eleven, I was classified "KV" (kriegsverwendungsfähig: "okay for wartime service," similar to "A1" in the United States) with the caveat that I ought to serve only in the artillery where I wouldn't have to run much. I have stronger than average bones and this assured that I would be able to lift 100 pound artillery shells. When I protested, the doctor changed his recommendation to "*Sturmartillerie,*" meaning the tank-like vehicles without the traversing turret of a normal *Panzer*.

My parents signed my enlistment papers for the Waffen-SS, "for four years, or for the duration of the war, whichever is longer," only reluctantly. Both thought that at 16½ years of age I was still much too young to be a soldier. I countered their arguments with the fact that my father's brother Richard had been only 18 years and 3 months old when he died at the Russian front in 1916, during World War I, and he had been about the same age as I was in late 1943, when he joined the Ulans, the light cavalry, in 1915. Besides, the fellows at the Waffen-SS recruiting office had told me that there was only a slim chance for me to be called up before my 17th birthday in April of 1944. At this stage of the war, efforts were still made not to send any soldiers into combat who had not reached their 18th birthday. But, obviously, there were exceptions.

My father, who was stationed at some desolate spot on the Norwegian coast, was objecting more to my enlistment than did my mother. Besides the issue of my young age he also did not care much for the Waffen-SS because of the pre-war antagonism, or rivalry, that existed between the leadership of the NSDAP (the Nazi party), to which he belonged, and the black or Allgemeine SS. (In fairness it has to be stated that he didn't care much for the SA, the brown-shirted storm troopers, either.)

It must have been soon after Christmas of 1943 when I received not just one but two induction notices within a few days of each other. Both were accompanied by proper marching orders and the papers needed to use the railroad system from Saarbrücken to the assigned place. Today I have forgotten which notice came first, but one was from the Waffen-SS with the assignment to some sort of noncommissioned officer's training school in Prague, and the other came from the RAD (the Labor Service) for a three months' tour on the North Sea island of Borkum.

I was elated to finally get away from the drudgery of the office. To be away from the family was never a problem for me. Even as a young child I did not tend toward *Heimweh*, homesickness, that affects many other people. But the receipt of two induction notices within a short time, giving me a choice in the matter, proved to be one of those numerous fateful "coincidences" that would impact my life greatly.

I often had the feeling that a "guardian angel" was watching over me, and this incident in the war was but one such occasion. I discovered the proof of the ramifications of this 1943 occurrence only about 20 years later during a visit to Germany when I met the person again who had reported to the Waffen-SS in Prague in my stead: Hans Balzert, one of the other apprentices at the office of the *Kohlenhandelsgesellschaft Westmark*, had been born in 1926 and should have been drafted already but, seemingly, none of the armed services was very anxious to have him. I assume that his physical condition was not up to par. Like myself, Balzert did not want to be drafted into the Army infantry and be shipped to the Eastern front. He also hated to keep on working at the "KHG Westmark," as we called the company for short. On the day I appeared at the office with the two induction notices in hand and showed them to my co-workers, Balzert was the first to ask me what was my choice. The fact was, I couldn't make up my mind. In assigning me (obviously because of my Hitler Youth leadership activities) to some sort of school, or, better, to a special course, the Waffen-SS had undoubtedly sweetened the pot for me. And although I had always liked the sea and was anxious to breathe the fresh air of the North Sea, I also knew that the weather up there in Northern Germany was much colder than either in the Saarland or in Bohemia at this time of the year. And I had always disliked both cold weather and cold water. It was Balzert's idea that in any case I ought to go to the island of Borkum and the "RAD" first. He did mention that after three months I would join the Waffen-SS no matter what, and perhaps get an even better assignment than Prague. (I knew that this was highly unlikely since it was well known that of all the areas within the realm of the Reich the food in the *Protektorat Böhmen und Mähren* was still the best. There, the milk was supposed to be still undiluted; the sausages were supposed to be as fine as we remembered them from before the war, and - allegedly - one could still purchase cake and cookies without ration coupons. Up to then there had also been no air raids on cities or towns within the former Czechoslovakia.) One day Hans Balzert begged me to go with him to the draftboard so that the civil servants there could just change my marching orders for Prague over to him, by replacing my name with his. And that is exactly what we did. He went to Prague, and I traveled to Northern Germany. Immediately after the war, when I was still in the Saarland and had resumed my apprenticeship at the "KHG Westmark", nobody knew what had happened to Hans Balzert except that he had been missing on the Eastern front since the middle of 1944. I also discovered that he had been assigned to the SS Division "Wiking," composed mostly of non-German, albeit "Nordic" volunteers, who had enlisted in order to fight Bolshevism. At our office, where his sister still worked, we all presumed that Balzert was dead. By the time I left my homeland to emigrate to the United States, the fate of my replacement 'alter ego' to Prague was still unknown.

Finally, in 1961, 16 years after the war, I was able to visit Saarbrücken again (in the meantime I had been busy trying to get all my family, except our parents, to immigrate to the United States,) and after being informed that Hans Balzert had eventually returned from a Soviet prison camp, we met again. Since this fellow's fate might have been mine, had I gone to Prague instead of to the North Sea island, I was especially curious to discover what had happened to him. This is what I found out:

Once Hans Balzert got to Prague in the winter of 1944, he was not assigned to the non-commissioned officer's training that had been planned for me. Instead, he went through a few short months of intensive basic training, and was soon shipped to a combat unit. When in the summer of 1944 the entire center of the German Eastern front collapsed, as a result of treason, and more soldiers went into captivity than had been lost at Stalingrad, Balzert was among the POWs who found themselves being shipped to the far reaches of the Soviet empire. A few years after the war, after having been held for about four or five years in the brutal GULAG (while all this time his family suffered from not knowing whether he was dead or alive), he was released due to illness. When I met him in 1961 he had still not fully recovered from his ordeal, and to the best of my knowledge he was sick for the rest of his life. - - - - Would that have been my fate if I had gone to Prague instead of to the *Reichsarbeitsdienst* on the island of Borkum???

Eight of the male apprentices of the KHG Westmark at Saarbrücken in late 1942. Eventually, four of us served in the Waffen-SS. Two died for Germany, Hans Balzert (bottom row on the left) spent years in a Soviet prison camp. I am standing in the top row, second from left.

Chapter 2

My decision to complete my Labor Service duty first had proved to be the right one. Not yet seventeen years of age when I arrived on the island of Borkum, I was still growing, and both the fresh, salted air of the North Sea, and the decent food we received in this agricultural area near the Dutch border, did wonders for our bodies. The physical labor we performed, most of it consisting of camouflaging heavy German coastal batteries with greenery, and erecting so-called "Rommel Spargel" (Rommel Asparagus: Telephone poles pounded into the beach sand to thwart potential glider landings by the Allies), strenghtened our muscles.

One day we camouflaged the emplacement of a 280mm (15") gun with sod so that it could not be too easily discovered by enemy forces should they try to land on Borkum (an unlikely event). Always being nosy, I discovered that the barrel of this gun had once been placed on the World War I battle cruiser *"Moltke,"* and was used against the British fleet in the Battle of Jutland (German: *Skagerrakschlacht*). Barrels of heavy guns have sometimes to be replaced after heavy use, just as is customary with the barrels of rapid firing machine guns, and I assume this particular barrel had been taken off the "*Moltke*" in 1916 and hidden from allied inspectors who roamed Germany after the signing of the Treaty of Versailles. Among many other things, Germany was allowed only a very limited number of such heavy artillery pieces by the World War I victors.

The *"Moltke"* itself was part of the German high sea's fleet that was delivered to the British Navy as a condition of the November 1918 armistice, and "interned" at the British Naval base of Scapa Flow in the

Orkney Islands. However, on June 21, 1919, when the harsh conditions of the Treaty of Versailles became known, according to which Germany was permitted no navy to speak of, and only an army of 100,000 soldiers, and no air force, Admiral von Reuter, the commander of the interned fleet, gave orders to sink all his ships in the Scapa Flow anchorage. In one day, 10 battle ships, 10 battle cruisers, 9 small cruisers and 46 destroyers sank beneath the waves of the North Sea.

In peacetime the Labor Service was not armed and did not receive weapons instructions, and all barracks drill was performed with highly polished spades. But during the war this changed, and besides the earth moving tools we were also issued military hardware such as rifles, gas masks, helmets and the like. Our rifles were leftover *Gewehr 98* from World War I. This weapon differed from the German standard rifle of World War II, the Gewehr 98k ("k" for kurz: short) generally only in that it had a longer barrel and was therefore somewhat difficult to handle for young boys. On the other hand, the longer barrel assured greater accuracy, and just as in the Hitler Youth, I did well in shooting competitions. Apart from the fact that the food was good and sufficient, to my surprise we were occasionally also able to purchase additional items such as figs and oil sardines from the commissary. And there were also a few days when we could buy half-litter bottles of cheap wine. That most of us were quite underage never seemed to matter in this respect. At the time I had not yet developed a taste for wine, and I used my allocation to buy myself out of KP and guard duty, both of which I hated.

The most memorable events of my three months on Borkum were the shooting down of an American P-51 (Mustang) fighter plane by the nearby anti-aircraft battery "Lüderitz": the American "Jabo" ("**Ja**gd **bo**mber" - fighter bomber) flew too low over our base, and finally crashed into the sea, and the discovery on the beach, and subsequent blowing up by experts, of a large round enemy mine that had been dropped into the Ems river estuary.

About the shooting down of the American P-51 I remember this: One day, we were sitting in the mess hall and enjoying our simple lunch, probably some heavy stew or soup fortified with a heavy slice of dark bread upon which margarine or jam was spread, when in the distance we heard the violent shooting of light anti-aircraft guns intermixed with the angry noise of an enemy fighter bomber making turns. There had been no alarm, but we knew enough to dive underneath the heavy tables where we were sitting. It took but a minute and the plane flew directly over our barracks, still spewing bullets from its machine guns. Being curious, we ran to the window facing the North Sea, only to see the P-51, already afire, crashing into the ocean. The plane had been flying so low that there was not the slightest chance for the pilot to have safely ejected. I doubt that I finished my meal.

The incident with the enemy sea mine, a huge round ball of steel filled with explosives lying on a stretch of beach where we were pounding telephone poles into the sand, is worth mentioning only because some of my comrades went within a yard or so of the thing, looking for who knows what. I clearly remember seeing the little fingers with fuses sticking out of the mine, the breaking of which upon colliding with a ship would cause a tremendous detonation. Being mindful of the explosive power of a mine, I kept what I considered a safe distance immediately after we had discovered the thing. But when demolition experts of the *Kriegsmarine* arrived to blow the mine up, they laughed when we showed them what we had considered a safe distance: More than three times further away than we had thought would *perhaps* have been okay.

Someone in Berlin, or wherever the assignments to the various RAD units were decided, must have had a macabre sense of humor when he selected young men from two different coal mining areas of Germany, namely, the Ruhr and the Saar valleys, to serve together at the *RAD-Abteilung 5/195* on the isle of Borkum. That was comparable to recruits from the most staunch Confederate areas of the United States being placed into the same barracks with Irish descendants of some of the most famous Union regiments.

Well, that is what happened to us. Not only were we placed in the same company but also in the same room that was to be the home for twelve of us for the next three months. The dozen of us boys were about equally divided between Saarlanders and, as we called them in an unflattering term, Polacks from the Ruhr. Severe friction was foreordained, especially because the Ruhr guys wanted to play the bigshots from inside the Reich while many Germans still regarded the Germans from the Saar as being only half-Germans as a result of their two decades' absence outside of German borders.

One day the obnoxious and high-handed attitude of the Ruhr guys got too much for us, and I stated our opinion in no uncertain terms.

Somehow it had happened that I had become the spokesman for the Saarlanders, and a heavy-set coal miner's son with a Polish surname acted as the unelected leader for the Ruhr fellows. The inevitable happened: When I once more complained about some *bagatelle,* the big Ruhr fellow told me to shut up or else he would use his undoubtedly strong physique to do so. I, not easily frightened, challenged him to try it. No sooner had I said that, and I was totally knocked out by the expert right-hander of an trained boxer. As it happened, I had challenged a former boxing youth champion of the Hitler Youth for a fight.

For a week or so I walked around with one of the largest shiners one can imagine. At the time I did not think that almost a year later a similar, visible injury would save me a lot of trouble while in American captivity. Alas, in the *Reichsarbeitsdienst* fights between the recruits were strictly prohibited, and especially those recruits who caused injury to someone else could get in lots of trouble. When I was asked by the company commander how I got the black eye I insisted that it happened at night when I allegedly fell out of the high bunk bed. I know he did not believe me but let it go at that. The non-commisioned officer who ran the everyday chores of the company was not as benign, he saw to it that for my alleged stupidity of falling out of bed (or was it because I did not snitch?) I was assigned to three days of KP, *Küchendienst.* To this day I remember the huge mountain of potatoes that had been boiled in the skin, and which I had to peel. My one-punch boxing defeat did not impair my reputation among my comrades. The Saarlanders were grateful that I had stood up for them, and the guys from the Ruhr appreciated that I did not snitch on my adversary. The result of this incident was a greater civility among all of us.

One incident of a somewhat tragi-comic nature has to be told because it shows how at a young age I reacted when faced with a difficult decision:

One day, during field exercises in a large dune area, our group of perhaps ten or twelve young RAD boys was accidentally separated from the company, and decided to make the best of it. In other words, we purposely stayed lost for longer than necessary. Suddenly we came upon a small enclave of prefabricated buildings that seemed unguarded but were surrounded by thick strands of barbed wire. The entire area was marked with large signs "BETRETEN VERBOTEN!" (Entry forbidden). Well, it was precisely this prohibition that piqued our curiosity, and it didn't take us long to crawl underneath the barbed wire into the forbidden zone and somehow enter one of the pre-fabricated buildings. What we had discovered was the officer's lounge of a secret command center of the German *Luftwaffe,* well equipped with soft arm chairs, comfortable sofas, and a refrigerator stocked with soft drinks. There might even have been some cigarettes for the smokers but of that I am not certain anymore. What we did was play "gentlemen" for an hour, lounging about in the cozy surroundings and enjoying some of the sodas. We took care not to damage anything. Once we were back at our barracks, we kept mum about our find, hoping that someday we could go back for a return visit.

A few days later the entire company was suddenly ordered to dress in the best uniforms, assemble in the center of the barracks area, and assume a parade position in the form of an open square. At the opening of the formation a lectern decorated with the swastika flag had been placed, and as soon as everyone stood at attention, our commander accompanied by a few high-ranking Luftwaffe officers marched scowling onto the square, and spoke to us from the lectern.

Due to the platoon I belonged to, and because of my size, I was standing right in the center of the first row of the middle platoon, facing our commander and the Air Force officers directly. As the commander spoke I had the feeling that he was really talking only to me. The officer explained that a few days earlier a group of Labor Service men had broken into a secret headquarters of the Luftwaffe, and there created havoc. Because the secrecy of this Air Force installation had now been compromised, the General in charge of the entire Northwest German area had demanded that the culprits responsible for this heinous act ought to be severely punished. However, a review of all RAD companies that could have been in the general area of these headquarters on that particular day did not point to a specific unit, and therefore this assembly had been called in order to discover who was responsible. Thereupon the commander ordered all those who participated in this "crime" to step forward and accept the punishment they deserved.

I was in a quandary. I knew that the entire company would face restrictions, punishment exercises and the revocation of certain privileges, like going to the movies on weekends, if no one admitted his part in the break-in. On the other hand I was also fairly certain that not one of the other guys who was with me inside the headquarters would step forward because most were essentially cowards. Furthermore, there were not many other RAD units stationed on Borkum (if any others at all) and, come what may, some sleuthing by the officers would eventually discover the real culprits. I had but a few seconds to make my decision, but then I gave myself a moral push, took three steps forward, out of the first line in the direction of the officers, and reported merely with "Arbeitsmann Schmidt zur Stelle!" ("RAD man Schmidt reporting, Sir.") At the same time I was listening intently whether anyone else had stepped forward with me. As I had expected, no one did. Our commander stepped closer to me, asking in a loud voice, so that everyone could hear it, whether I was at the secret installation on that particular day, something I readily admitted. Was I alone? What could I say but yes. Was anyone else with me in the headquarters? I denied that there had been anyone else with me.

After a few more questions our commander stepped back and spoke with the Luftwaffe officers. Then he ordered me to turn around and face the entire company. Instead of being scolded and punished, I found myself being praised as an example of honesty, courage and integrity. But because no one else admitted to having been in the installation, and since it was clear that *Arbeitsmann Schmidt* could not have been all by himself, the entire company but myself was ordered to undergo severe punishment exercises for a few days. On the following weekend I, and I alone, would even have been allowed to go "downtown" as the only one of all the recruits of the company, but in the interest of peace and good comradeship I declined.

In retrospect I must admit that what I had done on that day had little to do with courage and basic honesty. What really had happened was a quick and intuitive acknowledgment on my part that for all people concerned, for officers and men alike, and especially for our commander, it was better if one of the culprits stepped forward. I knew from the start that by being the only one to admit to the transgression (if I was going to be the only one, which I had guessed correctly) my punishment was not going to be very severe.

The reaction of my comrades surprised me: None of them saw through the charade. Actually I was admired for having been so courageous. It was a good lesson for the rest of my life.

Chapter 3

Having completed the RAD service, I went home again for a few days, where an induction notice from the Waffen-SS was already waiting for me. This time I was assigned to the replacement battalion of the Waffen-SS howitzers at Breslau-Lissa in Silesia. At this training center a special unit had been formed where young men who had shown leadership qualities in the Hitler Youth were being nurtured as future officers of the Waffen-SS. It was there that I remained for most of 1944, until receiving my assignment to the *Leibstandarte Adolf Hitler,*[1] the LAH, in early December of that year to take part in the *Ardennenoffensive*, the now famed "Battle of the Bulge".

The barracks of the SS I.G.A.u.E.Btl.1,[2] the official designation of the unit I was assigned to, was a brand-new installation, and some of the tall, three-story brick buildings were not even completed when I arrived. I still remember well my walk from the small railroad station of Breslau-Lissa, a suburb of the German city of Breslau, to the barracks. I had a tight knot in my stomach when from the distance I saw the guard house of the base with a huge SS flag flying above the entrance. For years I had heard many stories of the extremely tough basic training Waffen-SS recruits had to undergo before they were assigned

---

[1] After numerous changes, at the end of the war the official name of the division was 1. Panzerdivision "Leibstandarte SS Adolf Hitler". It was commonly referred to only as the LAH, I will use this designation or the name *Leibstandarte* (life guards) throughout this book.

[2] Short for "Infanterie-Geschütz Ausbildungs- und Ersatz-Bataillon Nr. 1" (Infantry Howitzer Training and Replacement Battalion Number 1)

to the combat divisions, and I feared that my general attitude of taking all things easy would be put to a severe test.

However, when I reported to the U.v.D., the *Unteroffizier vom Dienst* (the non-commissioned officer in charge of the guard house on that day) he was quite friendly, and even helpful, and there was none of the denigration I had seen doled out to the new recruits of the regular German army when I had visited their *Panzergrenadier* barracks at Landau in the previous year.

The swearing-in ceremony at Breslau-Lissa on Nov. 9th, 1944, which I missed due to my perennial shenanigans. Note the brand-new (still unfinished) barracks, and the Infantry howitzers (150mm to the left, 75mm to the right) in the foregound.

Within an hour I found myself in the company of about a hundred other boys or young men my age - like myself all new arrivals. Soon we were being outfitted with two well-made uniforms each (one being a regular field gray outfit and the other was new, 1944 SS fatigues of the "harvest" camouflage pattern) and provided with all the other accouterments that make a soldier, including a 98k carbine, bayonet, helmet, gas mask, belt with shoulder harness, and an entrenching tool (spade) among others things. It was up to us to sew the eagle with the swastika on the left sleeve of our uniform jackets, and the SS collar patches on the collars of the new field gray uniform. No name ribbons for the sleeve cuffs were issued since replacement battalions did not have any, and we were far from being assigned to specific field units. As was customary in the German armed forces, some of the equipment we received was registered in the new *Soldbuch* (pay book) that we were issued within the first week of our tour of duty, and which we were admonished to carry with us at all times. By the evening of the first day at the Lissa barracks, my soldier's life had begun in earnest. Not to forget: In the Waffen-SS the heads of new recruits were not shaved, nor did we have to have our hair cropped very close.

Perhaps this is the time to explain to the reader of these memoirs what the Waffen-SS actually was; how it came into being, and what bearing for the future of the European peoples on all continents the short existence of this German military elite unit had. Considering that by its proper name the "Waffen-SS" existed but 5 years, something that constitutes but a second in the long history of the Germanic peoples, its impact was great and it is felt to this day. Interestingly, nobody knows that better than the anti-Germans of our era.

The simplest answer to the question "what was the Waffen-SS" one can give to Americans is to make a comparison with the Marine Corps: Like the Waffen-SS, the U.S. Marine Corps is the fourth branch, besides the Army, the Navy and the Air Force, of the armed forces of the nation which it serves, and it is a generally acknowledged elite. Strictly by law the Marine Corps is part of the Navy, and the intent was that the Marines (*nomen est omen!*) should always be under Navy command when thrown into battle. Viewing the engagements of the Marines in both World Wars and other actions in-between these wars, and since then, it becomes clear that this intent was not kept. Well, similarly it can be said that the Waffen-SS fast outgrew its original purpose of being a small Praetorian guard at the service of the Führer. However, while the birth of the U.S. Marine Corps was derived from the need, more than 200 years ago, to have infantry soldiers permanently stationed on the ships of the U.S. Navy, the Waffen-SS was merely an outgrowth of the regular SS, a German paramilitary organization that was created in the late 1920s by the leadership of the National Socialist party, the NSDAP. The biggest difference between the Marines and the Waffen-SS probably lies in their different world view, or ideological make-up. Whether the Marines really are defending their country or merely safeguarding the special interests of the wealthy U.S. elite when they occupy such countries as

Nicaragua, Panama and (even) Vietnam remains to be questioned. Between the World Wars the former U.S. Marine Major General Smedley Butler wrote a book expressing doubts whether the engagements in which he had participated had really been in the interest of the people of the United States.

Conversely, there is no question that the Waffen-SS became a major force in preventing the capture of all of Europe by the Bolshevists, a calamity that would have set European culture back a thousand years. The planned and purposeful execution of the destruction of Christianity in the Eastern European countries that fell under the hammer and sickle between 1917 and 1991 speaks for itself. And I myself was in the 1980s able to see the devastating impact Bolshevism/Communism had on that part of Germany, namely the now extinct "GDR", that fell under Soviet suzerainty.

To this day the "world media" still writes of the allegedly uncalled-for attack on the (seemingly) helpless Soviet Union by "Nazi Germany". They are writing this even at a time when a heavily armed military super power like Israel claims to be "defending" itself against the overwhelming might of disarmed, stone-throwing Palestinians. The fact is that the Soviet Union was poised to attack Germany in the summer of 1941, and *only* the German preventive attack ordered by Hitler prevented the Soviet Communists from washing their horses in the Atlantic by the fall of 1941. (Probably the best description of the German reasons for marching against the Soviet Union in June of 1941 can be found in the book *"Stalin's War of Extermination 1941-1945"* by the German military historian Joachim Hoffmann, published 2001 by Theses & Dissertations Press, P.O.Box 64, Capshaw, AL 35742)

The genesis of both the NSDAP *(Nationalsozialistische Deutsche Arbeiter Partei* - National Socialist German Workers' Party), namely, the "Nazi" party, and two of its major associated formations, the SA and the SS, can be traced to the turmoil inside Germany following the defeat, in the First World War, of the German Reich in November 1918.[3]

---

[3] The designations "Nazi" party and "Nazis" were coined by the enemies of the National Socialists in the early 1920s, and had derogatory connotations, albeit without a specific pejorative interpretation except, after 1945, in connection with "Nazi Germany," for the never-ending wartime allegations. In the meantime though both designations have become part of everyday use, and in the minds

Upon the signing of the armistice on November 9, 1918, and the departure of *Kaiser* (Emperor) Wilhelm II into exile in Holland, the German monarchist system that had ruled the nation since the reign of Emperor Charlemagne in the 9th century collapsed. The central power of the Reich that between 1871 and 1918 had been located in Berlin vanished.

In some parts of Germany, but especially in Munich, Hamburg and the Rhineland, Communist agitators, generally under Jewish leadership (as they had also been abroad, for instance in Hungary, Rumania and Russia) called for outright revolution and the establishment of German Soviet republics. These actions generated resistance by the numerous German nationalists, among them many combat soldiers, and along with the creation of ever more political parties arose the establishment of paramilitary groups, both nationalist as well as internationalist in outlook, attached to these parties vying for power.

The German situation of 1918 is somewhat reminiscent of the political conditions which exist in the United States at the time of the writing of this book, namely, at the beginning of the Twenty-first Century:

So-called internationalist and human rights, "race-mixing" (my terminology) groups, for instance the leftist student associations, equally leftist unions and parties, Jewish, Black, Hispanic and Asian organizations, and all assorted Marxists cadres, can currently meet with in the United States anywhere and anytime with impunity and without fear of interference. Unfortunately, however, in this alleged "land of the free" doing the same is now almost impossible for patriotic American groups safeguarding their white, European-American background, the upholding of the Southern (Confederate) heritage, or the call for the separation of the races. The latter is viewed as criminal by the system. The lessons of Sri Lanka, Albania and Africa do not count. "Tolerance" is being promoted, albeit only for and toward those that do not question the current "liberal" system. Only a few days before these lines were written, on Tuesday, May 1, 2001, the notorious ADL (Anti-Defamation

---

of many Americans they do not generally contain a negative value judgment, obviously to the dismay of the public opinion molders in the so-called democracies.

League of B'nai B'rith), a self-appointed Jewish watchdog group that spies on American citizens in all walks of life and probably has files on millions of them, a fact for which it already got in trouble with the law, held a meeting attended by 600 of its most important agents from all over the United States in a prestigious Washington hotel, and not a single instance of an attack or harassment by nationalist, patriotic groups or by anti-Semitic individuals was reported.

On the other hand, should, for instance, one of the better-known militias of the United States try to arrange a national meeting of equal size in the nation's capital with attendant publicity, it would be impossible for them to rent a hall, assemble peacefully (as is guaranteed by the U.S. Constitution) and have the Attorney General of the United States speak to them. As a matter of fact, should such a meeting take place, we can be certain that assorted leftists under Jewish leadership would be in the forefront of hundreds of dirty, disheveled, venomous and ski masked, obscenity-screaming, leftist protesters. And what would these protesters profess to represent? Democracy, freedom, "tolerance", "equal rights", and "freedom of expression". Alas, they defend only freedom of expression for themselves and those who agree with them. But not for "fascists", their current bogeymen. (The constant misapplication of the words "fascist" to anything connected with "National Socialism" indicates how much the leftist protesters understand of the issues at hand. Alas, their knowledge and understanding of economic issues is even more worse.)

In the early 1920s an almost identical situation had developed in Germany, and there, just as now here in the United States and in Germany (again), it seemed in the interest of the prevailing system to suppress the patriots and pander to the goons from the left. At first, when for instance Adolf Hitler wanted to speak to his followers and to those who were curious about his message, there was not a single National Socialist gathering or convention that was not interrupted with physical force by leftist agitators. Their main complaint was that Hitler had pointed out the prevalence of Jews in the high cadres of the Communist and other Marxist parties in Germany and abroad. Rather than answer this allegation with facts of their own making, the leftists tried their utmost to keep Hitler and other high Nazis from speaking in public.

It was then that the SA (*Sturm Abteilung* / Storm detachment), the so-called brown-shirts, came into being. Both Hitler and Hermann Göring, the famed German Air Force fighter pilot of World War I, had realized that the Red terror could, in the absence of a patriotic-leaning police force and government, be broken only by counter-terror. Among the millions of unemployed workers in Germany, the result of the lost war, it was easy to recruit a sufficient number of hardened street fighters in most of the large cities of Germany who could henceforth guard the National Socialist party meetings and conventions as proud SA-men. The usual methods of the Reds to infiltrate Nazi meetings with their own street fighters backfired. As a rule they were recognized upon their entry into the meeting place (sometimes a circus tent, so large was the number of people who wanted to hear Hitler speak) and thus were kept under constant surveillance. Once the Red leader in place gave a certain signal to his comrades a melee broke out, the SA-men who had armed themselves with truncheons went after the "demonstrators", most of whom soon found themselves lying on the street with injuries of various kinds.

With the major Nazi leaders having managed to be able to speak freely in most large German cities, the party grew fast. Soon it became apparent that especially Adolf Hitler needed a personal guard of loyal and intelligent followers who could arrange for the security measures needed when traveling in territories where the German Communists were still dominant. Out of the tens of thousands of SA members, small squads of the so-called *Schutzstaffel* (Security Detachment) were formed to whom fell the task of guarding the party leaders, and performing other services. This was the beginning of the SS.

In his table talks,[4] Hitler himself described the founding of the SS thus:

"Believing that there are always circumstances when there is a need for elite troops, I created in 1922-23 the 'Adolf Hitler shock

---

[4] As reported in the book *Hitler's Tischgespräche* as recorded by Dr. Henry Picker, Seewald-Verlag, Stuttgart, 1972

troops'.[5] *These troops were made up of men who were ready for revolution and they knew that someday things would demand the utmost from them. In 1924, when I came out of Landsberg prison, the party was in disarray and scattered into many competing groups. I realized then that I needed a bodyguard, but a small, very restricted one, made up of men who could be depended upon without preconditions, even if it became necessary to march against their own brothers. I envisioned only twenty men to a city with one provision being that one could depend on them absolutely. Maurice, Schreck and Heiden formed the first group of hard fighters in Munich, and they were the origins of the SS; but it was because of Himmler that the SS became an extraordinary body of men, devoted to an ideal, and loyal to the death."*

On January 6, 1929, Heinrich Himmler, a somewhat shy and modest 29-year-old agricultural manager with a degree in farming, became the head of the SS, then a small unit of 280 selected men that was nominally still part of the million-man SA. The first SS men wore SA uniforms but with black trimmings, and black instead of brown caps that were adorned with a silver skull (death-head) insignia. The double S runes ("lightning bolts") on the collar would come later, as would the SS-motto *"Meine Ehre heisst Treue"* (Loyalty is my honor) on the belt buckles.

It was the decidedly unmilitary-looking Heinrich Himmler who created the *Order of the SS,* with religious overtones and ramifications far into the future of Europe and the white race, from a group of a few hundred dedicated party followers. Himmler, a man with a strict Catholic upbringing, must have known the history of the Roman Catholic Church well, for there is little doubt that he had taken some of his inspirations for the creation of *his* order from the teachings of Ignatius of Loyola who founded the Jesuit order in the early part of the 16th Century, just about the time when Martin Luther laid the foundation for the Reformation.

Here I must mention that probably because of his unmilitary bearing and looks, Heinrich Himmler was not much respected in the

---

5 The original German word is "Stosstrupp". It is of World War I origin and denoted the shock troops that were used to breach the enemy lines during prolonged trench warfare. A famous post-World War I war movie in Germany was titled "Stosstrupp 1918".

Waffen-SS, and I do remember that once someone had turned his picture to face the wall in the Waffen-SS barracks in Breslau-Lissa. Himmler was also derogatorily referred to as the "Reichsheini", with the term *Heini* being both the diminutive of Heinrich in the German language, as well as sometimes being used to describe someone who is kind of awkward or clumsy. In other words, Heinrich Himmler was regarded by some as the buffoon of the Reich. I myself have never been an admirer of Himmler but I am fairly convinced that those who denigrated him during the Nazi era and after World War II will be proven wrong. Besides Adolf Hitler, and probably Joseph Goebbels, it will be Heinrich Himmler who will leave a lasting impression long into the future.

In 1929 when Himmler became the head of the SS, the full name of the organization *Schutzstaffel* was still being used but soon the designation SS became commonplace, and I, for instance, never ever saw the Waffen-SS being called "Waffen-Schutzstaffel", except in allied postwar literature written by people who didn't know the facts.

It also deserves mentioning that before the advent of the National Socialists the swastika was in Germany only a little-known ancient symbol that could be found, for example, on Germanic steles, in Roman ruins or on American Indian jewelry, but there was no special connection of this symbol with the German psyche. *Or so it seemed.* In 1918, nobody would have dreamed that less than 20 years later almost every single German, young and old, would be wearing a uniform, or a pin or badge, adorned with the swastika. The allegation that the swastika has an anti-Christian connotation can be answered with the fact that some of the tombs of the early Christians, for instance the grave stone of a Christian martyr in the Middle East who died about 700 AD, were decorated with swastikas of various kinds.[6]

Even lesser known than the swastika was the S (lightning bolt) rune that in double form would in later times become *the* emblem of

---

[6] Before the Hitler era, and perhaps because of the American Indian connection, the swastika seemed to have been used in the United States more often than in Germany. Commercially, for instance, among others by a railroad company, and in San Antonio, Texas by the local ROTC-units, and even by an American Army division. The particular grave stone I am referring to can be seen at the Dumbarton Oaks Museum at Georgetown near Washington, DC.

a white Aryan semi-religious order that will probably survive for many centuries to come (even if at this time it is officially not in existence), namely, the SS.

Within a little more than two years after being appointed as the *Reichsführer* or national commander of the SS, Heinrich Himmler had managed to enlarge his organization to about 30,000 men. No mean feat for anybody. He also imbued his order with a mythology combing Germanic (pre-Christian) rites, a strict adherence to racial laws and unquestioned fealty to Adolf Hitler. Nobody could have predicted that out of this small group of dedicated men would eventually be created an elite army of nearly one million well trained and highly motivated soldiers that generated both fear in the enemies of Germany and the white race, as well as lasting admiration among many of those who were born long after the original SS men of the post-World War I era had died.

The majority of the German people became familiar with the "new" SS soon after January 30, 1933, when Adolf Hitler became the Chancellor (prime minister) of the German government, an event that was eventually referred to as the "*nationalsozialistische Machtergreifung*" (the National Socialist Assumption of power). Less than a month after this date, the Berlin Reichstag building (the German capitol) went up in flames set by a Dutch Communist. Hitler used this opportunity to incarcerate the most vociferous of his enemies, and for this reason 25,000 SA-men and 15,000 SS-men were appointed to the auxiliary police. Toward the end of 1933 was the first time that the black-uniformed, armed and barracked SS regiments, among them Hitler's own *Leibstandarte,*[7] took official positions outside a few major German government buildings and institutions. The *Leibstandarte*, along with other armed and barracked SS formations, would become the nucleus of the Waffen-SS.

The power of the SS within both the many (and in number ever increasing) formations of the Nazi party, and in the Reich as such, rose considerably after the so-called Röhm putsch in June of 1934.[8]

---

[7] This regiment would eventually become the division in which I served from December 1944 to the end of the war.

[8] Ernst Röhm had been a decorated officer in World War I, and with his talent for organization and foresight he had created the million (or more) man SA

As a result the SA, the old vanguard of the National Socialist revolution, was relegated to a second spot, and the SS became *the* organization to safeguard the party, its leaders, the ideology, the race, and not the least the German Reich and people from enemies inside and outside of the country. This new status would later lead to the development that all the major security services of Germany fell under SS command, including the Gestapo (*Geheime Staatspolizei* - Secret Police) and eventually also the regular German *Schutzpolizei*, the local police. Note the SS chain of command on page 213. There is no doubt that Himmler had created an efficient empire within an empire, with jurisdiction over nearly all personnel safeguarding the nation, inside and out..

Having in mind that work liberates (*"Arbeit macht frei"*), and that regular prisons are only breeding grounds for new and hardened criminals, the concentration camp system was created first under SA auspices and then came under SS command, with the "KL" (*KonzentrationsLager)* Dachau becoming the first concentration camp to be extensively written about in the German press. In the concentration camps not only habitual criminals but also known enemies of the system, particularly Communists, were kept under a strict regimen. The allegation that already in the early years after the assumption of power Jews were arrested and sent to the concentration camps "because they were Jews" is not true.

---

paramilitary army. However, like many other National Socialists, among them, for instance, the Strasser brothers, Röhm placed much emphasis on the socialistic ideas within the ns ideology while Hitler realized (rightly, in my opinion) that the interests of the German nation should be paramount. Based upon this divergence of opinion, Röhm would have loved to replace the archaic and often aristocratic ideology of the German Army with the revolutionary fervor of a new socialistic officer's corps. Hitler on the other hand realized that Germany's enemies would force a war sooner, and that he had to depend upon the generals and other offices now in command.

Whether or not in June of 1934 Ernst Röhm really planned a putsch against both Hitler and the Army in order to create a German *Volksarmee* is still a matter of conjecture. Considering the cards Röhm was holding it is easy to imagine that he tried to put Hitler under pressure. In any case, the *Führer* knew that Röhm and some othes of the SA leaders had gained too much power in the new Reich, and this power had to be squashed. In addition, Hitler had to placate the generals, the loyalty of whom he was by no means assured. The result was the brutal elimination of much of the SA leadership, and a few others, on June 30, 1934. As I wrote before: The SA would never again regain its former power: the SS was in the ascent.

They found themselves behind barbed wire because they were Communist agitators who advocated world revolution.

Beginning immediately after the war and even until now (Daniel Goldhagen's book "Hitler's Executioners" comes to mind) there is still the argument as to what the German people could have known about the so-called "Holocaust", and what not. One thing is certain: The leadership of World Jewry started their atrocity propaganda against the Reich immediately after Hitler's assumption of power in the spring of 1933,. At a time when most Jews were still in Germany, and when most Germans still frequented Jewish shops and department stores (among other businesses), Jewish leaders like Rabbi Stephen S. Wise and Samuel Untermyer, both of New York, already claimed that Jews were being murdered in Berlin and elsewhere. These flagrant lies contributed to the fact that the German people as a whole did not believe any allied claims *after* the war had started. Germans knew that so-called facts and figures disseminated by Jewish organizations and their allies could not be trusted.

In spite of all postwar claims to the contrary, it is a fact that something that did not happen, could not have been known. This simple truism led to the general German insistence after 1945, not to have known "this or that," especially about the alleged extermination of Jews in the concentration camps, or "death camps" as they are also called. However, seeing the photographs taken at the liberation of the prisoners at camps like Bergen-Belsen, Buchenwald and Dachau, the Allies simply did not believe the German declarations of ignorance. According to the Allies, if 11 million people (six million Jews and five million others) had been murdered by the "Nazis", this fact must have been general knowledge in Germany. When Germans asked members of the Allied nations for proof of their contention of mass murder, they were shown the often crude propaganda pictures (such as the famous one taken at Dachau, when an obvious delousing chamber for clothes was presented to a visiting U.S. Congressman as "the" gas chamber used to kill people.) Unfortunately, American Congressmen were then not any smarter as they are today.

In the 1970s I had a public argument about these points with a young Dutch Jew who, until the middle of 1944, had lived in the Netherlands, when he was arrested by German police forces and sent to Germany where he had to work in an armaments factory. He insisted that the German people must have known of “gassings”, “Zyklon-B” and the names of such camps as Auschwitz, Majdanek and Treblinka. I tried to disprove his statement without going into the cardinal question whether the “Holocaust” really happened as is now being told.

Since this Jew lived in Holland in relative freedom for four war years, and certainly must have had more access to clandestine information than I had, I asked him whether at the time of his arrest *he* had known of Auschwitz, Zyklon-B and alleged gassings. He answered in the negative.

My next question to him was, whether he did not see the incongruity in his answer: He, an alert Jew who undoubtedly was aware of the policy of the German Government regarding every Jew as an enemy alien, and therefore had a vested interested in keeping informed about such matters, had no inkling what was (allegedly) the fate of his ethnic and religious brethren at camps such as, for instance, Auschwitz, but he expected the German people as a whole, most of whom had to fight their daily battles of scrounging for food and other necessities of life, and who often suffered from allied air attacks, to be concerned about the fate of the Jews in general, something he himself obviously had not done.

What did the German people know? The existence of some of the concentration camps was general knowledge and there were even some articles written in popular magazines about the older camps such as Dachau and, I believe, Sachsenhausen. What happened inside these camps, whether good or bad, was generally not known. It is like in America today where in some areas, near the California/Nevada border for instance, heavily guarded prisons can be seen from the superhighways yet few people driving by know what transpires in these prisons, nor do most of them care. That is just part of human nature. As a matter of fact, I myself was then just as familiar with the name Sing Sing, the famous prison in New York state, as I was with the name of the Dachau concentration camp. What really transpired in either of these places I did not know, nor did I care.

Even though I was a member of the Waffen-SS I knew, *before* our capitulation, the concentration camps of Dachau and Buchenwald by name only. I knew of them because they had

Waffen-SS training areas nearby. Only after the war did names like Auschwitz, Mauthausen, Bergen-Belsen, Flossenbürg etc. also become familiar to me and most other Germans. They and camps (or whatever they were) such as Sobibor, Treblinka, and even Majdanek are today part of my general knowledge only because of my personal interest in Holocaust revisionism. Postwar Americans do not seem to realize that in wartime *all* governments, including those of the U.S., Canada and Great Britain, exercise a strong control over the media. In Germany that control was especially strict because of the important role propaganda played in World War I. U.S. citizens like to believe that due to the free press which (allegedly) exists in the United States there are few secrets the government can keep for long, or there is little that the powers-that-be can keep from the people. However, one only has to question Americans as to their knowledge about the human losses at Dresden and Hiroshima in order to discover that the witholding of important information was not a specialty only of the "Nazis". This bad habit seems now especially bad in the so-called "free democracies" pertaining to wrongdoings by their eilte, or, like in "democratic" Germany in all matters pertaining to the Third Reich.

Looking through old American almanacs and newspapers, it is interesting to note that few of them state the number of people that were killed by the atomic bomb dropped on Hiroshima. The Encyclopaedia Britannica of 1958 went so far as not mentioning any casualty figures altogether. In school text books the number of about 60,000 seems to be generally accepted. But on August 6, 2001, 56 years after the war crime, one was able to read in *the New York Times* that 145,000 Japanese fell victim to the Hiroshima bomb.

The casualty figures for the devastating - and from a military point of view totally unnecessary, therefore criminal - air raids on Dresden on Shrove Tuesday 1945 prove even greater attempts to lead the American public astray. Come February 14, one can expect that some AP or newspaper report will mention the "35,000" Germans killed at Dresden. Considering that at the time this seemingly safe city had been overfilled with refugees fleeing the marauding Soviet Army, the German claim of "more than 250,000 victims" might be conservative.

How many Americans know that during the so-called Nuremberg Trials of German wartime leaders no forensic evidence was presented by the prosecutors, nor permitted to be presented to the victor court by the defense? This important fact was mentioned *for the first time* since 1945 (!) in a publication available to the general public in an article published in the *New York Times* on August 1, 2001, more than half century after the German Generals were executed.[9]

In spite of all the Hollywood claims and false depictions, the Gestapo *per se* was never uniformed, just as the American FBI is not uniformed. However, it is logical that during wartime, when people look askance at young men who are not in uniform, Gestapo officers would don their SS uniforms in order to show their (important) duties and rank. I personally doubt that there were any high-ranking Gestapo officers who were not also high-ranking members of the SS. When the Communist German state, the "DDR", collapsed in 1990, it became known that the secret police, the "Stasi" of that Moscow creation, had nearly 20,000 full pledged officers and officials, and, in addition, hundreds of thousands of informers. Even during the war years, while Germany controlled friendly and enemy populations of more than twenty times the size of the 17 million inhabitants of the *Deutsche Demokratische Republik*, the Gestapo never reached the size of the Stasi. Furthermore, I can just imagine what a field day American movie makers and the media would today still have if they could show the Gestapo dressed in Swat team (Ninja-) attire, and dressed this way harassing and menacing Jewish civilians with submachine guns, similarly as we were able to see when little Elian Gonzales was "liberated" in Miami not very long ago, or if we remember what happened near Waco, Texas in 1995.

Apart from the activities mentioned above, the SS grew to be a "state within a state", as the Nazi regime transformed almost every

---

[9] As I will state several times in this book: The truth can be discovered by those who are willing to search for it. Unfortunately, the fiendish system operating under the guise of a free media knows exactly what to withhold from the public and where, knowing full well that few people take the time and effort to discover hidden facts. The Jewish Holocaust tale provides the best example for this statement.

facet of German life. A *Rassen und Siedlungshauptamt* (The Office for Race and People) concerned itself with the racial hygiene of the Aryan race. *Lebensborn* saw to it that unwed, pregnant girls of good racial stock received the best of care in special clinics, instead of being ostracized by their fellow villagers in rural areas.[10] The SS Medical Corps became a foremost institution not only for advanced German medicine but also in the fight against cancer, smoking, tuberculosis and illnesses related to environmental factors, among other health problems. In the cultural field the SS reawakened the dormant interest in the art of the pagan tribes that populated Europe before the often forced conversion to Christianity. The manufacture and distribution of such "primitive" art works became the task of a special SS bureau. Among collectors, items produced by the SS porcelain factory are today prized possessions.

By 1938 the black-uniformed SS had become "the" elite of the Reich, to which not only the idealistic youth of the nation flocked. For many members of the old aristocracy, important men of finance and industry, university professors and scientists, farmers and philosophers, it became a status symbol of the new German society to have an honorary title in the SS. Wernher von Braun, for instance, the man who along with other German rocket scientists came to America as part of operation "Paperclip" and later was responsible for sending the first American astronauts to the moon, had been a honorary major in the *Allgemeine* SS, as it was called during the war in order to make a distinction with the Waffen-SS. I doubt, however, that Wernher von Braun ever attended an SS meeting.

As a result of the so-called Treaty of Versailles that concluded World War I and which really should be referred to as the Dictate of Versailles, Germany, then a nation of 60 million people, was only allowed armed forces with a combined strength of 100,000 men. No airplanes, no battleships except two ancient (1906) battle

---

[10] The tale that *Lebensborn* was created as a sort of stud farm where SS men and girls of good stock were sent to copulate in order to provide "babies for Hitler" is one of the typical inventions of the sick minds of anti-German propagandists in the so-called Western democracies. The dilemma facing pregnant white teenage girls in America half a century after the demise of Hitlerism proves that a *Lebensborn* organization not connected to religious or leftist social service institutions would find a fertile field of operation.

cruisers, no U-boats, no tanks, no heavy artillery. Once Hitler had established himself firmly as the leader of the Reich, about 1934, he unilaterally abrogated the enemy dictate, and a slow rebuilding of the German armed forces began. However, from the start of his reign Adolf Hitler depended on the support of both the military and the so-called Ruhr barons, a group of wealthy and influential people we would today call the German military-industrial complex. For the first six years of his reign Adolf Hitler was in no position to antagonize either.

Particularly the officer's corps of the German army, a host of men tied to the traditions of the Prussian army and the former German General staff, looked with misgivings upon the aspirations of the new rulers of Germany to interfere in military affairs. By law and as a rule German military officers were not allowed to become active members of a political party, although once the war had started, this rule became unenforceable. As mentioned above, there was at first the attempt of the SA leadership under Ernst Röhm to create a National Socialist people's army out of the millions of men under its command, and later, after this attempt was squashed by Hitler, there arose to the Generals the threat of the SS as a military elite formation. Only after the "Röhm-Putsch" the SS became independent of the SA. By then it had reached a strength of 200,000 men, and it was in mid-1934 that the name separation began between the *Allgemeine* or general SS, and its armed formations, the nucleus of the Waffen-SS (albeit not yet with that title).

Already before the Second World War friction between the *Wehrmacht* Generals and the Reich leadership became apparent when Himmler and other SS leaders planned to have such permanently armed and barracked formations as the *Leibstandarte* and the so-called *SS-Verfügungstruppen* (SS detachments for special tasks) equipped with armaments heavier than the light infantry weapons they had then at their disposal. The dispute was solved when the SS leadership agreed to the following stipulations:

1. The SS was to remain a unit composed solely of volunteers.
2. In case of war, all Waffen-SS units would be under the command of higher ranking Army Generals. All arms and provisions for the SS would be supplied by the Army supply corps.

The first test of the Army/armed SS cooperation occurred during the Austrian *Anschluss* in March of 1938, when the *Leibstandarte* covered about 1,000 kilometers (600 miles) in 48 hours, and received high praise from none other than General Heinz Guderian, the creator of the German tank corps. The German liberation of the Sudetenland after the now (allegedly) notorious Munich Agreement, followed in October of 1938, and again the soldiers of the Army and the armed SS performed flawlessly together. On the 9th of October 1938 Adolf Hitler visited my home city of Saarbrücken, there to dedicate a new opera house, a personal gift from him to the Saarlanders for their fealty to Germany. My oldest brother Richard and I were among the hundreds of thousands of Germans lining the street of the city to greet the *Führer* of the Reich. (I know a newsreel exists where one can see Hitler and the both of us in the same frame, but I was unable to discover it in a German archive. It is probably hidden somewhere in an American, British or Jewish depository.) On that day it was also for the first time that I was able to admire the tall soldiers of the *Leibstandarte* in their neat black uniforms with silver and white trimmings, as they stood at attention in front of the hotel where Hitler was quartered. Little did I consider then that but six years later I would be a member of this elite. At the time the requirements for the *Leibstandarte* were very high: The volunteer had to be at least 6ft 1" tall and of excellent physical health. He had to prove pure Aryan (ie. no Jewish or Gypsy, and no colored) racial background going back to the 18th Century.

Less than a year after Hitler's visit to Saarbrücken, World War II broke out and the *Leibstandarte* and other armed SS units participated under general command of the German Army in the fighting. They performed so well that Hitler ordered the creation of an entire SS-Division. While the *Leibstandarte* had helped to defeat Poland, only a ceremonial company and a replacement battalion of the unit remained in Berlin.

In the book "SS, Himmler's Black Order, 1923-45" (Sutton Publishing, Stroud, Gloucestershire, GB., 1997) the British author Robin Lumsden describes the SS soldiers and their training as follows:

"Once in the armed SS, recruits were molded into very adaptable soldier-athletes capable of much better than average

endurance on the march and in combat. Great emphasis was placed upon ideological indoctrination, physical exercise and sports, which were made integral part of the training program and daily life. More time was spent in the field, on the ranges and in the classroom learning the theory and tactics than was practice in the army, while considerably less attention was given to drill, even in the Leibstandarte after 1938. This resulted in a standard of battlefield movement and shooting that was appreciably higher than that of the Wehrmacht. Maneuvers were made as realistic as possible, with the use of live ammunition and heavy artillery barrages, so that every SS soldier became fully accustomed to handling a variety of weapons, and also to being within 100 yards of explosions from his own artillery fire. The end product was a higher standard of soldier, a man who was a storm trooper in the best traditions of the term."

To the best of my knowledge it has never be ascertained exactly when the term "Waffen-SS" came into being, who introduced it, and when it really became official. The above-named historian Robin Lumsden states that the designation can be found in official correspondence as early as late 1939, and that by February 1940 it had become the official title. I see no reason to dispute this statement, except to mention that a correct translation of Armed SS (vs. General or *Allgemeine* SS) would be "*Bewaffnete* SS". We must admit that the title that eventually was used and became famous the world over sounds better.

On May 10, 1940, the so-called phony war that had lasted for more than eight months on the Western front came to an end. On that date, German armies crossed the borders of France, a nation that had declared war on the Reich two days after the German incursion into Poland, into Belgium, that was allied with France and Britain, and also into quasi-neutral Holland.[11] The newly-named

---

[11] In American history books one can often read that "in one hundred years the Germans attacked France three times," meaning of course during the Franco-Prussian War of 1870-71, and during the two world wars. While one could dispute who attacked whom in World War I, there is no question that both in 1870-71 as well as in 1939-40 the French Government had declared war on Germany. And without the French declarations of war that nation would not have been in danger of being invaded by German troops.

Waffen-SS was an integral part of the attacking force. The *Leibstandarte*, by now a fully motorized armored infantry regiment, fought along with the SS-Regiment *"Der Führer"* in Holland before turning south toward Belgium and then deep into France. Besides these two SS units, the SS-*Totenkopf*-Division and the SS-*Verfügungsdivision* took part in the campaign. They all performed well in battle, and earned the thanks of their *Führer* as well as the respect of the old-line Army Generals, a number of whom who had now been named field marshals by Hitler. *Der Feldzug im Westen,* (Campaign in the West,) as it was officially called, namely, the Blitzkrieg in Western Europe, saw for the first-time the extensive use in a great war of war reporters equipped with movie cameras. And the SS-*Kriegsberichterstatter* were among the best. That is why to this day we can watch, on our television sets, with a view from close range, the battles as they happened so long ago. And since it was the Waffen-SS that was the first army to be equipped with camouflage outfits, it is still easy to make a distinction between troops of the regular German Army and the SS.

After France had capitulated, the aerial fights of the Battle of Britain and the war at sea, fought between the forces of the Western nations, captivated the attention of the peoples of the world. Early in 1941, and while the German preparation for the eventual invasion of the Soviet Union (unquestionably a preventive measure!) took place, Hitler was forced to come to the aid of his Italian friend Benito Mussolini who had become mired in a no-win situation with Greece on the Balkan peninsula. It was the *Leibstandarte* that captured Athens on my 14th birthday. At about the same time I completed my eight years of *Volksschule* (elementary school) and got ready for my work year, actually only a semester, on the farm, as the law demanded. Ironically, exactly four years to the day after the capture of Athens and on my 18th birthday, Mussolini and his mistress would be murdered by Communist partisans and strung upside-down at a gas station in Milan.

When the war against the Soviet Union began on June 22, 1941, five Waffen-SS divisions were in the German front line. They were deployed separately among the three giant German armies that marched east. Battles such as those just before Moscow, at Minsk, Demjansk, Rostov, Kharkov, Kursk, in the Baltic countries,

Zhitomir and Cherkassy are indelibly connected with the heroism and sacrifice of the SS.

Eventually there were 38 Waffen-SS divisions defending the Reich, albeit some of them were divisions in name only. In the West, after the allied invasion, the battles in Normandy and in Holland against the allied "Operation Market Garden"-offensive deserve special mention. At Caen in Normandy, the new 12th SS Panzer Division *Hitlerjugend* whose cadre consisted mainly of officers and non-coms of the *Leibstandarte*, and the bulk of whose soldiers had been volunteers from the Hitler Youth, delayed the British advance far beyond the time set for capture of the city by the allied Generals. Considering that the average age of the "HJ" division, as we called it, was only 19 years, including general officers, this division will forever have a hallowed place in the annals of the German Reich (an institution that is temporarily out of existence due to allied fiat. In the meantime, units such as the division *Prinz Eugen* and others had to fight the ever more active partisan movements in the Balkan countries and elsewhere.

Then came the Battle of the Bulge, described in this book, and, almost simultaneously, ferocious fighting near the Reich border in Alsace-Lorraine by, among others, the SS Division *Götz von Berlichingen.* The last well coordinated attack in which Waffen-SS divisions were involved, and as a result of which the preset goal was reached, namely, the elimination of the Russian bridgehead at the Gran river northwest of Budapest, followed in February of 1945. Hungary itself became the graveyard for the SS divisions *Florian Geyer* and *Maria Theresia* that found their end during the two-months' battle for Budapest, and in March of 1945 of the Sixth SS-Panzer Army to which both the *Leibstandarte* and the *Hitlerjugend* divisions belonged. I myself had been badly wounded at the Gran river bridgehead, and spent six weeks in a hospital. Fateful six weeks of inactivity followed, during which my company was totally wiped-out.

The final battles in Austria in April of 1945, in which I took part, were only delaying tactics intended to prevent the rapacious Red Army from advancing deeper into the heart of Europe, and also to give the western powers the chance to gain more ground in the west. We also wanted to make certain that as many German refugees as possible from the ancient German settlements on the Balkan peninsula could reach safety behind our lines.

The crowning glory of the sacrifices of the Waffen-SS soldiers from all over Europe during a war that had lasted nearly six years was the battle for the *Reichshauptstadt Berlin,* the capital of the Reich. Units from many Waffen-SS divisions, or remnants thereof, took part, but it is especially noteworthy that it was French volunteers of the SS-division *Charlemagne,* and Nordic SS soldiers from the Nordic and Baltic countries, that at the time of Hitler's death defended the inner perimeter of the city in which the Reich chancellery was located, and where the *Führer* ended his life.

In the six years of war approximately 920,000 mostly young men from almost all European countries wore the uniform of the Waffen-SS. Of these 181,000 died and 72,000 are still missing, and presumed dead. About 400,000 were wounded in combat. I personally do not believe that their sacrifice was in vain, as the future will prove.

I am frequently making references to the chivalry that was imbued into young Waffen-SS soldiers, a spirit that was already absent in many enemy soldiers of World War II and which seems to have been totally abandoned at the beginning of the Twenty-first Century, even in the new German Army. Can one imagine the Israelis and the Palestinians treating each other "ritterlich" (chivalrous)? I can't! Instead, the teaching of hate has now reached a sophistication unimaginable (in Europe!) two hundred years ago.

Did Heinrich Himmler recognize where Western Civilization was heading, and did he try to turn the tide with his orders to the SS? Read the following of his orders:

"The following transgressions will be severely dealt with and have no place in lives of the soldiers of the SS:

Theft from comrades and others.

Seduction of underage girls, and rape.

Accumulation of debts and purchasing things on time payments.

Cheating at sports and other contests.

Serious fights between relatives.

Mistreatment of prisoners of war.

Finally this admonition: Always remain truthful and chivalrous: Both in battle as well as in your private life."

Chapter 4

The train that in 1944 took me across Germany from Saarbrücken to Breslau in Silesia (about 500 miles) then a beautiful 700-year-old German city of about 630,000 (99% German) population, ran amazingly on time. Along the route I saw a lot of destruction caused by the allied bombing fleets but somehow the Reich was still humming with energy, and the people I had to deal with were good-natured and helpful. At the time, the Silesian capital was a citadel of German high culture, with a great number of institutes of higher learning (including one of the best universities of Germany) and, due to the absence of French marauders who had for centuries devastated my own home state, Breslau had probably more important cultural monuments within its confines than could be found in all of the Saarland. Breslau received its German city charter in 1231, and both its Dom (cathedral) as well as the beautiful city hall (built in the 15th Century) made a lasting impression on me. I must also note that by the time I arrived in Breslau that city had not experienced even a single serious air raid in the entire war, and there were no ruins or even blown-out windows.

Little did the proud burghers of Breslau realize that in the following year their city would be largely destroyed as a result of a siege lasting from January to May 1945. Eventually (by 1946) *all* of the city's surviving inhabitants would be expelled by the Polish new "owners" of the Silesian capital with nothing but the clothes on their back, and shipped into the crowded remnant of what was left of Germany.

The borough of Lissa, where the Waffen-SS Infantry howitzer base was located, is only about 10 miles from the center of Breslau. The village became famous in the Seven Year's War (1756-1763), when immediately after the Battle of Leuthen (1757) which his forces had won, the Prussian king Frederick the Great rode practically all by himself to the little *Schloss* (castle/manor house) of Lissa, where he suddenly found himself among the top Generals of the entire enemy army (the Austrians, in this case) whom he promptly took prisoners of war. I remember visiting the little manor house of Lissa during my basic training. It had become a museum to the great Prussian king, and original uniforms, weapons and other accouterments of the era, including some personal belongings of the king, could be seen. In 1945, when the Poles expelled all the Germans from Breslau, they either destroyed or stole all the contents of the museum.

Also part of the greater Breslau during the time I spent there, was Krieblowitz, the last home and final resting place of the Prussian field Marshal Gebhard von Blücher who in 1815, along with the British General Arthur W. Wellington, won the battle of Waterloo that spelled the end of the Napoleonic era. The grave of this great hero of German history was also destroyed, his remains desecrated. In doing so the Poles followed the example set by French troops nearly two hundred earlier who played soccer with the skulls of the German emperors that had been buried in the crypt of the Cathedral of Speyer. In light of this I find it odd that the "absolutely evil" Nazis left the oldest Jewish cemetery in Europe, located in Prague, intact, just as they did not touch all the otherr Jewish cemeteries on the Old Continent. It was Hitler who in June of 1940 paid his respects to the great French emperor Napoleon at his tomb in the Dome d'Invalides in Paris, while ordering that honor guards were to remain at the graves of the Polish General Pilsudski, and, for instance, in Greece at the mausoleum of General Metaxas. He also had the remains of the young *Herzog von Reichstadt,* Napoleon's son, transferred from Vienna to his father's tomb. Can one imagine Dwight D. Eisenhower paying silent homage at the sarcophagus of King Frederick the Great? It would look ludicrous, wouldn't it. But why?

It deserves mention that with but a few exceptions the German "Nazi" Government generally left all major national institutions of the conquered nations intact, namely, the monarchies in Denmark, Belgium, Norway, Holland, Hungary, Rumania and Bulgaria, and the *legal* successor governments of France and the Baltic countries. The Soviet Government on the other hand was not as benign, and from the start created junior Soviet (Bolshevist/Communist) republics in all territories that came under Russian control. In addition, the Germans as a rule did not interfere with private business and property, while under the suzerainty of the Soviet Union, *the ally of the United States*, all private property except for some personal belongings was confiscated, and tens of thousands of Christian churches were destroyed or desecrated.

The basic training we received at Breslau-Lissa was hard, as expected. We were driven to the limits of our physical endurance and mental faculties. For me personally, the worst experience was the lack of sleep that soon became the norm. While at most or all regular installations of the German armed forces the reveille was at six o'clock in the morning, the Waffen-SS wake-up call came one hour earlier, and in order to steel our bodies, we had to take cold showers. Something I absolutely hated. Once, during a long and strenuous night training exercise, I seemed to have fallen asleep while marching, and instead of being in one of the front rows of the column, which was my usual spot, I found myself on the march back to the barracks at the very end of the company when we arrived at the base. Without much ado *Untersturmführer* Franz Budka, the platoon leader, had taken the MG-42 I had carried from my shoulders, and lugged it himself for most of the march.

Throughout our basic training, my comrades had much fun with my emphasis on good food and lots sleep. Incidentally, at the Breslau-Lissa training grounds I experienced or saw none of the harassment or hazing that seems endemic at U.S. Army, Navy, Air Force and Marine installations. There were also none of the stupid drills where new soldiers have to attack straw bags with their bayonet-spiked rifles, all the while yelling "kill, kill, kill." And while our *"Ausbilder"* (drill instructors) did yell at us and we had to run on the double all the time, they were not allowed to touch us, or to come too close to us without our permission (I believe the distance that had to be respected was about 2 feet). We retained both our dignity and our individualism. I never bought the American claim that it is necessary to destroy the individual characteristics of young men in order to make them better soldiers. I still believe that the will and the voluntary determination to be part of the unit, and to have sound reasons to be proud of it, was or is far more important. The *esprit de corps* of the Waffen-SS derived to a not inconsiderable part from the truth that most of our officers and non-coms were themselves good men, and good comrades.

The different training methods of the Waffen-SS compared with those other units or armies was clearly noticeable when we were shown training films of opposing or allied forces. Once, when we were shown a movie depicting the making of American soldiers, fun was made of the above-mentioned bayonet drill. And an SS-officer with obvious medical credentials explained to us afterward that the American method of conditioning the bodies of young recruits with all-too-many push-ups and sit-ups was of little value since it "contorted" the body, meaning of course that not all muscles were built up and strengthened at the same time. In retrospect I would say that the Waffen-SS training was geared to create the best combat soldier possible who kept his cool under fire, had retained his individualism, and at the same time was a good team player. We also did not have to forget to take things in good humor. All exercises had been designed with this goal in mind. It was clear that our officers did not want to lead groups of unthinking robots against the enemy.

What we were not told about the GIs was the fact that far more American soldiers had grown up with guns, particularly rifles, in their homes than was true in our case, and that especially the farm boys from the Midwest states were often expert marksmen. They were also quite trigger-happy and never needed to consider the cost of each bullet fired, as was the case with us. It may well be that the high German military command did not think this fact important, but it did have a bearing when German and American troops clashed. While private gun ownership in Germany was *generally*[12]

---

[12] By law only holders of German citizenship were allowed to own fire arms. After the Jewish declaration of war against Germany, promulgated by major Jewish world leaders (for instance Chaim Weizmann and Samuel Untermyer) in the early 1930s, the German Jews were at first relegated to second-class citizen status (similar to the French *Protégé Français,*) and later designated as enemy aliens. Identical American laws prevented many German-Americans from retaining their personal weapons in both world wars.)

not restricted during the Hitler era, it bears mentioning that German guns of high quality were expensive and that after the horrible depression times, when every *Pfennig* counted, most Germans were not inclined to spend much money on the shooting sport. Besides, crime rates in Germany had always been low (a fact that has now, with the advent of "democracy" and almost unlimited immigration of unassimilable foreigners, been changed) and few Germans needed guns for personal protection.

I clearly remember when we viewed a captured training film of the Red Army where it was shown how essential good camouflage is for a combat soldier's survival. On these occasions one would never hear any derogatory remarks about the enemy such as could be found in newspaper articles. As a matter of fact, our often-wounded and usually well-decorated non-commissioned officers obviously had a great respect for the bravery and tenacity of the Soviet soldiers.

During weapons training the sergeant instructing us in all small arms that were commonly used by the various Waffen-SS units pointed out that both the Russians and the Americans already had semi-automatic rifles in common use, while on the average the German infantryman had to rely on his trusted, single-shot 98k carbine. The fact is that in 1941 and 1942, during the advance into the Soviet Union, the German armies had captured great numbers of the Russian Tokarev SVT 40 semi-automatic rifles with sufficient stocks of the needed 7.62mm ammunition, and especially the ever adventurous Waffen-SS soldiers did not hesitate to exchange their 98ks for the Russian semi-automatics. This act obviously did not please the high *Wehrmacht* officers who were in charge of all German arms procurement, including for the Waffen-SS, and as a result the German armaments industry received instructions to produce a semi-automatic that would be better than anything the enemies of East or West could produce.

One day one of our sergeants was showing us both a Tokarev SVT 40, as well as an American M1, when he grabbed a new German *Gewehr 41* lying next to the others on a table, and then continued with approximately these words:

"This, *meine Herren,* is our rifle *Gewehr 41.* A wonderful product of German craftsmanship. It is well designed, beautifully manufactured, a pride to possess. It weighs about 11 lb., uses standard 7.92mm ammunition, has a good range of 800 meters, and holds ten cartridges in a magazine that allows the firing of ten shots in succession without reloading. And do you know what?"

As the sergeant asked this question he practically threw the *Gewehr 41* into a corner behind him, continuing:

"The thing is *Scheisse* (a piece of shit)! It is so well crafted and has such fine tolerances that in combat, where dirt, rust and mud are a soldier's daily companions, it is practically useless. Since in battle my life depends on a *reliable* weapon, I would prefer either the Russian or the American rifle anytime."

We were also shown a Russian submachine gun with the round magazine, a weapon much coveted by Waffen-SS soldiers.

During these months at Breslau-Lissa there were many lighter moments that ought to be told:

At the time of the hurried German retreat from France it appeared that many supply depots of the Wehrmacht located in that country had been haphazardly evacuated, and their contents brought helter-skelter aboard railroad freight cars into the Reich. This resulted in a rather sporadic allocation of some kinds of foodstuffs of which one could only dream in normal times.

Another time we received, along with our bread ration and the ubiquitous slab of margarine and some jam of undetermined fruit content, a small round box of top quality original French Brie cheese. Having learned the appreciation of finer foods from my father, who was a connoisseur of such things, I immediately realized that this Brie cheese was perfectly ripened, and ready to be enjoyed now. It tasted wonderful on our German Army *Kommissbrot* (regulation Army bread). I also noticed that most of my comrades did not appreciate this fine delicacy. They were not familiar with it (they preferred Velveeta and other processed cheeses) and most thought that the stage of ripeness of the Brie cheese meant that it was already spoiled. I immediately brought the surplus of my cigarettes into play: It escapes me how many of them I exchanged for each one half-pound box of *fromage de brie,* but when all the bartering was done, I was able to take a stack of about seven or eight of the Brie cheeses to my locker.

I really enjoyed my Brie for a couple of days when one late afternoon, minutes after we had come back from field exercises in the blazing sun, one of the inspecting UvDs - one of the non-commissioned officers in charge that day, - came barging into our room and started sniffing around. Suddenly he stopped in front of my locker:

"*Schütze Schmidt,* would you mind opening your locker?"

He could have opened it himself. In the Waffen-SS we were prohibited from using any kind of lock or other closure. *Kameradendiebstahl*, theft among comrades, was also severely punished.

"*Unterscharführer,* I do not think that is a good idea!" said I. But he insisted. The moment I opened the door of the locker, such a strong stench of overripe, decaying Brie cheese filled our room that all my comrades ran into the hallway as if gasping for air. At the time air-conditioning was unknown to us, and the hot summer sun had caused the cheese to melt and ran inside the locker down the sides into all of the crevices. It was a mess.

The UvD shook his head, mumbled something to the effect that I must be crazy or worse, and then I was ordered to scrub not only my locker with a strong cleaning solution but our entire room as well. By the time I was finished with this chore, it must have been around midnight, and with this fiasco happening after a day of extremely demanding field exercises, there wasn't a muscle in my body that did not hurt.

When weeks later we once more we received a portion of Brie cheese, I abstained from trading with my comrades.

Due to the war situation we had eight men to a room that was originally designed for perhaps two or four. The furniture was spartan: four double bunk beds, a table and benches sufficient for all of us, and each soldier had a locker. The racks for our rifles were outside in the hallway, while the helmets were normally placed atop the lockers when not in use. For the beds we received clean linen every week (I never noticed lice or bed bugs at the Breslau-Lissa barracks) but the mattresses consisted of a sack cloth type of material that was filled with straw. The straw was changed frequently both for reasons of hygiene as well as to retain a certain resiliency needed for restful sleep.

The heat of the summer of 1944 made us use the sizeable swimming pool of our barracks as often as we were allowed to do so. Unfortunately, there were usually so many of us that little thought could be given to proper swimming, namely, from one end of the pool to the other. Therefore I, who had never really learned to swim well because the Saar river had been off-limits due to contamination with raw sewage for as long as I could remember, usually stayed close to the shallow end. Ironically, I had been the recipient of a commendation from the government that ruled the Saarland in the spring of 1933, because at age six I had rescued a playmate from drowning in the flood-swollen Saar river.

Alas, as part of our officer candidates' course we had to pass a swimming test and this entailed a jump from either the 3 meter or 5 meter (9 feet or 15 feet) height of the tower, I don't remember exactly which. But whichever it was, it seemed awfully high to me, and on the day of reckoning I looked for all possibilities either to get out of this test, or to find a way that would not cause me to drown.

We had a number of expert sportsmen in our group, and watching them, the jump seemed easy enough. While most jumped with their feet first, a few of my comrades jumped head-first, coming out of the water almost at the other end of the pool without catching a breath of air in between. Because it was a required test, we all stood in the proper line-up, just as our names appeared on the list one of the examining officers had on his clip-board. There was no way for me to let others jump first, while I myself generated the inner courage needed when my turn came. But I did notice that those who had jumped feet first did not appear on the surface of the water in the same spot. Depending on how they had held their arms, they were either further or closer to the edge of the pool. I did not hesitate when my name was called and I jumped. Once I felt the bottom of the pool about ten or twelve feet deep in the water, I was more than anxious to get out of it again, and I stretched my arms in such a way that I was propelled as close to the side wall of the pool as possible. Only a couple of strokes that were more like helpless thrashings got me to the edge, and out I went. I had passed!

The fact that we had excellent sportsmen among us did contribute to our general prowess, and it helped when city boys like myself had overexerted themselves while, for instance, going over an obstacle course. One day in late summer of 1944 we read on the blackboard of our unit that we had a choice of attending either a 14-day automobile mechanics course at an SS barracks in Holland, or a skiing course for the same length of time in the high mountains of the nearby *Erzgebirge,* the mountain range that lies between Silesia and Bohemia. I thought for sure that all my comrades would volunteer for the skiing course but that was not the case. The choice was about 50/50. While I always liked fine mechanics (the inner working of watches, sewing machines, cameras and the like) I never did care for being a grease monkey. I opted for the mountains.

When we got to the *Sudetenbaude*, one of the mountain resorts that can be reached via the old, small picturesque city of Glatz, there was naturally no snow at this time of the year, and we received our basic skiing instructions on thick beds of pine needles. For me it was a well-deserved vacation.

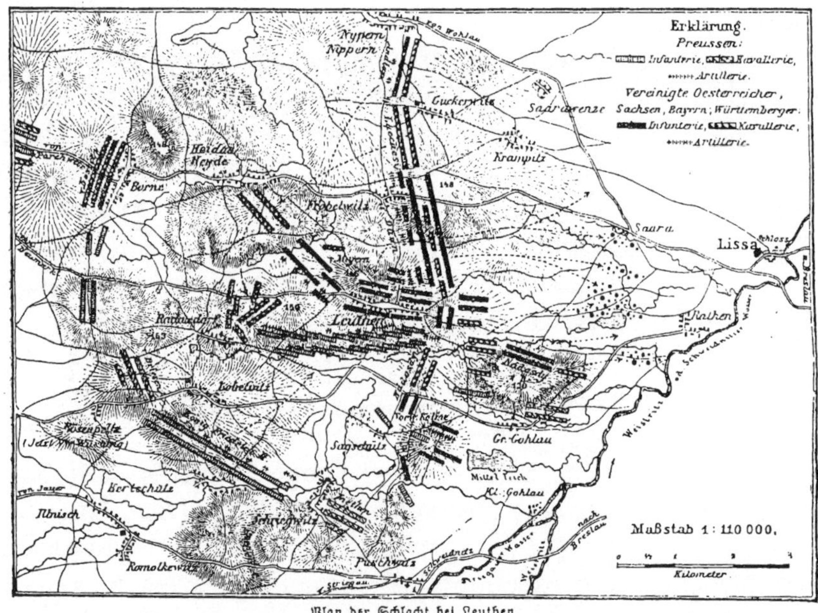

An old map of the Battle of Leuthen (1757) where the Prussian King Frederick the Great won a decisive victory over the Austrians, and, *ipso facto*, also the then German emperor. At the "Schloss" of Lissa, Frederick almost single-handedly captured most of the Austrian generals. The small dot next to the Schloss shows the location of our SS-Infantry howitzer barracks.

Chapter 5

Several times a week we had an hour of *"weltanschauliche Schulung"* (philosophical instructions), actually political studies. While the emphasis was on National Socialism I must state that every attempt was made to broaden our horizon. These instructions were as a rule not under the auspices of our normal superiors who were front-line soldiers more suited for weapons training and tactical and strategic planning, but given by highly qualified officers who had been sent by the SS-FHA (SS *Führungshauptamt*) in Berlin.

These efforts and others in our behalf lead me to believe that I belonged to one of the very last groups of volunteers that had, what one could call, normal Waffen-SS training with the aim of eventually turning us into good officers. Throughout 1944 we noticed that other groups of volunteers had arrived both in Breslau-Lissa and at the SS *Panzergrenadier* barracks in Breslau, received a rather short basic training, and then were immediately assigned to front-line units.

Among other things, we touched on such subjects as *Rassenkunde* (racial studies), culture, economics, European history from a national socialistic point of view, religion in general, and social progress. While I found much of the material interesting, I preferred service in the field. Incidentally, the many hours a week of our training were about evenly split between practical field service and theoretical instructions, the latter of which included tactics and strategy.

During our instructions about race no attempt was made to imbue hate of other groups of people in us, although it was quite clearly pointed out that most of the accomplishments of modern man, beginning with the ancient Greeks, came from white Aryans. Perhaps due to time limits we touched only on the various characteristics of the major races, ie. white, yellow and black. Jews did not fall in either of these categories, and were, with one sentence, merely defined as a mixed race seemingly not worthy of greater consideration. The term *Herrenrasse* (Master Race) still so dearly beloved by anti-Germans was never used.

One of the lecturers visiting us from Berlin had been in Africa during (German) colonial times, and he described the positives and negatives of the Negro race in such a fair way that I can still subscribe to his theories more than a half century later, myself obviously having learned a lot during a half-century of living in the multi-racial United States. The 1944-lecturer was obviously quite sympathetic to the black race, having taught black children in a school in Swakopmund. It was his opinion that no human race was closer to nature than are the Blacks, and that both their innate friendliness as well as that which we call criminal behavior derives from this fact. The officer believed that Blacks were be better off under German rule than was the case in the British and French colonies, and he predicted, quite correctly, that all of Africa would tend to develop "Haitian" conditions should the white man ever leave that continent altogether. This ex-Afrikaaner also spoke derisively of ns propaganda where the black man was often depicted as a brutal savage. He told us stories of the kindness of the black people he had experienced on the dark continent. Still, he warned against miscegenation, pointing out the unpredictable character of mixed-breeds.

Already by 1943 the German (NS) propaganda versus the Russians had laid aside the claim of the sub-culture of the Slavic peoples. This could have been partly because by then belated efforts were made to have larger numbers of the millions of Soviet POWs join anti-Bolshevist forces fighting alongside the Germans, but I am also certain that the common soldier of the Eastern enemy had earned the respect of the German fighting man as a result of his bravery and his ability to suffer for *Mother Russia.* Also, in the middle of the war, in 1943, a small, national German magazine issued in Berlin for a select group of readers interested in foreign policy, published articles where a close future cooperation of the German and Russian peoples was advocated.

The Japanese were our major allies, and this clearly prevented a negative depiction of the Asian race, or any talk of a Yellow Danger as seemed to have been the case in World War I. Japanese heroism was extolled in a movie about the attack on Pearl Harbor and the sinking of the two British battleships *Repulse* and *Prince of Wales* in Southeast Asia. Not being able to overcome our sometimes automatic rooting for the American Navy, due to our white kinship with the Americans, in its battles against the Japanese Imperial Navy, the emphasis was placed on the viciousness of the U.S. supercapitalist exploiter system. Having apprenticed at a *German* capitalist monopoly only a year before, a company that was not only not hindered by the ns regime but actually fostered as a necessity of war, I was personally not very sympathetic to people who tried to control others by virtue of their material wealth and their possession of money.

The German position vis-a-vis the Poles was ambivalent, to say the least. At the time (ie. during World War II) it was obvious to any German who was stationed in occupied Poland either as a soldier or a civilian that the derogatory term "*polnische Wirtschaft*" (literally, "Polish economy"), a term used for an economy where nothing works well, was appropriate. On the other hand, many of the older Germans extolled the good experiences they had with the "Prussian" Poles of the area around Posen (West Prussia) that had been part of the German state of Prussia from Napoleonic times to the reestablishment of the Polish state after World War I.

Shortly after the defeat of Poland in 1939, my father, then a public servant, was appointed the administrator of Wreschen, a small city between Posen and Gnesen (the seat of Polish Catholicism). It was at the very time when the German newsmedia made the most of the cruelties "the" Poles had inflicted on their German fellow citizens shortly before and after the war had begun. The "*Blutsonntag (bloody Sunday) von Bromberg*" (now Bydgoszcz), where many thousands of innocent German men, women and children were brutally slain by Poles on or about September 3, 1939, was undoubtedly one of those occurrences that from the start set World War II on the course of ruthlessness that would find its finale in the allied mistreatment of the entire German people after that nation's defeat.

My father seemed to have been too benign to the Poles under his administration, for soon he was transferred to a little town in Lorraine, not far from our home. But throughout the war the inhabitants from Wreschen remembered his kindness, and even while he was stationed as a common soldier on the Norwegian coast he still received food parcels from his Polish friends. (This also indicates that the food situation in that part of Poland was never as bad as it was, for instance, in the Saar area.)

The German attitude towards the Poles can perhaps be best compared with the way the American elite regards Germany: "It exists, but it would be nice if we did not have to contend with it." It is obvious that in both instances neither side understands the other.

The Polish elite still suffers from delusions of grandeur, and their leaders forget that history has placed their nation in the unfortunate vise of Germany on one hand and Russia on the other. Under the circumstances, Poland can never be truly independent. Many Poles also do not recognize their severe national shortcomings, and that is why their nation even found it necessary to claim Germans of world-renown, for instance such men as Nikolaus Copernicus and Veit Stoss, as their own. Even to this day, without massive infusion of (mainly) German capital, Poland would have a standard of living on a par with many Third World countries. This in spite of the fact that after 1945 Poland was able to annex a quarter of Germany, expel its population, and thus become the questionable owner of a totally built-up infrastructure (everything from thumb tacks to churches, factories, railroads and administrative buildings) of the size of Belgium. No wonder the average German does not understand the Poles, and there is comparatively little interaction between these two peoples bordering each other.

During *weltanschauliche Schulung* we obviously also delved into the causes of the war. Being a Saarlander whose family had suffered greatly as a result of the wrongful stipulations of the Treaty of Versailles, a treaty that the Germans had been forced to sign at gunpoint, I fully agreed with the German war aims, namely, the full restoration of German sovereignty; the re-establishment of Reich borders that did not leave millions of our people and great parts of Germany under foreign rule; the relief from financial slavery to other nations, and the right to have armed forces that were able to defend the nation.

Only recently I read a statement in a Jewish school book (The New Jewish History, by Mamie G. Gamoran, The Union of American Hebrew Congregations, New York, 1957) that *"Hitler's plans were (...) world dominion, and the extermination of the Jews."* It is difficult to answer such nonsense but since it seems to be a prevailing opinion among some parts of the American population, this subject matter has to be addressed:

If Hitler, and thereby the German Reich, had world dominion as its aim, the war would have taken a difference course from the start. Even to the most naïve reader it must be apparent that one cannot conquer the world with 50-man U-Boats and single-engine *Stukas*. In 1940, after the defeat of France, the Germans were not even able to launch an invasion of Great Britain across the 20-odd miles of the English Channel due to the shortcomings of the German Navy and Air Force. How, then, could the Germans ever have invaded the United States, 3,000 miles away, for instance? And for what reason?

It bears remembering that during the Second World War the Reich fought several nations that were really bent on world domination, or were already in possession of large parts of it, namely, Great Britain, Soviet Russia (World Bolshevism!), France, World Jewry and the United States. In the case of the latter, the argument that the population of this nation has never aspired to world domination is certainly true, but the American elite did so for financial gain, and there is no question that the U.S.A. is at this time the only superpower imposing its will on billions of people in this world (whether for the alleged good of all, and the mythical 'democracy', does not matter in this context). At any rate, the United States did not reach this position by a fluke of history but by the strong determination of some of its elitists.

Ironically, I can state unequivocally that if Hitler and his Third Reich had really aspired to world domination, Germany might have won the war. Then, almost from the beginning in 1933, the nation would have been put on war footing, and, most certainly, the development of such weapons as the atomic bomb and ICBMs would have been given priority. Later "Nazi" prowess in the production of super weapons bears me out. However, in 1941, while the United States was already fully engaged in war production, and as the Soviet Union had for years allocated 90 percent of its output of all goods to the war effort, the Reich still produced 40 percent of its manufactured goods for civilian use. In this context it bears remembering that the United States is 20 times as large as is Germany, and the USSR was even larger, with both nations possessing huge quantities of natural resources, something the Germans lacked almost totally, except for coal.

When Adolf Hitler came to power, his major aims were the breaking of the chains placed upon the German nation by the Treaty of Versailles, and the elimination of unemployment. In 1933, six million German men, a third of the work force, were without a job at a time when the men were usually the sole breadwinners of their families. For Germans, for whom work was the life's elixir, this was especially hard to bear.

Unfortunately, the National Socialist, or, if you wish, Hitlerian solution of the social problems of Germany, including that of unemployment, could not be accomplished without breaking the Jewish economic stranglehold over Germany. Especially in the short time span between 1918 and 1933, the German Jews had managed to take control of much of the economic, political, cultural and social life in Germany. They owned the major newspapers, the movie studios, the department stores and book publishers. They were the judges, the lawyers, the public administrators, and the people in charge of the teaching profession. They owned the most important banks and industrial cartels. In politics, they operated mainly through the leftist parties, and Communism was their fief. In short, they called the shots in a nation that for hundreds of years before the Jewish ascent was known all over the world as the *Land der Dichter und Denker,* the land of Poets and Philisophers. Goethe and Schiller, Beethoven and Mozart (and the innumerable other almost equally talented Germans) and leaders like Martin Luther and Frederick the Great, had all been real Germans, and suddenly these giants and others like them had been supplanted by an ethnically and genetically different tribe that believed it could do everything better. In other words, no German solution of German problems was possible with the Jews still in power. While, undoubtedly in Germany as elsewhere, there had always been calls to eliminate the Jewish problem of a nation by expulsion (it happened for hundreds of years all over Europe) it deserves mentioning that at first most of the National Socialist leadership had really only the disempowerment of the Jews In mind, not their expulsion. The first laws instituted after the NS *Machtergreifung* were passed with this goal in mind. One can assume that in 1933 no large-scale expulsion of the approximately 600,000 German Jews, about one percent of the German population, had been planned.

Unfortunately, it was also clear from the start that World Jewry would not permit the new Hitler Government to curtail Jewish power in Germany with impunity. Within weeks after the swastika flag was raised over the Reich Chancellory, a worldwide hate campaign and a call for the boycott of German goods was begun by prominent Jews abroad. One American Jewish leader, Samuel Untermyer, went even so far as to declare, in March of 1933, a Jewish holy war against the Reich and the German people. Undoubtedly these actions culminated in the Second World War, and finally in the fact that eventually most of the European Jews were largely displaced, and incurred greater human losses than if they had accepted the fact that it is against nature for a small alien and ethnically quite different tribe to try to rule a nation that by itself had reached great spiritual, cultural, social and scientific heights. But there was never any plan or order by Hitler to 'exterminate' all the German (or European) Jews. Had Hitler given such an order, then most likely there would not have been 500,000 so-called Holocaust survivors alive and in the Middle East at the founding of the Jewish state of Israel in the spring of 1948.

The late, well-known, excellent Jewish writer Walter Lippmann, who dominated the New York literary scene in the first half of the Twentieth Century, was totally disgusted with humanity after one of the U.S. Government's hare-brained schemes, in the development of which he was intimately involved had failed, namely, President Wilson's (World War I) "14 Points". In my opinion, this fact points perhaps to the greatest flaw in the Jewish character, namely, the inability to accept human beings as they are, and not try to go against nature and impose ideas and policies that are bound to fail. It is a pity that currently, due to 'PC' (political correctness) this aspect of Jewish behavior cannot be openly discussed. And as long as it cannot be discussed, no reasonable solution is possible.

During our political, respectively *weltanschauliche* education, much emphasis was also placed on proving to us the advantages of the *Führersystem*, namely the leadership principle as practiced in Hitler Germany vs. parliamentary democracy or the monarchies. Considering the social and economic mess Germany was in before Hitler's assumption of power, and the fact that Franklin Delano Roosevelt needed a war to get America out of the Depression, this was not a difficult task. Much was also made of the fact that in the United States people were able to vote who could hardly read, and who were therefore unable to really understand the issues at hand. In simpler terms we were told that a vagrant off the street was able to negate with his vote the opposite vote of a highly educated professor who had taken weeks to consider his choice. Needless to say, such draconian examples did not generate our sympathies for parliamentarism.

Just as the German movie industry did not produce even one anti-American film during the Third Reich, so I can honestly state that we were not taught to hate "America" or the American people. On the other hand, much was made of FDR's supposedly Jewish background (Rosenfeld) and that at least two of his closest advisers were Jews, namely, Bernard Baruch and Henry Morgenthau. Praise was heaped on Americans like Charles Lindbergh, Henry Ford and others who tried to keep the United States out of the war.

A similar emphasis as was put on Jewish influence in the United States, was placed on Joseph Stalin. He was depicted as surrounded by Jews like Beria, Kaganovich and others. We delved extensively into the fact that the great majority of the early Bolshevist leaders had been Jews, and that it was they, and not the Russian people, who were the real enemy.

At the time I personally never grasped or took special notice of the insistence on the Jewish background of enemy leaders. Up to then my view of Jews had been formed mainly by my voracious reading of biblical history during my school years.

Because the biblical events had taken place in what were for me alien surroundings, and a land far away, I was fascinated by the tales of the New Testament in which Jews played a major role. We were not taught, and it was never impressed upon our minds, to blame the Jews of our era for the fact that it was the Jewish High Priests of Jerusalem who had delivered Jesus to the Romans. In other words, I never made the connection.

The only Jew I had ever met before the end of the war was our beloved Dr. Fromm. Dr. Rudolf Fromm of Luisenthal on the Saar river had been our doctor during my childhood, and as a sickly boy who suffered through almost all maladies that can afflict a child, I had been under his care often. Besides, he obviously loved children in general, and due to his less-than-strict nature (at the time a rarity among German adults) we always enjoyed talking to him or greeting him when he, always dapperly dressed, made his house calls in our neighborhood.

Soon after the (now) so-called *Kristallnacht* on the 9th of November 1938, when, among others, the Saarbrücken synagogue was destroyed by arson, Dr. Fromm was told by some of his friends who had by then reached high positions in the party or other NS organizations, that he had better consider emigrating from Germany. He left early in 1939 for New York, where he died five years later. In 1952 during my mother's first visit to the United States, we both visited Dr. Fromm's grave in a Jewish cemetery in New Jersey (where, by the way, I noticed a monument to the "7 Million Jews" allegedly murdered by the Germans) and paid homage to this fine human being.

While I am certain that I was one of the few people in Germany who thought often of Dr. Fromm throughout the war, and even at the front, because he had been such an integral part of my childhood, the question might be justified whether we Germans (all?) were not shocked by the fact that Jewish co-citizens such as Dr. Fromm were forced to leave our German *Heim*atland for political reasons.

In this regard I do have to mention that only twenty years before, immediately after World War I, far greater numbers of equally innocent Germans were forced by the victors to leave their various border provinces, and emigrate somewhere else. I am speaking of Germans from territories that fell to Poland, Czechoslovakia, Italy, France, Belgium and Denmark, and also from the German colonies. Their number was in the millions. In the Saar, the French wanted to make sure that the most important of the German nationalist leaders of the territory did not attempt to impede their efforts to Frenchify the Saar population, and they expelled them overnight. The driving out from Germany of the Jews was for most people merely a continuation of the same injustice, and for the general population it was clear that in 1938 protests in Berlin were just as useless (and could be as dangerous!) as they had been between 1918 and 1920 in Paris, London, Warsaw and Washington. (In light of the fact that the Allies, including the United States, expelled 18 million Germans from their ancestral homes beyond the Oder-Neisse line after 1945, how many Germans would object if someday a government got the idea to expel all 10 million Czechs from Bohemia, and settle them beyond the Ural mountains, where their ancestors came from? I am mentioning such analogies to show Americans that in life not only good deeds are rewarded: Bad actions have a way of hounding the descendants of the wrongdoers.)

To prove how little effect the instructions, or, if one will, propaganda, concerning Judeo-Bolshevism and Judeo-Wall Street capitalism had on me, I must fast-forward to 1949:

In the fall of 1949, a few months after my arrival in the United States, I wanted to live right smack in the center of the world, namely, on the island of Manhattan. There I began looking for a job, and for a room to live. I still remember when I walked past the large news stand that was located on the north side of the *New York Times* building, just north of 42nd Street, when I saw a newspaper with the name "Aufbau" displayed. Looking closer I noticed that it was in the German language. I bought a copy, and within a day I had found, through the "Aufbau", a room on West 137th Street, and a job not far away on 125th Street, the major thoroughfare that leads into black-populated Harlem.

When I mentioned my change of address and the new job to a German acquaintance, and that I had found both through the "Aufbau", this man pointed out to me that this newspaper was in fact a German-language newspaper that had been founded in 1934 by German Jews who had been driven out from Germany. At the time I was still so unfamiliar with this subject matter that I had been unable to notice the difference between Aryan German names such as Uwe Peters and a typical Jewish German one like Ignatz Goldmann. As a result, both my landlord and my boss were German Jews. I also could never understand how German Jews, if they considered themselves as '100 percent' Germans as any other born citizen of the *Vaterland,* - as many did claim - could totally abdicate their loyalty to Germany just because one particular government had mistreated them. (I did not consider myself less a German because in 1995 the Bonn Government had incarcerated me for political reasons.)

Soon after my arrival in New York things would become even more interesting. I had to improve my English language skills and enrolled in one of the evening classes at a public school where "English for New Immigrants" was being taught. Since this school was in the general area of Manhattan where by then I lived and worked, an area the German Jews themselves called jokingly the "Fourth Reich", it follows that many of my co-students were also German or other Central European Jews. Most of them were young, like myself, most of them were DPs (displaced persons from various European countries), and a number of them had been held in either German concentration camps or work camps during the war.

Lo and behold, after a while they elected me the Editor-in-Chief of the school newspaper (only for the evening classes), and thereafter I sat many an evening editing the writings of my co-students and new friends. There were times when I had to rein in their writing enthusiasm as their vivid imaginations about the war experiences went too far off the possible. They knew I had been in the Waffen-SS, and once in a while I had to remind them that I had been "there" too, and that I knew what had been possible and what not.

On July 14, 2001, the American television "History Channel" showed a program about the last mass execution that occurred in an American prison. It was the ignominious and cowardly hanging of seven German U-Boat sailors in August of 1945, an execution that occurred months after the German capitulation and when these poor fellows were totally at the mercy of the U.S. victors.

In a POW camp holding so-called elite POWs, namely *Afrika Korps, Luftwaffe, U-Boat and Waffen-SS* soldiers, the Germans had caught one of their own being a spy for the Americans. A kangaroo court sentenced the spy to death and he was executed. The American military was obviously furious, and used medieval means to extract false confessions from the seven German soldiers who were eventually hung at Fort Leavenworth. Their real guilt lie in the fact that they had not been amenable to Allied brainwashing. The entire episode was an incredibly brutal tale of stupidity, revenge and - yes - hypocrisy for which some members of the American military and also President Harry S. Truman can be blamed.

What I found both shocking and interesting in this TV program was a sentence spoken by the narrator:

"Organized religion had been outlawed in Nazi Germany."

Hearing this, I was speechless. The fact is that the Hitler regime took absolutely no measures against the major churches, respectively religions, in Germany. 96% of the Germans were either Catholic or Protestant, and church attendance was as much as seven or eight times greater than it is today. *Nobody was prohibited from going to church or from belonging to a church.* Once the war had begun, conscientious objectors, among them Jehovah's Witnesses, were forced to do some service for the nation, and if they still refused they were incarcerated. But the same happened in almost all other warring nations, including the United States. If priests and in some cases even nuns could be found in the concentration camps, then they were there because they had transgressed against the stringent wartime laws. Among the Polish priests held at Dachau, for instance, the majority had been supporting the Polish underground. If after the war German priests had given aid and support to a Neo-Nazi partisan movement against the Allies, would the U.S. Military Government have abstained from persecuting them because they were priests?

How can one fight such constant lies about Germany, and especially Hitler Germany, as the History Channel broadcast in July of 2001, lies that are being told in America day-in, day-out, decade after decade. Rarely is a correction or a protest by a German published. No wonder most Americans, including well-educated ones, have a warped idea of what had really transpired during the Third Reich.

I remember this: Every Sunday morning two buses were standing by inside the gate of the Breslau-Lissa barracks to take potential church goers either to a Catholic or Protestant service. Absolutely no attempt was made to induce any of the Waffen-SS soldiers to abstain from church attendance or to leave their religion.

The allied invasion of June 6, 1944 certainly did *not* take us by surprise. It had been expected for a long time, and while I was in the *Reichsarbeitsdienst* on the island of Borkum, we had frequently delved into the various possibilities of time and place. I must say, though, that nobody guessed Normandy as a first landing place although the newspapers had written about all the other potential landing sites.

It follows that during our almost daily tactical, strategic and political instructions the invasion front was uppermost in everybody's mind. Almost all of the Waffen-SS elite units such as the LAH, the new *Hitlerjugend* division, and *Das Reich*, *Hohenstaufen*, among others, were engaged on the invasion front and we followed their battles intently. One day, shortly before the break-out of General Patton's forces from the Cotentin peninsula, one of our instructors, an older man with the rank of major (albeit not Waffen-SS), pointed to a spot on a map of France and stated flatly that *"if the Americans manage to break through here, and our soldiers are unable to close this gap again, then, judged strictly from a military point of view, the war is lost."*

The major had pointed at the city of Avranches! On one of the first days of August 1944 the fateful break-through was made, and Patton's Third Army began its dash through France that would only stop near the border of the Reich in the following month. Except for skirmishes with some hotheads in the French resistance (most of them belated heroes), Paris was abandoned without a fight on August 25th, at about the same time that we, in Breslau-Lissa, realized that the bulk of the Waffen-SS divisions fighting in Normandy had been caught in the Falaise pocket. Many of our best regiments had lost most of their armor, and had hardly any fighting units left.

As *Führerbewerbers* (cadets, officer aspirants) we regularly attended lectures by well-known personalities of the Third Reich. The subject matter could be almost anything: the military situation; new weapons; foreign policy; history, *Weltanschauung*, the economy and, I suppose, anything that in later years might sharpen our senses and increase our knowledge.

During tactics training at Breslau-Lissa we tested, probably in behalf of a Berlin headquarters, a new approach to infantry combat that was in the end never used in battle:

As a result of the storm troop experience of World War I, the infantry units of the new German Armed Forces under Hitler's command had placed the *Schwerpunkt* (focal point) of a squad of infantry around the machine gun. Especially after the development of the MG-42 this tactic proved very valuable indeed, when everything was geared to support both of the soldiers manning the weapon, and keep them supplied with ammunition. The MG-42 had such a tremendous firing rate (1550 rounds a minute) that it was sheer suicide for enemy infantry to try to make a frontal assault on a German machine gun nest. Over one million of these deadly weapons were produced during the war. Our test evolved around the feasibility of using not just one but two MG-42s in a single squad, leaving practically only the squad leader and a sharpshooter equipped with a special rifle (with a scope and night vision gear) outside of the machine gun support role. I believe that this test was made because by 1944 the production of MG-42s, a simply to produce weapon, had reached enormous numbers. One report I have states that 2,000 MG-42s were still delivered to the German military on Hitler's birthday, April 20, 1945, two weeks before the end of the war, even though the major industrial centers of the Reich had by then already fallen into the hands of the enemies.

Our test proved that two MG-42s in a single squad would use ammunition faster than could be supplied in a heavy engagement. Having only one machine gun under his command a squad leader was more prone to keep a lid on the excessive misuse of bullets.

One warm summer evening we were sitting on benches that had been placed in a kind of theater forum out in the open, when the lecturer of the week appeared, neatly dressed in the uniform of an officer of the Waffen-SS. It was *Sturmbannführer* (Major) Karl Ivanowitsch Albrecht, formerly a German Communist who had risen to the high rank of Deputy Soviet Peoples Commissar of Forestry in the Soviet Union, if I remember correctly. Albrecht had eventually been incarcerated in the USSR, and was one of the many people who had been exchanged for German-held Soviet citizens and German Communists when as a result of the Ribbentrop-Molotov (not "Hitler-Stalin", by the way) pact such individuals were traded.

I knew of Albrecht before he ever came to visit us since I had read his name in either *Das Reich* (the newspaper wherein Dr.

Goebbels' weekly column appeared) or in the *Völkischer Beobachter,* the major paper of the NSDAP, the "Nazi" party. (Incidentally, I preferred to read *Das Reich* above all other papers that appeared during the Hitler era. I practically never read *Gauleiter* Julius Streicher's *Der Stürmer* since I had absolutely no interest in the doings of the Jews, and I rarely read *Das schwarze Korps,* the newspaper of the SS.) Karl Albrecht had written a book about the failures and horrors of Communism, titled "*Der verratene Sozialismus*" (Socialism betrayed), that was sponsored by the so-called "Anti-Komintern" Committee, and sold in the millions.[13]

Albrecht's lecture was boring. It dealt mainly with the horrors of the Soviet concentration camp system, and the brutal methods of the GPU, then still the commonly used name for the Soviet secret police. While Albrecht claimed to have been tortured in order to get some kind of confession from him, to me he did not look as if that experience had left any permanent physical or mental mark. I can imagine that American school children are having the same thoughts when during Holocaust studies they listen to a spry, 90 year-old "Holocaust survivor" who could outrun them.

After that summer evening I never heard anything of or about Albrecht again, although I wondered at times what had become of him. Now, 57 years later, I received this information from a former Waffen-SS officer:

Almost immediately after the capitulation of the Armed Forces of the Third Reich, Karl Albrecht reverted to Communism. Soon he was one of the top promoters of that unholy ideology in the newly created West German *Bundesrepublik.* He also wrote an anti-"Nazi" book titled "...*wen die verderben wollen*"(...whomever they want to corrupt) that was somehow promoted by, of all people, the American occupation authorities. It seems that Karl Albrecht had never lost contact with the NKVD/MVD even while serving in the SS. If that is so then he did great harm to the German cause because for some time this man headed a special office in one of the secret services of the Reich where he was responsible for the

---

[13] Comintern: Communist International, one of the major vehicles of Soviet Bolshevism to foster the Communist world revolution.

interrogation and handling of Soviet officers who had defected to our side.

Der Feldpostnummer 21625 A — Zur Einlage ins Soldbuch

Merkblatt

über die Wegnahme von Feindesgut

Der Krieg ist nicht dazu da, daß sich der Einzelne — wie auch immer — bereichert.

Es ist unritterlich und SS-unwürdig, die wehrlose Zivilbevölkerung und Gefangene um Hab und Gut zu bringen.

Auch im Kriege und dem Feind gegenüber gilt der Befehl des Reichsführers-SS von der „Heiligkeit des Eigentums".

Vom SS-Standpunkt aus, und nach den auf Veranlassung des Führers verschärften Kriegsbestimmungen ist die

Wegnahme von Feindesgut eingeschränkt.

1. **Ohne Barzahlung und ohne Quittung dürfen nur weggenommen werden:**

   · **Nahrungsmittel, Wäsche, Decken, Heilmittel, Treibstoffe im Rahmen des persönlichen und augenblicklichen Bedarfes des einzelnen Soldaten.**

   Es können also z. B. nicht weggenommen werden: Silberbestecke, Zivilkleider, Stoffe, Damenstrümpfe u. a. m., kurz, was für Angehörige in der Heimat bestimmt ist.

   Kriegsgefangenen und Gefallenen darf nichts weggenommen werden.

2. Requirierungen (Beitreibungen) — das sind Beschaffungen für die Einheit — dürfen weder Männer noch Unterführer, sondern nur Führer vom Kompanieführer aufwärts vornehmen. Diese Requirierungen müssen durch ein unter dem Befehl eines Führers stehenden Requirierungskommandos erfolgen, und zwar gegen Barzahlung oder gegen Aushändigung einer von dem Führer zu unterzeichnenden Leistungsbescheinigung (Requirierungsschein).

   Männer und Unterführer dürfen also keinen Requirierungsschein ausstellen.

3. Alles andere ist Plünderung. Hierauf steht die Todesstrafe.

   Vom SS-Standpunkt aus ist Plünderung kein „Kavaliersdelikt".

4. Feindliches Staatseigentum (Beute) ist abzuliefern.

This is how my uniform looked in the spring of 1945. The *Hoffnungsbalken* (girders of hope - silver braids) around the shoulder straps showed that I was destined to become an officer but many soldiers took it for a sign of rank, which it wasn't. The ribbon on the chest denotes the Iron Cross, Second Class (the First Class was worn as Hitler had it on his uniform), and the *Verwundetenabzeichen* can be seen on the left breast pocket.
To the right is a *Merkblatt* (remainder) about how to deal with enemy property that was pasted in every Waffen-SS soldiers *Soldbuch*. The translated text can be found on page 77.

Chapter 6

Due to the fact that all of us were still under 18 years of age, and because our bodies were still developing, special care was taken that we received the proper nourishment, and good medical care. (In Waffen-SS units with many very young soldiers, especially in the divisions *Hitlerjugend* and *Adolf Hitler*, a porridge made from either oats, cream of wheat or rice was served in the morning. This caused army soldiers to call these divisions derisively the *"Milchsuppen-Divisionen"*: the milk soup divisions.) Yet, incongruously, we also received a daily ration of a few cigarettes. This in spite of the fact that pre-war SS-research had shown how harmful nicotine could be to one's health. I can only assume that the cigarette rations were distributed in the interest of fairness, and because the higher-ups in Berlin did not want to rock the boat while the fighting was going on. At any rate, since I did not smoke, and had no inclination to start then, I made the best of my cigarette ration. After a while I had the neatest uniform of all the recruits of our company, almost all new stuff and of the best quality available: The older privates and non-commissioned officers at the supply depot could be easily persuaded with a few cigarettes.

While the discipline in the Waffen-SS was very strict, and every measure was taken to keep us in line, so to speak, there were avenues where we showed our individualism even if, in fact, such ways were *verboten* or frowned upon.

Take, for instance, our uniforms. The name obviously implies "the same", and one would assume that all hundred or so of us would wear identical uniforms. But that was not the case at all. Part of the reason for the discrepancy was the fact that the German resources were exhausted after such a long war, but it also mattered how good or exceptional we wanted to look. While we all received the same brand-new "harvest-pattern" camouflage fatigues, and not much could be done with them, we had quite a bit of leeway as far as our field gray tunic and trousers were concerned. As the war had progressed, the wool used for the field-gray uniforms had gotten worse, and in 1944 they even brought out a short jacket patterned somewhat after the Eisenhower jacket the Americans wore. It was manufactured with coarse, recycled yarns, and quickly wore through when used too much.

As far as I was concerned, I saw to it that I received the best uniform in my size available. Then I began "customizing" it: When we received passes and tickets to travel by train or bus into the inner city of Breslau, and go there to the movies or ogle the pretty Silesian girls, I wore a white turtleneck pullover underneath my tunic, showing just a bit of white of it at the edge of the collar. I also wore white socks nicely rolled over the tip of my boots, just as the *Gebirgsjäger,* the mountain troops did, and to top it off I bought an Edelweiss flower stamped from metal that I fastened on the side of my peaked cap, also like a *Gebirgsjäger*. What surprises me to this day was the fact that I got away with it. But it may have been that due to the seriousness of the war situation our superiors did not want to bother with such minor details.

There were numerous times when we helped comrades that were somewhat older than we, and who had trysts with local girls, to climb over or underneath the fence surrounding our barracks area when, long after reveille, they returned to base. If caught, we all faced the customary three days' arrest with only bread and water as rations. It happened to me once but I was glad for the needed sleep I thus could enjoy. Because our company needed me in the office, I spent only about one day in the gaol.

The worst trouble makers among SS soldiers were those from the Low Countries, volunteers from Holland and Flanders. I personally really enjoyed the company of these spirited fellows, they were my kind of comrades. They were very good soldiers, and I was told that in combat they were unsurpassed for both bravery and death-defying actions. But their attitude was much more freedom-oriented than was evident among Reich Germans. An attitude many Germans viewed as a lack of inner discipline. The Flemish and

Dutch liked to argue, even with higher officers, and obviously they had different ideas as to how Europe should be reorganized after our victory than we had. There is no doubt that people of this kind would have played a major role in European politics if we had won the war. It is doubtful that the German NS leadership would have been able to railroad them into total submission.

I still recall reading in the fall of 1944 about Remy Schrijnen, a Flemish SS-soldier who received the coveted *Ritterkreuz* for destroying seven Russian tanks in a single action. While I would not want to say that Schrijnen's actions were "typical" as stated in the excerpt about him from the book "*Hell on the Eastern front*" by Christopher Ailsby (MBI Publishing Corp., Osceola, WI. 1998), Schrijnen nevertheless exemplified the spirit of the hundreds of thousands of non-German volunteers who fought alongside us against Bolshevism:

"Typical of the foreign volunteers in the Waffen-SS at this time was the anti-tank gunner SS-Unterscharführer Remy Schrijnen, Langemarck Brigade. He demonstrated his fortitude in many taxing situations. On 2 January 1944, for example, he destroyed three Russian T-34 tanks; on 3 March he was wounded for the seventh time. On the fourth day of the Russian offensive his gun crew was neutralized, either killed and wounded, and the support grenadiers retreated. Schrijnen, now alone, received orders to withdraw. He decided to stay at his post, loading, aiming and firing at the advancing tanks alone. As a dying naval radio operator directed artillery fire onto Schrijnen's own position, the enemy infantry attacked. Behind the infantry came 30 tanks, five being the new Joseph Stalin types. In a dramatic firefight, he destroyed three Stalins and four T-34s, putting others out of action until a Stalin blew up his gun no more than 30 m (98) ft. away, severely wounding him and catapulting him away. During a counterattack, he was discovered surrounded by the shot-up and glowing parts of a dozen Soviet tanks. For this bravery he was awarded the Knight's Cross on 21 September 1944."

In July of 1944 we received a contingent of "Dutch" SS soldiers from the *Standarte Langemarck,* to be trained with our howitzers, and it was then that things really became lively in the Breslau barracks. These fellows were obviously not awed by Hitler or other big shots of the NS regime, and they did not hesitate to criticize our leadership when they felt it necessary. Here I ought to mention that our general behavior in the Waffen-SS was already much freer than was customary among other German soldiers, and to this day I am convinced that we were more free in our thought processes than can be found today in the allegedly free and democratic American Army or other U.S. military units. For us there existed no political correctness, and we did not hesitate to express our opinion about others (other ethnic and religious groups, and peoples, for instance) when we thought there was a need for blunt talk. We had no fear of hurting someone's sensibilities. How else can one straighten out things that have gone bad except through often brutal honesty? Something that is dismally lacking in the United States at the beginning of the 21st Century.

How well I remember the conversations all of us had about the failed 20 July 1944 putsch against Hitler. We considered all the possibilities: What would have happened if the traitorous officers had been able to kill the Führer? Whom would we have followed? Would it have come to fighting between army units loyal to the traitors and us? Would it have been possible to keep all the fronts intact? I recall myself stating that I would unhesitatingly shoot any German carrying different flags than ours (meaning the ones with the swastika or with the SS runes).

We talked at length about the question when it would be permissible to try to overthrow the government of one's nation, but we all agreed that this should *never* be done in wartime, and especially not when the nation - - any nation - - is in a battle for its very existence. Having learned about President Wilson's 14 Points, and the fact that Germany capitulated in November of 1918 by trusting the assurances given by the American President, we regarded it as politically extremely naïve of the July 20th putschists to once more place their trust in any of the major enemies of the Reich. (The developments in Germany after the unconditional surrender on May 8, 1945, bore this out.) Incidentally, while we were informed of the fate of some of the treachorous officers like Field Marshal von Witzleben and a relatively small number of others, the true extent of the conspiracy became known only after the war. But then, obviously, the traitors were depicted as virtuous idealists, while the millions of German soldiers and officers who did their duty for the Fatherland to the last became pariahs.

Few Americans have an inkling of the great damage the (relatively few) traitors in the ranks of the Armed Forces did to the German cause. The Battle of Kursk did not turn into a decisive German victory; the supply of winter clothing to the troops on the Eastern front was sabotaged in the winter of 1941, and it is doubtful that the allied invasion would have succeeded as it did without the purposefully false disposition of some of the best German divisions after the Allies had landed.

During the war, listening to enemy radio stations was strictly prohibited, and could be severely punished. Unlike in the USSR, where few people owned their own radio sets and depended on the radio news that was piped into their places of employment and elsewhere through loudspeakers, many Germans had excellent radios, many with three different bands, and there was really no way to control the situation except by proscribing especially severe sentences for people who listened to the enemy *and disseminated* this knowledge to others. Similarly, the dealing in black market goods was often extremely harshly punished, at times with a death sentence.

For Americans reading this, the measures taken by the Hitler Government relating to both the dissemination of enemy propaganda and against any sort of black marketeering may seem unduly harsh and way out of proportion. However: It bears remembering that during World War II almost all of the major German leaders, including all the high-ranking military officers at the beginning of the war, with the exception of Dr. Goebbels, Albert Speer, Heinrich Himmler and a few others, had been veterans of the First World War. It follows that their entire world view was formed, or one could even say clouded, by that war and its aftermath, namely, the 1918 capitulation and the punitive peace enforced by the victors.

Most Americans interested in history have heard of the so-called *Dolchstosslegende,* the *alleged* claim that the German soldiers of World War I had been stabbed in the back by certain elements - let's call them anti-war protesters - inside the Reich.

The fact is that already in 1916 German soldiers at the front experienced severe shortages of ammunition because leftist (Communist and Social Democratic) agitators had promoted strikes in essential industries. Furthermore, the black market inside the

Reich blossomed, causing widespread hunger among the masses while a thin veneer of German society lived as if in peace time. Unfortunately, many of the leftist agitators who organized the strikes in the ammunition factories, and a great number of the best known black marketeers, were Jews from Poland and Galicia (the Western Ukraine) and this fact contributed to the growing anti-Judaism among German nationalists. (A comparison may be drawn with the fact that proportionally many Jews were among the leaders of the Vietnam era anti-war movement.)

When Germany accepted the Fourteen Points of President Woodrow Wilson's peace program in late 1918, the German leadership saw an honorable way out of the war, and accepted under these proposals. The fact that this occurred while German troops were still deep in France and Russia, and that the German industry was virtually intact, led to the *justified and true* claim or assumption by German soldiers in the field, soldiers such as Adolf Hitler, that they had been stabbed in the back, hence the *Dolchstosslegende,* the Legend of the Stab in the Back. It must also be stated that at the time the German soldiers had not lost a single decisive battle against the Allies.

With the onset of World War II, the "Nazi" leadership was mindful of their bad experiences during and after the First World War. Hence, strikes were absolutely forbidden, and so was all black marketeering and the dissemination of enemy propaganda, ie. the spreading of false news. The laws which prohibited these transgressions were extremely harsh, and in many cases the death penalty was pronounced and executed.

Hitler was of the opinion that the lives of malicious law breakers were not of any higher value than those of the German soldier at the front whose life was endangered every minute of every day. In one known instance, a hoodlum, a previously convicted thief and robber, was caught after he had grabbed, during the black-out, the handbag of a woman, breaking her arm in the process. A lenient judge gave the convict, a young man who had not been drafted because of his criminal record, a cursory prison sentence. After hearing of this sentence and of the fact that the victim was the mother of a soldier who had given his life for Germany, the *Führer* ordered the execution of the criminal under his wartime laws.

There are a couple of stories connected with rifle training that are worth telling:

We were still in basic training when for some reason I must have gotten on the nerves of a drill sergeant known for his strictness. Once, after training in the mud and dust of a freshly harvested field, we had to clean our rifles as well as we could, namely to a spotless condition. After we thought we had completed this task, the entire company assembled in the courtyard of the barracks for inspection. The first few of my comrades seemed to have done well, for no complaint from the inspecting non-commissioned officers could be heard. But once my turn had come, and I presented my rifle to this sergeant for inspection, he dressed me down rather loudly, claiming that I really had a nerve to show him a rifle the bore of which still showed rust. He immediately ordered me back into the barracks to take the rifle apart again, and begin the cleaning process anew.

A few minutes later it appeared that I was not the only one who had drawn the wrath of this particular *Ausbilder* (DI), because soon more fellows from my squad came inside and, immediately taking their rifles apart, began oiling and polishing them and whatever else had to be done to get in good grace with the sergeant again. I, on the other hand, did absolutely nothing. All the time while my comrades slaved with their 98ks, I was resting on my bunk, viewing the situation with a smile. One of my comrades couldn't believe that I had cleaned my rifle again so fast, and he questioned me about it. I told him that I had a secret helper in getting the thing in order. When he questioned who was my secret helper I merely said "psychology", and let it go at that. Obviously, my answer remained a puzzle to him and the others.

Once again outside and in the inspection line, we faced the same DI again, and as I had expected, he screamed even louder than before, however always keeping the two or three feet distance required by the Waffen-SS when *Ausbilder* spoke to their charges (in other words, none of that obnoxious behavior was permitted that seems endemic with American DIs who seem to like to practically spit into the faces of recruits). The DI claimed that we were a lazy bunch of no-goods who did not even know how to see with the naked eye when their rifle, their very life preserver in combat, is full of rust. Soon most of us were again back in our room, and the taking apart and cleaning the rifles began anew. Except myself. I rested while the others slaved. This went on once more, twice more. Each time a few of us fellows passed the inspection, and the remaining few were sent back for more of the same. Finally, after having done nothing at all to my rifle from the very beginning (because I believed that it was already as clean as it could possibly be!) the DI took the weapon from me, looked it over carefully, handed it back to me and then said, still in a loud voice, "now, why couldn't you have done such a good job from the start?" Then, giving the rifle back to me, he added, "this is the way a rifle should always look for inspection." I am glad the DI did not see me grinning inwardly. My comrades looked dumbfounded but kept their mouths shut.

I was a pretty good sharp shooter, having earned a proficiency badge while training with small caliber rifles in the Hitler Youth. Although I really disliked to shoot with the 98k because of the poerful recoil, I was soon one of the best shooters in the company, and especially our new squad leader, a 19-year old corporal whom I did not like, wanted to use my shooting skills to win some sort of trophy or certificate for our unit during a shooting competition.

It was apple pie, something that I really liked, that literally sweetened my shooting efforts: One of the major shooting ranges of Breslau was located just off the road between Lissa and downtown Breslau near the Oder river. A family, the father of which was a soldier, seemed to have the concession for the small eating place connected to the range, and while the husband was away at the front, his wife took good care of the soldiers that utilized the premises. One of the woman's specialties was freshly backed *Apfelkuchen*, actually more of a pie similar to the one commonly baked in America, and not the kind of cake the Germans are used to. I assume the lady had invented this *Kuchen* herself because it needed less flour, and she was able to use lots of sweet apples which were abundant in that part of Germany. The main thing was that sometimes she was able to sell her apple desserts without food ration coupons, or with fewer coupons than were normally required. These ration coupons were something young soldiers never seemed to have enough of. At any rate, there was no trip to the shooting range without me enjoying the woman's delicious apple pie. As a matter of fact, it was always the highlight of the week except when I received packages from home.

As our rifle training came to an end, our shooting competition also concluded. The very last day under the tutelage of the young corporal was the day when he expected me to do my best "for the good of all". And he tried to use peer pressure on me. I did not buy that. (In all my life I disliked it!) Besides, I really did not like this squad leader, I thought him an arrogant ass, and I acted accordingly. I will never forget his disappointed face when I showed him my hits on the target. Not once had I hit a bull's eye.

I did not visibly grin at his disappointment but he must have seen something in my face because he got awfully angry and told me to "wipe that grin off my face" that wasn't really there. Then, when all that did not help, he ordered me to take my rifle in my outstretched arms and with the weapon held in both hands perform 150 (!) knee bends. I don't remember how many knee bends I was able to do before I keeled over. But there were many. In the end the victory was mine.

Incidentally, this corporal had been captured by the Polish insurgents when the Warsaw uprising began on August 3, 1944. At the time he had been convalescing from a wound in a hospital in the Polish capital. He told us that for many weeks he lived with the Polish underground fighters in the sewers and cellars of the city, always being moved from one place to another when German troops came too close. He did not complain about the treatment he received at the hands of the Poles, being mindful of the fact that they themselves were in constant danger of discovery, and that they had no regular supply of food and medicine. His freedom came when the Polish uprising collapsed at the beginning of October and General Bor-Komorowski had to capitulate to SS General Von dem Bach-Zelewski.

While one can understand the Polish desire for freedom from both German and Russian suzerainty, the Poles always seem to forget that fate has placed them between two of the largest and most dynamic peoples on the European continent, and prudence would demand from them that they ally themselves with one or the other. In fact, they have no other choice. Instead, they always seem to look for their friends abroad: in the Nineteenth Century in the French Government; before World War II among the British, and just now, in 2001, they believe that the United States is the guarantor of their independence. Anybody well versed in politics, and especially in world politics as practiced by the major Western powers, knows that for the U.S. Government the Poles are only a pawn in their game that would be quickly abandoned if Washington deems it in its interest.

For the Poles to start the August 1944 uprising in their capital city at the very moment when the German soldiers of the Eastern front were in a desperate defensive battle with the Red Army proved a great miscalculation. It bears remembering that the numerous marshaling yards around Warsaw were the major railroad connections between the Reich and the Eastern front, and these connections had to be held at all costs. Consequently the German reprisals against both the partisans as well as against the general population supporting the underground fighters were both swift and brutal. The inner city of Warsaw was largely destroyed during the ferocious battles that lasted for two months. To make a special issue, as the Poles seem to do even to this day, of the fact that the Germans leveled the inner city of Warsaw during the uprising is ludicrous. By that time most German inner cities had been destroyed, and the Allies had even attacked targets in Rome and Paris, something the German High Command had always avoided. Considering everything, there was no reason for the German High Command to go easy on the residents of the Polish capital.

Tragically, the leadership of the Polish underground, the so-called "Home Army", believed that by stabbing the Germans and their allies, who were fighting in the defense of all of Europe against Bolshevism, in the back, this would be appreciated by the advancing Red Army and generate assistance from this source. At that time the Poles must have been aware of the fact that most of the Polish officers and officials who had been captured by the Soviets in September of 1939 had been murdered in cold blood by the Soviet Secret Police in the forest of Katyn and elsewhere on Stalin's orders. Somehow it did not seem to matter to the Polish leadership that approximately the same number of Polish officers in German captivity, about 21,000 in all, were well taken care of in German POW camps. Stalin rudely awoke the Polish leaders from their dreams of grandeur and equality with the world powers: Once his troops had reached the river Vistula and thus the outskirts of

Warsaw he stopped them cold, and no help was given to those Poles desperately trying to reach the lines of the great Soviet ally of Poland (and the U.S., Great Britain and France) in the east.

SS CHAIN OF COMMAND.
Himmler, the SS Reichsfuehrer and German chief of police, was responsible to Hitler alone. A "*Hoeherer SS und Polizeifuehrer*"—a superior SS and police leader—headed each of 30 territorial sections and reported to Himmler. At the end of 1944 Himmler ruled his "empire" with the assistance of the following 12 major adminstrative groups. (The precise structure of the SS was changed periodically; this arrangement, however, was fairly typical.)

Personal Staff of the Reichsfuehrer SS
Karl Wolff, who was also responsible for the *Ahnererbe* association and the *Lebensborn* program, headed this group.

Central Administration of the SS
This group was headed by Gottlob Berger, one of those responsible for the recruitment of the *Waffen* SS.

SS Central Command
Headed by Hans Juettner, the SS Central Command encompassed two subsidiary units:

Command bureau of the regular SS
Membership in the regular SS amounted to 240,000 men in 1939; by 1945 its strength had declined to 40,000.

Command bureau of the *Waffen* SS
Two units fell under this bureau's jurisdiction. The *Waffen* SS was created in 1940 as the *Verfuegungstruppen*, units for special missions, reinforced by "death's head" formations (*Totenkopfverbaende*). At the end of 1944 the total strength of the *Waffen* SS was 910,000 men. The death's head units (concentration camp guards) included 30,000 men at the end of 1944.

"Race and Population Resettlement" Administration (RUSHA, or *Rasse und Siedlungshauptamt*)
Headed by Richard Hildebrandt, this administration was responsible for all questions relating to "purity of blood" both within the SS and outside it.

SS Administration of Justice
This group, headed by Franz Breithaupt, administered the high court of the SS and the police, the regular SS and police courts, and the SS and police courts in the field.

Administration of SS Personnel
Maximilian von Herff headed this group.

Central Security Administration (RSHA, or *Reichssicherheitshauptamt*)
Ernst Kaltenbrunner, the successor to Reinhard Heydrich, administered the RSHA. Its subdivisions included:

Personnel, formation, organization

Administration—economy

SD
The SD encompassed both the SD *Inland* (Interior SD), headed by Otto Ohlendorf, and the SD *Ausland* (External SD), headed by Walter Schellenberg.

Security (Sipo, or *Sicherheitspolizei*)
Included under the jurisdiction of this group were the secret state police (Gestapo, or *Geheime Staatspolizei*), headed by Heinrich Mueller, and the criminal police (Kripo, or *Kriminalpolizei*).

Ideological investigations

General Administration of Civil Police (Orpo, or *Ordnungspolizei*)
This group, headed by Kurt Daluege, was the central administrative bureau for conventional local and regional police.

"Economy and Administration" Organization (WVHA, or *Wirtschafts und Verwaltungs Hauptamt*)
Oswald Pohl, the chief of this group, was responsible for concentration camps, construction, various industries (among others, 296 brick factories, porcelain plants and 75 percent of the nonalcoholic drink industry) and the administration and finances of the *Waffen* SS.

Department of the *Obergruppenfuehrer* Heissmeyer
This group was responsible for national educational policy and for the boarding schools.

General Administration for German Minorities (Vomi, or *Volksdeutsche Mittelstelle*)
Werner Lorenz administered this group, which was responsible for the techniques and organization of population transfers.

Department of the Reich Commissariat for Consolidating the German Nation
Ulrich Greifelt headed this department, which oversaw the planning and realization of population transfers.

Chapter 7

One day, fairly near the beginning of my training at Breslau-Lissa, I was called upon, along with others of our new company, to report for 24-hour duty at the guard house next to the major entrance of the Breslau-Lissa base. I discovered quickly that I did not like this assignment at all. In the German armed forces of the Third Reich it was customary that the entire watch detail of the guards on duty at a given time, usually a squad of nine soldiers, had to run out of the guard house and there salute in formation and in full dress (with rifles and helmets worn in proper alignment) whenever any officer above the rank of major was entering or leaving the base. And the same honor had to be shown any *Ritterkreuzträger* (similar to a Medal of Honor recipient), even if he was only a lowly private. After I did this once I managed, thanks to my stash of cigarettes, to never stand guard again as long as I was at Breslau-Lissa, not even at night around the perimeter of the base. The cigarettes that I did not need for bartering purposes I mailed to my father in Norway. Amazingly, the German *Feldpost* (APO) system still worked extremely efficient throughout 1944. (In some parts of Berlin the mail was still being delivered on May 2nd, 1945, two days after Hitler had already committed suicide.)

To alleviate the impression that the cigarettes enabled me to really shirk duties, I do have to mention that, for instance, instead of being at the guard house, I assisted in the company offices. I was pretty good at typing and doing other office work. Therefore I was often called upon to occupy the company office when the non-commissioned officers, including the *Spiess* (Staff Sergeant), went to town or had other duties. After a while I was entrusted with a key, and this enabled me to continue my extensive correspondence with relatives, friends and former work colleagues by using the company typewriter.

Following is a translation of a letter I wrote to my mother in August 1944, just about when my comrades on the Western front managed to make a break-out of the Falaise encirclement in the Normandy. (And a few days before Paris changed hands.) This letter was one of the few that survived the ravages of the war and postwar years, and the following four decades. Numbered notes coinciding with the various paragraphs will explain the details of my letter immediately following this translation.

Breslau, August 19, 1944

Dear Mother:

Thanks for your nice letter of the 11th of August and the two packages.Your letter reached me on the 15th but only now do I get around to answering it. I hope you don't mind that I am using a type-writer but with it the writing goes so much faster. Now to your letter (1):

I am glad you received my letters of the 1st, 4th and 6th of August. Others are on the way. Due to the fact that a) I have little time, b) there is really nothing to write about, and also due to my 'Schreibfaulheit' (lack of inclination to write), my letters are rather short.

I would have enjoyed it if there had been some edible goodies in the packages, but as it was it turned out okay. It is regrettable that now the mailing of packages is restricted, however there is nothing we can do about that.(2) Now that there are so many air raid warnings it won't take long before you will have used up the energies you gained in your vacation.(3)

On the radio I heard that Saarbrücken (4) had to suffer terror attacks (5) again on the 11th, 3rd and 9th of this month. That our neighborhood was hit also is not surprising. I am not certain which building you meant by "Marsong's house", you may remember that I don't really know the people in our town well. To me it is also not clear which railroad underpass was hit by bombs; after all, we do have three. It is certainly a pity that our chicken coop was destroyed but that it far better than if it had been our home. I am sorry about the loss of the garden. You had worked so hard in it all these years and now, in a few seconds, all is gone. I will miss the peach and plum trees. I am sure that you had anticipated the first harvest soon, and now this joy is gone also. How is it with the cherry trees? Where exactly did the bombs fall?(6) I won't be coming home for a long time now, and by that time the bomb craters may be filled in.(7) Exactly which trees in the garden were destroyed? That our radio is also "kaput" doesn't bother me as much as the other things but it really didn't have to be.(8) What kind of air raid damage do we have, A, B or C? In cases of B or C one can apply for "bomb furlough". Still, I would rather fight the whole war without coming home than to "earn" 14 days leave as a result of the destruction of our house.(9)

I have no idea where Richard is currently stationed.(10) I have already written him two letters, and did not receive an answer. I assume he is on the march to a different front, or else he might be with the V2.(11) In your present condition you should definitely not upset yourself unnecessarily, you know that is harmful. I do hope that Father can get leave when the time comes. Richard for sure won't be able to get home. I also hope that the enemy fliers leave you alone. Unfortunately, you won't be able to leave home for a more secure area.(12) How are Helga, Manfred and Harald? Tell them to write again.

Now about me. Although the training is hard (and will get harder still), I am fine. But all this doesn't matter if only this war is over soon, and if it weren't for the horrible human losses ... Since I am absolutely convinced that either of the two warring parties will soon try to bring about a decision in the war through the use of some ***new means to fight*** *......... (13)*

20 August 1944

Yesterday my duties kept me from writing more, and only now can I continue.(14) Today we experienced the first air raid warning here. Just a while ago I saw a huge "Gigant" plane fly by (15). You can't imagine how big these things are. It looks like a building with wings. A few days ago we marched past the spot where Colonel Mölders crashed with his plane.(16) The site is near the highway from Breslau to Lissa. The spot is marked with a big swastika, and on the other side of the road is a stone marker.

Here a few words about the packages: I was very happy with the first package with the little brush, the shoe shine brush, the candies and the razor brush, although I didn't expect the shoe shine brush. The second package was especially welcome because of the sneakers, but I did miss a cake. You may remember that here I am not as easily satisfied as in the Labor Service. Today we were able to buy some things at the quartermaster: A ½ liter bottle of white wine and candies.(16) And in addition to our normal food ration we got 1 piece of cake, 2 apples and 4 candies. This is the best they can do, and it only happens every six months at the most. (17)

Every Thursday we go to the movies. Last Sunday we had a Kameradschaftsabend where one of the best big bands, Bernhard Etê, played for us. The music was fantastic, and they played all the modern hits. I really liked it. Richard wouldn't have cared for it at all since he never liked "hot" music. (18)

That's about all for today. Tell Manfred and Harald that I am with the big cannons, and show them in the album "Die Deutsche Wehrmacht" in my room how infantry howitzers look. They are the same kind of guns that passed our house in 1939. I am not certain when I'll go to the front but it will probably be in December. Therefore, please prepare some extra winter clothes for me, just in case I will be sent to Russia, or more accurately, Poland, a possibility I don't really care for.(19)

Perhaps you wonder how I am able to use a typewriter: I sometimes help in the company offices, and when I do that I leave the typewriter unlocked so that I can use it at my leisure. (20)

Aunt Else promised me a package. I wonder whether I will still get it. Did you receive the extra food ration coupons I mailed you and Helga? In spite of that I was able to purchase a half a pound of butter for my own use. Please return some of the new coupons for baked goods to me, I mailed you enough for 4 pounds. I hope you still have some left. I always like to buy some cake when we visit the shooting range for sharp shooting.(21)

Now some little items I could use: I know you have little time to make packages but maybe Helga can help. I still have some things lying here for Father, and didn't get around to mailing them to him. I was also able to purchase a nickel-plated razor for him (22).

Now I am out of money, since I am having a beer or two with every meal.(23) But don't worry, every 10th of the month is payday.

Please mail me the following:

1. *Gray wool to darn socks.*
2. *One pair of gray socks. Here we received only two pairs instead of three as regulations call for.*
3. *My fountain pen. Helga will know which one.*
4. *Toothpaste.*
5. *Black shoe polish.*
6. *A brush to polish my boots, I can't do anything with the one you mailed before.*
7. *A folder for my mail.*
8. *The leather shoe laces from the Labor Service. The quality of the ones we get here is lousy.*

That's about all. I don't even want to mention cake etc. anymore because I know that is hard to get now, and not important for the war effort. Mail everything in one parcel but points 5 and 6 are most important, those you may mail in a letter.

How is the weather at home? Here it has been beautiful all summer long. Mostly clear sky, and since an airfield is nearby there are always planes in the air.

Now I'll finally close. Take care of yourself, and greet everybody, including the neighbors, from me, your son Hans

Commentary to my war letter of August 19th, 1944:

1. It sounds a bit incongruous that I was writing a letter home about every third day, and still considered myself "schreibfaul" (too lazy to write). Regretfully, very few of these letters are still in existence. While they were no masterpieces of literature, most of them probably were a compendium of information that increased in importance as the decades went by. For that reason I translated this particular letter in its entirety, not omitting items that are clearly of little interest to most readers in the new century. The fact that I was using a typewriter proves how I was quite adept at breaking rules and taking shortcuts. US ex-servicemen will appreciate it when I remember that in nearly a year of military training I managed to abstain from guard duty at the camp entrance (in the US Army generally done by military police), except for one single time. I just didn't like the drill and ceremony connected with it. Since I didn't smoke, I used my regular cigarette ration (which we received although most of us were but seventeen years of age!) to ingratiate myself with the non-commissioned officers in charge.

2. Judging by this sentence, there must have been some restrictions put on the mailing of packages after the successful Allied invasion of June 1944. I do remember using some kind of "permit stamp" in addition to the regular postage when mailing a package or parcel inside the Reich.

3. At the time my mother was pregnant with her seventh child. Through one of the social service organizations (affiliated with either the party or the church) she had been sent for a few weeks of recuperation to a home for expectant mothers located in a safer area of Germany. Two months later, as the time for the delivery of the new baby arrived, she was once more sent to a place in the Palatinate where my youngest brother was born.

4. Our home is part of the greater Saarbrücken area (only four miles from the inner city). It is one of the most industrialized territories in Germany. As a result, we (the Saarlanders) expected air raids right from the start of the war, and we were far better prepared than most other cities of the Reich. Although attacked numerous times and over 65% destroyed, Saarbrücken lost fewer than 1,200 people through air raids in nearly six years of war.
5. During World War II, in Germany the term "Terrorangriff" (terror attack) was generally used for Allied air raids instead of the (perhaps) more correct word "Luftangriff". In retrospect, and knowing of the Allied policy of trying to undermine the morale of the German population through attacks on their

homes, churches hospitals and cultural monuments (instead of on factories and transport facilities, for instance), and killing as many civilians as possible, there is no question that the use of the word "terror" was, in this conjunction, justified.

6. My mother's letter to me, telling me of the August 9th, 1944 air raid in which our neighborhood was hit, must have been cryptic. This accounts for my many questions. The raid occurred shortly after eight in the morning, and this indicates American planes from the Eighth Air Force. I assume it was twin-engine B-25 or B-26 bombers flying from a French airfield. Personally, I also have no doubt that the heavy concentration of industry, roads, railroad marshaling yards and a nearby important bridge surrounding our house had been the targets. While the Americans participated in many terror raids against the civilian population, it is also a fact that most attacks against real strategic objectives were flown by the U.S. Air Force. By "railroad underpass" I meant a nearby railroad bridge that had received a direct hit. This affected, at least for a day or two, the major rail line between Saarbrücken and Cologne via Trier. In our street, several houses were destroyed, resulting in some civilian deaths. Bombs that were probably aimed at the bridge fell a few hundred feet away, one of them putting a big crater smack in the middle of the important road that also goes from Saarbrücken to Trier and Luxembourg.

7. In addition, this cluster of bombs destroyed the post office and, what was worse for us, a 4-story apartment building with a groundfloor store that was owned by my family. It was behind this building where we had our garden with the fruit trees and the fairly new chicken coop. My mother recollects that at the time we had 38 chicken. All perished. Russians POWs did the repair work.

   (Note that there is no lament from me about the loss of the other property of my family. There was a war going on with properties being destroyed every day, and with the Schmidts being typical Germans, they accepted this rather stoically. Similarly it was ten and twenty years earlier when our formerly very wealthy family lost this wealth (tens of millions of dollars worth mainly in real estate) as a result of WWI and the inflation. Many of the Saarbrücken properties, for instances apartment houses, had been bought "for pennies" at foreclosure sales by Jews newly arriving from Eastern Europe. None of us would ever have dreamt to reclaim these properties on spurious grounds as is being done right now (2001!) even by distant relatives of German Jews who had to sell their businesses and houses after Hitler had decided that Germany would be better off without them. What amazes me personally about these actions is the emotional content of the collective Jewish outcry in this matter. As if, for instance, only they had lost "things" in the wars and their aftermath, and under the unstated assumption that property once owned by Jews remains Jewish forever.)

8. The story of the radio has a tragicomic slant: Our "old" trusted "*Volksempfänger*" (people's radio: a radio that was mass produced on orders of Hitler to make certain that every German family could afford one), had quit, and on the very morning of the air raid my mother took it to the repairman whose store was on the groundfloor of our other building (only a block from our home). Hearing the air raid sirens, she barely had time to get some necessities from the house before running to the nearby coal mine entrance that served as a bombshelter, and into which my sister and

my other siblings had already gone. (By then air raids had become a daily - and nightly - occurrence. Everybody knew exactly what to do.) Hardly had my mother entered, when the bombs began to fall, and soon someone came into the mine shaft and told of the damage, mentioned also that "Schmidt's house is gone". One can imagine how my family felt. But upon questioning, the man stated that he had meant "the other one of Schmidt's houses", and this brought my mother the confirmation that, along with the building, the radio was also destroyed.

9. It so happened that I did finagle some extra leave two months later, and by that time the major craters had in fact been filled in. It is doubtful that the raid, although moderately successful from a military point of view, slowed down war production much. My sentiments that I'd rather fight the whole (rest of the) war without any leave than see our home destroyed by bombs were sincere. Nevertheless, after Saarbrücken experienced its worst terror attack of the war on October 5th, 1944, that killed many people and flattened huge tracts of the city (but left our neighborhood unscathed),I managed to get a furlough, and once home I told a little white lie based upon half-truth in order to get a few more days of leave to spend with one of my best friends who had arrived on a convalescent leave after being wounded on the Baltic front.
10. Richard, my oldest brother was at the time in the German Navy, and assigned to a command encompassing the Balkan peninsula (including the Black Sea and parts of the Mediterranean Sea). After the war I found out that in August of 1944 he was stationed in Greece. Soon thereafter the sailors had to abandon their ships, and began a slow, fighting retreat that took them through Greece, Albania and Yugoslavia to the border of the Reich, which they reached in May of 1945.
11. In one of the last letters I had received from my brother he had mentioned volunteering for some of the new "*Wunderwaffen*" (miracle weapons) being put into action in 1944, among them the one- and two-man U-Boats, the "*Kampfschwimmer*" units (underwater demolition teams) and the like. Because just about then the V2 rockets had been mentioned for the first time, I may have been kidding my mother, knowing full well that the Navy didn't have jurisdiction over this weapon.
12. At the time our father was a private stationed near Stavanger in Norway. Obviously, it was more difficult to get leave from there than if one was located closer to Germany. He didn't get home until August of 1945.
13. I consider this the most important sentence of the letter. Unfortunately, it was never completed. As part of our (officer's candidates') training we had a lecture every week by some well-known academician, scientist or other important personality of the Reich. One day a professor came from Berlin who told us of new kinds of weapons being developed, one being a bomb which could destroy a whole city. Did he mean the atom bomb? I really don't know. But it is obvious that my opinion expressed in this sentence was the result of such a lecture. After the war we (German ex-soldiers) were chastised for being so naive and believing in the promises of our leadership concerning the "*Wunderwaffen,*" but being realistic about it, the fact remains that "Nazi" Germany was the spawning ground for most of the modern weaponry being used in the world's armies today, five decades later, from ICBM's to modern U-Boats, and from the assault rifle to the best battle tanks. The outward appearance of a (white) fully equipped US-soldier of 2001 is very much like that of a Waffen-SS soldier of 1944, and

has little in common with the GI of WW2. Even the latest American planes, like the B-2 and the F-117, look like planes "Nazi" Germany had in the developmental stage 56 years ago. We were that far advanced.

14. Breslau, then a city of 600,000, is the capital of Silesia (currently in Polish hands), and was in August 1944 totally untouched by bombs. Less than a year later it was destroyed, its population dead, expelled or sent as slave laborers into the GULAG. Ironically, Auschwitz is not very far away, yet I never heard that name until months after the war was over.
15. The ME-323 "Gigant" was the largest plane that saw service in World War II. Many of the features of the ME-323 were later incorporated in the "giant" planes of the victors. (Also in the summer or fall of 1944 I saw a jet plane for the first time. Comrades and I were standing somewhere in the fields when a single plane flew high above us that was making a - for the time - unusual noise. When I was wondering what that had been, one of the fellows volunteered that this was a *Düsenflugzeug* - a jet plane. Asking him what was meant by that word he explained that it was a plane without a propeller, where the forward movement of the plane was generated by a new kind of engine. Since we were great at kidding each other at all times I did not believe him. I thought that, except for gliders, a plane without a propeller was an impossibility.)
16. Colonel Werner Mölders was the first air ace to reach the magic number of 100 air victories, thereby surpassing Manfred von Richthofen's World War I record. The German people deeply mourned the accidental death of this fine young officer. Always being interested in aesthetics, I did not like the sight of a rather large and plain swastika on the side of the road. I would have much preferred a pylon with the German "Hoheitsabzeichen" (an eagle holding a swastika surrounded by a wreath) on top.
17. This paragraph shows the seriousness of the German supply situation. Still, we didn't really complain. Younger Americans will find it incongruous that at only 17 years of age I was able to buy wine (and beer). The "Labor Service" was the outfit in which every German boy and girl was supposed to serve (for the good of the nation) at about age 18, for one year. Due to the wartime exigencies I spent only a healthy three months in the "*Reichsarbeitsdienst*", building anti-invasion fortifications on an island in the North Sea.
18. During the Third Reich the German movie industry reached artistic and technical heights in movie making unsurpassed to this day. Immediately after the German defeat it was falsely stated that most of the German films of that time had been made 'for propaganda'. This lie enabled the Allies to promote their own films and movie industry, and, *ipso facto,* destroy the German one. To this day, more than 56 years later, the German movie industry has not recovered from this fall-out of our defeat. For instance, we cannot even guess how many wonderful movies Leni Riefenstahl would have created had she had the chance to prove her great talents as a director after 1945. As it happened, she is wrongfully and criminally still being ostracized to this day. The reasons given are her two "Nazi" cinematic master works "Triumph of the Will" and "Olympiade 1936", but the truth is probably that she would have turned out to be the best movie director ever, far surpassing any of her colleagues in the victor states. The fact is that of approximately 1,200 feature films made between 1933 and 1945 only about fifty can be called propaganda movies, far fewer than Hollywood turned out in the same time. I was an avid movie goer,

preferring comedies and musicals to war movies. The "*Kameradschafts-abend*" was akin to an American USO evening without any dancing. On this particular Sunday we had a top German group entertaining us. The Bernhard Etê orchestra had in Germany a standing not unlike that of the Benny Goodman or Ray Anthony bands in the United States. My reference to "hot" music (I used the English term) sounds funny today but was considered "in" at the time. Then I liked "swing" music, and although such music was frowned upon by the authorities, they couldn't prevent people from playing it or listening to it. This particular "*Kameradschaftsabend*" must have been very unusual because years after the war it was specifically mentioned in a book. That particular evening it happened that around midnight, after the higher echelon officers had left, the band leader asked us (hundreds of young soldiers) which tunes we wanted to hear, and I still remember that, among others, "Oh Marie" and "Black Panther" (in English!) were asked for, both of them tunes that were totally out of bounds. The evening ended like a jam session. And this in the barracks of Germany's best at the very height of the war, and after the Allied invasion! There were no serious ramifications for our transgression afterward, except that we didn't get any passes to town for a couple of weekends. The "system" was far more tolerant than is being acknowledged today.

19. German soldiers obviously had no say where they were going to be sent after completion of basic training or, as in my case, after passing some OC and special weapons courses. "Nobody" wanted to be assigned to the Eastern front, except those who belonged to older units and wanted to return to their former comrades. In the summer of 1944 Italy or France were much preferred over Poland, the Balkans and what remained in our hands of the Baltic countries. I think the major reason was because one had at least a 50/50 chance to survive if captured by the Western allies, but hardly any at all if one fell into the hands of the Red Army. My sentence mentioning Russia and Poland also seems to indicate that I expected the coming winter to be worse in the East than in Western Europe. Little did I know that exactly four months later I would lie in the deep snow of the Ardennes (Battle of the Bulge), and there experience one of the coldest winters that area had seen in decades.
20. My typing abilities came in very handy when trying to get special favors from officers and non-coms. I found out very early that people everywhere try to get away with things (including disliked work) whenever possible, and office work is not every man's favorite. In Breslau I also managed to have a look at my personal file (something absolutely forbidden), and discovered that my (voluntary) enlistment had been changed without my permission from 4 years or duration of the war (whichever would be longer), to "*aktiv auf Lebenszeit*" meaning that "they" anticipated to retain me as a professional soldier after victory. Obviously I must have been doing well, but little did the SS-FHA (*SS-Führungshauptamt* in Berlin) know that they would have had a big fight with me on their hands, had we won the war, for the order to change my enlistment conditions had been signed by the FHA .

An interesting addendum to this story is the write-up about me that can be found on the Web site of the notorious ADL (Anti-Defamation League of B'nai B'rith), the Jewish spy organization. In this write-up the ADL uses a curious sentence that goes somewhat like this: "Hans Schmidt, who was in the Hitler Youth, also claims to have been in the Waffen-SS." In a way this is an underhanded compliment to the Waffen-SS. Why would someone "claim to have been a member of such an allegedly *'murderous', 'brutal' and 'criminal'* military unit" unless it is an honor to have belonged to it? Furthermore, it is general knowledge among historical researchers that the so-called Berlin Document Center, where all the available and still extant personnel records of the Third Reich had been stored and that were until relatively recently totally under American control, were in fact most of the time in Jewish hands. In other words, it was usually a Jew in the uniform of the U.S. Army, or otherwise employed by the U.S. Government, that was in charge of these documents and it is easy to imagine that the world's Zionist groups made the most of it. I doubt that all ex-Waffen-SS soldiers who wanted information about themselves or who needed proof of this or that were too kindly dealt with by these "Americans" in charge. The odd circumscription used by the ADL regarding my war service seems to indicate that my file is missing. Someday, when I have time to do so, I'll look into the possibility of finding out what the gentlemen of the SS-FHA wrote or knew about me. (Decades ago I had the interesting chance to talk, for a few minutes, to Moshe Dayan, one of the best known Israeli Generals [he had lost an eye in combat, and his eye patch became his trade mark]. I purposely mentioned to Dayan that I had been in the Waffen-SS. I was *not* surprised when he praised the heroism and tenacity of the soldiers of my unit. As an Israeli soldier he did not feel the contrived Jewish need to express an abhorrence of being in the company of a former SS-soldier.)

21. Since all food was rationed in Germany by that time, soldiers needed some coupons when going to town, or visiting relatives. I was able to "amass" extra coupons to mail home by trading those cigarettes which I didn't mail to our father.
22. It is amazing that at this critical juncture for Germany, one was still able to mail packages to far-flung places like Norway. In retrospect it sounds asinine. The United States, although not really touched by war, mobilized its citizens far earlier and far more thoroughly and got the whole nation much sooner on a near total war footing than did Germany whose very existence was threatened. Incredible as it seems, in 1942, while less than 10% of the entire Soviet production went to civilian use, "Nazi" Germany still allocated 60% for the same purpose. I still remember when about 1942 the Saarland Tramways received brand-new street cars of the most fantastic quality: with brass fittings and an elegant interior. While I liked these street cars precisely because of their beauty, I thought it crazy that at a time of war they were still being produced in this fashion. It was similar with the German steam engines for the rail roads. I believe that it was only in the third year of the war when the so-called K-Lok *(Kriegslokomotive)* was manufactured, an engine totally bereft of unnecessary accouterments. It was Albert Speer (for whom, due to other reasons, I have in retrospect no sympathy) who finally managed to get the German industry on the war footing it should have been on from the start.
23. By 1944 German beer had an alcohol content of only a little over 3%, a fact that led to serious grumbling in Bavaria. That most of us were below 18 years of age didn't matter when ordering beer. Nobody gave it a thought. It was another matter when we wanted to sneak into movie houses where films with the notation "*Für Jugendliche unter 18 verboten*" ('verboten' for youths under 18 years of age) were shown. Then not even medals earned in combat, or our SS uniform made a difference. Our morality had to be

guarded. Ironically, all these movies would get only a PG13 rating in today's America, they were that benign.

My comments (footnote #20) that because of their unilateral declaration that I shall be a professional soldier after the war, the NS leadership in Berlin would have had a fight with me on their hands had we won the conflict, must not be taken as a belated claim on my part to have been sympathetic to the "Anti-Nazi" resistance. I was not in any way or form against Hitler or National Socialism, and to this day I find no excuse for those Germans who during the war betrayed the Fatherland, whatever their personal motives. But I know I would not have liked to be under military discipline forever, and thus my statement of personal independence.

Liberals reading my letter and the footnotes will be shocked to discover that in this letter (or any others of my wartime missives) I did not express any concern about the fate of the Jews. Nowadays the existence of such a concern, however late it is professed, seems to be a litmus test for a person's character. The fact is, we had other things on our minds; first and foremost the well-being of our families. I recall only one conversation concerning the Jews, and that was in the middle of March 1945, when I lay badly wounded in a hospital near Vienna. At that time another soldier in a bed near me "enlightened" me in regard to this wondrous people. Neither in the Hitler Youth nor as a soldier was I ever subjected to specific anti-Jewish propaganda akin to the insidious anti-German propaganda, camouflaged as "Holocaust studies", young Americans have to suffer now. It must also be mentioned that during the Third Reich all of three (3!) anti-Jewish movies were produced, and not one of them was shown at the Breslau-Lissa SS barracks because they had been declared "*Für Jugendliche verboten*" and, obviously, most of us were underage. The U.S. Army was not as coy when it came to propagandize underage GIs by showing them anti-German hate films, of which hundreds were made.

The question was asked how we young recruits dealt with the knowledge of the almost constant enemy air raids that devastated our home cities in the west while we lived in almost peaceful surroundings in Silesia.

In 1944, the daily *Wehrmachtbericht*, the communiqué of the German Armed Forces HQ, was purposely sparse and to the point.

For instance, the worst air raid of the war that largely destroyed Saarbrücken was reported with these words on October 6, 1944:

"Last night the city of Saarbrücken was the target of the British terror bombers." While in the same communique other cities likeWilhelmshaven, Dortmund, Koblenz and Rheine were mentioned as having been attacked from the air, only in the case of Saarbrücken were the words, *"target of terror bombers,"* stated, and this was for us an indication that it was this city that had experienced a major, and devastating raid.

Reading this, we could only wait for the mail to arrive in a few days that would bring the good news like, *"Wir leben noch!"*: "we are still alive" for telephones were then not in general use and available as they are now, and besides, as a result of air raids the telephone exchanges were often destroyed also. In early October I knew that our mother had been sent out of the city to a home for expectant mothers in a (relatively) safe area, where coincidentally on the day following the burning of the city my youngest brother was born. And I also knew that my two other young brothers were in some sort of a boys camp. My sister Helga, then still fourteen years of age, was home alone and took care of the house. It was her that I was most concerned about until I received a postcard from Luisenthal telling me that all was well.

I remember a particularly sad case that happened a few weeks earlier. One of my young comrades from another platoon was from Darmstadt, an acient German city of culture and for retirees, with a population of about 90,000, that lies midway between Frankfurt and Heidelberg. On September 12, 1944, the *Wehrmachtbericht* contained the following laconic sentence: *"Last night* [Sept.11!] *Darmstadt was the target of British terror bombers."* Not more.

As a result, the boy from Darmstadt began his long wait for news from home. After a week had passed without a message from his mother or any other member of his large family (the father was somewhere on the Eastern front,) we all feared for the worst. It must have been toward the end of September when a cryptic note from grandparents or some other relatives arrived: *"They are all gone!"*, meaning of course that his entire family had been killed. *Obersturmführer* Ludescher immediately saw to it that our comrade could get a couple of weeks furlough to travel to his home city, but if I remember correctly he never returned to Breslau-Lissa.

In the appendix I am going to reprint a report written by an unknown British amateur historian about this air raid on Darmstadt. In it is described what was meant when the *Wehrmachtbericht* reported, *"In der Nacht war Darmstadt das Ziel eines britischen Terrorangriffs."*

Chapter 8

While my earlier induction notice for the Waffen-SS had called for an assignment to a non-commissioned officers' course at Prague, it soon became apparent that at Breslau-Lissa a group of young men had been assembled upon which the top SS leadership in Berlin had placed even higher hopes. After a relatively short time of the basic training which every recruit receives, we soon found ourselves in a setting where everything seemed geared for officer's training. It was more like going to college than doing military duty. The prime prerequisite for all, or most of us, was that we had shown leadership qualities in the Hitler Youth, and that our report cards from school showed that we were of a good character. In addition, some of my comrades had excelled either in sports or in their chosen profession. I remember one fellow from the Sudetenland having been a 1943 national ski champion of the Hitler Youth, and another had made his mark as a winner in the yearly *Reichsberufswettkampf*, the contest where the best apprentices and journeymen of numerous professions, from draftsman to butcher, and from shoemaker to carpenter, were competing with each other.

The extent of our training can been seen from the fact that we did not only learn to handle the standard German carbine of World War II, namely, the *Gewehr 98k,* and how to throw *Stielhandgranaten* (hand grenades that look like potato mashers). In retrospect I can say that we learned the mechanics and proper use of every single German infantry weapon then in use, from the famous Luger pistol 08 of the First World War to the two "cannons" we had at the base, the 75mm l.I.G.18 (*leichtes Infanterie-Geschütz 1918)* and the 150mm howitzer s.I.G.33

(*schweres Infanterie-Geschütz 1933).* And in the case of the last two guns, we learned to fill, in an emergency, every single position needed to fire this weapon, including that of *Geschützführer*, the chief of the gun crew. I also remember learning to handle and disassemble the P-38 pistol and how to use the grenade-firing attachment to the 98k carbine. Efforts were even made to familiarize us with the gas masks that were issued to all of us. It was only in the very last two or three months of the war that gas warfare had become so remote that during the perennial inspections we did not have to prove to our superiors that our gas masks were still inside their canisters. The fact is that by then most of us carried other essentials such as additional food stuffs in them, because by then there was often no assurance that the promised chow would arrive.

As stated earlier, our training was about evenly split between the practical and the theoretical, with considerable time devoted to steeling our bodies through track and field exercises.

Ever since the death-defying reputation of the Waffen-SS arose around the beginning of World War II, there were two claims that seemed to have been implanted by enemy propaganda. One was the saying, "the SS doesn't take prisoners," and the other that during training young Waffen-SS recruits had to place a *Stielhandgranate* on a helmet while wearing the latter, and pull the fuse of the grenade to let the thing explode just above one's head. In theory this would be possible since the explosive force would dissipate above head and helmet, but logically it would be asinine to attempt this feat since a handgrenade, once charged, cannot be controlled. As far as the "taking no prisoners" claim is concerned, the many pictures showing thousands of Soviet POWs in Waffen-SS captivity belie it.

Interestingly, during my weapons training I did not have to learn how to disassemble and handle the firing mechanism of the MG-34, the British Sten gun and the *Stielhandgranate.* After the German victory over France in the summer of 1940, and soon after we had returned to the Saarland from our first evacuation (that had lasted nearly a year) we at that time teen-age boys combed nearby former German positions and battle fields for war souvenirs. Among other things we found the handgrenades, albeit without the fuses, and also parts of a German machine gun, 1934 model, of which we took the firing mechanism home. Both Richard and I soon learned to take the thing apart, and for a long time I was fascinated by its ingenious design, knowing that it had to fire several hundred times a minute when used in combat.

A few Sten guns were added to our arsenal about a year or two later. A British supply plane making a delivery of weapons and other material to the French underground had mistaken our area for French territory (or perhaps the open furnaces of the nearby steel mills as light markers set by the partisans), and dropped a parachute canister not far from my home town. By law we should have reported our find to the police but then we would have given up our guns. Therefore we kept quiet, and for a few weeks at least we played "soldiers" in our nearby forest with live ammunition, thanks to the generosity of the British Government. Oddly, I do not remember what happened to these guns. We might have traded them for something "better" once we had run out of bullets. I can just imagine the carnage that might result now, if 15-year-old boys of a normal American high school came into possession of real submachine guns with a good amount of ammuntion, and began playing with them.

One of the tracked vehicles at the Breslau-Lissa training grounds had been made to look like a Russian T-34 tank. On this vehicle we learned how we were supposed to disable such a *Panzer* even while it was traveling past us at a relatively high speed.

We had to take a *Hafthohlladung* (an explosive device that could be stuck to the side of a tank with its magnetic stand, and which upon firing practically melted the thick steel wall of the T-34 to finally create an explosion inside) in our left hand, grab some protrusion on the enemy vehicle, and let the force of the speed propel us aboard - a good idea which I never saw used in combat since the Russian tanks we encountered during the last battles in Austria were always surrounded by bulks of infantry. Besides, by the end of 1944 *Panzerfausts*, the single-use rocket-propelled anti-tank weapon was available in abundance.

One day at the end of our special course for officers-to-be, we traveled to an artillery firing range, probably the *Truppenübungsplatz*, training base, at Neuhammer not far from the city of Sagan, in Silesia, where our prowess in handling the infantry howitzers with real artillery shells was to be tested. Unfortunately, for lack of ammunition, we were not able to use the heaviest of the two types of cannon in earnest. At the time the Russians had come to within less than 200 miles of Breslau, and all available ammo had probably been shipped to the front.

It bears remembering that there was no serious natural obstacle between the German Eastern border not far from Breslau, and the Russian front. No major river, no high mountain range, and not even a thick impregnable forest. Breslau was already in harm's way while I was there, but few people seemed to realize it.

The test firing of the 75mm light howitzer went smoothly. I was able to prove my ability to fill every single position needed to operate this weapon. When my turn as *Geschützführer* (commander of the gun crew) came, I was highly praised when the first two rounds hit right on the designated spots in front and in the rear of the target in the far distance. Alas, the third shot, the very one that ought to have hit the bulls-eye, went so far off the mark that we almost had to search for the impact area with binoculars. On the one hand I was certain to have calibrated everything correctly, on the other hand I was devastated, fearing that I had not passed. But one of the higher officer present, probably a *Standartenführer* (Colonel), came over, looked at the gun sight and range finder, patted me on the shoulder and merely asked whether I knew what had caused the error? Certainly I knew. I realized it the moment the shell left the barrel (similarly as a bowler knows whether he has a strike or not the moment the bowling ball leaves his hand,) - - - I had forgotten to check whether one of "my men" had seen to it that the gun had been leveled correctly after the second shot, something that is essential for any artillery piece's performance. The Colonel smiled as he stepped back and said, "I am sure you won't make that mistake again." I assumed the same thing had happened to him when he went to artillery school.

On this day I also had my first and only close contact with concentration camp inmates in the entire war: With myself always interested in any type of new building that was being constructed, a trait inherited from my father and grandfather, I noticed that a new large building, probably a new barracks, was going up near the artillery range. As was usual in the German Armed Forces, the building was being built with bricks, and relatively thick walls, three stories high. Most of the bricklayers were concentration camp inmates wearing their washed-out blue-and-white striped camp uniforms.

We had just received our daily allocation of bread and were carrying it in our arms back to our quarters during one of the short stays at the range, when I decided to walk close by the new construction in order to look at something that had aroused my curiosity at the building site. The prisoners doing the work did not interest me. At this time of the war Germany was full of enemy personnel of all sorts, POWs, regular prisoners, voluntary foreign workers, forced foreign workers and so on. As a matter of fact, throughout Germany it was on any given day impossible *not* to have some contact with foreigners. Particularly the huge numbers of Polish and French POWs and free workers from almost all European countries could be seen anywhere, and they performed almost any function imaginable.

As I was walking by the construction site, one of the concentration camp inmates, probably a Jew, as I found out years after the war, saw me carrying my big stack of bread, came closer and asked me in German whether I would give him part of it. At the time I received not only the regular daily allocation of *Kommissbrot* (the regular dark German army bread) but two extra allowances, one for being in demanding physical training, and the other for still being under 18 years of age and growing. I believe it amounted to 850 grams, almost two pounds of bread per day, more than I could eat.

As a rule I gave my surplus ration to one of my comrades who ate like a horse, so to speak, and still didn't have enough. But on this day I did not see a reason why I should not give the cut part of my bread to the prisoner who had asked me for it. Incidentally, if he or the other concentration camp inmates had looked emaciated I would have remembered it. But I knew from reading books that people in prisons frequently were always hungry even if they ate more than on the outside.

I had no sooner given the prisoner half of a loaf of bread when another concentration camp inmate, this time one that carried some kind of stick and was dressed in a cleaner prisoner outfit, came running and tried to take the bread away from the man to whom I had given it. When he didn't succeed because others of the inmates assisted their comrade in hiding the bread quickly behind the newly constructed walls, the Kapo (trustee), for as that he introduced himself, admonished *me* loudly and in no uncertain terms that it was forbidden for SS soldiers to have contact with concentration camp inmates, and that he was going to report me to my commander. When he asked for my name I just laughed in his face and went on my way. Decades later, remembering this incident, I wondered whether this Kapo was not the now-famed Simon Wiesenthal who, according to some reports, was supposed to have held such a position at the Grossrosen Concentration Camp from which the inmates at Neuhammer had (allegedly) been drawn. There certainly was a resemblance.

Some readers may now ask whether I was not shocked at seeing people (Jews, we must now assume!) in concentration camp uniforms doing manual labor. The answer is simple: Not at all. I had my first contact with French POWs in the summer of 1940 when a group of about ten of them helped our family cut some fire wood. A year later I incurred an injury and spent weeks in a hospital in Neustadt in the Black Forest, and there the bed next to mine was occupied by a dapper young Polish cavalry lieutenant who had broken his leg while trying to escape from German captivity. Incongruously, the Pole, who spoke excellent German, was convalescing in a civilian German hospital without any guard. To pass the time he taught me to play chess, while at the same time flirting with all the pretty young nurses' helpers which had been assigned to the hospital by the Hitler Youth.

Another incident at the *Abschlussprüfung* (final inspection) occurred during the last field exercises. On this day we had to march hurriedly, heavily packed with all the gear one carries into combat *(feldmarschmässig)*, for a number of kilometers, covering the stretch in a certain amount of time. Then, without interruption, and still with all our gear, we had to cross an obstacle course similar to the ones also used by the American Army. The final barrier was a small creek that had to be crossed, monkey-style, while hanging up-side-down on all fours on a telephone pole that had been thrown across the water at a height of about six feet.

Just after I had hung myself on the pole and started to move across, a bottleneck arose. The second fellow in front of me, *Schütze* Bogdan (or a similar name), had frozen, and was now holding onto the pole with such force as if his life depended on it.

All admonitions and calls by us and the DIs that he get moving did not help. The DIs had no choice but to get some 10 to 12 foot long sticks from somewhere and pry Bogdan off, resulting in the poor fellow falling into the waist-deep water below.

Now came a scene that is indelibly imprinted in my memory. It is one of the tragi-comic incidents of "my" war:

Schütze Bogdan, if I remember correctly the son of a General or someone in a high similar position, crawled out of the mud obviously angry and disgusted. Right in front of a group of neatly dressed officers who were watching everything from a little knoll, Bogdan removed the shoulder harness-and-belt combination with all the equipment from his body, and placed it on the ground. Then, taking his rifle, he swung it around and threw it as far as he could, muttering: "And now I am going home!" before angrily stomping off to somewhere.

I don't know what happened to Private Bogdan. And no, I do not think that he got shot or ended up in a *Strafkompanie*, a punishment detachment. (The Waffen-SS penal institution near Danzig was greatly feared.) In such matters as in the case of a rather young Mama's boy like Private Bogdan, the SS leadership was much more lenient than one could expect, for instance, if something like that happened at one of the famous private or government U.S. military academies. My best guess would be that Bogdan was sent to an infirmary for a few days, and then transferred to his father's outfit outside of the Waffen-SS.

That the Waffen-SS went to extraordinary lengths to safeguard the discipline demanded from all of us can be seen from an incident that happened in the LAH a few years before I was able to join:

During occupation duty in France a love affair developed between a young Waffen-SS soldier and a French farm girl. A few months after the division had left French soil for redeployment in the east, the girl discovered that she was pregnant, and rather than admit the affair to her parents and others, she claimed that she had been raped. As a result, the girl's father reported the "rape" to the German occupation authorities.

In World War II, German soldiers convicted of rape in *any* of the occupied countries usually received the death penalty, and as a rule the sentence was quickly meted out.

Upon questioning, the young Waffen-SS soldier readily admitted to the affair with the girl, and his comrades who had known about it backed him up. In spite of this, the young soldier was convicted and executed.

To this day I believe that this harsh treatment of a young soldier was cruel and wrong. On the other hand, we must see the matter in the context of the time: The Waffen-SS was a new military unit and had to earn both its reputation as a viable military arm (and not as a barracked police force under jurisdiction of the Reich government, as had been originally envisioned), and also vis-a-vis the German Army, many of whose officers viewed the daredevil soldiers in their camouflage smocks as interlopers. In addition, the "anti-SS" propaganda by the enemies had managed to paint Himmler's creation as some sort of atheistic, blood-thirsty ignoramuses who went about shooting prisoners, pillaging homes and churches, and raping the girls of the subjugated nations. In order to overcome this negative image, the SS soldiers had to be more brave, better disciplined and even better looking than their compatriots in other uniforms. Finally, toward the end of the war, there were many occasions when a Wehrmacht officer whose unit was in dire straits somewhere at one the many fronts where Germany was under onslaught, praised the Lord for sending relief in the form of one or more SS divisions.

Special praise goes to both our company commander, *Obersturmführer* (First Lieutenant) Walter Ludescher, and my platoon leader throughout the time I was stationed at the Breslau base, *Untersturmführer* (Second Lieutenant) Franz Budka. Both were Austrians, and both were absolutely fantastic officers. Neither would ever ask us to do anything which they themselves were unwilling to do (for instance, at an obstacle course), and at all times their honest concern for their charges was apparent.

I met Walter Ludescher only once again long after the war had ended; a half century after we had left Breslau-Lissa for the "Battle of the Bulge": Almost exactly 50 years after the war we got together at his home near St. Pölten in Austria, not very far from where I had been in combat in April of 1945. It was a very pleasant meeting although, as could be expected, Ludescher did not remember me. Amazingly, he had quite a career as an opera singer after the war, and with pride he showed us his albums of some of his most memorable stage and movie appearances. Even at nearly 80 years of age, he still had the straight bearing (and the good looks) of a Waffen-SS officer. Unfortunately, he died soon thereafter.

Franz Budka became one of the heroes of the defense of Breslau when the city was under siege by the Red Army, and he was one of the last recipients of the coveted *Ritterkreuz* during the war. Following is an addendum to the *Wehrmachtbericht*, the official communiqué of the German *Wehrmacht*, dated 27th March 1945, where Franz Budka is mentioned:

"In the Fortress city of Breslau, the First company of an SS-Regiment under the able leadership of SS-Untersturmführer Budka managed to prevent all attempts by enemy forces to break through the German lines. The fighting frequently occurred in the basements of burning apartment blocks where the heat reached up to 60 degrees Celsius (140 degrees Fahrenheit). The enemy sustained heavy losses."

The fate of Budka seems in doubt. According to one report I have, he stepped on a mine at the very end of the war and was killed instantly. Other sources told me years ago that he fell wounded into Soviet captivity, and that in 1952 he succumbed to the cruel treatment of the Bolshevist GULAG system, while working as a slave laborer in the mines of Vorkuta near the Arctic Circle. In a book, FORGOTTEN LEGIONS, *Obscure Combat Formations of the Waffen-SS*, by Antonio J. Munoz, a work I purchased only recently, Budka, by then the 25-year-old commander of my former company (I had in the meantime been assigned to the *Leibstandarte),* is mentioned again several times. According to this book, Franz Budka, a native of Vienna, Austria, died of wounds received on May 6th, 1945, during a break-out attempt from the Soviet encirclement. Ironically, this happened on the very same day when I made my way to the American forces that had in the meantime reached the Enns river not very far from Vienna. SS-*Obersturmbannführer* (Lt. Colonel) Besslein, my battalion commander at Breslau, received the *Ritterkreuz* on the very day Hitler took his own life in Berlin.

One more incident from our final inspection comes to mind. While our ideological instructions had, at this late stage of the war, been relegated to a minor role, our leadership still wanted to know how well national socialist ideals had been imbued in us. In retrospect I can honestly state that we were not as brainwashed regarding Hitler's and our other leaders' (including Heinrich Himmler's) ideology as is presently happening to young people in the United States regarding democracy, racial equality, political correctness and, not to forget, "Holocaust studies". Even our German patriotism was not as much promoted as is customary with American patriotism in American schools.

During the final inspection it happened that we generally did well in our answers regarding the causes of World Wars I and II; the need for German rearmament after 1935; the criminality of the Versailles Treaty; the perfidy of Great Britain, and other pertinent matters. The Jews were not mentioned. The fact is, they were never mentioned. But then one of the attending higher officers asked that one of us answer the questions, *"Was ist der Nationalsozialismus? Was ist seine Bedeutung für das deutsche Volk?"* (What is National Socialism, and what is its meaning for the German people?")

Dead silence.

The silence lasted so long that it became uncomfortable. Nobody moved. As usual, I was sitting way in the back since I had no desire to be indivdually questioned about anything. I never minded arguing about almost any point in a smaller circle, but to provide answers to teachers in classrooms was not my forte.

This time I felt I had to rescue the situation. I lifted my arm, and I could see the relief on *Obersturmführer* Ludescher's face when he called my name.

"Schütze Schmidt, can you explain what National Socialism is?"

I stood up. I had no intention of giving a long speech or explanation. All I did was recite something that I had probably read in my father's NSDAP *Schulungsbriefe,* the thin magazine that was sent regularly to the political leaders (the ones that later in the war were derisively called the *Goldfasanen* - golden pheasants - because of their fancy uniforms).

What did I say? Since I remember the scene well, I stated something like this: "National Socialism is the manifestation of the political will of the German people. It found its best expression in the *Volksgemeinschaft* created by Adolf Hitler. The mottos of our German *Volksgemeinschaft* - Community of our People - are *'Einer für alle, alle für einen,* namely "One for all, and all for one" and

"Gemeinnutz geht vor Eigennutz" (the common good has priority over private gain)." Finally, I likely stated that "National Socialism means a free and willing social engagement for every member of the German *Volksgemeinschaft."*

After that I sat down, and on the satisfied faces of the officers I could see that I had rescued a ticklish situation.

German soldiers sang a lot. As a matter of fact, on our overland marches we *always* sang. Our repertoire of marching songs was great. It included not only the few *Lieder* of the National Socialist *Kampfzeit*, the era before Hitler assumed power, but marches from the First World War, from the Kaiser's empire, from the Thirty Years' War, and even some from Pathfinder and Communist youth organizations, and a couple of foreign ones. A favorite with all of us was the one with the melody of "It is a long way to Tipperary". The one song with American connotations had the words "Lore, Lore, Lore, you are the prettiest girl around," based upon *"Mine eyes have seen the glory,"* with the "Lore, Lore, Lore" (a girl's name) instead of "glory, glory, glory."

The song of the *Leibstandarte* had a difficult melody and was hard to sing. Much better was *"Als die goldne Abendsonne..."* (*As the golden evening sun was sending her last rays, a regiment of Hitler marched sadly into the little town, for they were going to bury a fallen Hitler comrade*",) which interestingly ends with the refrain, *"As the golden morning sun was sending her first rays, a regiment of Hitler continued to fight on...."*

My personal favorites were the old cavalry tunes about the *"Blue dragoons"* and *"Drei Lilien"* (Three lilies) and the march of the German *Schutztruppe* (military units) guarding the German colonies in Africa when Germany still possessed them up to 1919.

(The German colonies in Africa had been: *Deutsch Ostafrika*, now Tanzania; *Deutsch Südwest Afrika*, now Namibia; *Togo*, now Togo and Ghana, and *Kamerun*, now Cameroon. In Windhoek, Namibia, they still had a *Kaiserstrasse*, and even a *Göringstrasse*, the latter named after the father of Herman Göring, in the 1980s while I was visiting there.)

The song *"Deutsch ist die Saar"* (The Saarland is German) the tune about my home area, unfortunately doesn't have a good rhythm for marching. The official song of the Hitler Youth,

"Vorwärts, vorwärts, schmettern die hellen Fanfaren." (Forward, forward, the fanfares soun."), was equally bad for marching to.

I am frequently asked whether on our long hikes through towns and over land we also sang the famed *Horst Wessel* song, the title of which is *Die Fahne hoch*. The answer is no. During the Third Reich the *Horst Wessel Lied* was, whether merely by custom or by regulation I do not know, attached to the first verse of the German national anthem *Deutschland, Deutschland über alles.* I would assume that in the light of this *Die Fahne hoch* was not used at less than solemn occasions. Besides, the cadence of *Die Fahne hoch* also does not lend itself to marching in the German marching step.

On the floor of the barracks building in Breslau-Lissa occupied by our unit we had one good radio. At times, when no officer was around, we dialed a station calling itself *Soldatensender Calais,* a British propaganda station pretending to be a station of the German Armed Forces Network. We knew it was an enemy station and we had much fun with the really stupid propaganda they spewed out daily. What we liked was some of the modern music they also broadcast. I don't think we ever got in trouble for listening to this enemy station even though in our civilian life such behavior was strictly against the law.

In the Waffen-SS the officers and non-commissioned officers ate the same food as did the common soldiers. They had their own tables in the mess hall but there was no separation between theirs and ours. That does not mean that in the privacy of their apartments or rooms our superiors did not consume delicacies that were unavailable to us. After all, they were older than us and had more right to enjoy the finer things of life. However, at this stage of the war, few people in Germany had access to good food or exotic spirits. Real coffee - *Bohnenkaffee* - was only a frequently-dreamed-about pleasure.

As the summer of 1944 went by and the fall began, the German military situation became ever more serious. We followed the many battles closely, and our eyes were riveted by the heroic resistance of our soldiers especially on the Eastern front and in the areas in the west after Patton's breakthrough at Avranches. By now we were used to the frequent litany of the daily *Wehrmachtbericht,* the official communique of the German Armed Forces that always spoke of '*Im Zuge der geplanten Frontverkürzungen,..."* (In the course of the planned shortening of our front, ...) this or that city had to be abandoned. We knew that this was not always true. In order to get somewhat at the truth, I often - whenever possible - listened to the weekly radio commentary on the *Wehrmachtbericht* by a Lieutenant-General Dittmar. This high officer, obviously working in the services of the Reich, was nevertheless astonishingly frank. From his broadcasts I gained a much deeper understanding of the real military war situation. Dr. Goebbels, in his weekly columns in the newspaper *Das Reich,* delved into the political situation of the world. And he did so in a manner that permitted the forming of one's own opinion. (Except insofar as the belief in our eventual victory was concerned.) It was almost like today: For people who want to be informed, for instance about the so-called Holocaust, almost all the desired information is available, now especially on the Internet, even if at times one has to search for it. But most people seem satisfied with the pre-chewed opinions of the better-known newsmen. Neither Dr. Goebbels nor Generalleutnant Dittmar were the fare of the average Joe, or German "Michel". (The latter often preferred rumors to facts.) I do not recall that even one other of my comrades at Breslau-Lissa either listened to General Dittmar or read Dr. Goebbels' columns.

One day, during a day of rest, an *Unterscharführer* (corporal) of whom I knew that he had been transferred from the *Luftwaffe* to the Waffen-SS against his will, asked me to assist him in going to the Lissa railroad station with a little hand cart and pick something up from the baggage counter. I was surprised that this non-com asked me to go along with him since the two of us had never any personal dealings with each other before.

On the way to the station he told me why he had asked me to go along: He felt he had to talk to someone about the deteriorating war situation, and he wanted to hear my opinion. The man was about 25 years of age, married, and the father of two children. He told me flat out that he had no intention of giving his life for the Fatherland. His family was more precious to him.

I was not surprised that someone much older - - for a 17-year-old, the age of 25 years is much older - - wanted to have a serious talk with me. This happened already when I was still working at the *Kohlenhandelsgesellschaft* in Saarbrücken. Perhaps I looked more serious-minded than most of my comrades of my age. At any rate, if

I remember correctly, the family of this former Luftwaffe *Unteroffizier* lived in the vicinity of Breslau, and this soldier was concerned about the precarious strategic position of the Silesian capital. At the end of July the Soviet Army had conquered the Polish city of Lublin, and ever since then the Red scourge had slowly but steadily advanced in our direction. When the two of us had our conversation, there was no obstacle that could have held back the Russians but the bravery of German soldiers.

The question the *Luftwaffe* fellow had for me was whether I thought that Breslau could be in danger within a relatively short time, and if yes, what he should do with his family. I told him that my father had send us, his entire family, away from the Saar danger zone, which was in the *Westwall* fortifications' area, three days before World War II actually began. He did this not because he knew more than anybody else in our town but because he viewed the real situation differently, and he acted accordingly. The fact is that we ended up, of our own free will, with relatives in northern Germany where we were well taken care of, while most of our neighbors were ordered to board trains into the unknown (into the heart of Germany) a few days later. My opinion was that the corporal should send his family much further to the west.

Ironically, at the time I did not believe that we would lose the war. I knew (and we in general had often spoken about it) that from a strictly military point the war was lost but we had much confidence in the abilities of the German scientists to produce *Wunderwaffen* (miracle weapons) that could again turn the tide in our favor. Lest American readers laugh about this naivety I do have to mention that in 1944, with Germany outwardly totally devastated by Allied air raids, the output of arms and other accuterments of war was greater than in any other year of the war. Besides, by the time I spoke with the *Luftwaffe Unteroffizier* (for as such I regarded him still even though he was in Waffen-SS uniform), we had seen the new employment of the V1 and V2 rockets, the Messerschmitt 262 jet fighter and other new weapons of a quality and revolutionary kind, like the MG-42, our enemies did not possess. There was also still the statement, alluded to in the August 19, 1944 letter to my mother, by the scientist who told us of a new weapon that could destroy an entire city with one big bang.

In February and March 2000, mean-spirited attacks against the Waffen-SS appeared in almost all American newspapers as a result of the uncalled-for, and contrived, public outrage about Jörg Haider's rise in Austrian politics.

Reading the following depictions of the heroic Waffen-SS by major American newspapers, I cannot even be angry anymore. I know wherefrom this nonsense originates, and I feel pity for the non-Jewish cowards employed by the American media who, often unthinkingly, do the bidding of those whose never-ending quest is the destruction of our race and heritage.

"(Haider) glorified veterans of the murderous Waffen-SS... " The New York Times, Jan. 29, 2000

"(Haider) once called Waffen-SS veterans 'decent people with character who stuck to their belief through the strongest headwinds'." Chicago Tribune, Jan. 29, 2000

"Haider's record includes praise for ... former Nazi SS men." Christian Science Monitor, Feb. 2, 2000

"Among Haider's more disturbing sentiments is his praise of the 'orderly employment policies' of the Third Reich, and defense of the Nazi Party's military arm (sic! HS) as 'decent men of good character'." The Washington Times Weekly, February 7 - 13, 2000

"(In 1995 Haider said...) that many Waffen-SS veterans were 'decent people of good character who stuck to their convictions'." The Washington Post, Feb. 2, 2000

"Haider was quoted as saying, 'individual guilt is what matters. Hence, it can never be the Waffen-SS as such but only individuals who ... bear responsibility'." Washington Jewish Week, Feb. 10, 2000

"(Haider) outraged many Austrians by appearing at a reunion of veterans of Hitler's Waffen-SS, calling them 'men of character'." Associated Press, Feb. 2, 2000

The claim that Jörg Haider had outraged many Austrians with his statement looks very ridiculous when one considers that more Austrian-Germans than Prussian-Germans had served in the Waffen-SS, and that especially the officer corps of the Waffen-SS was more Austrian than "German-German". There exists hardly an Austrian family without one of its members having been a Waffen-SS soldier. *Kameradschaft IV,* the veterans' organization of Austrian former Waffen-SS soldiers, plays a greater political role than HIAG (*Hilfsgemeinschaft auf Gegenseitigkeit der ehemaligen Angehörigen der Waffen-SS* - The mutual assistance league of former members of the Waffen-SS) does in the German Bundesrepublik.

a Waffen-SS lieutenant

Chapter 9

By October 1944, our training at the Waffen-SS barracks at Breslau-Lissa seemed to have been sufficient so that we could be assigned to any one of the thirty-odd SS divisions then committed to battle. Before that, however, we were entitled to about ten days of *Einsatzurlaub,* "leave before going into combat". Thus, at about the middle of that month I traveled by train back to Saarbrücken, noticing on the way that the general situation in Germany had deteriorated seriously since I had made the 500 mile-trip in the opposite direction.

As mentioned, Saarbrücken had experienced the worst air raid of the war on October 5, 1944, causing nearly 700 dead, and many more wounded. When I arrived about 12 days later, there was still a pall of smoke from smoldering fires over the city, and the train from Frankfurt took us only to the eastern outskirts, forcing the few incoming passengers, mostly soldiers on leave like myself, to hike the rest of the way through one ruined street after another. Since the passage through the former business district was *verboten* due to still-unexploded enemy bombs, I had to make my way across the Saar river through the district called "Alt Saarbrücken", namely, the oldest part of the town. There, the devastation was thorough. The former castle had been heavily hit. Both the ancient "*Schlosskirche*" (castle church) and the beautiful *"Ludwigskirche"*, the church where my great-grandfather had been a deacon, were burned-out ruins. Of the quaint, old narrow old town that had always reminded me of the Middle Ages, nothing was left standing.

In front of the depot for the street cars (electric trams) I saw my favorite, No. 112, one of the large, modern electric engine cars that had been delivered only a few years earlier, and which had often taken me to work at the "Westmark" company, lying on its side, totally destroyed, across a number of the converging rails. A huge bomb must have lifted it and thrown it across the tracks. And not far away practically nothing was left standing of the well-built, solid brownstone Schmidt town house on *Kanalstrasse,* in which my great-grandfather had lived out his long and fruitful life. Near the ruin of the townhouse the contents of basements of some buildings were still burning ten days after the raid. I believe the archives of the major Saarbrücken newspaper had been in one of them.

When I finally got home after many hours of hiking in the darkness, I found only my sister Helga there. My mother had been taken to a safer area, out of the Saarland and Lorraine battle zone, to deliver, on October 6th, her seventh child, a healthy boy, appropriately named Siegfried (victory and peace) after one of the heroes of the Nibelungen sagas. The other two of my little brothers, 7-year-old Manfred and 5-year-old Harald, were in a boys' home not very far away.

I don't really remember much of this furlough except that the weather was miserable, and that because in our area now all places of entertainment, including the movie houses, were closed by the authorities, there was preciously little to do. The first few days were utterly boring. Things got a little more interesting when first my mother came home with our new-born brother, and a few days later my sister was able to pick up Manfred and Harald.

Living in an area of heavy industry, and astride several major transportation arteries, there was now no day when enemy planes could not be seen in the skies above Luisenthal, either bombers or the feared *Jabos*, namely, the Mustangs and Thunderbolts of the U.S. Air Force that seemed to shoot at anything that moved.[14] This made it very dangerous for us, including the children, to go outside the house, or take a train or tram, during the daylight hours. At this time, many civilians got killed by strafing Jabos: children going to school, farmers plowing their fields, a postman making his deliveries, and mothers trying to get some food for the little ones.

---

[14] The former P-51 pilot and later General of the USAF, Chuck Yeager, made a reference to this in his autobiography, "YEAGER", Bantam Books, 1985, pg. 63.

Near Merzig, not far from Luisenthal, a narrow-gauge passenger train was attacked, causing many civilian casualties.

I have been asked the question, what were the feelings of the German population regarding American fliers. Were they all lumped together as *Luftgangsters* (air gangsters) as the German Government propaganda depicted them?

There is no doubt that especially the people in Western Germany, who had to suffer much from the wanton killings of civilians by *some* of the American Jabo pilots, regarded them as cold-blooded murderers. Anyone who has flown in an airplane and noticed during landing and take-off how extremely well one can see the ground from a low altitude must realize that there simply was no excuse for a P-47 or P-51 pilot to attack and kill, for instance, a farmer and his horse on a field, or children walking to school. In my part of Germany there is hardly a village that did not lose some of its inhabitants through uncalled-for Jabo raids. Similarly it is easy to imagine that Germans who lost close family members in terror atacks hated *all* British, Canadian and American flights crews.

However, looking at the devastation wrought on Germany by the bombers one would think that the hate of the Germans would have been mostly directed at them. But this was not the case. One day I was standing outside of our house as Saarbrücken was being attacked. The *flak* fired furiously, and in order to avoid being hit by ragged iron splinters from the exploding *flak* shells we stood underneath some roofing, watching the spectacle high up in the air. It was then that one of the men standing around voiced the opinion that at this moment he would not want to be one of the "*arme Kerle*" - poor fellows - sitting in the thin-skinned aluminum boxes that flew overhead. We all agreed.

Another time, I believe it was in 1942, a British four-engine "*Lancaster*" bomber was shot down over our area and crashed onto coal mine property perhaps three or four miles away across the Saar river. Upon hearing of the crash, my brother and I took the street car to the nearest stop to the crash site, to view the horrible scene of the smashed bomber from as near as we could get. Very close to the road, and still accessible to all because no security detail from the German Air Force had yet arrived, I saw the bodies of most of the crew of the enemy plane lying side-by-side under some tarpaulin. One could not see their uniforms or their faces but I noticed that none of them wore boots or shoes. Later I was told that foreign workers or POWs working at the mine had absconded with them. Listening to the other Germans watching the scene because I wanted to hear details of the crash itself, it was clear to me that most Germans felt sorry for the (obviously) young men who had lost their lives in the crash. No expression of rancor or hate could be heard.

Searching in the area for some souvenirs, my brother and I discovered in the nearby forest the rear wheel of the bomber. It must have broken off during the crash, and been jettisoned for a few hundred feet. It wasn't easy but we did manage to get the wheel, rubber tire and all, back to our house. Taking it apart I saw that at least one of the ball bearings had been manufactured in Canada.

Depending on which way the wind was blowing, one could hear the distant rumbling of the vicious battles being fought in the Metz area of Lorraine between German and American troops but 40 miles away. After a breakthrough, an American Sherman tank could have traversed this distance in a little over an hour. There was no river or mountain between Metz and us that could have stopped the U.S. Army.

The older people in Luisenthal were amazingly good-natured, considering everything. Certainly they were griping about the shortages, and the black-out, and the other innumerable inconveniences and sorrow caused by the war, but they went to work, did their duty, and helped each other more than was the case in better times.

Mr. Fuerst, the old-time Communist, was still complaining about the what he called the "Nazis," while being grateful that the NSV, the National Socialist social service organization, assisted him and his invalid wife. And the old SA men boasted of their efforts in the *Kampfzeit* when they bested the Reds, the Liberals and others.

While at home I also visited our butcher, Wilhelm Bidot, whose brother Karl was the local NSDAP leader (and who as a result was to starve to death in a French concentration camp a year later). In the Bidot shop I again heard an exchange of words that was unchanged since the time when the Saarland again became part of

Germany in 1935. In other words, this sort of banter had been going on for years.

Mrs. Philomena Meyer entered the shop.

"Guten Morgen, Herr Bidot!"

"Heil Hitler! Frau Meyer!" answered the butcher.

Frau Meyer again:

"Herr Bidot! I wished you a good morning!"

"Frau Meyer, I heard you, I also wished you a good morning by remembering our Führer. What better greeting could there be this early in the morning?"

Frau Meyer was undaunted: "A simple *Guten Morgen* would have accomplished the same!" said she.

With that everybody laughed, including Frau Meyer, whose dislike for Hitler was known to all.

One day during my furlough I went to Saarbrücken to visit my colleagues of the *Kohlenhandelsgesellschaft* when to my dismay I discovered that the company had in the meantime been *ausgelagert,* meaning, moved from the danger zone in the city to a smaller town in a rural area. The former villa that had served as the main office of our company and where my big boss had his offices had received a direct hit, and the entire front of the house had caved in. Most of the other fine buildings in this area of upscale homes had been severely damaged in an air raid, and even one of my favorite houses, a huge single-family home from which I knew that it had been practically a living museum with beautiful Victorian furniture and furnishings, was but a burned-out ruin.

(The question may arise why people in the bombed cities did not put their pianos, fine furniture and other valuables into the basements (cellars) which all German houses possess, in order to have at least some chance that not everything would be destroyed by fire or explosions. Perhaps our own experience can provide a valid answer: Right at the beginning of the war a law came out that made it mandatory for everyone to reinforce the basements with heavy beams so that they provided a safe shelter not only for the inhabitants but also for passers-by caught nearby once the air raid sirens had sounded. This made it impossible for large parts of the basements to be used for storage. The same law that demanded the reinforcement of the cellars also ordered the people to *"entrümpeln"* - - remove unneeded 'junk' - - from their attics so that in case an incendiary bomb went through the roof there would not be enough flammable material to start a big fire. In our case the "*Entrümpelung*" was especially tragic because we had to send much archive material left from the Schmidt construction firm to the garbage dump, among other things hundreds of the most beautiful, hand-drawn blueprints of turn-of-the century houses, railroad stations and churches. When I was a child my father did not want me to touch these works of art too often because of their fragile state.)

While I had worked at the *Kohlenhandelsgesellschaft,* I had to trudge every working day (then six days a week) from the Saarbrücken central railroad station a mile or two uphill to our offices. On the way I passed some caves that had been hewn into a minor hill of relatively soft sandstone, caves that were then used as *Lager* cellars for their delicious product by a nearby beer brewery. As the air raids increased, some of the caves were emptied of the beer barrels, and refurnished as air raid shelters for the civilian population living in the area.

During one of the heavy air raids on Saarbrücken in late 1944, the very hill into the side of which the brewery caves had been dug received one or several direct hits of huge concussion bombs. As a result, the ceiling of one of the shelters where many mothers of small children were sitting on long benches that had been placed along the side walls caved in, burying all the babies and small children that had been sleeping in their carriages in the center of the room. None of the many children was still alive by the times rescuers had been able to remove the huge mountain of rock and sand that had covered them.

Possibly during this October visit to the inner city I met in the totally ruined and boarded-up main street a young, married woman, a former colleague of mine, who seemed incredibly happy to see me. Wondering what this was all about, she told me that she was soooo glad to see me because there was something on her mind about which she was not able to talk to anyone, yet she felt the desperate need to confide in someone who would understand her. And that was supposed to be me.

Frau Z's husband, a sergeant in the German Army, was one of the true heroes of the German Eastern front. He was one of the relatively small number of infantry soldiers who kept the Soviet

Army from breaking through the thin German lines (where the unequal battle often pitched ten Soviet soldiers against one single *Landser* [a German expression used similarly as GI in the U.S.] on the German side) for three years now. I remember having met this *Feldwebel* (sergeant) once. He wore a much-worn field-gray uniform with all the decorations that proved his service on the Eastern front: The Iron Cross, first and second class; the close combat badge in silver, the wounded badge in silver; the infantry assault badge; the *Ostmedaille* for the first horrible winter in Russia, and a *Panzervernichtungsabzeichen* for single-handedly destroying a Russian tank, and others.

Well, Sergeant Z. had been wounded once more and because of that he was able to visit his wife again in the fall of 1944. This happened after the American Army had reached Metz. The sergeant's wife thought that this meant the war was going to be over within weeks, and when her husband wanted to leave again for the Eastern front, which in the meantime had in some places been moved inside the borders of the Reich, she adamantly refused to let him go. The result was that she had hidden him - literally entombed him - in a cellar of relatives. In other words, he was a deserter, and if found by the MPs he would be executed. Medals or no medals.

Mrs. Z. wanted to know from me what I thought of the war situation and when everything was going to be over. She also wanted to know my opinion whether she had done right in keeping her husband home. What could I say? Actually, she placed me in a serious quandary. By law, and considering the oath I was supposed to swear soon (but which never happened), I should have reported her and her husband, and thereby would definitely cause not only the death of this brave *Ostfrontkämpfer* (infantry soldier of the Eastern front) but possibly hers as well. Obviously, I was unable to give her the proper answer regarding the outcome of the war. Hoping against hope I believed that the tide of war would turn again in our favor and perhaps bring victory. But that was not what this woman wanted to hear.

I did not report Frau Z. or her husband to the Gestapo. Throughout the war I had had dealings, inadvertently on my part, with people whom one could consider enemies of our cause. That was the fate of many Germans such as myself who lived in border areas of the Reich where enemies of Germany abounded, mostly people from neighboring states. In the case of the sergeant I knew that for all the war years he had given his best for Germany. Undoubtedly he was burned out. While he had fought almost daily against the often overwhelming superiority of the enemy, one could still see many - far too many - shirkers who had always managed to be as far removed from any shooting as possible. I could just imagine how it felt for the sergeant to have lost most of his comrades at Stalingrad, and then later to experience the incessant fighting of the 2000 kilometer retreat from the Steppes near the Volga river to the Vistula in Poland. Now the war had reached a point where the question of whether to stay and fight on (and possibly sacrifice one's life for a seemingly lost cause) or to look out for one's own personal interest, had become a primary requisite especially for the older generations. I knew what I had to do to retain my honor - namely fight to the bitter end, or, if the fortunes of war were still with us, to victory, but I also was realistic enough to acknowledge that the war situation looked dismal indeed for Germany, and that the former was more likely now than the latter. It was not up to me to judge individuals like this sergeant and his wife too harshly.

The sergeant survived the war. I never met either him or his wife again.

At the end of October 1944 I was just about ready to travel back to Breslau again because my leave was ending, when my former playmate (since the time when we were very little boys) and later co-worker at the "Westmark" offices, Kurt Seiler, arrived for a short convalescent furlough. Kurt was a year older than myself and had joined the Waffen-SS in 1943. In the summer of 1944 he had been fighting with the *Wiking* division near the Baltic countries against the Red Army, and it was there that he had been wounded.

Now that Kurt was in Luisenthal, things got a little more interesting, and suddenly I hated to leave so soon. It was then that I got the idea of using the previously mentioned loss of the apartment house belonging to our family in order to have my leave extended. Some time before, the German government had designated three different kinds of damages after bombing raids that were used to describe what had happened:

Bombing damage A meant broken windows and doors, heavy but repairable roof damage, shrapnel holes and smoke damage,

Bombing damage B indicated structural damage to a building, or loss of some rooms,

Bombing damage C described the total loss of a home, a building or business establishment.

The *Wehrmacht* had been ordered to grant, if possible, an emergency leave of short duration to soldiers whose family had incurred *Bombenschaden C.*

Our destroyed 3-story apartment building was only about 400 feet from our house, but three heavy American bombs had exploded in front and in the back of it, and there was nothing left standing of this solidly built brick structure after the air raid except one side wall. Since the Luisenthal bridge is very nearby, it is possible that this important river crossing was the intended target. Incidentally, no person living in the apartment building had come to harm on that day because, as a rule, when the sirens sounded their alarm, the Saarlanders went religiously into air raid shelters that had been prepared in nearby coal mine shafts. No doubt the destruction of our apartment building was *Bombenschaden C.*

It just so happened that one of the girls I had gone to school with worked at the local police station, and this enabled me to go to her (while the sole policeman who was normally manning the station was busy elsewhere) to ask whether she could provide me with a document that showed my family had sustained *Bombenschaden C.* Both the girl and I knew that this was true only in a legal sense but not in the way the order was supposed to be understood. Nevertheless, I got the document, and took it to the highest Waffen-SS authorities in Saarbrücken, asking for a few additional days of leave. A day later I received a telegram from the *Höhere SS- und Polizeiführer* (the higher SS and Police Commander) at Wiesbaden, extending my furlough not just 3 or 4 but for 8 days additional. Obviously, I was elated.

One day at the beginning of November 1944, Kurt Seiler and I were standing not far from the Schmidt home on the main street, when from the east, from the direction of Saarbrücken, we noticed a battle formation of military vehicles approaching at extremely high speed. Seeing us standing there in our natty dress uniforms (*Ausgehuniform,* shoes shined and all), an officer of the unit, a young *Obersturmführer*/First Lieutenant, and by the name band on his cuff sleeves, his demeanor, and the type of vehicles he was leading, obviously the commander of an anti-tank unit of the *Götz von Berlichingen* SS-division, had his half-track stopped right in front of us and called us over to him:

"Which way is the best and fastest way to Metz?" he asked us. "The Americans made a breakthrough."

On a not very good map he had of our area, we were able to show the officer how to cross the Saar river at the Luisenthal bridge only a couple of hundred feet away, the very river crossing near which in 1933 I had rescued my playmate Ludwig from drowning. The officer mentioned that as a result of the great destruction of Saarbrücken he had been unable to find the major road leading out of the city toward the south, namely, the Metzer Strasse. From the other side of the Luisenthal bridge the SS-*Panzerabwehrkompanie,* quite obviously a combat outfit in battle, could take the short road to Forbach, already on Lorraine (French) territory, then to Merlebach and past St. Avold, where a year later a giant American military cemetery would be established, and then on the well-constructed *chaussee* to Metz.

To me the entire scene looked surreal. Especially because it occurred in my hometown, in sight of our house, near the place where I was born, and where Kurt and I had played together; near where at this moment a great battle raged between German soldiers and those boys from America, tall, blond, good looking guys whom we remembered so fondly from our beloved Wild West movies. Our young comrades from the *Götz von Berlichingen* division looked as if they had been in combat for months, ragged and haggard, and - perhaps most of all - very tired. As soon as we had given the needed information to their commander, off they went, again at high speed, to repel the Americans.

Also in the first week of November, possibly on a day when because of inclement weather the enemy air forces had to stay in their hangars in Western Europe, Kurt and I went to nearby Völklingen to have pictures taken (Kurt, who only owned a field cap, wore my peaked cap for the occasion) and then we took the train to Saarbrücken where we went to the Hitler Youth administration for the Saarland to settle a dispute between the two of us, namely, which one of us had joined the *Jungvolk* (the cub scouts of the Hitler Youth movement) earlier, he or I. Amazingly, it didn't take the office worker employed at the *Bannführung* long to discover the facts: exactly ten years earlier to the day, on November 2, 1934, I had been accepted in the *Jungvolk.* Kurt had trailed me by a year. As a rule, only boys between the ages 10 to 14 were accepted into the *Jungvolk,* but 1934 was the starting year of the campaign for the Saar plebiscite that took place (under international supervision) on January 13, 1935, and German nationalists needed everybody, including seven-year-old boys such as myself, to hand out flyers and other propaganda material.

A few days later I was on my way back to Breslau. Saying good-bye to my family was not as difficult as one could imagine: I was convinced that I would survive the war. Little did I realize that apart from a few letters that I might still have received from my mother in the next few weeks, I would not know anything of my family's fate until the following August, after the war had been lost.

Kurt Seiler gave his live for Germany in March of 1945, a few weeks before his 19th birthday. He died during the heavy battles in Hungary, SW of Budapest, at just about the time when I lay badly wounded in a hospital near Vienna. Kurt's family did not learn anything of his fate for nearly half a century. Only after the collapse of the Soviet Union, and after the Iron Curtain that had split the European heartland so long had been lifted, was it possible for the German War Graves Commission to go to the countries of the former Eastern block and there look for the temporary graves of Germany's fallen heroes. Kurt's remains were discovered in the early 1990s, and they now rest in the German military cemetery at Deg in Hungary, not far from where he had died.

Although Waffen-SS soldiers could ask to be returned to their original units after having recovered from wounds or sickness (and most of them did so) there is a chance that Kurt eventually was assigned to either the *Leibstandarte* or the *Hitlerjugend* division after our mutual leave. The cemetery in Hungary where he is now buried is the resting place mainly of the fallen soldiers of these two divisions. How easily I could have ended up there also, for it was in March of 1945, and in that area of Hungary, that the company which I had joined during the Battle of the Bulge was totally wiped out. The shoulder wound I had received a month earlier had probably saved my life.

Chapter 10

Back in Breslau-Lissa on or about the 12th of November, we were soon being outfitted with clothes and equipment needed for winter combat. It was then that I was informed, but did not give it serious thought, that during my prolonged absence all the recruits who had successfully passed the tests of the Officer's candidates course were sworn in with an oath to Hitler, and, in addition, after a final medical examination, all my comrades had their blood type tattooed inside their left arm pit. In other words, I, of all people, never swore allegiance to Adolf Hitler, and the absence of the blood type tattoo would only a half year later (and for a much longer time thereafter) prove a very lucky fact indeed. I also do not recall ever receiving a certificate or other document proving that I had successfully completed the officer's candidates course and was entitled to wear the silver braids that we kiddingly called *Hoffnungsbalken* (girders of hope) around my shoulder straps. But I assume that it must have been noted in my *Soldbuch.*

One of the other platoon leaders of the company, a young *Untersturmführer* from Berlin, came to me and asked me (a private!) to make certain that it was he would get the long gray coat of my dress uniform which I had to turn in for a more bulky winter camouflage outfit. It seems that I had owned one of the finest gray coats of the entire company, namely, of fine wool, well cut, of good fit, and new when I received it. My cigarettes had accomplished wonders. I also do remember that against regulations I had sown the back slit of the coat shut so that it fit me as if taylor-made. Here I may mention that unlike in the other parts of the German *Wehrmacht*, in the Waffen-SS we did not address our officers with "Herr" (Sir), as in "Herr Leutnant", "Herr Hauptmann" (captain) and "Herr General". In the affirmative we would just say "Jawohl, *Hauptsturmführer* (captain)" and so on. This made for a better relationship between officers and men, but to the best of my judgment this usage did not infringe upon discipline, as the old-line officers of the regular services *Heer, Kriegsmarine* and *Luftwaffe* had feared.

In late November of 1944 the waiting for front-line assignments began. In spite of this our regular hours for both field training and theoretical instructions continued unabated. Because we had received special training in the handling of infantry howitzers, we were all supposed to be ordered to units that consisted of either the heavy 150mm or the 75mm (close infantry support) artillery batteries. This again assured that as a rule only a few of us would be assigned to each of the various regiments and divisions of the Waffen-SS. And, as one could expect, we all hoped to be assigned to the lowest-numbered SS-divisions like the *Leibstandarte, Das Reich* or *Hitlerjugend,* namely, the elite panzer divisions.

Then, beginning about the first of the month of December, typewritten notices with lists of names began to be posted on the blackboard in the central hall of our barracks, telling us who was assigned where. To my consternation, for a few days I did not see my name on any of the lists, and, presumably, all the slots for the top divisions had by then been filled. In my mind, I already saw myself trudging through the snow of the Eastern Carpathian mountains, fighting Czechoslovak underground brigades with an Ukrainian SS-division or, worse yet, on the Balkan peninsula keeping Tito's partisans in check. What I did not and could not have known was the fact that in the West a big offensive against the Americans and British had been planned, and due to the necessary secrecy (which, for a change, worked well in this case) perhaps even the SS-FHA (*SS-Führungshauptamt*) in Berlin, the unit that assigned us here and there, did not know where some of the howitzer companies were located. But about a week later I did notice my name, and I was assigned to the 13th Company of the 2nd *Panzergrenadierregiment* of the *1st Panzer Division Leibstandarte Adolf Hitler,* and the marching orders designated the small town of Lübbecke in Westphalia as the *Meldekopf* (reporting station).

Being the Number One division of the Waffen-SS, and having the honor of carrying the *Führer's* name on the sleeve bands, it follows that the LAH was the premier elite division of the Reich. As such it was larger than most other elite divisions of Waffen-SS and *Wehrmacht* (sometimes having a complement of more than 22,000 officers and men) and, although always under Army high command and being supplied by the Army, it was also better equipped than almost any other Panzer division.

When I joined the LAH in December of 1944, the Order of Battle of the *Leibstandarte* was, *to the best of my knowledge,* as follows (having undergone constant changes since its inception in 1933, and especially since its near destruction in the Falaise gap):

Division Staff
Security and Escort Company of the Staff
1st SS Panzer Regiment
1st SS Panzergrenadier Regiment
2nd SS Panzergrenadier Regiment
1st SS Reconnaissance Battalion
1st SS Panzerjäger (anti-tank) Battalion
1st SS Sturmgeschütz (assault gun) Battalion
1st SS Panzer Artillery Regiment
1st and 2nd SS Nebelwerfer (rocket) Battalions
1st SS Flak (anti-aircraft) Battalion
1st SS Panzer Pioneer (engineer) Battalion
1st SS Panzer Signals Troop
1st SS Replacement Battalion
1st SS Supply Troop
1st SS Truck Park
1st and 2nd SS Medical Companies
1st SS Bakery Company
1st SS Butcher Company
1st SS Division Administration Platoon
1st SS Field Post Office

(Some years after the war, when the supply of original "Nazi" memorabilia at reasonable prices became exhausted, unscrupulous dealers in militaria objects of all kinds began making fake medals, uniforms, insignia and the like pertaining to the Third Reich. Even to this day such things are in higher demand than are Allied, including Russian, products of the same era. Among the items replicated were also the sleeve or cuff bands of the Waffen-SS, and among those the ones of the *Leibstandarte.* Since in all other cases the full name of the division was used, ie. *Das Reich, Hitlerjugend, Wiking, Totenkopf* etc., someone must have believed that during the war cuff bands with the name *Leibstandarte* had also existed, and promptly went about faking them. Alas, the LAH cuff band we wore merely said *Adolf Hitler* in German *Sütterlin* [Gothic] script.)

There were about a dozen of us with marching orders either to the *Leibstandarte* or the *Hitlerjugend* division, who left Breslau-Lissa on or about the 10th of December 1944. I do not remember leaving the SS barracks at Lissa, or the train trip to Berlin, but I recall clearly when we stood on the damaged platform of the Berlin *Schlesische Bahnhof*, the Silesian railroad station, when a young fellow soldier of our group came to me (why me, I still wonder?) and told me that he lived only an hour by train from here in the province of Mecklenburg, and that he would like to visit his mother before going into combat. Without much ado I asked him to give me his marching orders, and where it said that SS-*Schütze* XXX had orders to report at the Waffen-SS *Meldekopf* in Lübbecke in Westphalia, and that he was supposed to travel from Breslau via Berlin and Hannover, I added in neatly written letters also the railroad station nearest to this soldier's home town between Berlin and Hannover.

"But what about the *Kettenhunde* (slang for military police)?" my comrade asked. "If they catch me, I'll be in real trouble."

Since I had helped type the marching orders, I was familiar with certain possibilities as to what one could do without really getting in trouble.

When the others saw that, I was asked to do the same for most of them also. I knew that what I did was not legal and could be severely punished if discovered, but considering the dismal situation of the Reich I felt it would be nice if the fellows could see their families once more. (There is a chance that some of the soldiers that traveled with me on that day were not from the officers' candidates course I had attended, and did not have the leave-before-being-sent-into-combat in the month before, as I did. The fact that I wore the silver braids around my shoulder straps also might have seemed to the young soldier who approached me first as if I had some kind of rank - which I hadn't.)

At the beginning of December 1944 I knew that our area of the Saarland had been totally evacuated for the second time in the war. It was clear that the U.S. Army had reached the Saar river, and this assured battle activities in the vicinity of Luisenthal due to the many pill boxes/bunkers of the *Westwall* located there. I assumed that my mother and the rest of the family had again found refuge in the small city of Preetz in the Northern German province of Schleswig-Holstein, where two of her sisters lived, and where we had already fled to when the war broke out in 1939. I therefore altered my marching orders by adding the city of Kiel, the port city on the Baltic Sea near Preetz, and Germany's most important naval base, between the Berlin and Hannover designations, and decided to travel there first.

From the *Schlesische Bahnhof* most of us had to get to other stations to catch trains going west. Due to air raid damage, the Berlin subway between these stations did not operate on that day. It had still been daylight when we reached the *Schlesische Bahnhof* (the Silesian Railroad Station), and I was shocked to see the tremendous destruction in the German capital caused by the Allied air raids.

Thankfully, the weather was miserable, with an overcast of low rain clouds, and this probably meant that the American "B-17s" and "B-24s" and the British "Lancaster" bombers also took a rest. Although I had never been in Berlin before, some of the other guys congregated around me, as though I was supposed to know what to do next.

On the platform of the railroad station nearly every person one could see wore one uniform or another: Army, Navy, Air Force, Waffen-SS, Labor Service, Volkssturm, Organisation Todt, Hitler Jugend and what not, were intermingling with Red Cross and NSV-personnel helping the wounded, serving some artificial tea or beef broth, and assisting those that were lost. There were also many foreign workers (the so-called slave laborers of today) traveling from here to there without escorts: Frenchmen, Poles, Italians, Spaniards and others. Nobody minded them, nobody bothered them. At the time there were about 7 million foreigners working in the Reich: POWs, volunteers, concentration camp inmates, forced laborers, and so on.

Although they wore exactly the same kind of uniforms as all other Army personnel, it was easy to spot the typical infantry soldiers of the Eastern front. The special kind of medals they wore, decorations like the *Ostmedaille*, the abundance of close combat clasps, special shields like that denoting fighting on the Crimea and at Demjansk, and the frequent *Panzervernichtungsabzeichen*. Also, the clean but much-used uniforms, and the soldiers' haggard, tired appearance was a give-away. Because it was customary in the German armed forces that all lower ranks had to salute the higher ones, for instance, all privates had to salute all sergeants, one could see a constant saluting with the right arm extended.[15] Except for the *Ostfrontkämpfer*. They obviously "had had it," and dared even nattily dressed, obvious non-combat officers, by walking past them as if they did not see them. But nobody missed saluting a young major, a *"Ritterkreuzträger"* (recipient of the Knight's Cross) dressed in a well-worn camouflage outfit, who was trying to catch his train. Soldiers develop a good eye for those deserving of respect, and for those who, by the look of things, were seemingly not doing their best.

Ironically, there were instances when some of our group were saluted by soldicrs of the other services because they mistook our officers' candidates silver braids as signs of rank. In a way I liked it, but then again I did not feel right about it. It looked unduly pretentious. Alas, there was nothing to do but to salute back.

It was already dark when most of us hiked in the cold winter night to another railroad station from where we were to catch our train to the west. I believe that it was the *Lehrter Bahnhof* (soon to be largely destroyed). All I remember is that we walked mile after mile, often in a circuitous route due to the destroyed streets, through the immense fields of ruins that had once been the population center of the German capital. It was a gruesome sight.

---

15 Up to the middle of 1944 the German military (Army. Navy and Air Force) used a salute not unlike that of the American armed forces. But after the failed July 20, 1944 plot against Hitler it was ordered that henceforth all officers and soldiers of the *Wehrmacht* had to give the Roman, or if you wish, "Nazi" (outstretched right arm) salute. We from the Waffen-SS who had never used the military-style salute in the first place had much fun when we saw the exertions of some of the older *Wehrmacht* officers when they had to return our salute in a way that was obviously to their dislike.

I had no idea where exactly Lübbecke in Westphalia, our destination, was located, so we went to the *Wehrmacht-auskunftstelle* (Armed Forces Information Center) at the station and asked how to get there. At the time all maps of Germany had been removed from trains and railroad stations. A soldier at the information booth pointed out that Lübbecke was not far from Osnabrück, but in order to get there, we had to travel first to Hannover, something I knew. "But there will be no train using this line for about 24 hours," added the soldier. "You can sleep over in the nearby *Luftschutzbunker*." (One of the extra-sturdy concrete air raid shelters constructed in large cities during the war.) I assumed that Hannover had experienced a heavy bombing attack. Hearing this, my guilty conscience about falsifying the marching orders was eased. I now *really* had an excuse to add at least Hamburg to my itinerary, and Kiel is not very far from Hamburg.

I found Kiel in total shambles. All the wonderful places where I had spent one of the happiest years of my youth had been bombed into heaps of rubble, or were burned-out shells.

In that part of the Kiel harbor right next to the railroad station where in 1940 the heavy cruiser *Prinz Eugen,* the warship accompanying the battleship *Bismarck* on her last cruise, was being outfitted, one could notice the heavy damage to the slips of the *GERMANIA Shipyards*, but U-Boats were still being built there, for everyone using the trains to see. Incidentally, this was also the spot where in May of 1940 I had watched the captured British submarine *Seal* being towed into a dry dock. This sub had been heavily damaged by a mine, and the captain of the *Seal* had no choice but to surrender to the German Navy.

To my dismay I found out that my family had not yet arrived in Preetz, but I assumed that, knowing our mother, she would be getting there soon. The Schmidts do not like being pushed around by bureaucrats and administrators, or being told that they have to remain in government-instituted evacuation centers. It was always better to get away from the crowds. My aunt knew only that our hometown had again been evacuated. There was nothing else to do but to tell my aunt that I had to report in Westphalia, and that I had no idea where we would be engaged in battle.

Leaving Kiel, I had an hour or so to visit the parents of one of my Breslau comrades who had been ordered to a division on the

Eastern front. There I was served what was, for me at least, a heavenly meal during these hard times: Freshly baked buns with butter and honey, and real, rich milk to drink.

Tragically, this comrade, Günter Bäringhausen, did not survive the war.

Continuing on my way to Lübbecke, I had to stop in Hamburg-Altona because an air raid had interrupted all rail traffic. I remember spending the time in a badly damaged movie house, watching my favorite film, *Der weisse Traum,* a Vienna-made musical about a beautiful ice skater, for the fifth time. (At the time, the German movie industry had three major production centers: Berlin, Munich and Vienna.)

Train travel in Germany in December of 1944 had become incredibly difficult and nerve-wracking. All trains were overfilled, and in the narrow hallways of the express trains it was almost impossible to move once the train had left a station. The simple task of going to the toilet at the end of the wagon meant stepping over sleeping service personnel or their luggage. Many of the trains had their glass windows shattered during air raids, and the haphazardly performed repairs were rarely sufficient to keep out the cold winter air streaming into the compartments. Add to this the soot from the overworked coal-fired engines that managed to cover everything.

Arriving at the *Meldekopf* of the *Leibstandarte* in Westphalia, I met two others from our Breslau group who had made it there, and together we were ordered to a reporting station in Siegburg, not far from Cologne, a couple of hundred kilometers to the south. For a trip that in normal times would take less than half a day on a main line, this time we needed about a day and a half, using tracks of secondary lines. However, this extra time on dirty, crowded trains turned into truly fateful extra hours, as far as my person was concerned. It was the reason for me missing the start of the Battle of the Bulge by perhaps 24 hours.

Anytime I had the opportunity to purchase or get some food, *"somewhere",* I made use of it. But that also took time. For older people traveling in these rickety, sometimes too cold, sometimes too hot trains was pure torture. I for one was okay when I could find a place to sit somewhere, or lie down and sleep.

In Cologne, we had just entered the main railroad station when the sirens sounded, and I remember taking shelter in an ancient cellar directly underneath the famous cathedral. Cologne was also full of ruins, yet people kept on working and - somehow - living.

At the time, some of the trains had cars for military personnel only. After the all-clear had sounded, and just after we had boarded a train that would stop at our destination of Siegburg, I looked out the window of our compartment when I noticed that far more civilians wanted to board the civilian-use passenger cars than there was room for them. And amidst the teeming masses stood an absolutely beautiful girl, not much younger than myself, trying her best to wiggle through the crowd and perhaps get aboard. Realizing that she would never make it, I motioned her to come to the platform just beneath our window, and by all of us (my comrades helping along) stretching our arms as far as we could, we got hold of her and lifted her through the window into our compartment.

The girl's name was Elisabeth, she was 16 years of age and she was returning to Siegburg, where she worked in the administration, after visiting her grandmother in Cologne. She was what I would call my ideal type: blond, blue-eyed, not too tall, with a fine face and a beautiful figure. It was heaven for me to sit, for an hour or so, very, very close to her (luckily, because the compartment was overfilled, this did not seem inappropriate) and listen to her golden voice. She also did not mind me holding her hand - - only to keep it warm, of course. For the rest of the war I dreamed of her. Alas, I lost her address, along with my peaked cap, about a month later during our last action in the Battle of the Bulge. When the war was over, there was no way to travel to Siegburg and look for her. Siegburg became part of the British zone, and we were under French occupation. Travel between the zones was severely restricted, unless one was an Allied soldier, or a Jewish black market dealer. At any rate, that was the end of a love story that never really got off the ground.

The interesting aspect of this part of my story is the fact that no matter how hard I tried years later, I was unable to establish *exact* dates for most of these experiences and those that followed. Winter days slipped into nights; gray, cold mornings with their semi-darkness could not be distinguished from gray, cold evenings equally opaque.

Chapter 11

After we had reported at the *Meldekopf* in Siegburg, the three of us, and a bunch of other Waffen-SS soldiers, were almost immediately put aboard a tarpaulin-covered Ford truck and driven across the Rhine river past Bonn, and the small cities Euskirchen and Münstereifel, into the direction of the Eifel mountains, a cold, snowy, Tennessee-like mountain range but 40 miles away to the west. Today I believe that this might have been either on the day when the *Ardennenoffensive*, the Battle of the Bulge, began, or more likely a day later. I do seem to recall that we knew something big was happening on the Western front, and we were going to be part of it.

Unfortunately the truck driver who had been compelled to take us along was seemingly in a hurry to get back to his own unit, by now engaged in battle, and at the important road intersection of Blankenheim he took off in a hurry while the rest of us were being checked rather thoroughly by the German *Feldpolizei,* the MPs.

One must wonder whether the German MPs were mindful of the havoc being created at this very time behind American lines by German infiltrators in U.S. uniforms? SS-*Obersturmbannführer* Otto Skorzeny, the officer who in September 1943 had been responsible for freeing Benito Mussolini from his high-altitude prison in the Abruzzi Mountains after Italy switched to the Allied side, had organized a unit of English-speaking German soldiers, *Operation Greif,* whose task it was to create havoc behind American lines in conjunction with the German *Ardennes offensive.*

Skorzeny's men had been outfitted with American uniforms and vehicles or, in some instances, German tanks made to look like U.S.

tanks, and they were successful in infiltrating American lines along with the U.S. troops then in retreat. They dismantled explosive charges underneath bridges; cut telephones wires; gave wrong orders to U.S. units; exchanged street signs, and did everything else possible to create confusion among the enemy. Although the direct success of Skorzeny's task force was less than expected, it had ramifications as far as General Eisenhower's command post near Paris, when the Supreme Commander of Allied forces was prevented from leaving his headquarters for a day.

Even though throughout the war the Allies had made extensive use of commando operations utilizing German uniforms, vehicles and insignia, they were seemingly shocked when the Germans did the same with *Operation Greif.* Suddenly, some American commanders remembered the laws of war that prohibited such actions, and a number of the German soldiers of Skorzeny's outfit who were captured by the Allies in U.S. uniforms were summarily executed.

Unfortunately, the Americans mistook some regular German soldiers who, like myself a few days after our stop at Blankenheim, had equipped themselves with pieces of American clothing in order to keep away the cold, as illicit infiltrators. In at least one instance an 18-year-old German Army soldier who was not a member of *Operation Greif* but wearing an American jacket underneath his German uniform was actually hauled before an American military court, found guilty and "properly" executed, with a priest standing by.

On the day of my trip into the combat zone, I did not give it much thought that because of my illegal trip to Kiel I had missed the opening stage of the now famous "Battle of the Bulge", a battle where the United States Army lost more soldiers as prisoners of war than in any other war or engagement in the history of the USA.

As for myself, I did not join the regiment I had been assigned to for almost two weeks. Instead, I was "captured" by various higher headquarters, and this resulted in my seeing the entire northern combat zone of the "Bulge" from a vantage point not normally accessible to a common soldier.

While the Allied invaders of the European continent, most of them Britons and Americans, had made surprisingly fast advances immediately after D-Day on June 6, 1944,[16] they soon got bogged down due to the tenacious German resistance. To reconquer the same area of France and Belgium which the numerically inferior German forces had captured in a little over a month in 1940, the Allies needed more than 3 months four years later, in spite of their overwhelming air superiority, and even though by 1944 the *Wehrmacht* had been bled white on the Eastern front.

By October 1944, the great Allied offensive actions had stopped short of the *Westwall,* the line of German fortifications that stretched from the Dutch border to Switzerland, just inside the Reich borders. The seemingly most quiet area along this 1,000 km front was the 120 km stretch that reached south from the small city of Monschau almost to the city of Echternach, part of the Duchy of Luxembourg but not far from Trier, Germany. And it was precisely there, in this heavily forested area, where the Germans attacked with powerful forces on December 16, 1944.

In retrospect, it seems awfully foolish for the German High Command (Hitler) to have embarked on the *Ardennenoffensive* (as we called the Battle of the Bulge). Germany had neither the essential air superiority nor enough fuel and other supplies needed to reach the harbor of Antwerp, the objective of the attack. Furthermore, in expending such elite divisions as those of the Waffen-SS for this questionable endeavor, the fragile Eastern front was left almost helpless, and at the mercy of the Bolshevist hordes.

"Why did Hitler spend his last reserves for this offensive?" is a valid question that ought to be answered.

In explanation I must backtrack to a lecture I had attended in connection with our officers' candidates training in the summer of 1944 in Breslau-Lissa, and the result of which was my alluding to *"neue Kampfmittel"* - new means to fight a war with - in the August 19, 1944 letter to my mother. By now I would have forgotten this lecture if somehow this letter I had written home immediately after the lecture had not survived, and remained in my possession.

---

[16] This was partially due to treason by high German officers who hated Hitler with a passion. Most of them must have been incredibly gullible politically, and obviously they were endeared by the charade of Western *"democracy"*.

What we had been told in the lecture was that, among other things, next spring Germany would have such a fearsome weapon wherewith one bomb could destroy a city of the size of London. The scientist lecturing us was obviously talking about an atomic bomb, although this word was never used.

How close was Germany to developing an atomic bomb? I personally believe that one of the two bombs dropped on Japan had been manufactured in Germany. The fact that the (mostly) Jewish scientists of the Manhattan Project had to wait for Germany's defeat to even test their own devil's weapon more than 2 months later, on July 17, proves to me that they needed German know-how (the trigger or fuse?) to complete their task. There is no question that the Manhatten Project, ie. the development of an Amerian atom bomb, was mainly undertaken with the aim to have such bombs ready for use against Germany. It must have galled the 'American' scientists in Los Alamos, New Mexico, and elsewhere, immeasurably that they couldn't complete their task without German input.

It is possible that Germany had at least one A-bomb ready by December of 1944, but that the delivery system was not. Remember, we did not have a fleet of B-29s that could carry heavy loads over long distances. The sole reason for the "Battle of the Bulge" may have been to gain time against the Western Allies in order to complete the delivery system, whatever that might have been, for the new German *"Kampfmittel"*. In light of this, the "Battle of the Bulge" makes sense. Would England have stayed in the war if London had been destroyed by a German nuclear bomb? And what would the effect have been of a nuclear attack on New York?

Supporting evidence for my thesis that the Germans might have been close to dropping nuclear bombs on New York and London came to light decades after the war when in an obscure book about the *Luftwaffe* I found references to a German long-range plane, the JU-390-V2. According to this report, these specially constructed planes were able to carry a four-ton-load from Europe to the East Coast of the United States, and still return to base in *Festung Europa.* As a matter of fact, in March of 1944, three months before the invasion, a proto-type of the JU-390 flew from an air base in

Southern France to within 12 miles of New York City and back. Was this a test run for a planned nuclear attack? I believe it was.

An added indication that one of the two atom bombs dropped on Japan might have been of German origin is the fact that the Hiroshima and Nagasaki bombs were so completely different in appearance and inner structure. Producing such totally different *Kampfmittel* required, in my opinion, two different teams of American scientists working toward the same goal. But that does not seem to have been the case. At any rate, so far I have not been able to discover proof of two different teams of "American" physicists creating the Hiroshima and Nagasaki 'nukes'.

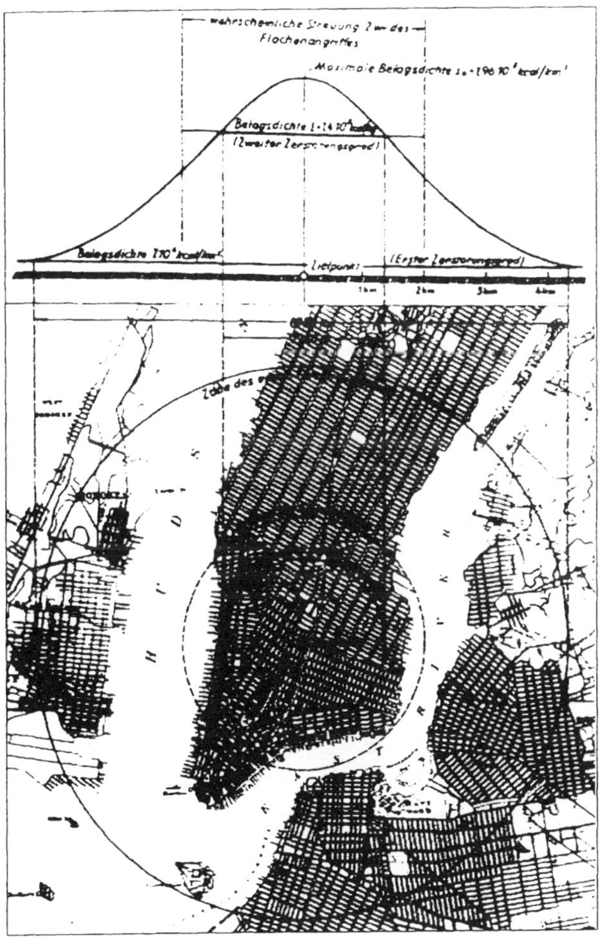

A wartime German blueprint showing projected damage to New York City. There is no question that the map was made in anticipation of the German use of an Atom bomb.

Chapter 12

Coming from Breslau-Lissa, and being assigned to the 13th Company, 2nd Panzergrenadier Regiment of the 1st SS Division *"Leibstandarte SS Adolf Hitler"*, I had entered the combat zone a day or two after the German armies had begun their move against the Western Allies. Having been held up at a German Military Police check point at Blankenheim in the Eifel mountains for more than an hour, a few of us soon found ourselves at a road fork outside of the city with two roads going west, and both of which had the "pass key"[17] tactical sign of the *Leibstandarte* pointing in that direction. I do not remember why most of my comrades decided to take the well-traveled south-westerly route; it could have been because this road seemed more heavily traveled than the other. But I had noticed that one of the tactical signs was of a better quality, and I therefore surmised that this would lead us, myself and a couple of comrades who went along with me, to the headquarters of the division, where they certainly would know where we could find our assigned units.

I must not forget to mention that on this particularly day (and a few that followed) the weather was miserable, and this prevented the Allied air forces from attacking the German columns with their fighter bombers. Just west of Blankenheim, however, the enemy artillery fired sporadically at pre-set targets, and I had no choice but to get used to incoming rounds. The soldiers of the U.S. artillery

---

[17] The German name for a pass key is "Dietrich". Sepp Dietrich was the creator of Hitler's SS *Leibstandarte* (body guard elite unit).

did not seem to know that they belonged to an army in retreat, for in some places salvo followed after salvo, forcing us often to take cover. In the following weeks I was going to learn to respect their pin-point accuracy, and eventually also the devastating proximity fuses of some their deadly shells.

My comrades and I moved toward the front by any means possible: sometimes aboard a truck, at other times as passengers on newly captured American Jeeps or other vehicles, and most of the time just by trudging through the deep, wet snow, always being on the lookout for enemy stragglers, and never forgetting to dive into the snow when incoming American shells sounded too close.

All headquarters of armies on the move are perennially short of soldiers to be used as runners, guards, observers and for other services. Thus it happened that my comrades and I were "captured" by the first major *Leibstandarte* headquarters we encountered, I believe it was at Ferme de Flamand, and from there on we were sent on errands of one kind or another, and no attempt was made to direct us to the assigned units. I do remember that one of the higher officers remarked, upon seeing my assignment to a 13th Infantry howitzer company, that the heavy "I.G.s," as we called them, were out of ammunition already, and because of that they didn't need me anymore. No new ammo for these artillery pieces could be expected soon. (Conversely, the American artillery *never* seemed to lack shells to fire at us.)

Being mindful that some American veterans of the Battle of the Bulge will be reading these lines, men who may also also want to refresh their memories, I shall now mention all the towns and villages that I "visited" in these first two weeks of the battle, and which I still remember. Later I will explain what I recall from each one. As mentioned before, these "visits" were constantly accompanied by exploding enemy shells, and once the clouds were gone just before Christmas, we were constantly harrassed during daylight by the forever dangerous and low-flying *"P-47s"*, *"P-51s"* and *"P-38s"*. At times, but not every day, I was close enough to the first line of the front where I had to take shelter from rifle and machine gun fire.

Meyerode, St. Vith, Recht, Born, Hünningen, Ferme de Flamande, Schöneseiffen, Vielsalm, Münstereifel, Sistig, Schleiden, Oudler, Ulflingen, Losheimergraben, Schmidtheim, Stadtkyll, Amel and Manderfeld, Kronenburg were the towns I remember best from the Northern tier of the combat zone.

Try as I may, I was unable to assign specific dates to my "visits" to most these places. Truly certain I am of only one, namely Sistig on the German side of the border, where I spent Christmas Eve sleeping underneath a heavy oak table in what must have been a country inn, and all I was able to scrounge from an army unit was a canteen half-full of noodle soup. A few hours before I had to take orders to a unit of heavy tanks - - not LAH but definitely Waffen-SS - - that had been held in reserve in the woods just east of the village. During the entire night American artillery shells were exploding in the area, although I do not recall whether the inn was hit: most houses in that area are built like fortresses, with thick walls of field stone and heavy timber used for the roofs.

Possibly on the very day when I entered the Battle of the Bulge combat zone, an incident occurred that would become known as the "Malmedy Massacre", where soldiers of the *Leibstandarte* had allegedly killed, in cold blood, upwards of 80 American POWs.

Meyerode, the headquarters village of the 6th Panzer Army, was, as the crow flies, less than 15 kilometers (about ten miles) from the crossroads where an incident, but not a "massacre", had occurred.

It is interesting to note that the high commanders of the SS 6th Panzer Armee heard of the American "Malmedy Massacre" allegations by radio while the area of the Baugnez crossroads was fast in German hands, and was being held for another month. In spite of this no attempt was made to obliterate the later-shown alleged proof of the massacre, namely the bodies of the American soldiers who had died on that spot. Furthermore, it was later proven that the personal effects of the dead GIs had not been removed or stolen.

Unfortunately, nothing exemplifies the false reporting, and the continuing propaganda against the Waffen-SS, better than the never-ending recitation of the alleged "facts" surrounding this so-called "massacre".

Many Americans may remember the scene in the 1960s movie "Battleground" (about the Battle of the Bulge) where a bunch of GIs are deliberately mowed down by a (World War I-type!) machine gun that had been hidden in a tarpaulin-covered German truck. Suddenly the ramp of the truck was opened and the SS-soldiers began shooting at the helpless captives. This movie was made forty or fifty years ago and yet the dastardly scene still has today the same anti-German effect on young, innocent Americans as it had then.

On or about 17 December of every year, so many years after "something" really did occur at the crossroads near Baugnez, Belgium, someone of the American news media always digs out the "facts" as depicted already during the war, and reports them as if it was God's honest truth, - - - as if no German side of the story exists.

The 2001 hullabaloo about D-Day ought to give us food for thought. Then, nobody had mentioned that Utah beach, for instance, had been defended by only a few hundred very young and some old German conscripts, with the younger ones mostly in the 18 to 19-year range, and that these boys had suffered through tremendous fire by some of the heaviest ships' artillery imaginable, before engaging the American elite forces (rangers) coming ashore.

In order to understand the "Malmedy Massacre" story, one must realize that the entire *Ardennen Offensive* was fought in extremely difficult to traverse, mountainous terrain, and in the worst imaginable winter weather. I remember vividly that even a couple of weeks after the German attack began on 16 December 1944, snow drifts permitted only one-way traffic on most roads, and often one could not see further than a few hundred feet. There were no such things as snow plows then, and certainly none with combat troops. In addition, it must be remembered that only few of the bridges in the Ardennes area were sturdy enough to accommodate heavy truck traffic, much less the 70-ton German "Tiger II" (*Königstiger)* tanks. Thus everybody was very restricted in their movements.

A day into the German attack, after the spearhead of the First SS Panzer Division under the command of Colonel Jochen Peiper overcame the initial American defenses near the Belgian-German border, the German forces ran into a column of nearly 200 American soldiers belonging to Battery B, 285th Field Observation Battalion that had been ordered to join other U.S. forces in the vicinity. This unfortunate American unit was traveling in their (no doubt well-closed - to ward off the cold) vehicles, seemingly unaware of the Germans nearby. Actually, both the German and American units ran into each other, with the Germans being the more alert since they were the very head of an entire Panzer army.

As can be expected, the German force (consisting mainly of five tanks and a few accompanying vehicles) opened fire when they came upon the enemy, immediately aiming at the very first and the very last of the American vehicles, as was a battle custom, and then raked the entire column with their machine guns and a number of shells from tank cannon, creating an inferno of burning and exploding American trucks and Jeeps. The GIs were totally surprised, and offered little resistance. According to everybody involved, the entire action lasted about ten minutes, after which most of the GIs surrendered.

Since the German commander, Colonel Peiper, had the order to reach a certain target at a given time, he did what can be seen in numerous WW2 newsreels of Third Reich war footage when rapidly advancing German tank units took enemy prisoners: the Americans were disarmed (but seemingly not body searched), and merely told to assemble in a clearing beside the road, lightly guarded by a few Germans in two vehicles, a half-track and probably a VW *Schwimmwagen.* The bulk of the German force continued, almost without interruption, on its way.

Once the tanks and other vehicles of Peiper's spearhead were out of sight, some of the Americans realized that they far outnumbered the handful of Germans guarding them. Knowing that American-occupied Malmedy was but a few thousand yards away, they saw an opportunity to escape into the nearby forest. The watchful Germans obviously saw this and fired at the escapees.

As a result, all hell broke loose. Many of the GIs had heard U.S. propaganda stories of the SS massacring their prisoners, and they believed that their end was near. They also tried to flee. Others remained on the spot where the had stood in the snow, and merely did what soldiers do when firing begins: They hugged the ground, and looked for cover. Still other GIs (actually only very few) pulled the handguns they had hidden, or grabbed rifles that were still lying around, and fired back at the Germans guards.

A few minutes later, after some of the Americans had made their escape, the German main force entered the area, traveling the same road as Peiper's group. Hearing the small arms fire, the

German soldiers on the first vehicles of the main battle group undoubtedly were ready for action when they came upon the scene of the skirmish, and they also fired at the Americans.

Several minutes more, and this shooting also ended again with the Americans surrendering. This time the captured remainder of the Americans were more heavily guarded until the German main force had passed, and then they were marched back toward the east, into captivity. According to one source I spoke to, about 120 GIs counted as survivors of the "massacre" but I was never able to get a confirmation of this number. I maintain that had it been the German aim to really 'massacre' the Americans at the Baugnez crossroads, they would have killed them all.

On December 17th, there was low visibility due to weather and terrain conditions in the Ardennes mountain region. And anybody who has seen the result of the rapid fire of a MG-42 on a column of soldiers can imagine the carnage that had occurred after the first GIs began to flee. This fastest machine gun of World War II could theoretically be fired at a rate of 1,550 rounds per minute, three times as fast as the 50-caliber American BAR (Browning Automatic Rifle).

Only few Americans had a chance to make it to their own forces stationed at Malmedy, and *some* of these honestly believed to have been the survivors of a premeditated massacre. About two decades ago I attended a meeting of American ex-POWs in Washington, DC. Many of these former GIs had been captured in the Battle of the Bulge. Fortunately, I was able to talk to one of the fellows who had managed to escape during the shooting at the Baugnez crossing and make his way back to the American lines. He was one of those men who testified after the war against the Waffen-SS soldiers at the infamous "Malmedy Massacre Trial". In essence he confirmed the story of the incident as I have explained it above. After all these years he still thought it wrong for the Germans to have shot at a couple of escapees since this action resulted in the pandemonium that caused additional American deaths. When I asked him what he would have done, had he been ordered to guard German captives and one or more had tried to escape, he answered that he would have shot them. I was unable to convince this ex-GI that this was all the Waffen-SS guards did in this case.

This type of thinking was and is not uncommon among American soldiers. Reading American military literature, one frequently can read of situations where the GIs got really mad at the enemy because 'their best buddies' had been killed in battle. As a result they let their anger out on captives. Compare this to the chivalrous attitude British and German fighter pilot aces displayed when during and after the war they were able to talk respectfully and without rancor to each other even though their "kill" numbers of enemy planes indicated that they might have been responsible for shooting-down and the resulting death of each other's most beloved comrades.

Sometimes it seems to me that the unchivalrous attitude of many American military men stems from the still unresolved experience of the War between the States (Civil War) that was fought so viciously, especially by the Northern victors, between 1861 and 1865.

Only recently I discovered another proof for my contention in this regard in a Honolulu newspaper: The family of a 19-year-old Japanese Kamikaze pilot who died in April 1945 while attacking the battleship *Missouri* wanted to honor the late Captain Callaghan who had given their son and brother a decent military burial at sea *against the wishes of many of the crew of the battleship.* At the time Captain Callaghan had even found it difficult to assemble an honor guard from the Marines aboard the vessel. Now, 56 years later, some former crewmen of the *Missouri* were protesting against the Japanese honoring Captain Callaghan aboard their ship that is now permanently berthed at Pearl Harbor. One of the ex-servicemen was asked about the reason for his protest and all he could answer was that, after all, didn't the Kamikaze pilots tried to kill the American sailors? How shameful.

I see from this that many Americans do not really know what it means to be a soldier. They suffer from the illusion that in a war only one side is right, namely the United States. It never enters their mind that war itself is insane, but that it also means killing *and being killed.* Hate should not come into play.

Recently, after a Palestinian suicide bomber had killed himself and more than a dozen innocents in a Jerusalem restaurant, the American President condemned the attack, calling it a "cowardly" act. Personally, I have serious reservations about this description. It takes a brave man to voluntarily blow himself up for what he considers a greater cause. How many sane young Americans would, at this time in history, be willing to sacrifice their life in this way for either the President, or even for their country and 'democracy'? I know of not one.

Today we know that in the three fire fights at that time and in the vicinity of the Baugnez crossroads, fewer than 70 American soldiers lost their lives. The number of fallen GIs shown on the monument that has been erected at the crossroads, close to where the incidents took place, is false.

About three days later, a German intelligence officer listening to American broadcasts heard for the first time of the alleged massacre at Malmedy. A questioning of the German troops in the area brought no results, they knew of skirmishes (some of many in these days) near the Baugnez crossing but could give no further information. While the territory was in German hands, and in spite of the fact that the German commanders knew of the propaganda campaign surrounding this alleged massacre, no attempt was made to remove the dead GIs. After the area was again in American hands, the bodies of the Baugnez crossing dead were found exactly where they had fallen, and their personal belongings had been left undisturbed.

In 1946 an "American" military court composed almost entirely of Jewish officers and interrogators (Rosenfeld, Perl and Thon - - the latter two both Viennese "refugees"- -, Kirschbaum, Ellowitz and others) found 70 Waffen-SS soldiers guilty. Their sentences were:

43 received the death sentence
22 were sentenced to life imprisonment
2 were sentenced to 20 years in prison
1 was sentenced to 15 years in prison
2 were sentenced to 10 years in prison.

The Jewish interrogation methods resulted in the death of some of the young German soldiers by suicide and permanent health problems for many others, and they were eventually the cause for Congressional hearings in the United States. But since a crime committed in the name of "democracy" is no crime, the Jewish war criminals got away with a slap on the wrist. At the Congressional hearings it came out that, *"All but two of the Germans in 139 cases that were investigated, had been kicked in the testicles beyond repair. This was standard operating procedure with the interrogators."*

And,

"The interrogators would put a black hood over the accused's head and then punch him in the face with brass knuckles, kick him, beat him with rubber hose. Many of the German POWs had teeth knocked out. Some had their jaws broken."

Furthermore,

"At least one fake Catholic priest was sent into the cells (one of those macabre Jewish jokes on people of other religions! HS) to hear confessions and give absolution, and then to advise the prisoners to sign anything the army prosecutors presented. The prisoners were told that in this way they could gain their freedom."

Why do I emphasize that most of the interrogators at Schwäbisch-Hall, where the investigation in the alleged Malmedy Massacre was held, were Jewish? Because it is the truth; because I do not see why the onus should be on Christian ex-GIs, and furthermore, because at the time of this writing (56 years after World War II) young Palestinians have to suffer the same cruelties at the hands of members of a people that likes to depict itself as the eternal victims of the meanness of others.

For years men and women both in Germany and in America fought to have the results of the Malmedy Trial travesty of justice reversed. However, General Lucius D. Clay, then the American High Commissioner in Germany, and one of those political Generals the type of which once in a while arises on the American public scene, wanted to see some of the death sentences carried out (although he personally had never taken part in any battle), and there were days when the hangman (not even a firing squad for German soldiers!) was held in readiness. Colonel Peiper himself was at least four times led in mock fashion atop the gallows, to experience that often his proverbial last minute. The cruelty of his jailers knew no bounds.

Fortunately, General Clay's orders for hanging the 43 Waffen-SS soldiers who had received the death sentences were each time reversed by higher-ups in Washington. Nobody fought more for justice in this matter than (former) U.S. Colonel W.M. Everett, a brave man who spent his health and his fortune to save America's honor.

Jochen Peiper (one of the most decorated German war heroes) was the last of the Malmedy prisoners to be released from the American military jail at Landsberg. He gained his freedom in 1956, 11 years after he went voluntarily into American captivity. Exactly 20 years later, on 14 July 1976 (note the date!), he was murdered by a communist Jewish terrorist gang in his retirement home in the Vosges mountains of Eastern France. He died, shot in his burning home, in a manner similar to what we are now accustomed to in the United States, when the "system" wants to liquidate inconvenient witnesses and anti-system dissidents (note: Kahl, Matthews, Waco, and others). They all suffered being burned in a building that had been deliberately set afire so that very few earthly remains were left of the intended victim. Ie. in a minor holocaust - a burned offering. Even at Ruby Ridge the FBI had a truck with flammable material standing by.

It bears mentioning that four of the German soldiers sentenced to death in connection with the "Malmedy Massacre" were only 18 years old when the incident at the Baugnez crossing occurred. I also would like to point to the symbolism of sentencing almost exactly the same number of Germans (70) as was the number of Americans who had allegedly lost their lives on that now famous crossing on December 17, 1944. As a result of the incredible hate propaganda directed toward U.S. troops after the first broadcast of the "massacre", untold numbers of mostly very young Waffen-SS soldiers were subsequently shot by GIs after their capture. Having interviewed many former GIs since 1950, I would put that number into the thousands.

The main reason for the entire "Malmedy Massacre" uproar was probably the fact that since the D-Day invasion too many American soldiers had expressed doubts about the "devilishness" of their German counterparts, and that especially the Waffen-SS volunteers had received high marks for their professionalism and *Ritterlichkeit* (chivalry) from Allied officers and men alike. Something had to be done to besmirch the honor of the Waffen-SS, and when some of the escaped GIs of the Baugnez crossing incident reached American lines and told of what some of them honestly believed was a premeditated massacre (after all, they had been propagandized to expect such things), it was precisely what the Allied brainwashers needed. This especially because it concerned the *Leibstandarte SS Adolf Hitler*, the *Führer's* personal and favorite division, an unit against which the Allied war crimes investigators so far had nothing or precious little to report. That my assumptions in this matter seem correct can be gleaned from the fact that even as late as 1951 the press officer of the American military government in Germany spoke of 142 "murdered" GIs at Malmedy, and some U.S. newspapers multiplied this figure to 400.

At the *very time* when the criminals of the American War Crimes Commission were combing the POW camps all over Europe for members of the *Leibstandarte*, and especially of *Kampfgruppe Peiper* (Task Force Peiper), declaring 18-year old recruits who had been without any authority at all murderers, millions of Germans and other Europeans were *really* being murdered in cold blood by the victorious allies. And nobody knew or cared about it.

A last thought about the Malmedy case: Obviously three fire fights occurred in short succession at the Baugnez crossing. The first happened when the German spearhead surprised the Americans in their well-enclosed vehicles; the second when some of the American POWs escaped, causing a pandemonium among the rest, and the third when the German main force appeared on the scene and began shooting at some of the Americans who had taken up arms again. According to the monument erected near the spot where the shootings occurred, "84 GIs lost their lives to indiscriminate German killings". No mention is made how the battlefield situation had really developed.

For someone like myself, for whom World War II is not just a historical event but even now still a real and unfinished part of life, current happenings with similar outcome have a particularly strong meaning. Concerning the "Malmedy Massacre" this came to the fore in late November 2001:

After the defeat of the Taliban forces in Afghanistan, thousands of their fighters capitulated to the rag-tag soldiers of the so-called Northern Alliance. At the time there was no question that the United States Government, as the major power which decided the outcome of the conflict, would also bear the greatest responsibility for what was going to happen in that unfortunate country after the "victory".

Just as the Taliban fighters were laying down their arms, I read ominous articles in major American newspapers concerning the anticipated fate of these men: In some of these essays there was a clear call for executing (murdering) them since "one will never be able to set them free, nor is it possible to keep them as prisoners for the rest of their lives."

Then, on November 23, the expected happened: Several hundred of the Taliban POW's who had been held at an ancient mountain top fortress near Mazar-i-Sharif *allegedly* mutinied, using weapons "including machine guns (!?!) they had brought into the fort", killing a number of the guards and, among others, an American CIA officer. A firefight that included attacks by American jets, and lasting several days, was the result. According to the reports, there were few Taliban survivors. One of them was an American boy, John Walker, age 20, caught in the turmoil. In a newsreel he is shown being interrogated by American CIA officers. Viewing this revolting scene I was wondering how I would have reacted in early June 1945 if I had being interrogated *in the manner employed in 2001* by such employees of an American secret service, instead of by the fair-minded and soldierly Captain Frye. (See page 349).

Red Cross offcials who visited the scene of the carnage a few days later reported seeing a number of dead Taliban prisoners with their hands or arms still tied behind their backs.

After being questioned about the obvious massacre, the Islamabad-based spokesman for the American forces engaged in the Afghanistan conflict issued a statement denying that the Taliban soldiers had been massacred. He said the fighting broke out only after prisoners overwhelmed their guards and grabbed their weapons. <u>"When that happened they became combatants and their status changed from prisoners to something else,</u>" he said. It seems that since 1946, since the "Malmedy Massacre Trial", the U.S. Army has altered its stance in this regard. Or is the entire happening proof of the hypocrisy that seems now to be so all-pervasive in western society?

Only a few hours after the Mazar-i-Sharif Massacre I received a call from Germany where both the tying of the hands on the backs of P.O.W's, as well as the presence of CIA officers instead of regular American soldiers was severely criticized. I was asked, but could give no answer, whether it wasn't likely that the CIA arranged for the subterfuge of an uprising (by smuggling arms into the compound?) so that the Northern Alliance thugs could murder the captured Taliban with impunity? The earlier mentioned newsreel filmed by the cameraman of a European station seems to confirm that.

On November 30, 2001 the *New York Times* topped the sanctimony of the current democratic rulers of the West with an article titled, "Unsure ground for a stand against killing of prisoners." According to this article, *"The responsibility for an inquiry (into the massacre, HS) fell to those who had custody of the prisoners - the United States, Britain and the Northern Alliance"*, and *"any summary execution of prisoners is a clear violation of the Geneva Conventions, but "there are a lot of gray areas,"* said Sidney Jones for Human Rights Watch. *"It was not even clear whether the Geneva Conventions applied,"* S. Jones added, *"although it is a basic principle in any law governing conflict that those who lay down their weapons must be treated humanely, the rules are different for internal conflicts and international conflicts - for which the Geneva Conventions were written and under which the United States would be directly responsible for the treatment of P.O.W's."* In other words, the U.S. attacks against the Taliban may only have been an American interference in an internal, ongoing Afghanistan war, and this means the Geneva Conventions did not apply. General Eisenhower's DEF (disarmed enemy forces) ruling comes to mind.

I suppose we shall not see anytime soon the commanding general of the U.S. Forces in Afghanistan defending himself before a kangaroo court similarly to the one that sat in judgment over Sepp Dietrich and my other comrades at the Malmedy Massacre Trial.

Chapter 13

In the early hours of one of the Christmas days 1944 (Germans count the 26th of December as an additional day of Christmas) a clear, crisp winter day, I had to make my way back to Meyerode near St. Vith, to the headquarters of the 6th SS Panzer Army. In addition to the constant detonations of the near and distant artillery shells, the Ardennes battle field had an odd smell to it. It was a combination of the smoke from burning houses, the odor of cordite (from exploding rounds), foul-smelling German gasoline, the fumes of the better American fuel, and the pleasant scent of the fir trees that forested the hills. Inside the farm villages one could add the stink emanating from the stables and from the manure heaps in front of the farm houses to this aromatic mixture. Because it was a cold winter, we were thankfully spared the penetrating, pungent malodor of decaying bodies. Nobody who was there during that horrible winter will forget the wet, cold snow that soaked our shoes and clothes. Thankfully, because of the cold, the many bodies I saw of both German and American soldiers, and of a few civilians that had been killed, were usually frozen stiff, and I do not recall the pervasive stench of decaying human cadavers that is a hallmark of battle fields in warmer months.

The fact that I had successfully passed an officers' candidates training course and was now a *Führerbewerber* (officer's aspirant), and the ease with which I was able to read military maps, besides my (to this day still) excellent *Orientierungsvermögen* (sense of direction), contributed to my being used as a messenger. In general, I was assigned either a captured American Jeep (there were many) or one of the Volkswagens (*Kübelwagen* or *Schwimmwagen* [an amphibious VW] used for that purpose by the German armed forces) with a driver. Due to the incessant American artillery barrages the telephone lines that had been strung by German soldiers were often down, and radio-telephones were then not yet in common use, and had only a short range. I can also imagine that many staff officers hesitated to use any sort of telephone for fear of having the enemy listening in.

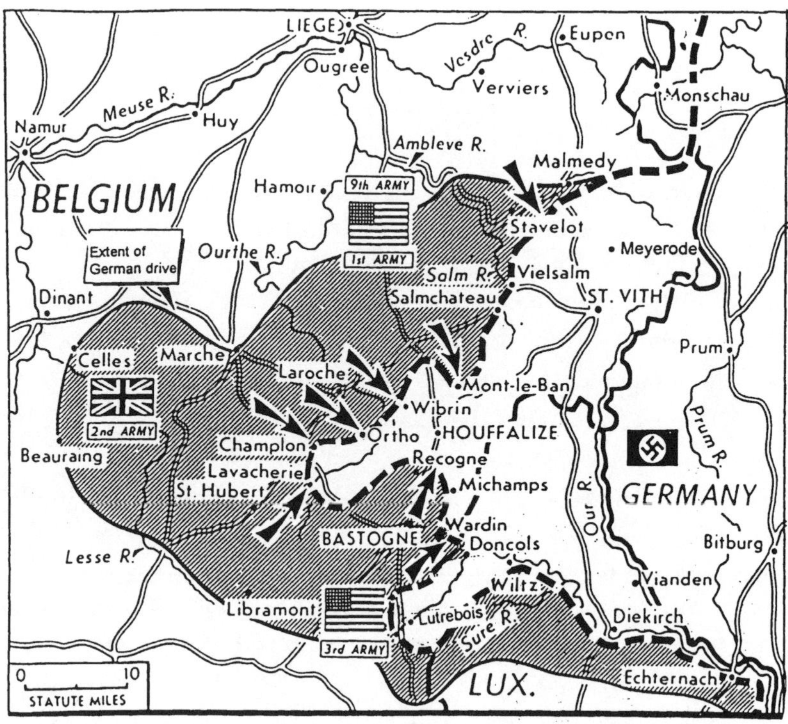

The Battle of the Bulge area shortly after Christmas 1944 when St. Vith was in German possession and Bastogne was not anymore encircled, having been relieved on Christmas Eve. This was the time when the Allied counter attacks began in earnest. Note the undecided situation around Vielsam.

Although I was with an elite unit, and even though I took part in three major campaigns in only six months, and my wounds prove that I was there, my soldierly "non-combat" reminiscences far surpass those of the days when I, or in our case "we," had been in direct and close combat. And even on such horrible days when the losses on both sides were considerable (January 4th, January 12th, and February 18th, 1945, and the street battles in Hainfeld in Austria come to mind), there was not one day when body parts were *constantly* flying around due to heavy enemy action (and direct hits), and when almost *everybody* acted with determination and like a hero, as is depicted in Spielberg's film "Private Ryan" that so impressed the world's movie audiences in 1999.

All one has to do is look at the real newsreels of D-Day, June 6, 1944, to see how it really was: Landing crafts are nearing the beach, and most, but not all, are obviously coming under German fire. Some sink, with many of the heavily laden GIs drowning as a result. Those American (and British and Canadian) soldiers finally having ground underneath their feet are, as a rule, widely dispersed, seeking cover, and are seemingly assembling at a leisurely pace before reconnoitering the cliffs above them, contemplating how to best get up there, where the German guns are located. Here and there one sees GIs fall, and then lie still, obviously they are either dead or badly wounded. But no scene justifies the *incessant* carnage Spielberg has depicted, where the viewers allegedly see "the war as it really was". To put it bluntly: I believe that few soldiers had to experience what Spielberg depicted at the landing on the D-Day beaches. If such incessant carnage had occurred, then few of the GIs would afterwards still be of sound mind, and they would therefore have been unusable for further combat. Even the best soldiers can only take so much horror before going crazy. My own guess is that the worst fighting in World War II occurred on the Eastern front, in Russia: incessant combat where row upon row of Soviet infantry and tanks attacked thin lines of German defenders hours and days on end after heavy artillery had pounded their positions to smithereens.

In his film Spielberg also did not show who was manning the German machine gun nests atop the cliffs, and the artillery batteries further to the rear: The aforementioned old men and young boys. To the best of my knowledge there was not one first-rate unit guarding the Normandy beaches. Only such strongholds as Cherbourg, Le Havre, Brest and Calais were better defended (that's why the Allies did not land there; the failed Dieppe raid was still on everybody's mind).

As mentioned before, instead of being a gunner with 150mm howitzers, I had ended up being a messenger for higher German headquarters located at the village of Meyerode near St. Vith. It deserves to be recorded that St. Vith is but a few miles from

Meyerode, and the former was taken by our troops only shortly before Christmas Eve. Once, a few days before that date, I was supposed to take orders to a unit fighting near Vielsalm, and the most direct route would have been through St. Vith. Not knowing that this small city was still in American hands, I got dangerously close to the enemy lines. From that trip I do remember inspecting an abandoned very heavy American cannon (probably of a 210mm caliber), and in the snow I found ammunition for a Colt 45, the largest pistol bullets I had ever seen. I put one of the bullets in my pocket as a sort of talisman.

Perhaps my most interesting trip occurred when I was sent to the northernmost units of the 6th SS Panzer Army to make contact with a unit of the 12th SS Panzerdivision *Hitlerjugend* (the very division that after the invasion so heroically delayed the British advance at Caen). The "HJ" division, as we called it for short, had bogged down near the *Westwall*, and did not reach its set targets at and near the famed Elsenborn Ridge. For myself and the driver assigned to me, it was impossible to take the direct route to the ridge since the main east-west road just north of Meyerode was clogged by regiments of the *Leibstandarte* and many American POWs on the march into German captivity. We had no choice but to make our way back to Blankenheim, then north to Schleiden, and from there west to the village of Schöneseiffen, from where a road lead to the famed Kaiser barracks (an old Prussian training ground) at the Elsenborn Ridge.

At and near Blankenheim the situation looked quite different from what I had seen a few days or a week earlier: The weather had cleared, and the roads leading to and from this small town were littered with the shells of burned-out or otherwise destroyed German gasoline trucks and other types of military vehicles, the result of American air superiority. And here and there in the snow-covered fields one could see the remnants of numerous V-1 flying bombs that had crashed before reaching their targets far behind the enemy lines. While my driver raced along the road, I had to be on the lookout for the low-flying *Jabos* that made life hell for everyone who had to venture away from the immediate battle zone. (In order to avoid that trigger-happy American pilots killed their own troops, there was an area, a forbidden red zone, very close to the front where German soldiers were relatively safe from air attacks.)

It may have been on this trip when the vehicle I was on had to move to the side of the road, onto a slightly higher elevation, to let a huge column of American POWs, I am guessing now between 300 and 500, walk by. They were on their way into POW camps in Germany.

While I was looking at the GIs with some curiosity, noticing again how much like us they were, the SS soldier next to me got all excited and, pointing at one of the Americans shuffling by, called out "ein Jude, ein Jude!"

I had no idea what he meant. As it turned out, he was surprised to see a Jew among the American soldiers, explaining to me that Jews as a rule allegedly cannot be found among frontline troops. That still did not make sense to me since I couldn't understand how one could discern someone's religion from his appearance, and it seemed unlikely to me that an entire group of people could manage to stay away from combat. Especially not if he wore a uniform like hundreds of his comrades. Seeing my noncomprehension of the subject matter, the non-comissioned officer, an *Unterscharführer*, gave up. I knew that in the First World War many Jews had fought for Germany, although I had also read that the alleged number of 12,000 Jewish soldiers who had given their life for the Fatherland was an inflated number used by Jewish organizations. It was way out of proportion to the number of Jews then living in Germany.

I vaguely remember that the corporal who was all excited about allegedly seeing a Jewish American soldier among the captured GIs had arrived at Meyerode a few days earlier in a crisp new Waffen-SS uniform, sporting the *Kriegsverdienstkreuz* (KVK) *Erster Klasse*, the war service medal 1st class, a decoration given to civilians who were commended for extraordinary civilian deeds toward the war effort. For years he had held an important position at a Berlin radio station. One of the first things an officer at Meyerode told him was to take off the medal since it might create difficulties for him. He was still a relatively young man (albeit not from my vantage point), and the question might arise what *fighting* he had done so far during the war. (While the railroad men who kept the trains of Germany running throughout the war, and the factory workers who continued working even after they had lost their families and homes in Allied bombing raids, certainly deserved their KVKs, there remained the skepticism among front-line troops that this medal was often given to the wrong people.)

Incidentally, the long line of American POWs walking toward POW camps in Germany all had their hands in their pockets to ward off the cold. Conversely, Allieed newsreels and photographs of the same time show German POWs being taken to the rear invariably having been forced to have their hands high up in the air, cold or no cold, or whether they wore gloves or not. (Similiarly it bears mentioning, and can be seen in ancient newsreels, that nearly naked survivors of German U-Boats that had been sunk, were often heavily guarded by gun-toting U.S. sailors immediately after their rescue by ships of the U.S. Navy. Kind of silly, it seems to me.)

Schleiden, an old medieval city with narrow streets, had recently been bombed, and it was difficult to maneuver through the ruins. While asking an MP post for the best way to get out of the town, we had to pass by a group of Russian POWs repairing some damage near the railroad station. Seeing that we were alone, one of the Russians ventured to say to me in broken German, "soon you will be either dead or prisoner, and I shall be free." What could I say or do about that? We trudged on. Neither I nor the poor fellow realized then that most Soviet soldiers who had fallen into German hands as POWs soon would end their lives in the Bolshevist GULAG.

The village of Schöneseiffen west of Schleiden was in an area under constant American artillery bombardment. We had hardly entered the village, and were near the cemetery, when a salvo of American shells began detonating about us. I took a flying leap over the low wall surrounding the cemetery, and fell atop one of the graves. A minute later, when the danger had passed, I looked up and discovered right next to me the body of an older, immaculately dressed staff sergeant of the German *Marine Infanterie*, the German Marines, who must have been killed much earlier, for his body was already frozen stiff. How someone of the German Marines, recognizable by the gold-colored braids of his uniform, got to this God-forsaken place in the Eifel mountains remained a puzzle forever. I could not help but look at this dead soldier who rested so peacefully in a cemetery, and I wondered about the family he had left behind.

Soon the driver and I were on our way through the village, traveling on a narrow road that was freshly covered by snow, leading toward the west. I remember speaking to two Army infantry soldiers in foxholes besides the road, and asking them whether they had seen either SS soldiers passing by, or had contact with the enemy. Their answer was negative.

Only a few hundred feet further down the road we suddenly came under fire from the Americans while we were looking at a large caliber self-propelled gun of the U.S. Army standing in a well-camouflaged clearing. Around the vehicle, and in my opinion much too close for the gun to act as a safe shelter from German fire, I counted the corpses of about a dozen GIs, obviously infantrymen. Their frozen young faces still were showing the emotions of their last minutes of life.

Due to the increasing American fire (both from small arms and artillery pieces like anti-tank guns) my driver and I were forced to beat a hasty retreat. Obviously, this was no way to get to the Elsenborn Ridge. Coming by the two soldiers again, I chastised them for not telling us that they were in fact the foremost German post. Their laconic answer was simple:

"You didn't ask."

Halfway back to Schöneseiffen, less than a mile away, we thought we came under attack by an American Jabo, a *P-47* "Thunderbolt". The plane came out of the sun all guns firing, and we could do nothing but lie helplessly in a ditch next to the road as bullets hit the snow quite close to us. When the plane flew past us, he was so low that we were able to see the face of the pilot. After several strafings the *P-47* made one more low pass and left westward toward his home base. We continued, unscathed, on our way to Schöneseiffen, only to discover, well camouflaged but recognizable, a battery of 20mm (four barrel) German anti-aircraft guns somewhat off the road, the real target of the American plane.

Back in the village we decided to call it a day, and join some Army soldiers for a meal of thick soup and dark bread. (I do not recall ever having been denied food in the chow line of a strange unit when on my numerous reconnaissance trips but, obviously, I would not have been allowed to push myself ahead of others.) Later, as we stood on the east side of the farm house, the side away from the danger of getting hit by an American artillery shell, we watched numerous V1 missiles flying rather low over the village, coming out of the already dark sky in the east toward targets in the west. At the time the port city of Antwerp was under heavy bombardment by these *Wunderwaffen.* They did great damage but did not really stop the supply of war materiel flowing to the Allied armies.

Suddenly, the odd-sounding lawnmower noise of the engine of one of the V1s whose flight path led directly over us stopped, and all we could hear was the swooshing sound of the wind gliding over the wings of the missile. We had no doubt that the thing was going to crash very close to where we were standing, and we knew that these new miracle weapons carried such a heavy load of explosive that it could blow all of us to bits. The five or six of us standing around jumped as fast as we could, and one on top of each other, down into the outside stairs leading to the farmhouse cellar, just making it, when we heard the V1 crash into a house less than a hundred feet away. Then - - - nothing.

What we did not know then was the fact that such a cruise missile had to arm itself while flying. Since this V1 must have been launched only a few minutes before, the fuse for the explosive had obviously not been charged. For safety's sake we waited for a couple of minutes, and then we sauntered to the wreckage. The missile had hit the side of a farm house constructed of field stone, made a large hole in the wall, but fell, shattered in many pieces, into the courtyard. The only thing seemingly undamaged was a large ball of something about 2½ feet diameter in size that was held together with very many metal straps criss-crossing each other. When I inspected this thing and gave it a kick, one of the other soldiers got all excited, telling everybody that this was the explosive charge. Well, in the darkness we never discovered the real cordite charge or whatever explosive was used, but decades after the war I found out that the apparatus I had kicked contained the missile's gyroscope.

(In the 1970s I visited Schöneseiffen again. It was then that I discovered that the people in the farm house never knew that their home had been hit by an errant V1. They had ascribed the hole in the wall to artillery damage.)

Chapter 14

We never made contact with the *Hitlerjugend* division on our mission to the Schleiden area, and could only report that, as far as I could find out, the northern approaches to the Elsenborn Ridge were still in American hands.

A few days after our return I had an interesting experience with an American prisoner of war: A *P-38* twin-rump *Lightning* fighter/bomber had been shot down by the *Leibstandarte,* and I received the order to take the pilot all the way back to the city of Münstereifel, about 25 miles behind the front, where the German Air Force had some interrogators. That was one task I really did not care for because the farther one was from the front, the more dangerous it became to travel the snow-covered roads. In some areas the American *Jabos* sounded like horse flies buzzing a cow, there were so many of them.

(Why, after so many decades, I should still remember that the pilot had flown a *P-38* Lightning remains a puzzle to me. I do not recall seeing a plane being shot down, but then again, except for the many *Jabos* behind the front, I do not remember seeing <u>any</u> planes over the the battle field during the entire Battle of the Bulge, not even the Dakotas (C47s or DC3s) dropping supplies to the defenders of Bastogne, something I must have observed from our lines.)

There was also the fact that many of the captured Jeeps had no top cover at all except for the skimpy windshield. It was like driving an open convertible during a Nebraska snowstorm. Twenty minutes of this, and I felt as if I was one of the explorers of the North Pole. I thought I could solve the problem of not traveling an hour or so to Münstereifel by having the American escape in a stretch of forest where the Jeep would have difficulty driving up a steep grade. Since I did not know the English language then, and in order to made my intentions known to the dashing young officer in his leather jacket (he had a mustache like Clark Gable) I took my place next to him on one of the back seats, making certain that he would notice how I dealt with my rifle: I pulled the leather strap of the weapon over helmet and face so that it was in front, while the rifle was on my back. It would have taken me awfully long to get the gun in firing position, and shoot at an escapee. At the time I had not yet been issued a handgun.

The American must have realized what I was up to, for all he did was grin at me and offer me some chewing gum. Then he settled leisurely in the Jeep and let us drive him to Münstereifel. I assume that he had seen enough combat, and a few months in a German POW camp seemed better than to die for FDR. As luck would have it, at the precise moment when we approached the center of this small, quaint old town (founded 830 A.D.) a flight of about a dozen B-25s or B-26s twin-engine American bombers attacked it. The three of us just had time to bail out of the Jeep and take cover inside the doorway of a solidly constructed building, when the bombs came whistling down and exploded in a crescendo of fire, smoke and debris. But it was over quickly. We remained unscathed. Even in the confusion and chaos following the attack I was able to find a post of the *Feldpolizei* who accepted the American for delivery to the nearby *Luftwaffe* base.

Driving out of Münstereifel again, I noticed that a large hospital that was clearly marked with the Red Cross had been hit by several bombs, and in spite of the cold many of the sick were congregating in their hospital gowns in front of the building, seemingly not knowing what to do next.

Another experience with the American Air Force occurred soon after St. Vith had been captured by the Germans:

For reasons that I cannot remember anymore, I was trudging through the deep snow of a forest outside of Meyerode, when I came upon a hill from which I had an unobstructed view of St. Vith about 7 kilometers (4 miles) away. It was a beautiful, sunny winter day, and apart from the never-ending barrages of American artillery fire, everything seemed peaceful and even Christmassy. Looking westward, I saw far away in the sky something that looked like a menacing swarm of locusts approaching, but due to the distance no noise could be heard. Then, as soon as this huge swarm of flying somethings, that looked quite odd from the front, was nearly over the church steeples of St. Vith, I noticed a dark cloud falling from the swarm, descending almost dreamlike - seemingly slow - onto the little town. At first there were innumerable explosions, big and small, but still nothing could be heard. Only a few seconds later the ground shook and I was able to hear the sound of the detonations. After that fires broke out, and a thick pall of smoke covered the devastation wrought by man.

On this day, several hundred inhabitants of St. Vith and allegedly as many as 1200 German soldiers were killed. The town was nearly totally destroyed.

While the bombs were bursting in St. Vith, I realized that at this very moment many people were losing their lives. Being a strong believer in ESP, I wondered by myself whether I would be able to make contact with the souls of the departing. But there was nothing. Having seen all that before, I was not even horrified. Seemingly, for any contact to be made with the souls of dying or dead people, prior communication or acquaintance might be a prerequisite.

Incidentally: Although inside Belgium, St. Vith is a town populated by Germans. It was part of the many German-populated border areas given to the victors after World War I. Even the old name of Bastogne has a German ring to it: it is *Bastnach.*

Once during these forays, I stayed overnight in a farm house in the village of Oudler that is part of the Eupen-Malmedy enclave cut off from the Reich after 1918. Obviously, soon after the 1940 German victory in the West these territories were re-attached to Germany, Versailles Treaty or not. The farmer's wife, who had a daughter about eight years of age, told me that immediately after the U.S. Army had occupied the area in September of 1944, her husband had been arrested because after the reunification of the village with Germany he had become a member of the NSDAP, the Hitler party. At the time I was there, the woman believed her husband to be in a prison in Malmedy. I still wonder whether he survived the war.

In Oudler I also had a chance to inspect an interesting small anti-tank cannon that must have been "forgotten" by a German Army unit passing the area during the great retreat in the fall[18]: The muzzle of this gun was visibly smaller than the circumference of the shell being pushed into the breech. I assumed that such a design would considerably increase the velocity of the round leaving the barrel, and thereby also increase the *Durchschlagskraft*, the ability to penetrate the hull of an armored vehicle.

American equipment was everywhere. I saw almost brand-new Sherman tanks, probably abandoned because they had either run out of fuel, or due to a mechanical defect. Although there was a *very slight* chance that such equipment was booby-trapped, I made it my business to "inspect" all tanks, trucks and Jeeps the U.S. Army had left behind or that lay damaged on the side of the road. After a few days I was well supplied with "Ami" cigarettes, chocolate, chewing gum, soap, tooth paste, candy bars, C and K-rations and - - - toilet paper.

Sometimes when I returned to the headquarters at Meyerode one of the junior officers would inquire whether I had been near the front, and upon receiving an affirmative answer the next question was whether I had some American cigarettes to spare. As a rule I was generous with the Chesterfields, Camels and Lucky Strikes. I knew that on my next assignment I would be able to find more. In one of the destroyed trucks I had found one of the zippered field jackets many of the GIs preferred at the time. For added warmth I wore it over my field gray tunic but underneath the more spacious camouflage smock for about a week, when one day a young lieutenant advised me not to wear American clothes such as the jacket, or even socks or gloves. When I inquired why not, the officer told me that there had been reports of captured German soldiers being shot by the Americans because they wore U.S. Army clothes. The GIs were in the belief that such equipment had either been pulled off dead American soldiers, or had been taken from their captured comrades. Regretfully, I had no choice but to part

---

18 Since the gun was seemingly not damaged, I assume that the German artillerymen had run out of ammo for it, or due to the activities of the U.S. Air Force there was no truck or tractor available to take such war materiel back into Germany in this hasty retreat.

with my GI jacket. It is obvious that, due to strict secrecy, none of us ordinary German soldiers knew of Otto Skorzeny's *Operation Greif.* Incidentally, had I seen some abandoned equipment from that endeavor, for instance a German tank with *American* markings, I would still remember that today.

After the war I discovered that numerous German soldiers had been haphazardly executed by GIs after their capture because their pockets were full of American "luxury" items such as cigarettes, soap and candy bars. I could have easily been one of the victims, for I had become an expert in scrounging for such things in abandoned tanks, Jeeps and other vehicles. The misunderstanding arose mainly because few GIs could imagine the large amount of American war materiel of all sorts that fell into German hands in the first week of the Battle of the Bulge.

The officers at the Meyerode headquarters were both tight-lipped as well as too busy to explain to a lowly private like myself what the German offensive was all about. I had the Allied war propagandists to thank for giving me at least an overview of the scope of the attack, and of the terrain included.

Although my hometown is only about two hundred miles from the B.o.B. area, I had at first not the slightest idea where we were except that the name of the "Eupen-Malmedy" area had stuck in my mind from my school days, and obviously I remembered being somewhat west of the city of Cologne. One day I found in the snow [to this day I remember almost the exact spot!] a recently-dropped enemy propaganda leaflet that had the form of a small tabloid newspaper. In order to befuddle the German soldiers it was called *"Nachrichten für die Truppe"* (News for the troops) and was allegedly the means by which German authorities informed German soldiers of things of interest. I knew it was an enemy leaflet but, as always, I read it from A to Z. There was little chance that I would be unduly influenced by the Allied propaganda. However, in order to keep up the subterfuge of a German-issued newspaper, the *Nachrichten für die Truppe*-leaflet had to have some kernels of truth, and thus I was able to learn in general what German units were involved in the attack, and who were the commanders. I distinctly remember reading General Rundstedt's name, and probably also that of Sepp Dietrich. I am also pretty certain that the date on the newspaper said 27 December 1944, and I am sure that while I was at Meyerode I did not meet or see either Sepp Dietrich[19] or one of the other German Generals.

It is an irony of war that the enemy is often better informed of the general details of what is happening than the own soldiers in the field. I doubt, for instance, that American soldiers received a newspaper such as the fake *Nachrichten für die Truppe* that had even included a map of the B.o.B. area. (Similarly it is today, when Chinese Generals are shown the secret war rooms at the Pentagon into which ordinarily only people with the highest security clearances are admitted.)

I knew that the famed Belgian Rexist leader, and at the time a high Waffen-SS officer, Leon Degrelle was at Meyerode because one evening his orderly came to the farm where I was housed and asked to purchase a chicken. Being a voracious reader with a keen interest in politics, the name of Degrelle, by then a legendary Waffen-SS hero, a *Ritterkreuzträger* with more than 50 days of

---

19 In German postwar literature Dietrich is often negatively depicted. Writers born long after the war who do not have any combat experience seemingly believe that only someone who has had the normal training to become a general can fulfill such a position. Undoubtedly, Dietrich's closeness to Hitler engenders such a view but there is also the fact that Sepp Dietrich rose from the ranks, and this, just like Hitler's common soldiers status, still rankles many people. (Ironically the very same people who generally try to tell the masses in the United States that everybody has it in him to become a president.)

Richard Landwehr, the American-born publisher of SIEGRUNEN magazine (q.v.), supplied the following excellent depiction of Dietrich's persona and accomplishments in issue No. 71 of his publication:

"(In my book).. Sepp Dietrich was a "founder" and a personification of the Waffen-SS. I think he has been highly underestimated and belittled at times, mostly because of his background and lack of higher education. But he had a very good instinctive grasp of command; knew how to treat subordinates and take care of his troops; had a very charismatic personality and always had a terrific staff with him. He was also an individual of great personal courage who certainly deserved all of the decorations given to him during the war. I have no doubt that he was a much greater general than many of those who were trained to be such. In addition, of course, those that served under him continued to hold him in great esteem and affection long after the war ended. And that is often the true measure of a man. When he died in 1966, more than 7,000 Waffen-SS veterans and many hundreds of others from all walks of life attended his funeral, and it drew world-wide press coverage. There is no question that he was one of the most distinctive and truly great military personalities of his or any other era."

hand-to-hand combat on the Russian front to his credit, was not strange to me, and in Meyerode I made certain that I saw him at least once. Degrelle and I would meet again in Madrid, Spain, where he had lived in exile since the end of the war, on April 20th, 1989. We commemorated the *Führer's* 100th birthday in his apartment together along with a few other stalwarts of times and battles from long ago.

In the fall of 2000, one of my dear friends of many years, Elmer Libby, last of Reno, Nevada, died at 74 years of age partly as a result of injuries he had received during the Battle of the Bulge and before, and partly because of the unavoidable deprivations in German POW camps at the very end of the war, and also, perhaps mainly, because of neglect by the U.S. Veterans Administration.[20]

I find it proper to insert into this "Battle of the Bulge" report the story of one of the true American heroes of that campaign, for if it had not been for the courage of mere handfuls of GIs like Elmer Libby, located "here and there" in the first line of American defense, divisions like the *Leibstandarte* might have reached their set targets earlier, and gained the smooth roads beyond the Ardennes faster: straight and level highways where there might have been no stopping them.

Before I transcribe Elmer's own report, and before I forget it, I would like to mention what he told me happened when he rejoined American troops again in April of 1945:

Elmer and a group of about 20 American POWs had been on a work detail out of the Moosburg POW camp, when one of the two old German soldiers guarding them (very leisurely) heard that U.S. forces had made a breakthrough, and were racing east on the autobahn not far away. The Germans, regular Army infantry soldiers, gave the Americans a choice of immediately trying to reach their comrades, in which case the German soldiers would

[20] When the war was over, the U.S. Government decreed that only those GIs who had spent more than half a year as an enemy POW were eligible for all benefits accruing from having been POWs. This left out most of the huge number of GIs that were captured in the Battle of the Bulge. This action by Washington caused great injustice. There is no question that the last four months of POW-time right at the end of the war was far worse than several years in a German Stalag between 1939 and 1944, after which the entire situation in the Reich deteriorated rapidly.

declare themselves POWs of the work detail, or else they all could march back to Moosburg and see what happened.

The Americans, obviously being hungry and anxious for their freedom, opted for the first choice, and soon all of them, Germans and Americans, were walking toward the west.

If I remember correctly, the first tanks they saw were from the 14th US division and we can easily imagine the joy Elmer and his comrades must have felt when their hard times were over. But soon American MPs of that division joined the "celebrations", and what did they want to do first? Shoot the German soldiers who had brought the GI-POWs back to their comrades! According to Elmer, he and his buddies had an awfully difficult time stopping the MPs from murdering the German soldiers who were now POWs of the U.S. Army. (This was not as rare a happening as many WWII ex-GIs still living seem to believe now. It may well be that the mind-set of MPs had been altered by different training methods.)

Following is the story, in his own words, of how Elmer Libby was captured by the Germans soon after the beginning of the Battle of the Bulge:

"The 106th Infantry Division, of which I was part, took over the 2nd Division territory in the Ardennes forest around the 12th of December. It was then that we marched to the Elsenborn Ridge area. On the 16th we were told to get ready for attacks on German pill boxes near the Roer river dams on the following day.

However, in the afternoon of the 16th it started snowing heavily, and therefore we crawled into our pup tents and sleeping bags relatively early, for what we hoped was a peaceful night.

It must have been around 7 p.m. of the 16th when we were suddenly told to take our weapons and ammo, and ordered to board a line of open trucks that immediately took us on a grueling ride through the snow-covered forests, with us being for hours exposed to ice-cold wind, wet snow and sleet. After midnight the trucks were unable to continue due to road conditions, and we trekked the rest of the way on foot, arriving at the village of Hünningen at about 5 am of the next morning.

Eleven of us were left at a house on the edge of the town, with six ordered to man two 30-caliber water-cooled machine guns. I remember that we were told that more units and food and additional ammunition would be arriving soon, but that never happened.

As far as I was concerned, the lonely farm house assigned to us as our defensive position was the most stupid place one could select for such a task. It was about 1,500 feet in front of the village, and nearly the same distance from a forest where we could expect the Germans to come from. It reminded me of a wagon train in the Wild West that was just about to be attacked from all sides by the Indians.

The locale was part of the front assigned to the 394th Regiment of the 99th Infantry Division, a green outfit that had never been in combat. We were obviously very unhappy about having been placed in a position where it would take a miracle if we got out alive once the shooting began.

I had been seriously wounded at St. Lo in France on the 22nd of June 1944. As a result, I had developed gangrene in my left leg, and I still carried a shrapnel in my left lung. The records of my gangrene had allegedly been lost, and thus I found myself back in combat before I had healed properly.

On one of the last days of November, a German lieutenant surrendered to us, and it was he who told us that a big German attack, "a second Pearl Harbor," was being planned. We were chagrined to notice that nobody on our side seemed to take this news seriously.

Not many hours after we had prepared that farm house near Hünningen for defense, the Germans attacked in force. Somehow I only remember three of us facing the enemy, a 26-year old Mexican, a 20-year-old private and me, then age 19. The Mexican never even fired a shot before being killed. The 20-year-old fired the machine gun left there by the 394th Infantry Regiment. It soon jammed. I knew that the odds of surviving a machine gun outpost under such conditions were small indeed, but my stepfather, a Mohawk Indian, had always told me that if one has to die young, it was best to go down fighting. Which I did.

I managed to get the weapon unjammed, and went on firing. How my wrist and arms survived this battle is still surprising to me, so many bullets from small arms hit the machine gun until it was finally put out of commission.

Once a small, round hand grenade landed right next to me. As I reached over to throw it out of our machine gun nest it exploded, leaving me with a splitting earache, headache and some piece of shrapnel in my left hip. After that the German infantry just bypassed us on their way forward.

It was a German medic who first attended to my wounds. But soon the German grenadiers from the 277th Infantry Regiment left the area, and others took over. It was then that I almost got into an altercation with the biggest and tallest enemy soldier I had ever seen. It looked as if this German was ready to use his rifle as a baseball bat on me, but then he suddenly walked away.

Of my four months as a German POW I remember the transport, mostly by rail, from the Battle of the Bulge area to the Stalag at Moosburg as being the worst time one can imagine. The cold freight cars, and the constant hunger of that week left an indelible impression.

The wounds I received at St. Lo and in the Bulge would bother me for the rest of my life. Tragically, after all these many decades I can unhesitatingly state that I was never properly treated."

I have forgotten how many years I was in contact with Elmer Libby, or as I would call him "Lib", but I guess it must have been 20 years. Therefore I was quite familiar with his troubles with the VA and other U.S. Government offices. To me it is obvious that the United States Army was so busy manufacturing phony evidence with which to prosecute alleged German war criminals that little care was taken to safeguard the records of men like Elmer Libby who had fallen wounded in German captivity. Although his scars proved his wounds, his sacrifice was never really acknowledged. I stick by my assessment that from an soldierly point of view Elmer Libby was a hero. Without the relatively few GIs like him tenaciously defending their positions, the soldiers of the German Army who were supposed to breach the American lines in that part of the front so that Waffen-SS Colonel Peiper's panzers of the LAH could move forward, would have gained an easy victory.

Being in possession of numerous German books and articles pertaining to the Battle of the Bulge I know that the few GIs defending Hünningen put up a stiff resistance and were instrumental in delaying the German advance. While Elmer deserved a Silver Star, he was not even recommended for the Bronze Star. He did receive the Purple Heart. Thus Elmer Libby's, a brave American soldier's story. May he rest in peace. I'll miss his letters.

In one of my earlier reports I had written how meticulous the German armed forces were when providing the items necessary for soldiering to new recruits. In my now-lost *Soldbuch* (pay book) even the number of the rifle I had been supplied with was carefully noted. How was this handled at the front?

When we left Breslau-Lissa we had all the equipment needed, including the helmet, except for weaponry. But once we had entered the battle zone I felt naked without either a rifle or a pistol, and at the first opportunity I had armed myself. The best place to do that was near a First Aid station or some other place where the many wounded arrived fresh from combat. Having had a 98k carbine for a few days, I remember stopping at a week-old battle scene (ruins, burned-out vehicles, some freshly dug graves of German *Fallschirmjäger*/parachutists) near the eastern entrance to the village of Losheimergraben, where the first skirmishes had taken place on December 16th and 17th, and there I found an undamaged assault rifle *Sturmgewehr 44 (StG44),* the forerunner of most of the assault rifles being used today. Since there were a few full ammunition magazines lying around also, I exchanged the 98k for the *Sturmgewehr,* believing that I had made a good trade. Soon thereafter an officer told me that it was not wise to have the new type of rifle: The bullets needed for it were not only in short supply but almost impossible to obtain. I had no choice but to abandon my find again. Henceforth I stuck to the 98k no matter the occasion. It is interesting to note that Hitler had long favored the development of such a weapon as the StG44, as a result of his World War I experiences. The famed Russian AK-47 Kalashnikov assault gun looks much like its "father".

In Losheimergraben I also tried to be a good Samaritan and pulled on a man's arm that was sticking out of the snow from atop the ruins of a farm house. But it was only an arm without the attached corpse, and so I left it where I had discovered it. Interestingly, I do not remember seeing any civilians there, although many of the villages we had passed were still populated.

Earlier in this report on my experiences in the Battle of the Bulge I had written that in many instances I cannot remember the exact date when I was at a given place or town during these fateful weeks. Sometimes, however, it is possible even after many decades to establish a date by researching other historical works.

For instance, about 10 km NW of St. Vith lies the village of Recht. I remember getting there one day on some errand while it was under steady American artillery bombardment. While standing smack in the middle of the inferno, trying to find my bearing on a map, an SS-soldier walked by me looking as if he had just escaped from Stalingrad: He was totally covered in uniform pieces that did not fit together, and instead of boots his feet were wrapped in sack cloth. Looking closer, I discovered that the fellow was one of our officer's candidates *Lehrgang* (class) from Breslau-Lissa. He had been assigned to the First Panzer Regiment of the *Leibstandarte*, and was one of the 800 or so survivors (out of 3,000 members) of Colonel Jochen Peiper's spearhead task force that had been surrounded by strong American forces at the village of La Gleize in Belgium. My Breslau comrade and the other survivors had to wade through icy mountain streams in order to reach the German lines near Recht, and he appeared to be badly frostbitten. When I saw him he had not yet had care from German medical personnel. This enabled me only recently to ascertain that the date of our chance meeting in Recht might have been the 25th or 26th of Dec. 1944.

This likely occurred on that day when I received orders to reach someone or some unit in the small city of Vielsam, just captured from the enemy, or so we thought. To get there I or we (it is doubtful that I was all by myself) had to travel through Recht that was some sort of a cross roads. The straight route from Recht to Vielsam, however, was impassable because German tanks had caught retreating American units in a devastating crossfire, and for several kilometers the meandering road was clogged by burned-out and otherwise destroyed American vehicles. I had no choice but to use an unpaved field road to get to my destination.

I do not remember having been able to find the officer or unit I was supposed to reach. It seems that Vielsam was not entirely clear of enemy troops, and there was lots of confusion and also some shooting while I was there. But what is still clearly in my memory is seeing German soldiers from an Army unit, probably from an old Eastern front *Volksgrenadier-Division,* plundering a small grocery store, and none of the officers in the vicinity was doing anything about it. This was the only time in the war when I saw wholesale thievery by German soldiers. Although in this case the stolen goods consisted exclusively of foodstuffs.

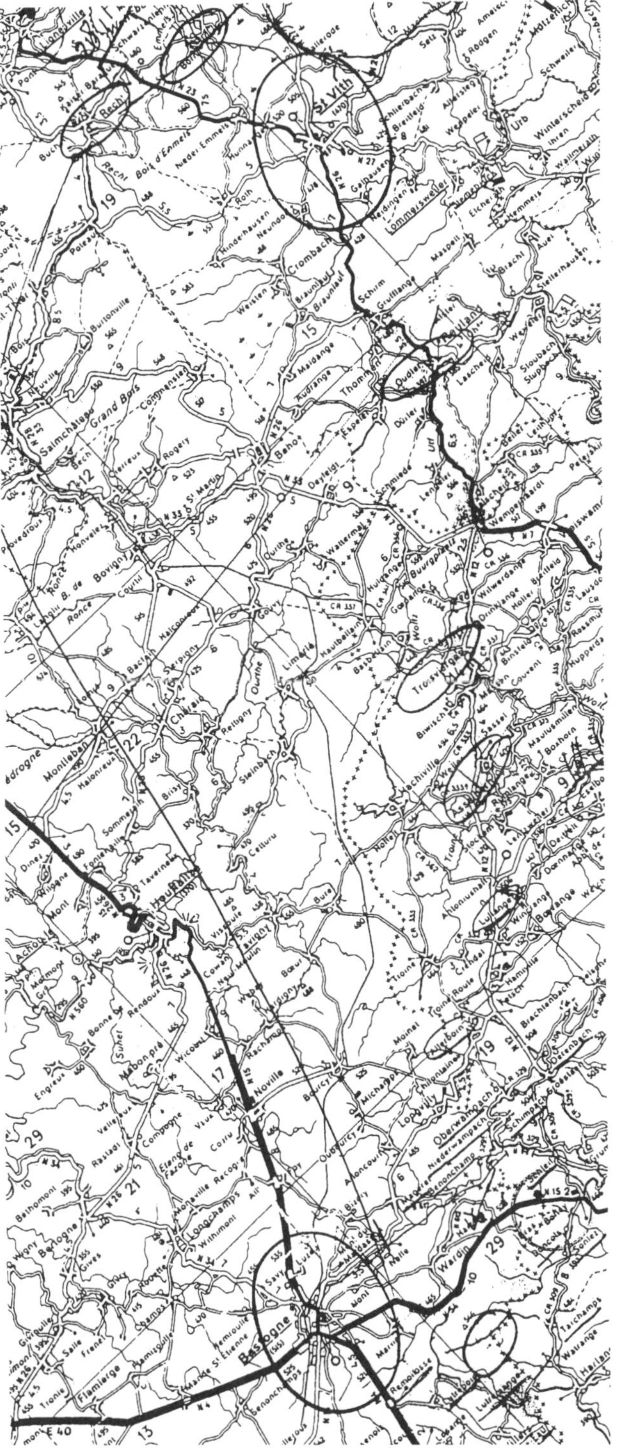

On the map to the left one can discern the route the LAH took from the battle-ground in the Northern tier of the Battle of the Bulge to the Bastogne area. I encircled the names of the towns that are best in my memory. However, some like Lullingen (Lullange) are, for whatever reason, in the French language.

The encircled area to the right (south east) of Bastogne is the Bois de Jean Collin, the forest where I spent some horrible days and nights in the first week of January 1945 amidst unrelenting American artillery fire.

The names of the hamlets Bras, Bohey and Doncols directly east of Bastogne show the spot where on January 12., 1945 we were caught in an American ambush and lost somewhere between 100 and 200 dead. This was the last serious engagement of the LAH in the west during World War II. The *finale furioso* of the war was only a few months away.

Chapter 15

As explained earlier, the German main thrust through the Ardennes forest consisted of two large German armies, the Sixth SS-Panzer Army, the backbone of which was my division, the 1st SS Panzer Division *"Leibstandarte SS Adolf Hitler,"* in the north, and the Fifth Panzer Army of the German *Heer* in the south.

Less than a week after the initial assault on Dec. 16, 1944 it became clear that the attack in the northern end of the "Bulge" was not only bogged down but had totally failed. The reasons were manifold: the failure of the German infantry units in the frontline to clear the way for the panzers in the very first hours of the attack; impossible road and weather conditions, lack of fuel and ammunition, lack of German air power and, not the least, the tenacity and bravery of small pockets of American GIs who had taken it upon themselves to delay the German advance long enough so that Allied reinforcements could be brought to the front.

The units of the German Army attacking in the southern tier of the B.o.B. area were more lucky: they reached passable roads much earlier, and it seems that the American resistance was not as tenacious as it was in the area of the Sixth SS Panzer Army. Some *Panthers* (Mark Vs) of the 2nd Panzer Division were stopped just short of the Meuse river after having bypassed the Bastogne crossroads.[21] However, it was there that the fate of the entire German offensive was decided in the last days of December.

---

[21] The bypassing of lightly defended strongholds was a normal procedure of the German armies in the early years of the war, when there were enough reserves to mop up enemy resistance that had remained in the rear of the

After performing my last duties at the Meyerode headquarters, which if I remember correctly was probably connected with the reconnoitering foray to the Recht and Vielsam area, I was finally given leave and ordered to report to the unit to which I had been originally assigned, namely, the 2nd Panzergrenadier Regiment (Second Armored Infantry regiment) of the *Leibstandarte.* Following the suggestion of an officer at Meyerode I traveled to the nearby *Ferme de Flamande,* where this unit had its command post, only to discover that everybody was ready to move out by nightfall. New orders had come in from Hitler: The *Leibstandarte* was to move south into the area of the Fifth Panzer Army and assist in the capture of the city of Bastogne.

Before we left the *Ferme* I was told that henceforth I was a member of the First company of the regiment, *Feldpostnummer* (APO number) 09088B. This meant that I was now part of the armored infantry, and therefore a *Panzergrenadier*. My hopes to be assigned to the artillery (150mm howitzers) for which I had been in training were finally squashed. Most of these heavy guns had become useless because large amounts of ammunition for them had never arrived in the combat zone.

Not knowing anybody, I made myself comfortable on the back of one of the many trucks with the famed passkey tactical sign of the LAH traveling the 50km (about 30 miles) south, and ended up in the village of Lullingen, about 16 kilometers as the crow flies northeast of Bastogne on Luxembourg soil, where the supply units of our First Battalion were stationed.

After the war I discovered that shortly after Christmas, and after the German ring around the city had been broken by Patton's forces, the German high command had ordered that Bastogne should be taken with superior forces, including my by then relocated division, as soon as possible. In case this goal was accomplished, the major attack toward the west was supposed to be renewed on December 29, with the *Leibstandarte* as the spearhead of an army group also consisting of the Third and Fifteenth (Army) Panzergrenadier divisions. Three other Army

---

German front. In the case of Bastogne, however, the failure to take the city when it was still lightly defended proved to have been a costly error.

divisions were supposed to assist in this offensive as soon as they became available. This never happened. The fast developing situation negated all German plans.

The transport of the 1st SS Panzer Division (the *Leibstandarte*) took place mainly on two days, namely the 28th and the 29th of December 1944. Some of the *panzers* and other vehicles had not been able to make the trip in time because they had no fuel or were still being repaired. Also, at the time the German Generals in charge of the battle had little correct information about the situation around Bastogne. Only one large German formation, General Remer's (the hero of the 20th of July 1944 anti-Hitler putsch) *Führerbegleitbrigade*, a unit mainly composed of experienced combat soldiers who had up to the loss of East Prussia to the Russians been guarding the outer perimeter of the *"Wolfsschanze"* headquarters of Hitler near Rastenburg, had reported that it was under heavy attack by American forces in the southern sector of what became known as the Bastogne Salient. (In some history books this "finger" in the American lines was also called the "Harlange Salient".)

Early on the morning of the 30th of December "my" battalion was part of the first *Leibstandarte* attack against the Americans in and around Bastogne. The unit was part of the forces to retake the villages of Villers La-Bonne-Eau and Lutrebois that were in the hands of the 134th Infantry Regiment of the 35th U.S. Infantry Division. Both of these villages were between the German-held part of the salient, and the major Arlon to Bastogne road that was the highway used by the U.S. 4th Armored Division to relieve the encircled American garrison of Bastogne.

The fact that I did not take part in the first attempts of the LAH to take Lutrebois and Villers-la-Bonne-Eau leads me to the conclusion that it may have been on that very day when I arrived at Lullingen. The soldiers taking care of the *Tross* (the supply) were mostly "older" fellows who had been with the division or other Waffen-SS units since the early days of the war. By "older" I do mean from the vantage point of a 17-year-old. The relatively few men left or still alive in the LAH who were now in their mid-twenties had seen it all, and were undoubtedly more skeptical about the final outcome of the war than were the newcomers. Most of the older guys had earned numerous medals for valor. The ubiquitous

Verwundetenabzeichen (similar to the Purple Heart) in silver worn by many, proved that they had sustained four or more injuries. It was the comrades from the *Tross* who saw to it that the soldiers in combat had at least one hot meal daily and were well supplied with ammunition, and other such necessities. One thing I soon noticed was that there was little chance to become friendly with the *Tross* fellows. They were a closely-knit bunch who had known each other probably for years, while we were the continuously changing, and in a way expendable, cannon fodder. There was no meanness involved in this "separation of duties". It was a fact of life and war. Due to the high attrition of officers in the SS frontline troops, even the platoon leaders and company commanders sometimes did not have a chance, at this stage of the war, to become closely acquainted with the *Spiess* (master sergeant - "the mother of the company") and other non-commissioned officers really running the unit. I learned quickly not to get in trouble with the master sergeant, or to become too friendly with him.

Very soon after my arrival, and after my name and other essentials had been written down, I was given a new rifle (the one I carried earlier I had left in Meyerode), and better winter clothing, and I guess within an hour I was sitting in an open (and therefore ice cold) Volkswagen *Kübelwagen*[22] loaded with insulated canisters of good hot pea soup on the way to the front. Since the weather was miserable - - low clouds almost touched the tops of the trees - - we did not have to fear American *Jabos* strafing us, but the driver,

---

22 In the meantime, the Waffen-SS divisions had quite a number of captured Jeeps at their disposal. But it was just about this time when we received the order from higher-ups not to use American equipment of any kind, including clothing and Jeeps, because it would mean almost certain execution if captured. This was the direct result of the Allied propaganda broadcasts concerning the alleged Malmedy Massacre. That did not stop me, however, from always keeping a fair supply of Chesterfields and Lucky Strikes and other American goodies in my pockets.
It was during this drive in the VW that I was becoming familiar with a minor road that in peace time led to a few insignificant farm villages but which had now become the major supply route for one of Germany's most famous armored divisions. And within the next couple of weeks I was going to use this road, the lifeline of the "Bastogne Salient", more often than I care to remember. Eventually there would be times when I was going to sit in a Jeep or VW and the driver was trying to speed through the worst of the road stretches that were continuously targeted by the enemy.

an experienced old-time corporal, warned me that some stretches of the road were under close surveillance by the Americans, and that he had no choice but to outrun the artillery barrages to be expected.

I ought to mention that the area around Lullingen, where the supply column was located, was within range of the heavy artillery of the Americans, and even during the short time I spent at this village I had to take cover because some shells were exploding too close for comfort. As a matter of fact, when the driver of the truck on which I was traveling from the St. Vith area to the Bastogne battleground had to stop not far from Lullingen to look at the map,[23] to discover which side road to take to the village, it seemed to me that the Americans must have had a forward observer in the area. Every time we even slowed down we had to fear being blown to bits. On the final stop I used the opportunity, while the driver took cover in a culvert, to "inspect" a brand-new Sherman tank without any visible damage standing on the side of the road. It had either run out of fuel or had been abandoned because of mechanical defects. Unfortunately, except for some chewing gum, I did not find anything of interest in it for me. (Come to think of it, it must have been this tank where I closely looked at the interesting viewfinder above the driver's seat.)

The trip from Lullingen toward the front took us first about six kilometers in a southerly direction on the major two-lane highway that connects St. Vith in Belgium to the city of Wiltz in Luxembourg. (Incidentally, all these German-speaking areas are now, in 2001, again outside of the German realm.) Just before the village of Derenbach we made a sharp right turn, stopping at a farm house where the driver smoked a cigarette and where I promptly lost my canteen when I tried to get drinking water from a partly frozen cistern. Then the driver admonished me to hold on for dear life as we drove downhill at high speed through a thick forest for a few minutes. As we neared the deep end of the narrow valley, I realized what my comrade had meant. Before me was a scene of such desolation that it was reminiscent of pictures I had seen

---

23 Both friend and foe had made it their business to remove most of the directional street signs. And those that had not been removed often pointed in the wrong direction.

showing the effects of prolonged trench warfare on a landscape during World War I: a formerly undoubtedly bucolic spot of nature had been, by almost constant artillery barrages, turned into an indescribable scene of horror and destruction:

Around the remnants of a small bridge,[24] one could see bodies of frozen dead German soldiers and many cadavers of equally dead horses. There were burned-out shells of trucks, and parts of what had been artillery pieces. And, what struck me most, in the entire vicinity of the bridge there was not one single tree that still stood tall. All one could see were the pitiful remains of what once must have been a beautiful forest of old firs, oaks and beech trees.

The driver knew what he was talking about. As soon as we had entered the bridge area, we heard a barrage of oncoming American shells. I expected him to stop suddenly so that we could take cover among the debris. But nothing doing. Instead of stopping, the fellow drove at such a high speed through the shell craters and over other obstacles that not only I but also the canisters with the pea soup, which he had wisely tied down, almost flew out of the VW. Luckily we made it without getting hit.

The recent revelations of U.S. Senator Bob Kerrey that during the Vietnam War he and his Navy Seals unit (an assassination squad, according to some reports) had killed a number of Vietnamese women and children in cold blood, leads me to the following comment. I am doing this especially because of a quirk in the American character to view an enemy's actions with unforgiving harshness while at the very same time explaining similar or worse actions by American soldiers with lame excuses, such as calling them "collateral damage". (Tim McVeigh made it a point to indicate this inability of many Americans to view both sides of an issue.)

In the book *Battle of the Bulge* by Danny S. Parker, a former research consultant to the Joint Chief of Staffs, I discovered the following interesting paragraphs. I believe that no further comment by me is necessary except to say that someone as prejudiced as Parker should not have had a research position at the Joint Chief of

---

24 *Many years after the war, and during a visit to the area, I was told that the rebuilt bridge is now being called the *Teufelsbrücke*, the Devil's bridge.

Staffs, and obviously, I excerpted these paragraphs and placed them as follows in a certain sequence to prove the incongruity of this American historian's thinking:

"The Germans were greatly feared and hated by many people in the Ardennes - particularly the fanatical soldiers from the dreaded Waffen-SS.

"Knowing the dangers of war, many citizens left their villages at the first sounds of gun-fire. Remembering the terror of the previous four years, some 200,000 Belgian and Luxembourg citizens took to the road...

"A good example was the town of Diekirch in Luxembourg. On December 19th, 3,000 civilians streamed from the village...

"The townsfolk were particularly worried because members of the local gendarmerie had (against the then existing laws of war! HS) fought alongside the Americans in September. Twenty German prisoners from this episode were still housed in the local jail.

"The citizens of the Ardennes (civilians!!! HS) often aided the Americans during the battle. Over the month long campaign, they helped to provide the Germans with "misinformation", directing panzer columns down bad roads, overestimating U.S. strength just over the hill, while warning the Americans of German moves. Some citizens even went so far as to fire guns from village windows at the German intruders. Soldiers from the 1st SS Panzer Division killed over a hundred Belgians supposedly in retribution for their having fired on German soldiers nearby. At the village of Bande, the dreaded SD (or Gestapo? HS) killed 32 Belgian youth in cold blood as a vendetta against the local resistance movement that had been active there the previous summer (when the German armies were retreating through this area, HS).[25]

"Although they did not commit monstrous atrocities like those of the SS, at least an equal number of deaths of citizens of the Ardennes must be ascribed to Allied forces. This is true if only

---

25 The fact that either the SD or the Gestapo was involved in the Bande village case seems to point to German knowledge that during the German retreat from Belgium a war crime had occurred in Bande, and furthermore, that the "youths" in question had participated in it. In his memoirs the famed Waffen-SS General Kurt Meyer (Panzermeyer) described such an incident in Belgium.

because of the effusive use of American artillery fire and bombs on villages suspected of harboring Germans.

(Remember: It seems as if only American soldiers have a right to safeguard themselves and even get angry at the enemy, - - and make errors of judgment in the heat of the battle -- but woe to soldiers of the other side who feel and act similarly. HS)

"In some cases, mistakes were made, so that bombs fell on towns such as Malmedy that were not even occupied by the enemy. At least 125 villagers and 37 U.S. soldiers were killed there.

"Of course, American GIs were no angels either. Some American soldiers broke into houses and plundered. Other GIs were rude and threatened (raped? HS) local women. U.S. airborne soldiers were perhaps worst in this regard. General Bruce Clark, the U.S. defender of St. Vith, was only half joking when he characterized American soldiery as "Two shooting and one looting."

(The following is abbreviated, but leaving the context intact, HS):

"At Houmont, southwest of Bastogne, the Americans launched an assault on December 30th to recapture the village. Renée Roland, his wife and their children from nearby Chenogne had sought refuge there. An artillery shell set their shelter ablaze. The refugees fled the burning building. As soon as they emerged from the smoke, however, a machine gun opened fire on them. It was an American gunner who had mistaken the group for fleeing Germans. Mrs. Roland was the first to be killed. As Mr. Roland crawled along the ground he was horrified to see the other six members of his family being chopped down by the machine gun. Somehow he dragged himself into a nearby farmhouse where he was found by its owner. 'They are all dead,' he wept."

Driving with full speed through the shell-cratered landscape of the steep valley below Derenbach, with one enemy round after another exploding on all sides of us, we finally made it to the opposite side of the ravine where there were some stretches of road seemingly in a dead corner for the American artillery.

While on the way up the hill, and due to the different angle again in relative safety from the enemy fire, I noticed that the Americans continued to pour shells into the valley. This led me to believe that they did not have a human forward observer in the area but some kind of listening device with which they heard German vehicles traversing the valley.

Before I could relax, the driver told me to get ready for another run for our lives. On the top of the hill before us we had to cross a road intersection that for friend and foe had become extremely important - - and was to remain so for a couple of weeks - - namely the crossing of the Bastogne - Echternach road with that of the narrower route between the villages of Derenbach and Lutrebois. But the driver of the VW again outguessed the American artillery, and soon, while angry rounds of 105mm and 155mm shells still pounded the crossing, we were rolling into Doncols, the first of the farm villages that was part of the salient.

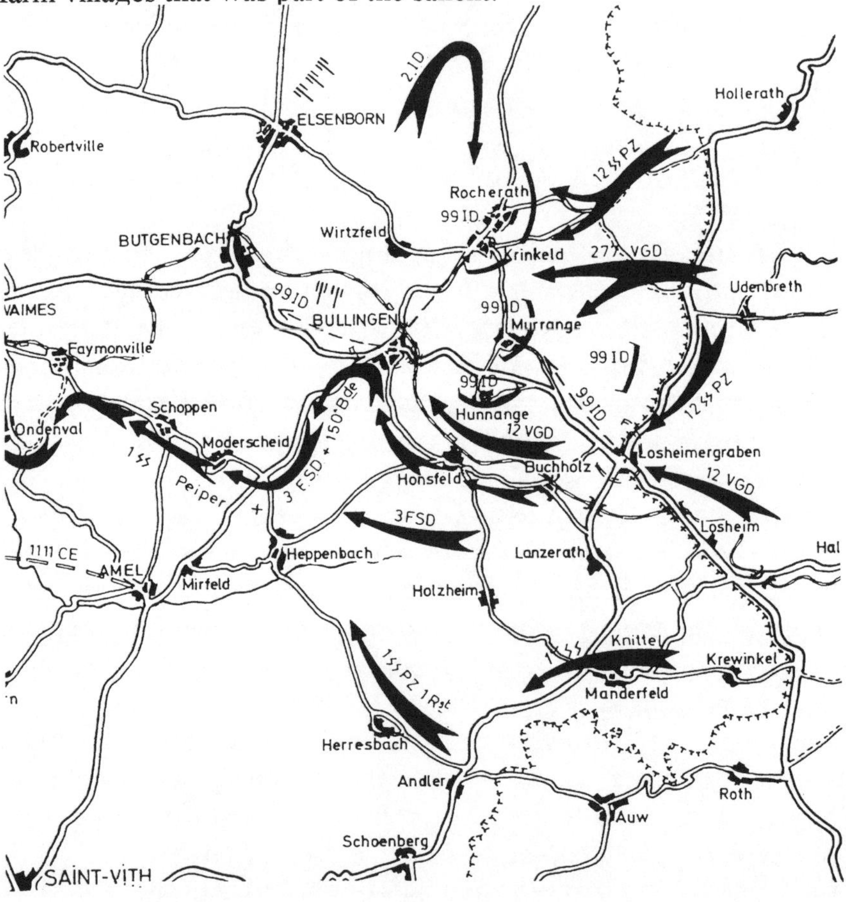

This map shows the Northern tier of the BoB during the very first days of the German attack. Note the village of "Hunnange" (Hünningen) in the center of the map where the American soldier Elmer Libby (see pg. 159) was one of the (relatively) few GIs to hold up the German advance.

Chapter 16

The finger of German-occupied territory around the southern perimeter of Bastogne began in the forest valley of Schleif, probably an unscheduled stop of the narrow-gauge railroad that before the war ran between the cities of Wiltz and Bastogne, and near Doncols.

The route that led from Schleif to the battle zone near the villages of Lutrebois, Lutremange and Villers-la-Bonne-Eau (and others) passed through the hamlets of Doncols, Sonlez, Tarchamps and Watrange. This narrow farm road became the major highway into the Bastogne (or Harlange) Salient not only of the *1st SS Panzer Division* but also the German *5th Fallschirmjäger Division,* the *Führerbegleitbrigade* and the *167th* and *9th Volksgrenadier Divisions.* All these small farm villages would become indelibly imprinted in my memory in the days following my arrival in the battle zone on or about December 30, 1944.

Opposing the abovementioned German units were the following American divisions: the 101st Airborne Division, the 4th and 6th Armored Divisions, the 35th Infantry Division, the 90th Infantry Division and the 26th Infantry Division. The hardest battles of the *LAH* were fought with the 35th Infantry Division. Ironically, this unit, essentially a National Guard division composed of men from Kansas, Nebraska and Missouri (largely "German" states), had in the weeks before the "Battle of the Bulge"-engagement been fighting in the Lorraine area just south of my home town. It may have been artillery of the 35th Infantry that had lobbed a 105mm shell into our home within sight of the Saar river, and caused considerable damage. From January 3rd to January 7th, 1945, the artillery of the 35th Infantry Division fired 41,000 rounds against our positions SE of Bastogne. In retrospect it seems to me that I heard them all detonate. (I am kidding.) The battle for Villers-la-Bonne-Eau and Lutrebois lasted mainly from December 30th to January 11th, with the 35th Infantry and the 4th Armored being the two American units successfully trying to keep the LAH from closing the road into Bastogne again.

To get safely over the crossing where the Schleif-Doncols road intersected with the road between Bastogne and Echternach became a cat-and-mouse game with the American artillery. At times we could see the low-flying observation planes (Piper Cubs) watching every movement on our side, but even in bad weather it seemed as if the enemy knew when vehicles tried to get across the intersection. The first houses of Doncols (probably Dunkholz [dark forest] in German), sturdy farm buildings with fortress-like walls, were a good place to have a little rest after the exertions of the Schleif and Doncols crossings. It seemed that most houses of the village were full of wounded soldiers, most of them victims of the American artillery.

Many years ago I was told the following story about Doncols by a former American lieutenant who was a tank commander with one of the independent tank battalions operating in the area on January 11, 1945:

While a vicious skirmish between American and German units was taking place at the famed Doncols crossing only a few hundred feet east of the village, a few American officers, including my acquaintance (who later became the mayor of the small city of Aurora in Nebraska), stood next to their white-washed Shermans awaiting further developments. A badly wounded German soldier was lying next to one of the houses, screaming because of pain. Suddenly one of the American officers, obviously bothered by the crying of the wounded German pulled his pistol and shot him dead.

Tragically I know that at the time there had been civilians taking care of wounded from both sides, and it should have presented no problem to take the wounded man into one of the houses.

Near Sonlez I saw a *Nebelwerfer* (rocket) battery in action. It was quite an impressive sight. But this also meant that the enemy was not very far away, since the range of these rocket guns was limited.

Tarchamps, whose German name is Ichpelt, would become very familiar to me because it was there that I found the command post of the 1st Battalion, 2nd Panzergrenadier Regiment of the LAH.

Two incidents relating to Tarchamps come to my mind, and since I do not remember on what day they occurred, I might as well relate them now:

Some of us young SS soldiers were in a farm house next to the battalion command post when we heard the farmer and his wife speak to each other in a language which seemed unfamiliar to us. At any rate, I couldn't understand a single word, and my comrades were just as puzzled as I was. Hoping that he would understand me, I asked the farmer in "my" High German what was the language he had just used with his wife? He looked surprised.

"Deutsch," he answered somewhat amused. "What else could it be?"

This proves how important was Martin Luther's endeavor when he translated the Bible from Greek and Hebrew (or Latin?) into a kind of German that could be understood by all people using the numerous Germanic *dialects* in the heart of Europe. To this day it is the Luther-German which is (essentially) the German we read in books, hear on the radio, and use when going shopping. Independent of this, the local dialects are by no means out of style. As a matter of fact, there seems to have been a resurgence of the use of German dialects in some localities.

American GIs from Pennsylvania Dutch families rarely understood High German but I had no difficulties conversing with them when I used the broadest slang I had learned from some of my fellow students in grammar school.

About the same time when Martin Luther translated the Bible, Johannes Gutenberg invented the printing press with movable type. This made the mass production of Bibles and other printed matter possible for the first time, and this fact contributed greatly to the literacy of the population at large. In other words, Luther and Gutenberg were the spiritual unifiers of the Germans. (Many or most people in Luxembourg are using the *mosel-fränkisch* German dialect at home but, oddly, the major newspapers of the small duchy are published in the French language.)

The other story about Tarchamps involves a *Volkswagen Schwimmwagen* (amphibious car): The constant bombardment by the American artillery caused not only considerable human casualties but also the destruction of lots of war material, among other things of our vehicles.

Our battalion headquarters was in desperate need for either a VW *Kübel-* or *Schwimmwagen* or a captured Jeep in order to keep in constant touch with the soldiers engaged in battle only a mile or two away. Finally our request for a new vehicle of this type was approved, and the battalion commander's driver was sent to pick it up somewhere in the rear.

Returning from his foray, he came down into the basement where we had taken quarters and reported to the officer that we finally got a brand-new *Schwimmwagen.* He had parked it in a presumably safe spot next to a stone barn, away from the American artillery fire, and we were all invited to look at the vehicle. But just then a horrific American artillery bombardment descended on Tarchamps. I remember that as a result a house across the street started to burn. When the smoke cleared and the artillery fire had died down, we finally ventured outside. The driver almost started to cry when he saw his vehicle: The *Schwimmwagen* had suffered a direct hit, probably by a heavy American 155mm shell, and was just one sorry heap of shredded metal. The safe spot had not been so safe after all, because we received American artillery fire from three directions: From the East, mainly barrages from the 35th Infantry Division, the 4th Armored, and from U.S. Corps artillery; from the North, "greetings" from the 101st Airborne and the 6th Armored Divisions, and from the South by batteries that probably belonged to the 26th Infantry Division.

Many decades after the war I visited Tarchamps, and I spoke to the farmer again where our command post had been. Realizing that he had made some changes to the house and its outside, I asked the man what he had all done. He told me that immediately after the fighting had stopped he began filling in the low lying area between the house and the barn, using the available war debris as a filler, so that the spot could be reached more easily from the street. When he did this he had left the wreckage of the small vehicle that was lying there exactly where it had been hit, and buried it under the war refuse. In other words, "our" VW will remain forever in Tarchamps, slowly but surely rusting away under the farmer's driveway.

Left photo—My brother Richard (left), then not quite 8 years of age, and a friend, on August 26, 1933 before departing for a Hitler rally that took place on the following day at the Niederwald monument near Rüdesheim on the Rhine, where the *Führer* made a speech to the Saarlanders. Note the absence of any patches on Richard's uniform. At the time there was no money in our family to purchase them. I still remember well when my mother sewed Richard's uniform from previously used material. While our mother was quite supportive of our being in the Hitler Youth at that young age, she did not *ever* permit our sister to join the BdM (*Bund deutscher Mädel*—the girl's branch of the HJ) although the law demanded it. She claimed that a girl's place was in the home, especially when there were younger siblings to be taken care of.

Right photo—This photograph of my sister Helga and myself was taken on January 27, 1935 in front of the gazebo located in the garden of the Schmidt mansion. January 27th was the birthday of Kaiser Wilhelm II who had abdicated 17 years before, and by then lived in exile in Holland. Our mother, who was a lifelong monarchist at heart, never missed to bake a cake, and, as seen in this picture, large pretzels for "Kaiser's birthday". She did this throughout the Third Reich and up to the war years, when food became scarce. I am in a *Jungvolk* (small boys of the Hitler Youth) uniform, and both Helga and I are carrying swastika flags because this was the month when the Saarlanders had voted by an overwhelming margin to rejoin the Reich. Another photograph taken at the same time shows our house bedecked with a large swastika flag and garlands for the occasion. Although normally a boy had to be ten years old to become a member of the *Jungvolk*, an exception was made for boys from the Saarland during the campaign leading to the internationally supervised plebiscite in favor of our reattachment to Germany. I had joined the previous November at seven and a half.

The (then) 25-room Schmidt mansion in Luisenthal, built in 1875, where I spent most of my youth. This picture was taken in 1908, with my father and his sister standing on the sidewalk. During World War II an American 105 mm artillery shell broke the sandstone rim of the window to the left of the balcony, and detonated in the center of the house between the first and second floors. Due to the fortress-like construction of the house, the damage was minor.

The Schmidt townhouse in Saarbrücken in 1906 where my great-grandfather lived in retirement. This building was totally destroyed in a British air raid on October 5, 1944.

Myself, approximately 1942 or 1943 in the uniform of the Hitler Youth fire brigade, at a time when we assisted after air raids.

My brother Richard, then still 17, in the Labor Service (left) and a few months later in the *Kriegsmarine* (Navy) in Libau, Latvia, in 1943.

Myself, not yet 17 years of age, in the Labor Service on the island of Borkum in the North Sea. Note my hands are swollen from hard labor building fortifications against the allied invasion of Fortress Europa.

Visit by a high-ranking *Reichsarbeitsdienst* officer at the end of our tour of service.

Viewing the troops. I am one of the RAD-men in the first row on the right.

A final inspection of our work on the anti-invasion fortifications.

Four young Germans from my hometown who during World War II volunteered for the Waffen-SS, and gave their lives for Germany: Kurt Seiler (upper left), my good friend whom I last saw in November of 1944. Kurt was wearing my peaked cap for the picture since his own field cap looked too shabby. Kurt Thiel, upper right, a distant cousin who died as a lieutenant in the *Leibstandarte*. Heini Jähne, lower left, was the first leader of the Hitler Youth in our town. His brother Kurt followed in Heini's foot steps. They were the finest fellows one can imagine: intelligent, upright, trustworthy, tolerant and always helpful. For Germany and our race it was a tremendous loss to have so many young men of this caliber die so young.

This photograph was taken November 2, 1944, ten years to the day after I had joined the Hitler Youth (*Jungvolk*). I was 17½ years old.

Just ten months later, after the German defeat. Combat in the "Battle of the Bulge," in Hungary and in Austria, and having been wounded twice and twice suffering from frostbitten feet, plus contracting swamp fever show in my face. I am wearing a jacket of the German Navy which my mother had wisely "liberated" when the townspeople of Preetz in Holstein plundered a *Kriegsmarine* supply depot at the end of the war.

The German s.I.G.33, a 150 mm howitzer, that was one of the four guns shooting too short on January 12, 1945 near the Doncols crossroads. Many of the rounds detonated among the German dead and wounded lying in front of the American lines. I discovered this gun 25 years later in the village of Niederwampach near Bastogne from where it was fired at us. It has now been restored and graces the village entrance atop a well-built pedestal.

This is the German armored vehicle, a *Sturmgeschütz* IV/70 of the *Leibstandarte*, that hit an American mine the same day next to the borderpost between Belgium and Luxembourg. As this and other incidents were happening, I was lying for hours, and unable to move, in the clump of bushes indicated by the arrow, within easy sight of the American GIs.

On the December day when I first came to Tarchamps, I did not remain long at the battalion command post. Within minutes after our arrival I was on the way to the front, still holding on to the hot pea soup canisters.

The sun having just passed the winter equinox, daylight was still very short, and especially in this part of the world it already got dark in late afternoon. By the time I reached the First Company, all fighting had died down except for the sporadic, never ending greetings from the American artillery.

My new company commander, a young, decorated first lieutenant, was glad to have one more replacement when I reported to him. However, after hearing of my nearly two weeks' meandering for the high headquarters in Meyerode, he also realized that, except for being very proficient in eluding American artillery shells, I did not have any real combat experience. As a result, he did not immediately assign me to one of the infantry platoons fighting somewhere between Lutrebois and Villers-la-Bonne-Eau but kept me in his own personal vicinity.

The first serious shooting with my new rifle, a brand-new war production that showed, in small details, that Germany was running out of manpower and materials, occurred the following day: A reserve platoon to which I was assigned was lying alongside another unit of German soldiers on a ridge overlooking a small group of houses that sat astride the Arlon-Bastogne highway several hundred meters away. We were told that these houses were occupied by the Americans and that it was our duty to keep the GIs down through intermittent fire while comrades from other companies of our battalion tried to attack the Americans from the rear. I never even saw one of the enemy, but less than a half hour after we had begun our action, all of us, including the attacking companies coming from the other side of the hamlet, had to make a hasty retreat because such a hurricane of American artillery fire descended upon us that it made a successful conclusion of the action impossible.

(This action seems to have been originally planned with a strong *panzer* force assisting us. However, a day before, the very tank unit that was supposed to lead our attack was badly mauled by tanks of the 4th Armored Division and American fighter bombers:

On the 30th of December, the 7th Company of our 1st SS Panzer Regiment was almost totally wiped out during an ill-fated attempt to close the Arlon-Bastogne road and thereby complete the encirclement of Bastogne again. Had the German armies controlled the air, things might have turned out differently. I remember seeing only American planes, Piper Cubs, *Jabos* and, high above us, the armadas of two and four-engine bombers flying into the Reich.)

Soon I found myself exactly where I did not want to be, namely standing guard against American surprise attacks not far from the aforementioned major highway, or lying in deep snow near the rim of the forest of Lutrebois.

Almost nothing surpassed the horror of the nights we spent in this large forest that straddled the heights between our supply route and the city of Bastogne. To me it seemed as if the Americans were bombarding this forest from all sides, and there was no escaping the never-ending cavalcade of shells that were raining down on us. At times, seemingly only when they were available, the Americans used a new type of grenades with so-called proximity fuses that did not detonate on impact, as do general-use shells, but that explode when they are in close proximity of a target, for instance, at tree height. One night shortly after New Year's Day was especially bad, and it seemed that every few minutes after the shells had detonated one could hear the screaming of the wounded and the calls for medics.

I must not forget to mention that almost the entire Battle of the Bulge area was under constant American artillery barrages *even when the Americans were in full retreat*. And this bombardment was especially vicious at places like St. Vith and Bastogne, where major battles were fought. A number of the enemy batteries were excellent in the pin-point destruction of German targets, while others were obviously assigned to what we called *Störfeuer*; "harassing fire," an almost haphazard covering of a set area with exploding shells. For us, there was not a place nor a minute where one could feel secure.

The following text is from a 1945 booklet, *"The 4th Armored from the beach to Bastogne"*, that provides some idea of what we had to go through:

"Stopped cold, the Germans clung to the Lutrebois pocket[26]. *They kept it for more than a week at terrific cost. The 4th's three artillery battalions poured the heaviest barrage they had ever fired into the small area.*

"From December 30 to January 6, a total of 24,483 rounds of 105mm howitzers cascaded into Lutrebois and the woods north and east. The New Year came in with a bang as armored artillerymen greeted it with 7,000 shells on December 31. The 66th FA alone fired 3,046 rounds."

Postwar reports showed that during the Battle of the Bulge most of the losses of men and material of the German divisions had been caused by the generally accurate American artillery. I believe the figure for losses in personnel was around 60 percent.

By the end of December 1944, about halfway through this gigantic battle, American artillerymen had fired about 1,255,000 rounds against us from 4,155 artillery pieces, most of them probably with 105mm guns.

(Incidentally, during a desperate last-ditch effort by the German *Luftwaffe* on December 31, 1944 the attempt was made to attack in one single "giant" strike the Allied planes that were now located on the West European airfields captured not long before from the Germans. On that day the *Luftwaffe* was able to muster only 550 planes of all sorts against 3,550 Allied aircraft. While in abstract numbers the *Luftwaffe* may have been the winner, the fact remains that on this day many of the most experienced and highly decorated German pilots lost their lives. The *Luftwaffe* would never recover from that blood-letting.)

After a few days of guarding, with others from our battalion, the German perimeter around our salient, and at night lying cold and frightened in shallow, lightly covered dug-outs that stopped neither the frigid air nor the shrapnel from the American cannonade,

---

26 If one envisions an encirclement where the enemy is held in the grip of a hand, with only a small opening where the tips of the forefinger and the thumb meet, then one has a good idea how the situation around Bastogne looked around New Year's Day 1945. We were right in the tip of the thumb and had the hopeless task of closing the gap that was breached on December 24, 1944 by tanks of the 4th Armored Division, the spearhead of General Patton's Third Army.

I looked for a way out of my predicament. Being of the opinion that anything was better than to constantly hope that the next incoming shell would not be directed at me, I decided that it was best for me to volunteer for *any* action that came up, no matter how dangerous it might be.

Incidentally, I do remember New Year's evening, when exactly at midnight the American positions exploded in a giant fireworks that gave us clear indications where the enemy was located. Not being so abundantly provisioned, I envied the soldiers from the opposite side for their seemingly inexhaustible supply of everything, including ammunition. Little did I know that General Patton had given the order to his troops to shoot at us at that moment with everything they had. I assume Patton did this with the knowledge that his soldiers would use their arms, at the stroke of midnight anyway, permission granted or not, and why not direct the fire at the enemy? Not seeing us, however, many GIs directed their firing skyward for a nice fireworks display.

In the first week of January I volunteered for a night patrol in an area that was not normally in our assigned region. Most of my new buddies thought I was crazy to take this risk. Alas, it would be the last time I would see most of them. The forest of Lutrebois, the correct name of which is *Bois de Jean Collin,* took its daily toll.

The patrol consisted of about a squad of soldiers. Our aim was to discover the location of the American positions just east of the center of Bastogne. I remember that we assembled in a farm house in a village named Oberwampach, where we were able to fry some potatoes with a slab of bacon we had scrounged somewhere. Thus fortified we set out aboard a half-track just before sunset to the village of Benonchamp, where I remember seeing, next to a bridge of the narrow-gauge railroad, a captured American heavy howitzer on a half-track that had been marked with crayon in large letters, *"Z.b.V. des OKH."*, namely, "Retained for special consideration of the High Command of the German Army." Seemingly this weapon was a new model that was supposed to be evaluated. Considering everything I doubt that the OKH ever had a chance to look at this weapon.

After we had disembarked, we waited in Benonchamp until full darkness had set in, and then hiked through the deep snow (2 ft. or more) in a westerly direction, one man behind the other, with me being the last. This time, I had been appointed assistant squad leader.

I must mention that we had left some of our equipment, such as the metal gas mask containers and the spades we usually carried, behind in order not to create too much noise. The road we took was probably an unpaved path that was part of a farm. A thin strand of barbed wire nailed to willow trees along a creek guided us for most of the way.

It was eerie to walk in a zone where we did not have to fear being hit by an incoming artillery shell from either friend or foe, although we heard both the American and German rounds traversing overhead, and noticed their detonations in the distance.

Suddenly we saw, not very far away, the silhouette of neatly planed rows of trees, and beyond that some houses. The leader of the patrol assumed that it was the little village of Neffe, and since we heard non-German (male) voices coming from there he had reason to believe that Neffe was occupied by the Americans. We also had orders not to engage in a fire-fight unless this was absolutely necessary. Having thus fulfilled our task, we began our hike back the same way we had come.

At the time I had the feeling that the Americans were watching us but it is possible that during this night the GIs, likely as cold as we were, had no intention of starting trouble for themelves and us. After several hours we arrived safely back at our command post, and the leader of the patrol was able to report on what we had seen, or not seen.

Unfortunately, at the time the patrol leader did not confer with me with on the 1:100,000 German Army map he carried. These maps were especially valuable in combat because on them 1cm always meant a distance of 1 kilometer. Thus it was easy to figure out how close we were to the enemy or to a destination we had to reach.Later, in Hungary, I discovered that I was better at map reading than he was. After he had reported back from our patrol I had a hunch that we had not been close to Neffe, as he had assumed, but that the buildings we had seen were in fact the first houses of Bastogne itself. This would also account for the fact that we had not received any fire. Few GIs quartered inside the city would have considered that a German patrol could reach almost the heart of the city unseen, and it is likely that nobody watched the direction where we had come from because just about there was the dividing line between the 101st Airborne and the 6th Armored Divisions, as I discovered years later.[27]

I ought to mention that in late December 1944 and the first two weeks of January 1945, the situation around Bastogne was extremely fluid. Reading of this battle a half century later, one would assume that the German and the American fronts each were closely connected lines facing each other, with a few soldiers covering each 100 feet or so. This was not the case at all. Once I had been ordered to take three men and a machine gun to a small hill overlooking an American-occupied village (I believe it was Magaret) and keep watch. On this day the German front had a gap of at least one kilometer that was covered by just four soldiers.

We must have been on guard for a few hours when we saw a Jeep occupied by three American soldiers leave the village and drive up a narrow, snow-bedecked field road that was leading directly toward us. Probably noticing that he was going in the wrong direction, but oblivious to the fact how close he was to German soldiers, the driver made a smart turn in easy shooting distance from us and then drove unhurriedly back into the village, the other end of which was outside of our view. As the Jeep had come closer to where we were lying behind a cover of fir trees, the gunner of my MG-42 lifted the weapon in anticipation of destroying both the vehicle and its occupants. I, on other hand, had the order to keep watch and immediately report greater enemy movements by sending one of the soldiers back to a command post with whatever message was necessary. It was not in my or the German armed forces' interest to make the enemy aware of our location by killing the three Americans. Thus I signalled the MG *"Schütze"* to hold fire. Personally I felt better that such an outcome of this small incident of war was possible.

Except for this Jeep's outing nothing happened during our watch, and by nightfall we retreated to the warmth of a farm house. Similarly it was on January 12, 1945, after the one-sided battle

---

[27] When I visited the area in the winter of 1970, I made it my business to check out this particular place. Retracing our 1945-hike starting from Benonchamp, I discovered that very likely I had been correct. We had almost reached the center of Bastogne that night.

described at the very beginning of this book: We, the four or five final survivors of the blood-letting, made our way back to a German First Aid station without encountering even one German post between it and the Americans. The German front was wide open.

These are the M5 tanks from Task Force Harper which, in January of 1945, I passed several times without even once "inspecting" them. I saw them from the road from which this picture was taken.

For whatever reason, and just about this time (ie. after I had volunteered myself out of the Lutrebois forest area), one of my buddies, a boy named Werner, and I ran along a road branching off from the major St. Vith to Wiltz highway. It was near the hamlet of Fetsch, where four or five American M5 tanks stood nicely side-by-side in a row, a little off the road in a forest clearing, as if their crews had just left them in the snow, soon to return. These American tanks had been part of a Task Force Harper that had been overrun by the German (Army) 2nd Panzer Division on December 17. The M5 Stuart tanks were 15-ton light tanks equipped with a puny 3.7 inch gun. They were no match for the 75mm guns of the Mark IVs and "Panthers" of the Germans. I remember passing these American tanks at least three or four times during my stay in the area, for what reason I don't recall, but I never "inspected" either one of them. The reason could have been manifold: either the artillery fire by the American was too strong in the vicinity, or the snow between the road and the tanks was too deep, or I was certain that I would find nothing of value to me in them, since obviously they had been there for more than two weeks. Years later I heard that during the final battles in the area, ie. a day or two after our January 12 fiasco, these Stuarts were used by retreating German troops as unmoveable defensive positions, as a result of which they were heavily damaged by U.S. artillery. They remained at this spot near Allerborn at least until 1947.

Getting close to Allerborn, Werner and I came upon a German tarpaulin-covered Army truck standing still in the middle of the road leading to Longvilly (I remember seeing a sign *Achtung, Feindeinsicht* [Attention, road being observed by the enemy] pointing in the direction of this village.). The truck looked from the rear as if soon intending to continue in the same direction as we were going. Hoping to get a ride, we noticed as we came closer that the vehicle was slightly damaged by an American artillery shell and seemingly abandoned. But to our joy the rear gate had been opened, and we could see that the truck was chock full of mostly edible goodies.

By now being used to just grabbing all abandoned things from destroyed vehicles, whether American or German, we immediately proceeded with filling our pockets with as much of that good stuff as, especially canned goods, we could handle. Only then we decided to look into the truck's cabin to see whether there still was anybody around. We found the driver all right: An American shell must have exploded very close to the left side of the front of the truck, and one of the larger shrapnels had sliced the truck driver's, an older soldier's, head neatly in half so that from the passenger side the poor fellow looked as if he was sleeping, while from the driver's side the place of his face, ears, hair was just one bloody mess. It was all gone.

Now my buddy Werner did something I never understood. He was so shocked by this horrible view that he immediately emptied his pockets of all the goodies we had "liberated" from the truck. As if there was a connection between these things and the poor soldier's death.

Werner, a good-natured fellow normally with a nice sense of humor, grew ever more morose as the days went by. One cold night a bunch of us were sitting out in the open, near the edge of a forest, feeding a small fire with cordite from a nearby abandoned American artillery emplacement. The explosive was burning harmlessly, not creating much warmth, fast flaring up as if we were every now and then burning an entire box of matches all at once, when someone asked,

"I wonder who will get it tomorrow?" meaning, of course, who would be killed the following day during the planned attack on American lines.

Without much thinking I said, "*Ich nicht!*" (Not me!) whereupon Werner said. "Hans, how can you know that with such certainty. None of us know their fate!"

I could only answer what I then firmly believed and what I also wrote in letters to my family: I was convinced that I would survive this war. Although I was afraid to get badly wounded I did not fear death seemingly because it was not in the offing for me. Particularly such wounds where a shrapnel had torn open a comrades' belly and all the innards could be seen while the fellow was quite conscious bothered me tremendously. Invariably such physical damage would lead to the death of the wounded soldier, since we had not enough bandages to stem the loss of blood, or the knowledge how to close the wound even temporarily. There were never enough trained medics around.

Werner gave his life for Germany on the morning following this conversation. I was always wondering whether he had a premonition of his death. He was killed a few feet behind me, shot through the head.

It may have been during this same talk when we opened various small containers of American canned goods that we had found in the abandoned enemy position. Spam, corned beef, pudding and the like found our approval. Saltine crackers we could do without. But then one of my comrades opened a small olive-green can with something of a reddish color in it; by the looks of it we assumed that it was some kind of sweet dessert. Obviously we had to try that too, only to spit it out again as fast as we could. This can turned out to be a Sterno container, the fuel GIs used to warm their food when no other means to do so was available. The reason why we had been unable to notice the unmistakable gasoline smell of the Sterno was simply because the burning of the cordite, and probably also the smoke from burning houses nearby had dulled our sense of smell. The German *Wehrmacht* used something similar as Sterno for the identical purpose: small cubes of odd-smelling, hard-pressed fuel that could be easily lit with a match. These cubes came in thin metal boxes that were supplied to front-line troops when no hot food came through. I do not recall ever using these cubes.

Stopped cold, the Germans clung to the Lutrebois pocket. They kept it for more than a week at terrific cost. The 4th's three artillery battalions poured the heaviest barrage they had ever fired into the small area.

Chapter 17

Perhaps the most interesting incident of war of this first week of January 1945 occurred in that farm house in Tarchamps where our battalion HQ was located, and where the *Schwimmwagen* is still buried.

Comrades from another company had brought ten captured GIs into the cellar. All suffered either from slight wounds or from frostbite. It was said that they were the survivors of an American company that had been wiped out in hand-to-hand combat. While the basement was barely heated, it was still much warmer than the minus 6 degrees Fahrenheit that it was just then on the outside. It did not take long, and several of us and the ten Americans were sitting in a smaller room of the basement atop a huge mount of potatoes, and began to talk. At least one of the Americans spoke some German, and one of us (not I!) knew some school English.

One of the first things one of my comrades did was to open a bottle of Schnapps he had found hidden underneath the potatoes, and, polite as he was, he offered some to our involuntary guests first. They declined in unison. Only after the GIs had noticed that we did not hesitate to drink from the bottle, and after a little coaxing, did they also imbibe. Later it came out that they had suspected that we wanted to poison them. The conversation went something like this:

Americans: “Why don’t you guys quit? Don’t you know when you are licked?”

Germans: “Who is licking whom right now? And why didn’t you stay in America where you belong?”

Americans: "Well, Hitler wanted to conquer the world, and somebody had to stop him!"

To which we Germans could only laugh. And so it went for a while.

I myself was surprised to discover that the Americans could not understand that on the very day of our battling against each other, with dead comrades on both sides, we could talk reasonably to each other. Speaking only for my person, but knowing that most of the young Waffen-SS soldiers in our company were feeling similarly, I can unhesitatingly state that we did not hate the Americans. We knew that, drafted or not, they had no choice but to join the armed forces of their country in a great war such as this, and that personal animosities were out of place. Hate against the enemy would not have made us better soldiers. (Does a big game hunter in Alaska have to hate a Grizzly bear he tracks and eventually kills?) The "Never forget, never forgive"-mentality that is so prevalent at the beginning of the Twenty-first Century was and is totally alien to us.

Suddenly one of the GIs said, obviously feeling pretty good (the bottle had been making the rounds!): "Am I glad we were not captured by the SS."

It was then that we realized that, considering the all-concealing winter outfits we wore, and with each of us covered with different layers of uniform pieces, the uninitiated could not know that we were members of the Waffen-SS, and so far the Americans had not seen one of our officers whose collars with the SS runes were quite noticeable.

We were curious to find out why the American thought that he was lucky not to have been captured by the SS, and so he was asked. It was then that I heard, probably for the first time, all the horror stories about the alleged brutality that became so prevalent after the war and remain so half a century later. The GI really believed that "had he been captured by the SS, he would have been shot". He also mentioned an alleged massacre of "hundreds" of GIs who were supposedly killed by "the SS" immediately after the beginning of the *Ardennenoffensive.* Now I am certain that he referred then to the so-called "Malmedy Massacre" that would cost so many young Waffen-SS captives their lives during the last months of the war.

After a while I had heard enough, and, opening my collar, I showed the GI who had made the statement the taps with the double-lightning bolt runes on it. Seeing it, he turned white. I myself got angry because of such stupid talk, and because of his in my opinion equally dumb reaction, and I refused to participate in any further conversation.

Soon the adjutant to the battalion commander came into the room and ordered me to take the Americans to the regimental headquarters which I knew would be close to the small railroad tunnel near Schleif. One other German soldier was detailed to me as additional guard. Having trodden the Tarchamps-Schleif route before, I knew we would have to traverse at least 6 kilometers (4 miles) through deep snow since a straight hike on the road between the villages was too dangerous. The constant shelling by the American artillery was mostly concentrated on the villages and the roads which connected them. Therefore I decided to avoid both, and to hike with my charges across the open fields. Due to the unavoidable deep snow drifts this would make our trip much more difficult and time consuming but would also increase our chances for survival.

While the Americans helped their wounded and frostbitten comrades by often carrying them between the two of them, I had difficulties with the German soldier. He believed it was prudent to have his rifle at the ready in case one of the Americans tried to escape. Realizing that none of the GIs was in any shape to get far, I ordered my comrade to carry his rifle on his back, and to assist one of the Americans who had difficulty walking.

Due to the bad shape my charges were in, it took several hours, but we finally got to the village of Sonlez. It was there where a few days earlier I had seen the German *Nebelwerfer* (rocket launchers) in action. Having gotten awfully thirsty by walking through the deep snow and also because often we had to take cover from American artillery rounds that detonated near us, I decided to stop in one of the houses alongside the road with the GIs and just to ask for some water to drink.

No sooner had we stepped into the farm house when a young Army lieutenant barked at me what I was doing, bringing captured enemy soldiers into an important post of the *Hauptkampflinie,* the main battle line, seemingly some line drawn back there where the

Generals made their decisions. I could only answer that I thought the *Hauptkampflinie* was there where the fighting took place. As we left the farm house without having gotten anything to drink, one of the German soldiers sitting by the door said to me, "Why don't you just shoot'em?"

"If you are captured you want to be treated decently too!" I retorted. These German soldiers had been part of either the 9th or the 167th Volksgrenadier Division, in other words, not Waffen-SS.

After passing through Sonlez and Doncols we had to cross near the dangerous intersection mentioned previously and soon, in the little valley below, I could see the few houses, one of which I knew was our regimental headquarters. Getting closer, I noticed that something was very wrong: The building must have sustained a direct hit only a few minutes earlier, and numerous soldiers were at work digging out the living and the dead.

We had no choice but to keep on going.

In the meantime I had noticed that the strength of the GIs was faltering. We practically had to stop every few yards. I knew that only a few hundred feet away from our regimental headquarters was a small railroad tunnel in which the 5th German Parachute division had a First Aid station and probably also an enclosure of some sort for POWs. When we got there I was informed that the parachutists already had nearly 300 GIs in the tunnel, and that they had neither enough food nor space for any additional captives.

What to do now?

Another two or three kilometers away was the small railroad station of Schimpach right next to another tunnel, and it was there where the LAH divisional staff was located. Not wanting to endanger the GIs by leading them through the valley that looked like a World War One scene, I decided that we would walk along the railroad tracks for the rest of the way. This route had the advantage that it was behind the hills and almost out of reach of the American artillery.

The going was rough and slow. Finally we reached the southern end of the Schimpach tunnel, but for one reason or another we could not enter it from that side. We had to practically slide down the steep, frozen embankment and crawl over large boulders until we again again firm ground under our feet. For the wounded GIs this part of our hike must have been hell.

Finally we got to the small railroad station and I was able to report to a staff sergeant assigned to the LAH headquarters and present him with the POWs. This decorated non-commissioned officer, obviously an intelligent man who realized what we had gone through this day, immediately saw to it that we were well taken care of with something hot to drink. While I was ordered to remain for the rest of the day and the following night in the warm main building of the small railroad station, he led the Americans into the station master's house that now served as a First Aid station.

When I wanted to leave the Americans by just waving good bye, one of the GIs, the one who probably was a non-commissioned officer, called me over, shook my hand and gave me his brown Bakelite compass. I am sure he realized that it had not been easy to get him and his comrades this far out of the worst danger zone. The fact that he still had his compass indicated to me that he and his buddies had never been properly searched, but having gone through all the difficulties of this day I thought it prudent to keep this knowledge to myself. For the rest of the war, until April 28, 1945, this compass would serve me well. A minor wound that day ended the fighting for me, and I gave the compass to one of my comrades who remained in the line. Years later, when I had settled in the United States, I was able to buy a replica of the compass in an Army-Navy surplus store as a memento to the winter "hike" from Tarchamps to Schimpach.

(This incident happened in the first week of 1945, likely between the 3rd and the 7th of January. It is my belief that these 10 GIs were from either the U.S. 35th Infantry or 6th Armored divisions. However, ex-POWs from the 4th Armored Division might also be interested in trying to remember their first day in German captivity. So far, during my 50+/year residence in the United States I have been unable to make contact with any of these men. I would still like to know what was their fate after I had delivered them to the LAH headquarters. If they were not killed by Allied planes while on the way from the Battle of the Bulge area to a German POW camp, they should have survived. At the time I estimated that the age of these GIs was about two to five years greater than mine, and that would make the oldest of them about 80 years now. Hopefully the detailed description of this incident in this book will generate some response.)

Writing the above brought back another incident that had been hidden in my memory:

I do not recall what happened to the other soldier from my battalion who had assisted me in taking the American POWs to the Schimpach station. It may well have been that he already had different orders when we left the battalion command post at Tarchamps. But I do know that on the next morning, after a good rest in acceptable surroundings (a pot-bellied stove kept the waiting room of the railroad station warm), and undoubtedly after having a substantial meal, I had to make the trip back to Tarchamps by myself. Since Schimpach was in the area of constant American shelling, I remember that inside the waiting room I had been very careful in selecting a safe spot to sleep.

Taking the same route I had come, I passed by the two small railroad tunnels, both of which incidentally had been shored up on their ends with enclosures manufactured from heavy wooden planks. Near Schleif, only a few hundred feet from the spot where the parachutists had claimed to already have 300 American POWs inside "their" tunnel, I passed a team of Waffen-SS "strippers", soldiers of a *Nachrichten* (radio and telephone) company repairing the telephone lines that had been destroyed by American artillery fire during the night. Suddenly one of the soldiers sitting atop one of the telephone poles called me by name. Today I assume he was either one of the fellows I knew from the *Reichsarbeitsdienst* or from our company in Breslau-Lissa. After a little talk he told me that his outfit was in need of replacements, and why didn't I just stay with them. I thought that was very funny, but he meant it.

On the way back to Tarchamps I again avoided the roads whenever I could, but it is vividly in my mind that in the middle of the Doncols crossing sometime earlier on that day a German supply truck must have been hit, for the street was littered with cookies. Unfortunately, the constantly incoming American shells made it unwise to remain and pick some of them out of the snow. A few kilometers further, just beyond Sonlez, I was almost hit by an incoming artillery round. In the meantime I had become very proficient in discerning which of the shells was going to become a danger or not, and this time I knew by the sound of the whistling that it was going to be close. Taking cover had by then become an instinctive reaction. Before me I saw a small, very low wall, probably part of a culvert, jutting out of a snow drift. I had barely flung myself on the street side of it when the shell detonated on the other side, not more than a few feet away. A lot of dirt flew atop of me, but I was unhurt.[28]

This column of assault guns driving in the snow-covered landscape could possibly have been the one that was on the way to the Doncols crossing on January 11, 1945. Of seven or eight *Sturmgeschütze* going to the front only two ever reached the American lines, all the other did not reach their target, for one reason or another. This left us without the needed cover.

---

28 When I visited the area with my father in 1970, I was able to show him the culvert and the pockmarked side of it that had borne the brunt of the exploding shell.

Chapter 18

Soon after New Year's Day, the German high command realized that the *Ardennenoffensive,* as we called the "Battle of the Bulge", had failed. By then the mangled divisions of the Waffen-SS were desperately needed on other fronts. The orderly withdrawal of my division from the Bastogne area began probably on the morning of the 10th of January 1945.

In his book "Hitler's Last Gamble", Colonel Trevor N. Dupuy, a renowned American military historian, describes our last couple of days in the Bastogne salient as follows:

"The 35th Division, still facing the dedicated and resolute soldiers of 1st SS Panzer Division, made only limited gains in its continued attacks in the Lutremange-Lutrebois area. Some elements of the division cleared Wartrange but were unable to fight their way into Tarchamps before making contact with units of the 26th and 90th divisions near Sonlez."

The LAH had already disengaged from the battlefield when the meeting of three American divisions at Sonlez occurred. However, the fact that both the U.S. 26th and 90th divisions had been able to reach Sonlez before the German retreat from the most exposed positions near the Arlon-Bastogne highway had been completed, led eventually to the encirclement and destruction of large parts of the German 5th Parachute Division. I was never able to discover how the 167th Volksgrenadier Division fared that had fought alongside the *Leibstandarte.*

I am pretty certain that sometime on the 11th of January my comrades of the fighting part of the First Company and I found ourselves again at Lullingen where the supply detachment was still located. The LAH was preparing to leave the Bastogne battlefield. As was usual in such circumstances, the day was likely spent with cleaning the weapons, seeing to it that the rest of our gear was complete, eating hot food, washing-up, and (especially in my case) sleep somewhere in the corner of a farm house where I had found a warm spot. Little did I realize that, as far as this *Ardennenoffensive* was concerned, the worst day was yet to come, not only for me but for most of my closest comrades.

Imagine sitting in a vicious snow storm atop a speeding *Panzer,* a steel hulled, tracked fighting vehicle that hurries at nearly twenty-five miles per hour toward the enemy, and also against a biting cold wind that drives tears to your eyes. Every few minutes enemy shells detonate dangerously close to the rough, pot-holed road, and at times one can hear shrapnel hitting the vehicle. All the while you have to hold onto some protruding part of the Panzer, the gun, an antenna, or some heavy clamps that normally hold some sort of equipment, lest you fall off and under the tracks of the other vehicles following yours. Yet if you grab the icy cold iron too hard, and if due to the holes in your gloves the bare flesh of your hands touches the steel, your hands may suddenly be fused to the metal, and almost impossible to get off again without the aid of hot water.

Thus began our trip from Lullingen back to the Doncols crossing on the morning of the 12th of January 1945. As a newly appointed assistant squad leader I was sitting with a machine gun crew atop the first of seven or eight armored vehicles, most of them assault guns, that had the lead of the newly created *Kampfgruppe* (Task Force) Keil, with other *Panzergrenadiers* (Armored Infantrymen) following in trucks, or even by foot, depending how close to the point of assembly were the companies from which they had been culled. The ad hoc *Kampfgruppe* was under the command of *Obersturmführer* Keil, the commander of the 8th Company of our regiment.

The vehicle I was sitting on was a *Sturmgeschütz III* (assault gun), a tank where the main mechanism of the long 75mm gun was not in a traversing turret but inside the hull.

In order to get to the assembly point near *Bahnhof Schimpach,* the little railroad station where about a week earlier I had delivered the ten American POWs, we had to turn off the major road that connected St. Vith with Wiltz, and make a right turn just before the village of Derenbach onto a smaller road going somewhat downhill toward Oberwampach. While this alleviated part of our worst exposure to the elements, namely the strong wind that had up to then blown into our faces, a new danger arose when we noticed that the tracks of armored vehicles are not very good on icy roads. While such vehicles are excellent in overcoming obstacles when they drive forward, they are almost helpless when they begin sliding sideways. And that is exactly what happened to our *Sturmgeschütz.*

In a narrow downhill curve where the driver had to do his utmost to remain on the road, his speed dropped to the point where he lost control of the vehicle. When we, the involuntary passengers atop the tank, noticed the sideways acceleration of a slide down a steep embankment, we had to fear that we would get buried by the overturning monster at the bottom, should it flip over. We had no choice but to immediately jump off, leaving our weapons behind.

(For decades after the war I believed that the tank had actually flipped over. But when speaking to local historians sometime in the 1980s, I found out that at the spot I so well remembered no overturned *Sturmgeschütz* had been found after the battle. I can explain this discrepancy best by pointing out that at the moment of the slide I envisioned the vehicle overturning with some of us being buried underneath it, and that this thought was retained, while the details of the actual occurrence were forgotten. It is probable that the assault gun was merely lying on its side after the slide had stopped, and that a recovery vehicle was able to pull it upright again and onto the road in the couple of days while the area was still in German hands.)

Once the vehicle had come to a stop in the deep snow at the bottom of the embankment, we retrieved those of our weapons that had fallen off during the slide, and some which we were able to pull from underneath the tank. I was able to find my rifle, but the MG-42 was a total loss. Bent out of shape, it was lying underneath one of the tracks. We had no choice but to continue our way to the assembly point without it.

The loss of this armored vehicle and of the main weapon of our squad should have made us extra cautious. But somehow this was not the case. In retrospect I assume that our oficers were convinced that the Americans had occupied the Doncols area only with light forces, and that our intensive knowledge of the village and its surroundings would be in our favor.

According to a note I had written long ago, we arrived at the *Bahnhof Schimpach* area around noon. We were cold and undoubtedly hungry. But instead of being able to warm ourselves in the little station and get something to eat, we found only desolation. The station was heavily damaged. The station master's house where a week before I had delivered the American POWs was a burned-out ruin. The small road nearby seemed impassable. Anticipating that we would soon commence our operation against the Americans, we, by now more than a company of mostly young soldiers, were ordered to take cover on a steep, forested embankment or hill behind the station building where we would be somewhat safe from the constantly incoming artillery rounds.

It didn't help that we were already thoroughly frozen from the earlier drive atop the assault gun. Sitting or lying in the snow between the trees, for I don't know how long made the situation only worse.

Today I assume that our waiting was caused by the fact that U.S. troops had in the meantime advanced in the area of Wardin, and this made it almost impossible for our commanders to bring the armored vehicles into a position where they could support us in our attack. At any rate, this all delayed the action far beyond the time necessary for it to be successful. I personally also believe that it made the results of reconnaissance excursions of the previous night invalid since it allowed the Americans to occupy positions that were by now unknown to our officers. But once the armored vehicles could not be brought in position to assist us, the attack should have been called off.

While we were lying behind the Schimpach station, a couple of non-commissioned officers came to us with bundles of extra coats and heavy camouflage jackets that had obviously been removed from wounded (or even dead???) comrades and were to be sent to be cleaned. The non-coms thought that we might have better use for them at this very moment. I was thrown a beautiful, heavily quilted camo jacket that had the army pattern of camouflage on one side and was supposed to be (but wasn't anymore) white on the other. I thought I was going to put it over everything I was wearing already - - it seemed large enough - - but then I checked the inseams and discovered that the jacket was totally infested with lice. Well, I remained rather cold than add more of the vicious critters to the relatively few lice that I knew were hiding in my clothes. (The crushing of lice had by now become a daily chore. The German armed forces did not have DDT. Our uniforms were periodically collected and disinfected with the now-notorious Zyklon-B insecticide.)

Finally we received the order to get going. Our slow and cumbersome steep uphill hike took us, single file, on a well-trodden field path from Schimpach station along the rim of the forest to the Bastogne-Echternach road only some two kilometers away.

For many years therafter I remembered passing by a substantial piece of iron standing straight in the center of the narrow path. In my mind, it had over the years taken the shape of a piece of iron rail, as if from a railroad, perhaps 4 feet tall. Walking the same route decades later I saw what it was: A round, tall, cast iron marker denoting the border between Belgium and Luxembourg as it had been delineated in the mid-nineteenth century. The unpaved field path was obviously the route take for many decades by people from nearby villages when they wanted to walk a shortcut down to the Schimpach station of the narrow-gauge railroad. To this day the border marker shows indentations of the many shrapnel that must have hit it in the winter of 1945.

Soon we crossed the Echternach-Bastogne road where the field way ended, then we ran, one after another, to a row of hedges on the other side of a larger field, and finally began to hike, still single file, in the direction of the important crossroads which I knew to be 1½ km (approximately one mile) to the south. It was foggy. One could see only a little more than a hundred feet ahead. We believed that we were still at least one kilometer behind the German front, a position perhaps being held by an anti-tank gun and some regular infantry. No order had been given to keep our weapons at the ready, and so most of us, including myself, had our rifles slung upside-down (so that the snow didn't get into the barrel) on the leather strap over our right shoulders.

To the left of us two additional columns of *Panzergrenadiers* could be seen, one hugging the road, the other in the open field between us. I assume other units were to the right of us beyond the hedges where I could not see them. The idea was that we all would spread out once we had reached the outskirts of Doncols and the few houses of the hamlet Bohey right next to it, and then attack the American lines with the assistance of the seven or eight armored vehicles that had been assigned to the *Kampfgruppe Keil.*

To the left of us, across the main road, was the deep, dark forest that covered the entire area down to the Schimpach station, the "devil's crossing" of Schleif, and the two railroad tunnels. In a small clearing of trees on the other side of the road I saw a low building that later on turned out to have been the official border post between Luxembourg and Belgium. I didn't give it much thought when I saw a seemingly destroyed or damaged Sherman tank, its gun turret awry, standing near the custom house, narrowing the road considerably. But it was perhaps my curiosity that kept my eyes longer than normal on the enemy vehicle, and thus I noticed a slight movement of something in a higher-elevated tree line a couple of hundred or so feet further alongside the road.

One second I saw out of the corner of my eyes an American soldier, probably someone in command, standing tall between the trees, the next instant he was down on his knees. I acted instinctively, yelling something to my comrades while throwing myself into the nearest earth indentation, while at the same time getting the rifle into a firing position. But at the same time the Americans, obviously well led, laid a fusillade of small arms fire on us that within two or three minutes left almost every German soldier in sight dead or so badly wounded that he could no longer move.

My rifle neither fired when I pulled the trigger, nor was I able to move the loading mechanism when I tried to unjam it. Even to this day I can only surmise that it had been damaged when it fell off the *Sturmgeschütz* alongside the MG-42. The only other weapons I had were the two hand grenades I had stuck in my belt. But although I was good at throwing hand grenades, I was not as good as a top baseball player, to to throw the things far enough to reach the American positions.

Where is our tank support? Where are the machine guns of the others squads? I did not recall hearing even one "MG-42" hammering away in all the racket. Suddenly I found myself alone and much too close for my own good to the Americans on a field strewn with German corpses. I could move neither forward nor backward. As a matter of fact, any move on my part would have meant certain death. For American sharpshooters I was a hare on a silver platter.

The furious shooting of the Americans had just abated when I heard from behind the familiar clanking noise of a couple of *Panzers* traveling the main road in our direction. They weren't going fast, and soon I watched the leading *Sturmgeschütz* of the *Jagdpanzer* IV-type going even slower when it tried to by-pass the "destroyed" Sherman tank on the little opening that was left between the road and the border post building. Just about when the German tank was side-by-side with the American vehicle, I heard a mine go off and the Sturmgeschütz stopping cold. Then, almost immediately after the explosion, I saw the crew of the *Sturmgeschütz* deftly booting out of their vehicle and, being covered by their comrades in the second panzer, make a hasty departure. I doubt that the remaining Geman tank fired its long 75mm gun even once before it began a slow withdrawal.

Almost the very moment when the mine exploded and incapacitated the *Sturmgeschütz,* one could hear loud, victorious jubilation from the American positions. They had reason to be joyful.

Then my excruciating wait began that is described in the beginning pages of this book: the shooting of the boy soldier; the "friendly fire" by German artillery; the slow freezing to death; the long wait for the darkness that might make a retreat possible. I assume that once in a while I fell into a kind of numb stupor, to be awakened every time I heard sporadic firing coming from the Americans.

From the moment when I first saw the American soldier - - whoever he was - - suddenly kneel down, probably giving some kind of command that was immediately drowned out by the furious rifle and machine gun fire of the GIs, I knew that we had walked into an expertly designed ambush. While the attention of most of us had been directed forward to a few farm buildings that lay between us and the Doncols crossing, and while we were expecting the command to fan out in attack formation, almost none of us had an inkling that an American unit had dug in to the left side of us and was ready to spring the trap with devastating results. Long after the war a historian told me that between 150 to 200 corpses of German soldiers were found in the vicinity of this engagement. I doubt that on that day, and at this place in the Ardennes, the Americans sustained any losses caused by German infantry.

There is a possibility that I did not even wear my steel helmet when the shooting began. In general I hated to wear the helmet and as a rule I put it on only when the situation got dangerous. Not expecting to be in an attack formation for another 500 meters, and noticing only sporadic firing by the enemy artillery, I may well have been in no hurry to exchange my warmer peaked cap (the one with the illegal Edelweiss emblem) for the cold steel of the helmet. What I do know for sure is that it was then and there that I lost my cap.

As it got darker, I began slowly sliding back into a clump of bushes beyond which I knew was a little incline out of view of the enemy. Then, always keeping an eye on the American position where by then, incidentally, nothing moved, I was finally able to scoot in a crouched position back to where I assumed the German lines were. Whether I took the hand grenades along escapes me.

Years later I estimated that I had been lying almost motionless for about four or five hours in that icy ditch. In retrospect I don't know what I then feared most, being shot by the Americans or the slow and quite noticeable freezing to death. The fact that most of the clothes I wore had been wet either from snow, or from sweat (when we hiked up the hill behind the Schimpach station at a good pace) greatly contributed to my physical discomfort.

While I was still crossing, ever so slowly the field of dead to the rear, and passing a German corpse every few yards - - the remains of soldiers, many of whom I had gotten to know in the last couple of weeks - - I suddenly heard the low whimpering of a wounded comrade. While crawling over to him through the deep snow, I must have been noticed by another SS-soldier who was, like me, seemingly unhurt. Together we pushed the wounded fellow onto a piece of tent canvas and then began pulling him toward the rear as if he were on a sled. Eventually one or two other survivors of the ambush joined us, and together we made our way back through the deep snow, away from the enemy.

Eventually, possibly a mile down the road, we entered the very first building we saw, and that turned out to be a German First Aid station, a farm house overfilled with wounded and frostbitten soldiers from the day's *malheur*. I realized that between the

Americans and this house that could be construed as a German line of first defense, we had not seen even a single German guard watching the road.

After delivering our wounded comrade, whose name and condition I never knew (seemingly I did not even ask, possibly being not altogether myself) a doctor came to me and asked me whether I had been shot. After hearing my "no" he inquired where I had been since the failed attack. I told him. Thereupon he asked whether I was suffering from frostbite. My answer was another "no". Then he ordered me to take off my boots so he could look at my feet, to which I replied that I could not do that, for if I did that I could not possibly put the boots back on again since my feet were that swollen.

"That means you are suffering from frostbite of unknown severity! Take the boots off!"

Following this direct order I had no choice but to comply. And after having taken off both boots and socks and looking at my discolored toes, I knew that the doctor had been right.

Thus my fighting days in the Battle of the Bulge were over.

Amazingly, the other parts of my body had survived the day's ordeal without any serious after-effects. If there were any, I did not notice it. (It took me 30 years to discover that a swamp fever contracted during the fighting in Hungary about a month later had caused my spleen to be enlarged to twice the normal size.)

For historians it bears remembering that this failed attack was the very last serious engagement of Hitler's *Leibstandarte* on the Western front. After that, nearly four months of fighting to the bitter end followed on the Eastern front.

Later I discovered that of the seven or eight armored vehicles that on the morning of the 12th of January set out from Lullingen only the two that I saw ever reached the front line. All others had mishaps of one sort or another. But the major factor for our defeat was the lack of good reconnaissance. It may well be that *Obersturmführer* Keil had received reports that the Americans were well entrenched just around the Doncols crossing, and that the area around the border post was still in German hands. Unfortunately, this *Obersturmführer* Keil died in the early 1990s before I was able to contact him.

Whoever was in charge of the American troops defending the Doncols crossing was an expert infantry commander. He placed his troops at the right spot and, rare for Americans, he was able to keep trigger-happy GIs from shooting too soon and thereby warning us before we came very close. I am not certain but I also believe that the seemingly destroyed Sherman tank was not damaged at all but placed on the spot close to the border post building so that a German tank - - almost sure to come - - would hit a mine placed on the narrow gap between the Sherman and the house. Luckily, someone took a photograph of that small battle ground soon after we experienced our catastrophe. (See the picture with the pertinent caption in the photo insert.) The German *Sturmgeschütz* shows obvious damage to one of the tracks, while the American tank that had been positioned directly on the road has obviously been moved.

Following is a translation of a chapter from volume IV/2 of the history of the *Leibstandarte* that was published in 1987, describing the action of the 12th of January. In compiling these facts my comrades of the LAH veterans organization had to rely mostly on the reminiscences of the still-living former soldiers of the division since most of the original documents of the division, including after-the-battle reports, did not survive the war (or else they are still hidden in American or Russian archives):

"After the bulk of the division had been withdrawn from the battlefield, and parts of it had already reached the Blankenheim area where the various units were temporarily quartered, a task force was formed from parts of the Panzergrenadier-Regiment 2, the Panzerjäger-Abteilung 1 and from Panzer-Regiment 1, and placed under the command of Obersturmführer Keil.

"The task force received the order to assemble in the Oberwampach/Schimpach area, and from there to attack Doncols so that the nearby important road crossing would be wrested again from the Americans.

"By noon of January 12th all units of the task force had been assembled in the designated area. However, none of the armored vehicles, except for two tracked assault guns (Sturmgeschütze), reached Oberwampach, and as a result our unit failed in this mission. During the attack on Bohey the bulk of the soldiers of the task force were stopped in front of the enemy lines, and then cut

down by the tremendous fusillade coming from the Americans before finally retreating with considerable losses."

An interesting sideline to this story is the following small item from Col. Dupuy's book mentioned earlier:

"The 90th Division's 357th Infantry finished securing Sonlez and then pushed on to take the high ground southeast of Bras. The 359th Infantry repelled a strong counterattack by the 1st SS Panzer Division, directed against the crossroads just east of Doncols. The 1st SS Panzer had been pulled into reserve on 11 January, and this counterattack was undertaken as a desperate emergency measure to open an escape route for the remnants of the 5th Parachute Division. However, the 90th Infantry Division, backed by its own tanks, held firm against these efforts, which petered out at dusk."

To the above, Col. Dupuy had added this footnote:

"Since the 90th Infantry Division was not really stressed by the counterattack, U.S. commanders did not realize the importance the Germans had attached to it until after the war, when German military records came to light and the real plight of the 5th Parachute Division became clear."

During the very early hours of the following morning, January 13th, while it was still dawn and before the American *Jabos* got busy, I was taken, along with some others, aboard an open vehicle (truck, Jeep, VW *Kübelwagen*?) toward the rear. The reason I remember it was an open vehicle is because it was the first time I was able to see the entire battle area of Schimpach, Oberwampach and Niederwampach unobstructed by trees and not during a snow storm. Eventually I ended up in the church of Eselborn, a small village near Lullingen, where nurses took care of my feet and where I spent another night sleeping fitfully at the base of the altar.

A few days of convalescence in the small city of Kronenburg not far from Blankenheim followed. My division had requisitioned a large part of a tavern, where as many of us as could fit into the large main room were lying as close together as possible on beds of straw, being well fed and also being tended for our frostbites.

The only thing of this episode I remember is the pot-bellied stove that stood in the center of the room and kept us warm, or too warm, depending on where we were lying. One day a young soldier was brought in who was surprised to see us searching our clothes for the ubiquitous lice we all had to contend with by then. He insisted that he was free from the blood-thirsty little beasts. After we had asked him how long it had been since he had taken a bath and changed his clothes, he guessed about two weeks, whereupon we insisted that he take off his uniform and look for any of the crawling, bloodsucking parasites. Since he was the newcomer he had to lie closest to the hot stove, and obviously he placed his wool pullover between himself and the stove in order not to scorch his bare skin that to us showed the tell-tale signs of lice infestation. Well, within a minute his pullover almost took off by itself. It was swarming with lice. Never before nor since did I see that many of them in one place. Since it would have been impossible to kill that many lice one by one, as we were doing every day, one of us just stuck the newcomer's pullover into a pail of water and placed it outside of the door into the cold. It is doubtful that any of the parasites survived in the sweater encased in the clump of ice that was presented to the young soldier the following morning.

I do not remember exactly how long I stayed at this make-shift hospital in Kronenburg while my feet and the tips of my fingers were treated for frost-bite. It could have been as long as two weeks.

Chapter 19

My feet were not completely healed and still needed light bandaging when one day I and a few other survivors of the *Kampfgruppe Keil* were transported to the aforementioned assembly area of the LAH. The remnants of the First company, fewer than 20 men, were quartered in a village not very far from Blankenheim. The name of this village shall, for reasons of propriety, not be mentioned. Too many years have passed since the two shameful incidents which occurred there, and told by me now, they might make some of the present inhabitants of this village feel bad about them.

Upon arrival at the company command post I noticed that one of the younger non-commissioned officers wore the nearly brand-new tennis shoes that had been a going-away present from my mother and which I had worn only a few times during off-duty hours. The comrade wearing the shoes immediately gave them back to me when I told him that I was the owner. He apologized profusely, telling me that the personal effects of those soldiers who had been officially missing since the ill-fated Doncols crossroads' action had been distributed among the living. I was thus informed that a missing-in-action report on me had already been filed, and that my family was informed. (Luckily, my mother, by then evacuated from our home in the Saarland and with a new address in Northern Germany, never received this message.)

After again being newly equipped almost from head to toe, and again in the possession of a rifle and other utensils necessary for combat, I was appointed a squad leader in the First platoon. With the company having incurred such heavy losses, I was at first in command of only three soldiers, all of them young boys approximately my age. I was still a mere private but the silver braids denoting that I was a *Führerbewerber* (officer aspirant) sufficed to create the aura of rank.

The LAH began the *Ardennen Offensive* with nearly 18,000 soldiers, and at the end had a final tally of about 14,000. Between December 16, 1944 and January 16, 1945, 774 LAH-soldiers were killed, 2,279 were wounded and 634 remained missing in action. Had it not been for the January 12th, 1945 engagement, the losses of the First company would have been slight. As it was, the company was devastated. - - Obviously I had been counted among the missing.

According to official U.S. Government sources, about 600,000 American GIs, and 55,000 British soldiers (of whom I did not see even one!) fought against 500,000 Germans. The alleged casualties were:

Americans: 81,000, including 19,000 killed.
British: 1,400, including 200 killed
Germans: 100,000 total

The German Historical Institute (an official arm of the present German Army) has provided us with these corrected German losses:

17,000 killed, 34,500 wounded and 16,000 fell into enemy captivity, for a total of 67,500.

Perhaps this is the place to answer the question whether I realized at the time that this momentous battle in which I had taken part for nearly a month would someday occupy a special place, if not necessarily in the annals of German but in American military history. The answer is no.

For the American armed forces the Battle of the Bulge was undoubtedly the greatest land engagement they had ever fought. In addition, at no time before or since, was a greater number of U.S. soldiers forced to lay down their arms and march into captivity as happened in the Schnee Eifel mountains in December of 1944.

For Germany the *Ardennenoffensive* was the last serious attempt to regain the initiative, and thereby gain the necessary time so that the new miracle weapons, among them possibly the Atom bomb, could be used against the major enemies.

As for myself, I only realized the extent of our offensive because I read every enemy leaflet I could get hold of. This provided me with a general overview of the situation, but our adversaries were obviously careful not to increase, among German soldiers, the belief in the Reich Government's abilities, and thus enhance our fighting spirits.

As the evening of my first day as a squad leader arrived in that small village near Blankenheim, a little farm house not far from the village church was pointed out to me, and I was ordered to take quarters there with my subordinates. In proper German fashion I was given a document to be presented to the potential hosts, announcing that they had to provide us with quarters. No time limit was stated.

It was already dark when we walked through the cold night toward the farm house. The star-studded, cloudless sky indicated that on the following day we would experience *Fliegerwetter*, a clear day where we had to reckon with constant attacks by the American Air Force. In the distance one could hear the rumbling of artillery fire near the front lines. My feet were still hurting as we walked in the deep snow, the frozen top layer of which cracked under our boots.

Arriving at the farm house I knocked at the door, hearing a little shuffling and talk inside before the door was opened slightly. Not seeing anybody in the darkness, I merely stated that we had orders to take quarters in this house, and that there were four of us.

I was totally taken aback when I heard the screechy voice of an older female saying so loud that we all could hear it, *"we do not take any SS into our house!"* And with that the door was slammed in my face.

For a moment I had to convince myself that we were still in Germany, on soil of the German Reich, and not in any of the occupied countries where one could expect such an insult. And what made matters worse in my opinion was the fact that it was extremely cold and that the four of us had just gone through a hard campaign lasting an entire month. All of us suffered from the after-effects of the ordeal.

I didn't even consult with my comrades about what to do next. Instead I pulled one of the long-handled hand grenades from under my belt and used this dangerous piece of weaponry as a door knocker, holding it in my hand in such a way as if I was going to detonate it any second.

Again there was some talk inside the house, some shuffling, and then the slight opening of the door. Due to the blackout very little could be seen, but I made sure that the dim light from within the house shone on the hand grenade.

"Do I have to blow the door to bits before you give us quarters?" I said, pointing menacingly at the hand grenade. With that, the old woman opened the door, and silently we entered a narrow corridor leading to the various rooms. Without saying anything, the woman led us through the small house, past the living room, kitchen and bedroom and finally opened the back door leading to the stables connected to the house, pointing to the hay or straw where we could sleep.

Later I discovered that the old couple were brother and sister, neither one of whom had ever been married. They did not look friendly or hospitable, and did not even offer us young soldiers as much as a glass of water, much less something to eat.

As combat soldiers we were used to sleeping in barns and stables, and in the four weeks of the Battle of the Bulge there were many days when we would have considered ourselves lucky to rest on a bed of straw in a stable oozing from the warmth of the animals. But in this instance, with a barely populated but heated house assigned to us as quarters, I felt that the offer of the stables was an insult to my comrades and myself, and I did something not quite charitable from the vantage point of today: I ordered the couple out of their living room and bedroom, demanding these rooms for the four of us, and told them to make themselves comfortable on the kitchen floor or in the stables, if they wished. Obviously none of us had any desire to sleep in a bed, and so the bedroom remained unused for that night, but we had our revenge.

We stayed in this farm house only one night. On the following day we helped prepare our battalion for a long trip to another front, packing weapons and supplies for a long trip.

Mentioning our bad experience of the previous evening at company headquarters, we discovered that others of our unit had had similar stories to tell. It seems that a few days before the arrival of the LAH in the area, the pastor in this fanatically Roman Catholic village had warned his flock during his Sunday sermon that the "SS" was going to be quartered there, and that the farmers should especially guard their young daughters from the beguilements of the equally young SS soldiers. The pastor allegedly had also told the villagers that all SS soldiers were heathens and had to disavow their Christian religion before donning the uniform with the SS runes.

One of us asked our young company commander whether something ought to be done about this traitorous pastor. He said no, "one can find such idiots everywhere!"

With that we left the village. I am not certain whether I would have been as benign as that officer, had I been in his stead. We were, after all, in Germany, and we did fight for Germany and, *ipso facto,* also for Christianity. (During the Hitler era most Germans still belonged to either the Catholic or Protestant churches, and on Sundays the churches were full. It took 50 years of "democracy" to bring down church attendance in Germany to a mere five percent (!) by 2001, and to see the transformation of many churches into museums, concert halls or the like. In the 12 years of the Third Reich more than 1000 new Christian churches were erected in Germany, none were destroyed by the regime, albeit thousand were destroyed in Allied air raids.)

I remember that during the Battle of the Bulge I once saw a German V2 rocket streaking high into the sky, probably on the way to London or Antwerp. And during a night watch in some village I saw a well-camouflaged, large trailer rig parked underneath a covering of trees, upon which something large was loaded that had only round forms. Lifting the all-covering tarpaulin (and taking care that a nearby *Luftwaffe* guard did not see me) I saw what could only have been one of these German miracle weapons. In retrospect I am pretty certain that this happened in the village with the mean-spirited farmers and the traitorous pastor.

On January 12, 1945, on the very day of my ordeal near Bastogne, the Soviet Union began its final assault on Germany that within a few weeks would bring it to the gates of Berlin. At the time the Red Army had been positioned at the Vistula and Narew rivers in the center of Poland. On this cold January day, three million soldiers of the Red Army crossed these rivers after a tremendous artillery barrage, and in some spots broke through the thin German lines defended by 750,000 German soldiers that were often lacking tanks, half-tracks, anti-tank guns and other artillery pieces. In spite of heroic resistance by the German soldiers, the *Ostfront* was breached, and within a fortnight the important industrial centers of Silesia were within sight of Soviet guns. Breslau was declared a fortress city, to be defended to the last man. The *Götterdämmerung* of the Third Reich had begun.

FPO No. 21825A To be placed into the pay book

NOTICE
about the taking of enemy property

It is not the intent of war that the individual shall enrich himself, come what may..

It is not chivalrous and certainly against the principles of the SS to take possessions from helpless civilians or from POWs.

The order by the leader of the SS regarding the sanctity of private property is also valid in the war.

Due to the principles of the SS, and as a result of the more stringent laws of war promulgated by the *Führer*, the removal of enemy property is sharply curtailed:

1. Without payment or receipt only the following items may be taken under special conditions:
Food, laundry, blankets, medicine, and
fuel. And this only for the very own
personal need under special circumstances
It is forbidden to take any of the following:
Silverware, civilian clothes, women's
stockings, etc. In other words, anything that
might be taken for relatives at home.
Nothing may be taken from POWs or from the dead.

2. Official requisitions (for the entire unit) are not allowed to be made by common soldiers or noncommissioned officers but only by officers from company commander on upward. These requisitions have to be made by an official unit which acts on orders from a higher officer, and they can be made either through payment in cash or with an properly signed requisition document.
In other words, common soldiers and non-commissioned officers may not issue requisition documents.

3. Everything else is considered an unlawful taking of plunder, the punishment for which is a death sentence. From the viewpoint of the SS, the taking of war booty is not merely a "gentleman's transgression'.

4. Property belonging to the enemy government is to be given to the proper authorities.

Chapter 20

As the end of January 1945 neared, we traveled by trucks and half-tracks to the extensive halls and buildings of a large plant, by the looks of it an iron foundry, at Bonn-Beuel, the suburb of Bonn that lies on the opposite side, on the right bank, of the Rhine. The plant was ideal for hiding our vehicles, and provided us with a place to assemble without being observed by enemy planes. It was there that we were ordered to remove the *Adolf Hitler* cuff bands and the interwoven LAH shoulder strap sleeves from our uniforms for reasons of secrecy. On our tanks, trucks and other vehicles we had to cover with paint and other means the famed passkey tactical sign of the unit. We were also forbidden to write letters home telling our relatives that our engagement on the Western front had come to an end. Being inside Germany and having access to both the regular post offices and even telephones, I doubt that this order was strictly obeyed. Henceforth, or at least for the time being, we were supposed to belong only to an *Ersatzstaffel Totenkopf,* the alleged replacement unit of the *Totenkopf* Division. (Our sister division, the SS-Panzer Division *Hitlerjugend,* traveled under the designation *Ersatzstaffel Wiking.*) The ruse worked so well that our enemies east and west really did lose track of the *Leibstandarte* for more than two crucial weeks.

Little did any one of us think then that in but four more years the sleepy little university town of Bonn on the Rhine river would become the German capital, and remain so until being replaced again by Berlin about half a century later. And none of us could have anticipated that the nearby Remagen bridge was going to become famous as the first bridge to fall into American hands only five or six weeks after our embarkation at Bonn-Beuel. Furthermore, who would have believed that U.S. Army stockades in the nearby Rhine river meadows would soon become the starving grounds for many tens of thousands of German POWs, and would become notorious as General Eisenhower's death camps known as the *Rheinwiesenlager*?

Long before and during World War II, but not anymore today after its "privatization," the German railway system was both incredibly extensive and extremely well-run. It contributed greatly to the fact that Germany, along with some allies, could fight nearly the entire world for six long years against overwhelming odds. The diversity of the German railway net assured that even after the heaviest air raids against a city that was a very important junction, cities such as Cologne, Hamm, Hannover, Berlin or Frankfurt, important trains could be easily re-routed, and traffic rarely came to a standstill.

The train that would take us to an unknown destination, but, we assumed, most likely to the Eastern front, was loaded within the confines of the Bonn-Beuel factory. It was still very cold. During the night those of us who had to stand watch were ordered to start the motors of the trucks every few hours, and let them run for ten or fifteen minutes so that the water in the cooling system did not freeze. It is possible that at this late stage of the war no regular anti-freeze was available. Thankfully, we did not have to worry about the air-cooled Volkswagen engines.

For our long trip to an unknown destination we boarded a number so-called German *Güterwagen,* the notorious cattle cars of "Holocaust" fame. These rail cars had been equipped with lots of straw for us to rest on, and in the center stood a pot bellied stove to keep us warm. All weapons and other equipment remained in our possession, including ammunition, hand grenades and other explosive devices. The wagon I was assigned to held most of the survivors of the First company, by then about 20 or 30 soldiers in all. After all the vehicles had been placed and fastened on flat-bed railcars attached to the same train, the engine was steamed up, and we began rolling east. Judging by the general direction the train had taken on the first day, we anticipated that we would be joining the battle against the Red Army somewhere east of the German capital.

By the following morning we had not traveled very far. It must have been shortly after five o'clock, still quite dark, and the first commuters were waiting to board their trains on the small station platforms we passed, when we traveled slowly through the railroad station of Marburg on the Lahn river, due east from Bonn and Cologne, and but 250 km as the crow flies from our starting point. We had opened the sliding door of the *Güterwagen* to see whether that early in the morning young girls were to be seen but we were out of luck. Offices and schools would open two hours later. Otherwise, all the people we saw were friendly and waved to us. Some looked surprised when from one of our railroad cars they could hear the sounds of American swing music. Music that was frowned upon but not forbidden by the system. It seems that some of our comrades had captured an American hand-cranked gramophone with modern records, and they made the best of it.

German troop trains were not very long, often consisting of but 30 of the relatively small wagons. It was nothing comparable to the mile-long trains we are used to in America. But most troop trains had anti-aircraft gun units attached to the front and rear of them, generally the deadly 20mm *Vierlingsflak,* the four-barreled kind that was the bane of Allied fighter bombers.

Throughout the war the SS Panzer divisions were used as some kind of combat fire brigades. This accounts for the fact that the LAH saw action in the Netherlands, in France, on the Balkan peninsula including Greece, on the Eastern front, in Italy, Hungary and finally in Austria. During *all* of the movements from one battle zone to another my division was transported by rail, *never* on the excellent German autobahn system. This belies the still-heard allegation that Hitler had the autobahn constructed for military strategic reasons.

Because of the cold outside, we kept the door of our 'cattle car' closed, and whiled our time away by playing cards, reading and sleeping. Our officers saw to it that we did not neglect our weapons, and that we attended to our personal hygiene. I do not recall standing watch even once on this trip.

Suddenly and unexpectedly one morning we found ourselves at a railroad siding near Nürnberg, the very city where within a year our surviving leaders would be hauled before a kangaroo court of the victors. I remember seeing, in the distance, the newly-built edifices of the *Reichsparteitagsgelände,* the huge open-air arena where Hitler made his memorable speeches to the German nation during the party rallies. The huge stone swastika whose back I saw atop the major building would be blown up by American engineers soon after the war's end.

At Nürnberg I got quite a scare: The weather must have been nice, and I had ventured out of our railroad car dressed only in uniform trousers and my pullover. I had no papers on me. If I remember correctly I had gone somewhere to get some *Ersatz* coffee or tea from the Red Cross or the *NSV,* the National Socialist "USO", to put it in American terms, that took care of soldiers on the go. All I was I was carrying was my canteen.

When I returned to the spot where I had left the train not long before, it was gone. And there was nobody around to ask what happened to both the train and my comrades. Since this was a major switch yard I decided to try my luck at a narrow, tall building at the end of the platform, and asked the switch yard master whether he could tell me what happened to my transport. Seeing that I was really concerned, and that I had absolutely no papers on me, he exacerbated the situation by telling me that the train had left fast and full steam for a destination that, due to war time secrecy, he was not able to divulge. Only after he had gotten the most out of my obvious anxiety did he tell me that the train was parked in a safe spot not very far away for the coming night. He even sent one of his employees with me so that I did not get lost again. Returning to the train, I noticed with satisfaction that my comrades had been just as worried about my getting lost as I was.

Our unexpected arrival at Nürnberg opened up a number of possibilities as to our destination, and immediately the rumor mills began operating. One thing was now certain: we were not going into battle east of Berlin. Since we had been freezing so much in the *Ardennenoffensive* it follows that we would have loved a transfer to the "warm" Italian front, obviously none of us realizing that the weather in the Apennine mountains can get just as cold and miserable as it was in the Ardennes forest. Sure enough, within a few hours someone knew 'with absolute certainty' that Venice would be our next destination.

Once we got on the way again we could see by the names of the towns which we passed, and by the general direction of the train, that we would probably end up in Hungary. Already I regretted not having been very attentive when years ago in our Luisenthal school the Kingdom of Hungary was the subject of our instructions. As a matter of fact, I once got in trouble for not knowing which major rivers, besides the Danube, ran through Hungary.

I don't know how long it took, it could not have been more than a day, but suddenly we stopped during the night at a huge marshaling yard outside of Vienna. Always being curious, but also being mindful that the train could start moving again any minute, we opened our sliding door and in spite of my scare at Nürnberg I jumped out to "inspect" the manifest of a railroad car on the track directly next to us. This car was part of a freight train obviously traveling in the opposite direction, toward the Reich.

It was pitch dark but with a match I was able to make out that this car was from the *Wehrmachtverpflegungsstelle Bukarest* (German Army Food Supply Depot in Bucharest, Rumania) going to a similar unit in Germany. That was just what we were looking for. This railroad car must have been loaded a few months before, for I did remember that Rumania had fallen to the Soviets some time in the fall. In a jiffy a few of us had broken the seal of this car and slid the door open a few feet. What we saw made our hearts (and stomachs) rejoice: the wagon was brimful with boxes, barrels and other containers probably holding the most wonderful things to satisfy our palate. Just then we heard in the distance a loud whistle, and our train started to move ever so slowly, continuing on our journey east. There was no time to think or to be choosy. Speed was of the essence. First we grabbed an incredibly heavy barrel of what we believed was nice, sweet Rumanian wine, and in the last minute also a large box of nearly 100 pounds of something coming from a well-known German cookie factory. Then we closed the doors of both wagons again, and continued our journey.

To open the plug of the barrel was no problem. As usual we used our all-round tool for this task, namely, a bayonet. But to our dismay we discovered that the barrel was not filled with wine, as we had hoped, but with sweet sugar beet molasses, something we called "Fenner Harz" in the Saarland, named after a factory for this stuff on the opposite side of the Saar from Luisenthal. Harz *Schmier* or spread was just about the cheapest bread spread one could get in the depression times that had lasted until Hitler came to power. It was the poor people's preserves, and a favorite of the coal miners (who also liked the many kinds of sausages that were offered in the grocery stores and butcher shops). Incidentally, sugar beet molasses cannot be compared with the similar product made from sugar cane. To this day I like *Fenner Harz* which tastes best with lots of freshly churned butter spread on German *Mischbrot,* bread made of several different kinds of grain. American sugar cane molasses are good only for baking.

The 100 pounds of bakery goods we had captured from the Army railroad car turned out to be *Aachener Printen;* Ginger bread. We made the best of the situation and stuffed our bellies with ginger snaps which we had dipped into the black molasses.

Months later the thought occurred to me what would have happened if instead of 100 kilogram (220 lbs.) of sweet molasses we really had "liberated" a barrel of wine. There certainly would have been some happy faces and unsteady walkers upon our arrival at our destination on the following morning.

On one of the first days of February 1945 our train arrived at the important railroad juncture of Raab, or Györ in the native tongue, in Hungary. This industrial city on the Danube river, then with a population of about 50,000, is nearly 60 km east of Vienna, and is the most important municipality in Western Hungary. In ancient times it was the Roman city of Arrabonna.

Opening the door of our wagon we saw row upon row of trains such as ours, and others with brand new tanks, assault guns and SPWs (*Schützenpanzerwagen* - armored personnel carriers) obviously shipped directly from the manufacturing plants in the Reich. I was amazed that our enemies had not yet discovered this trove of armaments, and smashed everything to smithereens with their bomber fleets.

For us this was the end of the line. We knew that the combined German and Hungarian garrison of Budapest, reinforced by some Waffen-SS and Army divisions, was surrounded by the Red Army, and we assumed that we would be sent there to relieve the encircled units. However, later it came out that probably at the very same time when we arrived at Györ, the last defenders of the Hungarian capital attempted a break-out that ultimately failed.

As we were unloading our train, we scrambled to find enough containers for our molasses, the bulk of which was still in the barrel. We were very generous with the stuff and at one time there was a long line of soldiers filling their canteens with it. Eventually though, we still had to lift the half-empty barrel onto one of our trucks, come what may, under the circumstances the molasses had a certain value, and we did not doubt that we could use some of it for bartering purposes.

Of Györ I only remember a short march through dark, dreary streets to a building in which we were housed for just one rainy night. Along the way I found on the cobblestone streets small leaflets with the red hammer and sickle on one side, and some Communist writing in both German and Hungarian on the other. In the leaflets the Reds announced that the "liberation" of Györ by the Soviet Army would happen soon.

While we were stationed in Hungary during these two first weeks of February 1945, the Red Army created havoc in the German provinces of East and West Prussia, Pomerania, Silesia and Brandenburg, east of Berlin, murdering and raping hundreds of thousands of women in front of their children, while the Anglo-Americans destroyed, on and after Shrove Tuesday, February 13th and 14th, the beautiful cultural city of Dresden, killing probably 250,000 or more civilians. We heard very little of that. It may well be that we were too much concerned with our own fate.

One night two of us, both privates doing non-commissioned officers' duty, walked through the center of a Hungarian village, checking the guards of our respective squads we had placed at strategic positions. Among other things we talked about the partisan movement that was so very active on the Balkan peninsula. I do remember saying that if one of my soldiers were killed by an armed person in civilian clothes, I would have no compunction about having this person shot. While I understand people fighting for their freedom, I do believe that this should be done by soldiers in uniform and within the conventions of war. The current mode of making heroes out of partisan assassins and hunting real soldiers for legal acts of war bodes ill for the future.

After we had delved into the matter of underground movements, this other squad leader and I talked about our favorite subject matter, namely, girls. Hearing that he was from Cologne, I mentioned that during a vacation in the summer of 1943 I had been quite smitten with a beautiful girl from his home city whose voluptuous body had attracted not only me in the swimming pool at Bad Bertrich, the little spa near the Mosel river where my relatives owned a hotel. Hearing Bad Bertrich, mentioned his ears perked up.

"Do you remember her name?" he asked.

"I sure do," I answered, telling him. After all, we had even gone to the movies together. "I do recall her address," I added, mentioning the Cologne suburb where the girl lived. "Adolf Hitler-Strasse 12."

After that he was crestfallen. It turned out that Agnete, that was the girl's name, was his high school sweetheart. Thankfully I was able to tell him that really nothing happened between Agnete and myself. Politely I also forgot to mention the smooching that had kept Agnete and me from watching the movie.

The next stop after Györ was the agricultural town of Kisber, about midway between Vienna and Budapest. We were quartered in a school house at the edge of the city and, if I remember correctly, I never even once went into the heart of Kisber. It may well be that we were forbidden to do so due to the proximity of the Red Army, and the uncertainty of the war situation.

In Kisber our company almost reached full-strength through the arrival of about one hundred new recruits, mostly boys born in 1928. They all had had some cursory basic training but nothing like I had been fortunate to receive at Breslau-Lissa. As a squad leader I ended up an *Ausbilder* - a DI teaching the new guys how to be good soldiers.

Finally I was entitled to wear a handgun on my belt. It sure enhanced my "stature". The weapon I received was a beautiful, new, Polish-made Radom pistol. Except for target practice, I would never use this weapon in earnest. Not even during the house-to-house fighting in Austria in late April.

While we were at Kisber, we were very generous with our molasses (the carton with ginger snaps was emptied much faster). One day the barrel was sufficiently emptied that we decided to put it out to pasture, namely, in the school yard. I will never forget the following scene: A few young Hungarian children had been hanging around the school house hoping to get some hand-outs like chocolate, candy or cake from us. Watching as we were putting the empty barrel outside, but also seeing that we licked our fingers after having touched the rim of the container, some of the boys immediately went to check about the contents of the barrel the moment we had returned to our quarters.

I watched the children from a window on the upper floor as they called to each other in a language of which I did not understand a single word, a rarity in our part of Europe. Soon they were milling about the barrel like a swarm of bees, licking, screaming with joy, pushing, shoving and time and again coming back sticking their little hands into the open top of the container, and then licking their fingers again and again. The commotion did not even stop when a little tyke, too small to reach the top of the barrel, climbed on the back of one of the larger boys and fell head-first into the large round opening. In order to get the little guy out of the barrel again, someone turned it on its side, and before I had to attend to my duties again I saw the child crawling out of the thing, covered from head to toe with *Fenner Harz,* triumphantly licking not only his fingers but both of his hands that were black with the sweet, delicious treat.

Another incident that happened in Kisber stands out in my memory because it could have had very serious consequences. During an hour when we had to disassemble and clean our weapons, one of the new recruits had forgotten one of the cardinal rules when handling small arms for cleaning, namely, to see to it that the magazine holding bullets was removed first, and that the firing chamber was empty.

On this particular day I was cleaning both my rifle as well as the Radom pistol on a corner table, when suddenly the tack-tack-tack sound of a submachine gun or assault rifle being fired filled the room. We did what good soldiers do in such a case, and hit the floor of the room with a speed that would have made any staff sergeant proud. For a moment I thought that a Russian unit had managed to sneak through to Kisber and surprise us in our task.

Thankfully, the young culprit, one of the new recruits, had at least learned the lesson to *never* point even a (seemingly) empty gun at another person, and *always* hold the weapon so that its barrel pointed up toward the ceiling when not firing at an enemy or at the shooting range. A number of bullet holes in the ceiling were the tell-tale signs that he had heeded that lesson.

There must have been more than a dozen soldiers in the room when the gun went off. I am sure that for a moment we were all scared. The result was that the inadvertent shooter was beaten up by some of his comrades, but not to the point where he incurred any permanent damage. I am sure this was a lesson he was not ever going to forget again.

After we had managed to create an acceptable fighting unit out of our new recruits, we were part of one single large field exercise that took us through numerous villages in this part of Western Hungary. One of them, named something like *Mariakollnock,* was populated entirely by German farmers, and showed the prosperity I would decades later also see in the Lancaster County of the United States where the so-called Pennsylvania Dutch, Germans like those in Hungary, lived. The farm villages of the Hungarians we saw looked poor when compared to those of their German neighbors.

I never was able to discover whether our transport to Hungary from the Western front was from the start planned for the offensive operations which we commenced on February 17, 1945. It may well be that at first we had been shipped to Southeast Europe in order to relieve or even recapture Budapest. I do know that the last major German attempt to break out of the encirclement of the Hungarian capital occurred on February 11, while we were already in Hungary and still busy trying to integrate the new 1928 recruits into the fighting units. On the 15th of February the official communique of the *Wehrmacht* reported that the battle for Budapest had ended.

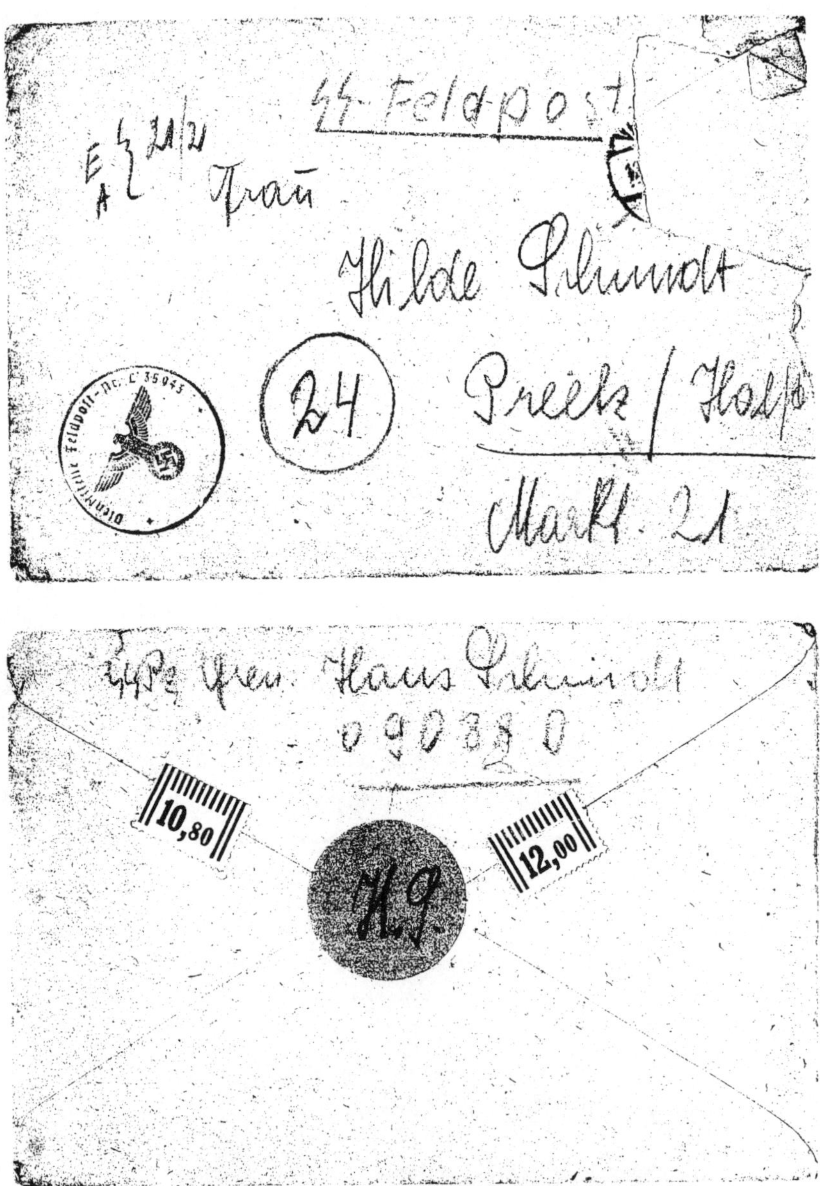

This envelope is from a letter I mailed from Hungary to my mother on or about February 5. Unfortunately, after the war, while I was already gone, someone of the family had removed the stamp and with it the postmark. This precludes discovering from where this letter had been mailed. Note that my mother answered on the same day she received the letter (Feb.21) but by then I was in the Burg Judenau hospital near Vienna. In case someone cannot make out my scribbling, I wrote "SS Pz.Gren. H.S." as sender. Probably because I was then a *Ausbilder* (D.I.) of new recruits I gave the APO No. 09088-0 of our battalion HQ.

Chapter 21

We did not know anything of our impending attack against the Russian *Granbrückenkopf* (the Soviet bridge head on the west bank of the river Gran NW of Budapest) when we left Kisber with all our vehicles and equipment, but this is par for the course for all soldiers: They rarely have an inkling of what the higher commands have in store for them. Secrecy requirements have priority over "the right to know."

It must have been on February 16th when we crossed the Danube river. A few hours later we moved by truck into positions not far behind the Eastern front that in this area was held by a relatively thin line of German Army infantry. The fact is, there were so few of these German soldiers that I did not even see one on this day and the next.

It was already dark when some of our officers and we non-coms got together and tried to find our bearings on a foreign-made map that seemed wholly insufficient for military purposes. Finally, one of the officers admitted that he had no idea whether we had reached our assigned destination or not. Worse yet, he wasn't even sure anymore where, in the dark, the battalion headquarters was located. I piped up: "I know where it is!"

As was my custom, I had watched certain landmarks pass by while we traveled on the half-track to the front, and I was certain that the command post of our battalion from which we had started out was not more than about 3 or 4 kilometers, less than an hour's hike, away.

The officer asked me: "Would you really be able to find battalion headquarters in this darkness?"

I was quite sure that I could, and soon I was on my way, this time alone, back to the command post, there to explain our predicament with the lousy map.

It was a clear, pleasantly cold night, and the ground was slightly frozen. Here and there one could still see patches of snow. Unlike behind the German lines in the Battle of the Bulge area, there was no enemy artillery fire here that interrupted my walk, or interfered with my thoughts. As a matter of fact, everything was very quiet.

At the battalion command post it did not take long until I had solved the riddle about the exact location from which our company was going to participate in the attack on the following morning. We had missed a narrow road leading to a small hamlet where we were supposed to spend the night by only a couple of hundred feet.

Taking the same route back, I was surprised to suddenly see in the distance, at about the half-way mark, a truck burning fiercely. From the looks of it belonged to the Red Army. While the flames lit up a larger area, I also noticed the wreck of a Russian T-34 tank behind a row of trees. But that must have been destroyed days earlier.

Loading a bullet in the chamber of my rifle, and holding it ready to shoot, if necessary, I approached this scene from the side, expecting any second to be jumped by either a German or a Soviet soldier. But nothing happened. There was absolutely nobody around, and no corpses of dead soldiers could be seen. Because of the potential danger I did not waste much time, but while I checked out the truck I removed a big round loaf of freshly baked bread from it, and then resumed my way back to the company, this time being more careful than when I had walked the same stretch an hour earlier.

My comrades were glad when I returned safely. They laughed when they saw me approach with the rifle at the ready in one hand, and clutching a big round loaf of bread with the other arm. Incidentally, it was deliciously baked bread made from sourdough. I liked it better than our *Kommissbrot.* During my absence my buddies had heard rifle fire in the distance, and they thought I had met an unfortunate end.

None of us could explain the puzzle of the Russian truck burning in the middle of nowhere. We could only assume that the truck driver and his comrades had lost their way and were surprised by a patrol of the German Army units still operating in the area. It may well have been that the Russians started to burn their vehicle before surrendering.

Once I had shown our location on the bad map it did not take the company long to reach the small hamlet that had been assigned to us.

The following scene is one of those that remains so clear in my mind as if it happened only a few days ago:

Soon after we had reached the village, I was ordered to report to the chief of our company, *Obersturmführer* (First Lieutenant) Teich. Entering the small, straw-thatched hut where the officer was quartered, I had to bend down in order not to hit the frame of the door, it was that low. Inside the hut it looked as if I had been transported back to the Thirty Years' War that more than three centuries earlier had devastated Germany. A fireplace constructed from field stones warmed the entire room that seemed to be kitchen, living room and bedroom in one. A small side door led to the stable. The room was lit by crude lamps fueled by oil or pitch. Our company commander, a young, very good looking officer resplendent in a beautifully tailored SS-officer's uniform which he had worn underneath his camouflage outfit, with the Iron Cross First Class and other decorations shining in the dim light, sat at an obviously hand-made table and wrote some report.

I myself, was dressed rather sloppily in a three-quarter length camouflage smock atop of which I wore on the belt and on shoulder halters all my accouterments of war. As was usual with many soldiers in a combat zone, but not in rear areas, I had the top button of my gray uniform unbuttoned, and, also as usual, for me, anyway, I wore my helmet against regulations pushed toward the back, away from my forehead because I did not like the leather of the helmet liner to press too hard on my skin.

For the short walk to the company commander's quarters I had left my rifle in the building next door, and when I walked into the hut I assumed a rather nonchalant position of "attention", lifted my right arm in the customary salute, and reported,

"Panzergrenadier Schmidt *zur Stelle*!"

I must add that this officer had been newly assigned to us and did not know me well.

At first the *Obersturmführer* commended me for finding my way in this pitch darkness to the battalion command post, and coming back with the needed information about our location. But he also mentioned the unsoldierly attitude displayed when I reported back to everyone assembled carrying a large loaf of bread. Then he asked some personal questions where I came from, what kind of training I had in Breslau-Lissa, and the like. After that he got to the point.

Looking at me, or rather at my disheveled appearance somewhat disdainfully, the officer then asked point blank:

"Schmidt, do you think you are a good soldier?"

I followed his look from my wrongly-worn steel helmet down to the unorthodox Italian hiking booths I was now wearing, and realized what he was getting at. In spite of standing somewhat at attention I shrugged my shoulders and answered him with a clear "*Nein*!" (No!).

Then, dismissing me and shaking his head at the same time, the *Obersturmführer*, a fine, brave SS-officer who would give his life for Germany but two days later, made a rather prophetic pronouncement:

"Schmidt, I would advise you go to America when this war is over. That is where you obviously belong!"

(Here I have to explain that Teich did not mean this as a compliment. He had probably fought against the Americans after the invasion or during the Battle of the Bulge, and might have been abhorred by the sloppy appearance of many GIs who had been taken prisoner. I probably had reminded him of that.)

I also must mention that before that incident I had never thought of either visiting or immigrating to "America". Our family was not one of the many families in the German lands that had contact with somebody overseas. This officer was possibly the cause for my arrival in the United States a little more than four years later.

As to the question whether I was a good soldier or not, that is even now - - more than a half century later - - difficult to answer. I personally never thought so. There was a war. In a great war all young men are expected to fight for their country. There was no doubt that I was going to fulfill my duty to Germany, and if necessary give my life for this greater cause. But I did not think that

I was really cut out for the soldierly life. I hated to get up before dawn every morning and take these awfully cold showers. I disliked sometimes being ordered around by lowly superiors whom I did not consider very smart. More than anything I did not care for the endless waiting for orders, standing watch, marching mile after mile on dusty roads, and all the other uncertainties and inconveniences that are connected with being a soldier. Quite simply, I yearned for civilian life in peacetime.

However, reading the biographies of exceptional German war heroes like Hans-Joachim Marseille, a ME-109 fighter ace with 158 victories (17 in one day!), or Erich Hartmann, with 352 aerial victories; SS-Captain Michael Wittmann, the most successful tank commander of World War II, with 138 tanks and 132 artillery pieces destroyed, and Hans-Ulrich Rudel, the famous Stuka-Pilot who destroyed 519 tanks, and innumerable other enemy material, including a battleship, it becomes apparent that neither of them was from the start what one would call a "good" soldier with perfect discipline who excelled under the authority of superiors. From that point of view I would have fitted in well with them.

Was I a hero? Most certainly not. I had received excellent training for the positions I was occupying at a given time, and whatever I did had been in the execution of my duty as a German soldier. I doubt that I exhibited signs of special bravery. Apart from a certain inherited audacity I had one other trait that separated me from my comrades of the same age group: the worse a situation got and the more stress we were under, the calmer I got. But in general I was as scared at anybody when the real shooting began.

The attack against the Russian bridgehead over the Gran river commenced in the very early morning hours of the 17th of February 1945. Soon after dawn, by the time we were picked up by a group of SPWs at the hamlet where we had been quartered for the night, the breakthrough had already been achieved by Peiper's *Panzers.* Our duty was probably only a mopping-up operation designed to provide our new recruits with the feel of the battlefield. Or it may well have been that we were the reserve for the following day's actions.

Soon after we had passed what had obviously been the main line of defense of the Red Army, a battle scene of smashed anti-tank guns and other arms, dead Soviet soldiers and haphazardly constructed defense positions, we disembarked from the half-tracks. At first we spread out in a long chain of soldiers combing the area as if we were on a fox hunt in Britain, but after an hour or so of hiking through the mud of thawing fields without any enemy contact, our officers decided that it would be better if we walked single file in platoon strength until forward observers made contact with the Russians.

The weather was clear, and one could see far. In the very far distance we heard the rumbling noise of artillery fire but where we were there was absolute quiet. No explosions of artillery shells, no rapid firing of machine guns, and no shots fired by rifles or pistols. Interestingly, we were also not harassed by Russian IL-2 ground support planes or others of their machines. (A couple of nights before we experienced our first attack by the Russian "sewing machines": Very slow, low-flying planes, possibly old bi-planes flown by women pilots who each dropped hundreds of small bomblets on our positions, often causing severe personnel losses among soldiers bivouacking in the open fields.)

The landscape was a typical farm area such as one can find in many parts of the United States: Slightly hilly with fair-sized fields that the year before had been planted with grain or corn, and that were now lying fallow. Thin, small patches of snow could still be seen in the lower elevations. Here and there I noticed little stands of trees or bushes. The tanks that had traveled this route before us had left deep furrows in the moist soil but they were so far ahead that we couldn't even hear the distinct noise of their heavy motors.

We must have been hiking in the direction of the artillery fire for about a couple of hours when we saw in this middle of nowhere, far from friend and foe and not within sight of any kind of dwelling, a single lone figure walking on a snowy field as if in circles. When we got closer, this human being turned out to be a Soviet soldier whose entire face was just one bloody mess of bones, sinews and flesh. The eyes were gone; where his mouth had been there was just a bloody opening. Even his chin was missing. I assume that his face had been destroyed by either a shrapnel or an explosive device such as from a direct hit from a bullet of a 20mm cannon. The poor creature walked only in large circles, not uttering a sound. I doubt that he was able to hear anything.

For some time I had been walking next to my platoon leader, a very experienced and well-decorated sergeant who, as it turned out, had been wounded no less than 16 times during the war. If I remember correctly, he had once lost an eye on the Eastern front.

The sergeant and I had been talking about rather mundane things when we came upon the wounded enemy soldier. When we came closer and saw the horrible shape the fellow was in, the sergeant quietly lifted his submachine gun, aimed at the wounded man, shot him dead with a short burst of fire, and then walked on as if nothing had happened.

I was shocked. I knew that there was nothing we could have done for the Soviet soldier. We had no way to transport him back to a field hospital. Yet I felt that we should have done something for him, at least console him for a few minutes in his agony. But a short burst from a submachine gun ended his life, and he fell down like a sack of potatoes, hiding his smashed face in the clean snow.

I am certain that people who have never been in combat will be reading of this scene with utter horror. Therefore I must point to the fact that war is about killing, and the more dead human cadavers one sees, the more callous one becomes. Perhaps I should even say that one "has to become callous" in order to survive in the type of carnage I and millions of other combat soldiers from all nations have experienced.

Without a comment about the incident we continued our hike, with myself being in deep thought and the sergeant nonchalantly smoking a cigarette.

Then, less than a half hour later, one of those inexplicable incidents occurred for which mankind probably will never find a satisfactory answer:

I had mentioned that during our mopping-up operation we did not receive any fire from anywhere. Except for the distant rumbling of the ongoing battle, nothing disturbed us as we hiked over the snowy fields. Then, suddenly, totally out of nowhere, came a single mortar round and detonated very close to the sergeant and myself, spewing shrapnel in every direction. I was unhurt, and so were the recruits following us, but the sergeant had received a deep flesh wound in the neck that was bleeding profusely, and it looked as if that was the end of him.

To the uninitiated I must explain that incoming shells fired from artillery pieces can be heard shortly before they detonate, and often there is time to take cover, even if only falling to the ground and hugging the soil. Mortars, on the other hand, are weapons for close combat, and sometimes the only warning one receives is the slight "click" one hears when the enemy launches a mortar grenade into the air. In addition, the trajectory of a mortar round is very steep, and it might fall almost vertically on the target, (like the V2s that hit London and Antwerp,) preventing an easy tracing of its source. I am certain that we did not hear the firing of the mortar round that wounded the sergeant before it exploded so close to us.

I was now in charge of the platoon, and I gave our medic the order to remain with the sergeant for as long as possible and see to his welfare. I was hoping that a vehicle would follow us soon and take the wounded man back.

(During the last battles in April I met the sergeant again. He had completely recovered from this wound. He told me that he and the medic had to wait for several hours until they both were picked up. I believe this happened after we had made contact with Peiper's *Panzerregiment,* and I was able to report the loss of our platoon leader.)

After the war, as my comrades and I were faced with the allegations that the Waffen-SS was nothing but a band of murderous villains, I often thought of this incident of war. Was it a war crime? If it was, it would have been the only incident I saw with my own eyes that could be viewed as such. But considering everything: the situation we were in, where we had not even been able to get immediate help for our own platoon leader, and the horrible shape of the wounded enemy soldier, where even the best front-line doctors on our side wouldn't have been able to help the poor guy except alleviating his pain somewhat, I came to the conclusion that the sergeant's act was a justified mercy killing.)

After we had reached both our target area as well as the limits of our physical endurance on the evening of the 17th of February, without anything else exceptional happening, we received orders to dig fox holes for the night's rest in a small valley. But just before it got completely dark I was able to reconnoiter the next day's prime target, a treeless hill, on the very top of which, about 1000 to 1200 feet away, the Soviet infantry and possibly anti-tank guns had built a strong defensive position.

I realized then that it wasn't going to be easy for us to dislodge the enemy on the next morning. I wished my platoon leader were still with us. As a squad leader I was in charge of 9 "men", most of them under 19 years of age, and half of them boys who were born in 1928. Some still didn't know how to handle our standard carbine 98k well, or even less the fast-shooting MG-42, in spite of our efforts in the previous fortnight.

During the night there was little chance for me to get any rest. It was awfully cold. In spite of that I had to go constantly from fox hole to fox hole and admonish the soldiers on watch to stay awake. Earlier I had attended a meeting of platoon and squad leaders where we were given our orders. Mine was to wait with our attack until I heard a specific signal from the new platoon leader who was to arrive shortly.

Sometime during the very early morning hours, just as dawn was breaking, the front came alive, and all machine guns on our side started firing without having been given orders to do so, including mine. I was puzzled. Standing straight up (and above) the fox hole of my two machine gunners, I tapped on their steel helmets from above and behind with one of my boots, and asked them why and at what they were firing. Scared, they pointed toward the hill. All I saw were fog shrouds rising from a small meadow between us and the hill. No Russian was in sight.

At about the time when we were supposed to attack, I heard battle noise in the distance, seemingly on both sides of our company. By this time it was light enough that I could see the positions of the other squads and platoons of my company. Nothing moved. Then, suddenly, a motorcycle with a side-car attached came from the rear directly to where we were lying. It was the *Bataillonsadjutant* (the assistant to the battalion commander) a junior officer, and his driver. He called me over to him: "Schmidt, *Obersturmführer* Teich and your new platoon leader just got killed. You must lead the company up the hill." Having said that, he took off again.

Here I must explain that I was the leader of the first squad of the first platoon of our company (incidentally also the first of the regiment). As such we held the central position of the attack (at least in our small sector). Thankfully, I had that excellent training throughout 1944, including being squad leader. There was nothing else for me to do but to send a couple of guys to the platoons to the right and the left of us and tell them that we would attack within a few minutes, and that they should watch either my signal, or the movement of my squad. And so it went.[29]

On the morning of the 18th of February, the Soviets were expecting us. Going up the hill our soldiers hugged the earth as they had been trained, and we had relatively few losses. Once I had given the order to go forward, there was little else for me to do but to always remain in the forefront. The noise of the battle was deafening: German and Russian tanks and anti-tank guns were firing, hand grenades were exploding, and everywhere one could hear the short bursts of small arms fire. Of interest was the different and slow staccato of the Russian machine guns versus our fast MG-42s. And, not to forget, the series of explosions caused by Russian Katyusha rocket launchers, the ones we called the Stalin organs (although my division was equipped with German rocket launchers, the so-called *Nebelwerfer*, I had not noticed them being deployed in this engagement).

We took the hill, and the Russians that were not dead or wounded took off downhill on the other side of the elevation. From the top of the crest I could see a wide valley in front of us. I presume that it was the Danube river valley (never having been

---

[29] From later reports I discovered that our unit of armored infantry did have the duty to conquer the more difficult-to-traverse terrain that was between the twin attack columns of the panzers of the *Hitlerjugend* Division, to our right, and of Jochen Peiper, to our left. In connection with the recent discovery - after 56 years! - of the burial place of Lt. Col. Bernhard Krause, the commander of the Panzergrenadier Regiment 26 of the *Hitlerjugend* Division, who died on the following day in the general area as a result of shelling by Russian Katyusha rockets, I am able to provide this small report of our attack as published in the October 2001 issue of the Waffen-SS veterans' magazine *Der Freiwillige, an excerpt* from the book *"Michael Wittmann und die Tiger der LSSAH"* by Patrick Agte (MUNIN Verlag):

"The attack reminded of our best days in the previous years; Royal Tigers, Panthers and SPWs drove as fast a possible and seemingly unstoppable toward the enemy. Soon the first vehicles hit mines, and became immobile. Both sides were shooting wildly but soon the mines were removed, and the way was free to continue the attack. (The villages that had been our targets) were retaken. The population was happy to see us, they had to suffer from the inhuman treatment by the Red Army soldiers. Women of every age had been raped - many had been kidnapped and taken into the Soviet trenches."

back to this area, even today I cannot be sure, but I know the battle took place 10 miles northwest of the Hungarian cathedral city of Esztergom).

Just about when we had reached the bottom of the hill, as some of our units were already on the flat expanse before us, and while everybody was still firing at the fleeing Russians, the soldiers manning our MG-42 motioned to me that they were going to be out of ammunition shortly. It was then that for the first time since we began the attack I looked back. A few hundred yards behind me, almost still on the top of the hill, I saw our "M.G. Schütze 3" (machine gun soldier number 3) the soldier who had the extra metal box of ammunition needed, lying in a shell crater. He didn't move. Since no one else was around, I had no choice but to run back, amidst exploding artillery rounds and machine gun fire, to where he was and get the ammo.

At first I couldn't see whether the soldier, one of the 1928 replenishments, was dead or alive but when I came closer I noticed that he was unhurt but hugging the wet earth in fright, crying. I crawled to him and yelled, begged, cajoled him to get moving, telling him that this spot was the very worst one in which to remain. Suddenly he grabbed the ammunition box and took off like a scared rabbit. He also did exactly what one should never do in such a situation: he ran straight downhill, without taking cover, without the ubiquitous short spurts of running hither and thither that are the life savers of a good infantry man. As expected, the Russians concentrated their fire, with rifles and mortars, on him from the distance (which endangered me also), and it didn't take long until the boy collapsed after being hit.

I ran to him but saw that, under the circumstances, he was as good as dead. His entire stomach had been torn open from side to side, probably from a large piece of shrapnel. I had only one First Aid kit with me. That wouldn't even have covered a fraction of the wound I saw. There was nothing I could do for him except tell him that we would get him to the First Aid station soon. As I took the ammo box and again made my way downhill, I could hear him cry for his mother. There was no doubt in my mind that he would soon die.

I must have been about halfway between the wounded soldier and the machine-gun, and running as fast as I could while intermittently still taking cover as I had been trained to do, when I suddenly saw out of the corner of my eyes a series of large shells exploding, making their way toward the spot where I was. A barrage of Katyusha rockets, perhaps as many as 32, was on its way to me.

I was just diving down, my rifle in my right hand and the ammunition box in my left, when a tremendous, powerful bolt - as if I had been hit full force with the sharp point of a pickax - slammed into my right shoulder and swung me around. One of the rocket shells had exploded right in front of me but only one jagged-edged shrapnel tore through my skin, partially severed the main artery to my right arm, and then got stuck on the shoulder blade, cracking it. I must have lost consciousness, for when I awoke (shortly?) my upper body was already totally soaked with blood.

I knew I couldn't stay there and let myself bleed to death. Leaving the rifle and the ammunition box behind, and grabbing something to hold against my wound in order to stem some of the considerable blood flow, an incessant stream pulsating out of the ugly opening in my body with every heartbeat, I made my way uphill again except that this time I chose a lower ridge to the left that had been taken by a neighboring company. "Our" hill would have been too steep for me.

Although my hearing had already been impaired by the loss of blood and I was probably in shock, at one time I heard, seemingly in the far distance, a Russian machine gun firing, and at the same time I saw the earth around me being churned by bullets hitting the ground. It neither scared nor bothered me, I just kept on walking. Then I passed two higher Waffen-SS officers who were watching the unfolding battle with their binoculars. One of them put a cursory bandage on my wound while asking my name and unit, and how things were progressing. When the officers asked me to remain with them until one of their runners arrived so that he could take me to a First Aid station, I declined. I was sure that I could make it by myself after they had pointed me in the right direction, a small Hungarian village perhaps only three quarter of a mile away. I told them that they needed the runner more than I did.

I do not remember how long it took me to reach the village with the First Aid station. But later (in a hospital) we discovered that my blood had reached the tips of my toes, and there was a tremendous amount of coagulated blood above the belt line, between the field gray uniform I wore and the camouflage smock that covered it.

Before I got to the First Aid station, a large, stately building, probably a manor house at the opposite end of the village that was marked with the Red Cross flag, I had to make my way through the single long street of the hamlet, oblivious to the shells of the Russian artillery sporadically exploding on and between the houses. German army soldiers who had taken shelter in the basements of the houses tried to convince me that I ought to join them. But I knew I needed immediate medical care, and kept on going.

I assume that I fainted on the steps of the First Aid station. I have never been able to recall my entering the building. When I awoke again (due to the noise of an exploding artillery shell), I noticed that I had been professionally bandaged but no medics were to be seen anywhere. I was lying on some sort of large table, possibly a pool table, shivering from cold and being covered with only one blanket. Next to me on the same table was a soldier who had four blankets over him. Although I could hardly move, I tried to wake the other fellow (punching him a bit), only to discover that he was dead. It wasn't easy but after I knew that he was gone I pulled all the blankets off him and used them for myself.

The First Aid station belonged to one of the regular army divisions that had been fighting alongside us. They must have contacted my outfit, for after a while (I remember it was still light), a half-track of the *Leibstandarte*, my division, came and picked me up, and within hours doctors of this famous unit operated on me, removing the shrapnel, and put my arm and shoulder in a cast. To this day I am proud of the fact that I was valuable enough to the most famous division of the Third Reich to be retrieved all by myself from a neighboring unit with an armored half-track.

It bears remembering that in February of 1945 I had still not reached my 18th birthday. Two months later, a day after my "18th", I was wounded once more, although lightly, and this meant the end of the fighting for me (albeit not necessarily of the still-ongoing war).

Chapter 22

March of 1945 -- the very month when the German Reich was being devastated beyond recognition beneath the onslaught of its enemies, and daily tens of thousands of my countrymen died - - was for me absolutely beautiful. It seemed as if nature had decided to make up for the mayhem which man was at that very moment causing all about us.

I spent that entire month convalescing, and being well taken care of, in the small castle of Judenau ("Jews' meadow", of all places) which is located about 40 miles west of Vienna in the so-called Tulln plains, part of the fertile Danube valley. According to old Nibelung sagas it was here where Attila the Hun met Krimhilde, the Burgundian princess and widow of Siegfried, for the first time. (Even at that time, more than 1,500 years ago, swarthy men preferred Germanic blondes. But in the light of recent discoveries of blonde mummies near the Chinese/Siberian border, do we know for sure that Attila was swarthy?)

In the early afternoon of the 18th of February 1945, shortly after a SPW of the *Leibstandarte* had picked me up at the First Aid station of the regular German army and taken me to a field hospital of my division, I was *almost* immediately operated on. Due to the great loss of blood, and the fact that the shrapnel had nearly severed the main artery of my right arm, there was no time to lose.

I remember waking up once during the operation - - coming out of the stupor induced by chloroform or ether - - only to throw up lots of green bile before being put under again. One of the medics later told me that the doctors had worked quite long on me. After I was "repaired", and lying on a stretcher in the long hallway of a building which I assumed to be a schoolhouse, I found myself quite immobile: My entire upper body was in a cast, with the right arm almost in a perpetual "greeting with outstretched arm"-position. Obviously bones had been broken or grazed. So that my wound could be tended to, the doctors had sawed a generous window in the cast. They had also discovered that my frozen feet, a souvenir from the "Battle of the Bulge", had not yet healed, and all my toes were swathed in bandages. In addition, I had somehow acquired "Volhynian fever" (a sort of swamp fever) while being in Hungary, and this was being fought with compresses and heat packs on my legs.

The field hospital must have been close to the front, for once in a while I heard the building being hit on one side by low trajectory shells, either from tank or anti-tank guns. Still, the doctors and (male) nurses operated with an incredible calm and patience. In the several hours while I was lying in the hallway watching the goings-on I noticed that the Waffen-SS medical personnel did not differentiate between the wounded, whether they were Waffen-SS, regular Army, Hungarian soldiers or even Russian POWs.

One very young soldier of my division spoke to me. He was also from the Saar region, from Dudweiler if I remember correctly, and had at very close range been hit in the lower right arm by several bullets from a Soviet submachine gun. One could clearly see the entrance wounds but no exit ones. The boy had been at the hospital for several hours, permitting other wounded to get ahead in line because he felt no pain. When he showed me his bullet holes, a medic noticed the absence of any bleeding, and immediately sent him into the operating room. Unfortunately, it was too late. The tourniquet around the arm of the young soldier had been too tight, and for far too long no blood had been allow to seep through the wounds. When I saw him next, his arm had been amputated.

Another young soldier who had been operated on just before me died while not yet completely out of the anesthetic-induced stupor. Due to the great lack of space in the room where we were all lying on stretchers, the medics came immediately to take the body away. But before they did so, they distributed his meager possession among the living. At that time of the war it was not possible anymore for combat units to mail personal items back to relatives. I inherited a small case with a foldable razor that years later accompanied me to America.

My memory of the next few days is rather hazy. I remember being loaded aboard a train in a small city named Neuhäusel in the German language, now Nowe Zamky in Slovakia. It is due north of Komarum on the Danube. Next I awoke in a hospital in Vienna, and (I assume) from there I was assigned to the convalescent hospital in the small castle of Judenau. How I got there escapes me today.

The several hundred wounded soldiers in the Judenau convalescent hospital were from all services of the German and other Axis forces. My bed was in a large room holding about fifty patients. The nurses, nearly all female, were either Catholic nuns or from the German Red Cross. One of my bed neighbors was a Hungarian cavalryman who could not speak a word of German, the other one was a very young, somewhat fat German infantry soldier, a *Mamasöhnchen* (a Mama's boy) who had been shot in the buttocks and made more noise crying about pain than other soldiers who had really been badly hurt. One night the Mama's boy overdid it with his crying and moaning, and some of the walking wounded took it upon themselves to give him a good but harmless spanking. Thereafter he only cried in his pillows.

One day higher ranking officers arrived and presented some of us with decorations for having been wounded in combat, and in other cases also for valor. I noticed the embarrassment of one officer when he did not know how to pin the Iron Cross, Second Class, and the *Verwundetenabzeichen* on my cast. Except for my head and my left arm there was very little of the flesh of my upper torso one could see. He finally merely laid the medals on my plaster cast, and shook my left hand.

Not having much to do, most of us wounded engaged for hours on end in long conversations about truly silly things, for instance whether we had ever eaten caviar and pineapple in peacetime. The fact is that talk about life in peacetime occupied most of our interest. On other occasions we conversed about the causes of the war, and what were now our German options. Among the fifty there was not one who still believed that the war could be won. I distinctly remember when one of the soldiers, a very Christian one, ventured the opinion that, "Adolf should have left the Jews alone, for in going against them another World War had become a foregone conclusion." It bears special mention that we spoke extremely openly and freely, far more so than is the norm in today's allegedly 'free' United States, and definitely more freely than is officially permitted in present-day 'democratic' Germany.

But being young and bored, we could also be cruel: One day a boy soldier who happened to be a farmer's son was assigned to our room and, for lack of other things to talk about, told us of his house pet, a white rabbit with red eyes. We all knew that white rabbits have or can have red eyes but that didn't stop one fellow from loudly disputing the fact that any animal, rabbits included, can have red eyes. When the rabbit's owner insisted that he was right, we all chimed in on the side of the detractor, and for days on end we assembled "scientific proof", including getting some wounded fellows from other rooms involved, that the farm boy was in this matter suffering from delusions. It took a week or two but after that the poor fellow sincerely admitted that he had been wrong. I guess that is the way the Bolshevists and do-gooders in America brainwash the gullible.

Another game we played was one called "two choices". It was a macabre game that was 'played' without interruption, day and night (someone was always awake), for an entire month. It began like this: We have two choices: Either we win the war, and then everything will be all right, or we lose it. If we lose it, we have two choices, we can stay here in the hospital and be captured, or we can try to make our way home on our own. If we get home, things will be all right but if we are captured, we have two choices: Either we are captured by the Americans, or by the Russians, whoever gets here first. If we are captured by the Americans, things will be all right but if the Russians come here first, we have two choices: Either they shoot us outright, or they transport us into the depths of the Soviet Union. If they shoot us, we are O.K. but if they transport us East, we have two choices, either we end up in Siberia, or we work in the coal mines of the Donez basin. If we end up in Siberia, this means the end, and nobody will ever hear of us again, but if we find ourselves in the coal mines in the Ukraine, we have two choices: Either they feed us enough to survive, or we die from hunger. If we die from hunger, we don't have to worry anymore, but if they feed us decently, we have two choices, ad nauseam - - - you get the point, I am sure.

We followed the course of the war on the radio and through the local newspaper. After six years of war most of us had become adept at reading between the lines, and when one day the news was broadcast that German forces had been successful in tightening the noose around the Remagen bridgehead of the American Army, we realized that one of the last major natural defenses of Germany in the West, the Rhine river, had been breached. I still remember when Patton's forces were fighting around Aschaffenburg, and somehow I was one of those who expressed the hope that the German defenses against the Americans were only cursory, for I wished that the Americans would join us in the battle against Bolshevism.

Toward the end of March I heard that my hometown had fallen into American hands. I wondered whether our house was still standing, for I knew that for about three months it had been within range of the American artillery. I believed, but still was not certain, that our mother with my younger siblings had again been evacuated, just as had happened in September of 1939 when the war broke out. Our home was smack in the red, or battle zone, along the French-German border, and in an otherwise strategically important area. However, the Saar basin is overpopulated, and has, apart from the coal mining industry also major manufacturing companies for all sorts of goods. I could only hope that the American artillerymen and bombing planes would find better targets than our home.

When writing to my family, in care of relatives in Northern Germany, from the Judenau hospital, I gave that facility's APO number (Feldpostnummer 35521) as return address but it seems that the letters took such a long time to reach them that I never received an answer.

I wrote the following letter nearly a month before Easter 1945 which during that year fell on the 2nd of April:

8 March 1945

Dear Mother:

I haven't heard from you but in case you wonder, I am wounded in a hospital near Vienna. I expect to be fine again soon. Since I am totally bored I will write you a letter.

When you receive my letters telling of me being wounded you may ask whether I am going to get convalescent furlough. The answer is no. After my recuperation, which I hope will be in about two weeks, I will probably join the battle against the Russians in Upper Silesia. That's still better than being in monotonous rural Hungary, where I was wounded. There I did not see a single two story building. But they do have much wine, tobacco and paprika, and in all three of these things I am not interested.

Even though the battles in Hungary were not fought with such intensity and great amounts of war material as I experienced in the west, I must say that all battles are executed by both sides with great tenacity.

Now that I have so much time on my hands, this gives me cause to think a lot, and I am also reading many novels, all of which deal with a normal life in peace time. This then creates a tremendous anger about this stupid war in me. How nice it would be if this damned war had not torn us apart. I can imagine that now, with the family that large (my little siblings growing up! HS) *we couldn't all fit at the kitchen table anymore and we would have to take our meals every day at the dining room table. But I wouldn't want to miss the little ones for anything. I hope they are all right. Please give my regards to everyone.*

Your son Hans, who today is dissatisfied with the world and himself.

PS: Did you ever get to Preetz?

PPS: Please answer to FPNR 09088B, or else your letters might not reach me.

28 March 1945 Dear Mother: Still no mail from you or anybody else.

I wonder where you and sister and the little ones are, now that the Saarland is in enemy hands. If you are in Northern Germany, as I expect, stay there, I doubt that it will come to a prolonged trench war there. And don't worry about me if through enemy action the North-South connection in Germany gets cut. I am certain that we will all celebrate next Easter together again. I haven't heard from Father, is he still stationed in Norway? And Richard? The last I heard from him he was with the Navy in Greece. I will be here until Easter. Then I go back to the front.

These letters reached their destination in Northern Germany shortly before the German armed forces capitulated. I am still surprised at the openness with which I wrote. At the time I was but one month away from my 18th birthday. Ironically, I then held the same rank as my fallen uncle Richard, my father's oldest brother, in 1916, when he died. However, since I did not know of my promotion to corporal in that week, I still used the designation "SS Panzergrenadier Hans Schmidt" as the sender.

My father's brother Richard, born September 1, 1898 in Luisenthal, died for Germany on the Russian front on December 11, 1916. Reading parts of my uncle's letters and diaries below, and comparing them to my writings, one great difference stands out: He seemed to have a premonition of his own death, while I was always convinced that I would survive the war (I clearly remember saying so, even when close combat was imminent). I also realize that in my uncle Germany might have lost a great future writer:

January 1915

Dear parents: "I would never have imagined that I would participate in a war, and have the honor to fight for the Fatherland. But as yet I am still at school, and await the call from the army. How can I stay at home when I hear of the heroism and the sacrifices of our brave soldiers? I simply have to be with them, even if a thousand chains hold me and the tears of my relatives make my decision ever more difficult. If I should die for my country then I will merely have joined so many others, braver than myself.

Today Aunt Mathilde told me "Richard, you will never come back again!" Yes, that's possible. But not every bullet finds its mark!

16 February 1915 *Today I was accepted as a volunteer to the* 7th *Ulan (Light Cavalry) Regiment at Saarbrücken.*

Summer 1916 *(Back at the front in Russia after having been wounded.) It has been eight days since I returned from furlough. How difficult it was to say goodbye to Mother, Father, sister and brothers. I could hardly hold back my tears when I heard their "God be with you!" and "Return home soon and healthy!". But why should one not cry when one's heart is so heavy? We all know a soldier's fate: Today his heart still beats, and the life's sun shines above him. Yet tomorrow the hand of death takes hold of the brave hero, never to let him go again. He will not experience the return of the victorious troops, and he will never again see that beautiful spot of earth where he spent the days of his youth in peace and happiness!*

23 October 1916 *In Poland, behind the front lines. I met a Jewish family in whose house I like to spent my free hours. But it is not just the "gemütliche" atmosphere in their home that attracts me, much stronger is the beauty of their young daughter Fanny. She has raven black hair, beautiful white teeth and a fine, rosy skin. She is the second Salome.*

26 October 1916 *It rains a lot. In the evening I ran to the people that have become so close to me. F. is very happy to see me. She doesn't want me to wear the ring my mother gave me when I left home.*

4 November 1916 *A beautiful day. Real spring weather. My thoughts are at home. Why can't we have peace?*

10 November 1916 *Last night we left the place where I have made such nice friends. It was very hard to say goodbye to Fanny. She is such a nice, dear girl who loves me deeply. I shall never forget her, and will always be thankful for the happy hours she gave me.*

It was still light when we rode out in the evening. I can't get over the separation from the girl who won my heart. Her father had tears in his eyes when I left.

2 December 1916 *We named our underground shelter "Villa Fanny"!*

11 December 1916 *All day long the Russians fired with heavy artillery on our fortifications. In some spots the trenches are totally destroyed ...*

Unteroffizier (Corporal) RICHARD SCHMIDT, age 18 years, 3 months, died a hero's death for Germany in the evening of 11 December 1916, when he inspected the trenches assigned to his squad.

Addendum to Chapter 22

Back to 2001 AD for a moment: As a result of undemocratic actions by the allied-instituted German *Bundesrepublik,* I cannot now travel to either Germany or most other countries in Western Europe.[30] An arrest warrant for my apprehension is still out, and if caught I could face a prison sentence of up to five years for no other "crime" but writing things in the German language that I am free to state here in the United States, but which are forbidden, likely by allied fiat, to be uttered and disseminated on German Reich territory.

Thus I cannot, at this time, visit my 97-year old dying mother, nor search in the place of my birth for important documents that might enhance the contents of this book.

As the manuscript was receiving its final editing, I was fortunate to receive from a relative a few of my war and postwar letters, the existence of which had escaped me.

Of special interest to the readers of "SS Panzergrenadier" is a letter dated February 25, 1945. It was the letter where I first informed my relatives of having been wounded in Hungary:

"Dear Mother:

Please excuse my bad writing and the fact that I did not write for quite a while. You ought to know that I am currently recuperating in a hospital, after having been wounded in the battle for the Gran bridgehead in Hungary on the 18th of February. My feet are also again frostbitten. On the 19th of February a shrapnel was removed from my right shoulder, but there was no damage to the bones. I can say that I was very lucky again.

Unfortunately, my right arm and upper body are in a tight plaster cast, and I am only able to move my right hand. It is assumed that the wound will take four to six weeks to heal. I like it

---

30 *The reasons for this injustice can be found in my book *"Jailed in 'democratic' Germany"* that is a true eye opener for Americans who are still believing in the benign influence of the so-called "American Way of Life" and its form of "democracy" on other nations.
My mother died on September 25, 2001, on her 97th birthday. Her last major wish to see me once more and say good-bye could not be fulfilled.

here very much. The food is very good. Unfortunately, I can barely walk because of the frostbite of both feet. As a matter of fact, I hardly feel the shoulder wound but the feet seem to hurt so much more. At the moment I am listening to radio music. Last night we heard a radio report from the front near Saarbrücken.

Please answer immediately. The last time I heard from you was on November 29, that is almost a quarter of a year ago. How are the siblings? And did you hear from Richard. Say hello to everyone. Your son, Hans

PS: I could use some writing paper."

This letter deserves a special commentary:

Please note in the text of Chapter 22 as it was originally written, that in the intervening years I had obviously believed that on February 18, 1945, soon after receiving my injury and after I had been cursorily taken care of in an Army field hospital, I was on the same day picked up by a *Leibstandarte* SPW and operated on within hours. This letter belies this. I can only assume that I was unconscious most of the time when I was in the care of the Army doctors and medics.

Furthermore, and perhaps most interesting, is the fact that I am writing of again having suffered frostbitten feet. I had totally forgotten this fact, and after so many years I am unable to remember how and where this injury did occur.

With this letter I was obviously trying not to alarm my mother. Reading of a needed convalescence of four to six weeks, and that my entire upper body was in a cast, she must have realized that the shoulder wound was not as benign as I had depicted it. The existence of the cast must also have told her that some bones had been hurt. And I must point out that I did not mention the swamp fever that I had contracted in Hungary and for which I was also treated at the Judenau hospital.

In the fall of 2001 it would have been a simple matter to correct the text as I had written it earlier. However, I decided to write this addendum in order to show how selective our memories can be after so many years have gone by. In another letter that was recently discovered I had written that in Hungary we were quartered with German farmers in a German village. Apart from remembering the *probable* name of such a village, my mind is blank about these days of rest, and of the people I must have met then.

Chapter 23

As soon as I was able to walk, I enjoyed going outside of the hospital area into the fields surrounding the village of Judenau. To be close to nature did wonders for my health. One after another the bushes, trees, flowers and grasses began to bloom and sprout new leaves, showing me that, no matter what, life will be going on, and even the most horrible of wars could not stop nature from creating new life.

There were days when I watched the Allied air armadas flying high above the Danube valley, only little hindered on their imperturbable way to their targets by small - all too small - formations of attacking German fighter planes. I counted hundreds of four-engine bombers with their death-bringing loads that not only killed indiscriminately but also destroyed irreplaceable cultural values which had been created over many centuries. It seemed odd but there were days when I felt that I had totally removed myself from the war, and that all I had to do was think of a peaceful future. No doubt I was sick and tired of the war and its associated restrictions and deprivations.

Although by the middle of March of 1945 the fighting on the Eastern front was much closer to Judenau than the battles against the Americans along the Rhine and Main rivers (120 miles vs. 300 miles distant), our main attention was directed toward the West and the advance of the U.S. Army. Sometime toward the end of the month, however, I heard from a recently wounded soldier of the *Leibstandarte* that our division had been engaged in battle against overwhelming Soviet forces almost continuously since I had left.

Particularly the fighting near Lake Balaton had been hard and costly. Tragically, my company had been in the center of a Russian breakthrough, and had ceased to exist. (Except for running into my former platoon leader during the last weeks of the war, the very same person who had been wounded in my presence on the first day of the attack against the Soviet bridgehead over the Gran river, I never met nor heard from anyone of the First Company in the decades since. I assume most of my comrades did not survive the war.)

As a result of the chaotic situation on the Eastern front where the Red Army had reached the outskirts of Vienna, all the roads leading toward the west were clogged with retreating troops and refugee treks. I went out of the Judenau burg as often as possible to talk to soldiers and civilians in order to get some idea of what was really happening. Under no circumstances did I want to fall into Russian hands. It was no secret that most German prisoners taken by the Soviets would end up in Siberia, perhaps never to return to the Fatherland. I also realized that, come what may, I had to regain my freedom of movement in the days and weeks to come, and I had to get a gun.

Already a few days before Easter I began pestering the doctors at the hospital to discharge me to my unit at the earliest opportunity. Invariably they refused since my wound had not yet completely healed, and the shoulder blade needed more time to mend. Other soldiers in my ward (none of them of the Waffen-SS) thought it was best for them to avoid going back to their units in what clearly was going to be the final death throes of the Reich, and one or the other placed strange matter, such as copper pennies, on their open wounds overnight so that they would not heal properly. Considering that the war was irrevocably lost, I did not regard such actions by these comrades treasonous. I was of the opinion that from now on each of us had to do what he thought best for himself and his family.. But I thought that it was utter foolishness to expect the Russians to abide by the Geneva Conventions and treat our wounded decently, and I said so. The fact is that in many instances the Soviet shot all the badly wounded they captured in German hospitals in order to make room for their own casualties.

It must have been on Easter Monday when I went outside of the hospital compound and discovered a supply column of the Waffen-

SS division *Das Reich*, one of the oldest elite divisions, moving westward. I immediately went to the officer in charge and asked him about the whereabouts of the LAH. He was not certain but on a small map of Eastern Austria which I had somehow been able to obtain (and which surprisingly is still in my possession more than half a century later), he pointed south to the likely area where I could find Hitler's best. It was only 30 or 40 km (20 to 25 miles) away, in a straight line.

Now nothing could stop me. The following day a friendly medic removed my cast and saw to it that I was well bandaged. Next I went to the *Kleiderkammer*, the supply room where the clothes and other personal effects were kept, and received, after having bribed one of the orderlies with a gift of rare cigarettes, my old but nicely cleaned uniform. The blood was gone, and the doctors who had operated on me had been so kind and put the piece of shrapnel that had slammed into my body in one of the pockets of the jacket. Alas, both the jacket of the field gray uniform, as well as the camouflage smock which I wore when I was being wounded, still had the holes made by the shrapnel. As it happened, to the very end of the war I never got around to mending the damage.

I also got my relatively new Italian-made mountain boots back, the belt with (now empty) ammo pouches, and the shoulder straps, among other things. My pistol was also without bullets. Missing was the steel helmet (although I discovered, incongruously, the camouflage cover of the helmet in one of the pockets of the uniform). Next I went to the doctor who headed the hospital and again asked for my discharge. Obviously knowing more of the precarious situation southwest of Vienna than I did, this time he gave me no argument about any advantages to be gained from staying at the hospital, but while he was signing the discharge papers and also made out marching orders (an absolute must in such disintegrating situations when deserters were shot without much ado), he cautioned me to be careful not to infect my wound. He told me that so far I had been very lucky.

The following morning after breakfast (probably consisting of Oatmeal, *Kommissbrot,* margarine, jam and *Ersatz* coffee) I walked out of the Judenau castle, and began my way south. Not a day too soon, as I discovered years later, for within a week after I had left, the first Soviet troops arrived near Judenau, having bypassed Vienna on the south from the area of their breakthrough through the German defenses near the city of Baden. By the end of the week German troops had drawn a perimeter around the Tulln area, including Judenau, that for a few days was defended as part of the Tulln bridgehead. An attempt was made to prevent important Danube bridges near Tulln from falling into Russian hands undamaged but the entire situation was so fluid that German forces were forced to dynamite the bridges before all heavy weapons could be brought to the other side of the river.

Searching my memory, I still see myself hiking southward along little-traveled roads, purposely bypassing larger towns which were most likely filled with refugees and soldiers and where accordingly it would have been more difficult to scrounge for food and drink. This area of Lower Austria is dotted with farm villages, and for me, a lone soldier, it was much easier to stop at a farm house and ask for something to eat than it was for a group of people, with or without uniform.

Somewhere I must have been able to get or liberate a rifle with some ammunition (in retrospect I presume that I received it from one of the Waffen-SS supply columns I saw near Judenau), but until I reached the *Leibstandarte* I was without a steel helmet, purposely I assume, since I never liked to wear these things in the first place. In place of my peaked cap, which I had lost in the Ardennes on January 12th, I wore a simple field cap that was a little too large.

What is most strongly in my mind is the beautiful rural landscape during sunny, mild spring days. I was neither scared nor worried, and actually marched rather leisurely toward what was certainly going to be new combat. It felt wonderful to be on the go again after nearly six weeks of enforced idleness, even though after a few kilometers my knees became wobbly. Somehow I also 'knew' I was going to be home in the Saarland again soon…

In the far distance to the east I did hear the rumbling noise of battle (it sounded like a continuous thunderstorm), and once, still on the very first day of my journey, a Russian IL-2 fighter bomber tried to strafe a rather small and unimportant bridge while I was still on it, surprising me while I was thinking of everything but war. Whoever was flying that plane was not a very good pilot, for he (or was it a she?) missed the bridge and me by a hundred yards. If that had been an American *Jabo* I would not have had a chance. But henceforth I made it my business to also watch the sky.

I ought to mention that walking south also meant walking from the lower elevation of the Danube valley toward the higher ranges of the Alps mountains. In other words, I had to walk uphill almost continuously. This made me tired much sooner than expected, and it must have been in the early afternoon when I quartered myself among other soldiers and refugees in the small school house of a tiny village.

On the following day a funny situation occurred, the likes of which happen only in the chaos of an ending world conflict, when empires fall apart, or in a revolution:

Having reached roads leading into the narrow valleys of a lower mountain range, probably still part of the famous Vienna Forest, I entered a small village where many of the townspeople were standing in front the guarded entrance to a natural cave that had obviously been transformed into some kind of air raid shelter. As always being curious to see what was happening, I went to the Army sergeant in charge of a small detail of soldiers being busy laying wires, and asked him about it. He told me that the cave contained a *Lager* (depot) of manufactured goods made by the famed Philips Corporation of Holland, which at the time also had a factory near Vienna, and that he had the order to dynamite the cave with everything in it so that it would not fall into the hands of the enemy who was as close as ten miles to this particular village.

Upon my request the sergeant permitted me to go into the cave, a well-lit underground storage brim full of boxes goods, and have a look around. But he also cautioned me not to linger, as he had in mind to dynamite the cave within twenty minutes. From the imprints on the boxes I could see that this storage contained mostly Philips radios of various sizes, from relatively small table-top models of the size like a car battery, to elegant "concert" apparatus the likes of which only rich people could then afford. (I ought to mention that for the last few years of the war no new radios could be freely bought in German stores.)

Without much ado I took three of the boxes with a small table radio each, tied them together with string that was lying around, and walked out of the cave. Before resuming my way I went again to the sergeant, thanked him and suggested that he let the villagers have some of the radios - this might be the last time for a long time they would be able to obtain such things.

Today I am not certain whether the sergeant followed my suggestion, but I believe he did heed it. If that happened then the villagers would have been able to enjoy their new property only for a few days, since the Russians, like the Western Allies, made the confiscation from the Germans (and Austrians) of all means of communication, including radios, one of their top priorities.

By noon of the same day the going got rougher as the inclines into the hills got steeper. I had hung my three radios on my rifle, and so carried them on my back. They were not particularly heavy but I was not very strong yet, and I felt the weight pressing on my back. Walking uphill through another small farm village, a boy of about five or six years of age walked beside me for a short distance, aping my larger steps as children are wont to do, when he asked,

"Soldat, what do you have in those boxes?"

"Radios!" I answered truthfully.

"Will you give me one?" was his next question.

Why not. I surely did not need three of them. Besides, two radios are easier to carry than three. So I parted with one of the sets, and the child ran happily home with it.

Hours later I was resting on the side of the road, and near the top of a steep hill, when I heard the noise of a truck coming from the valley below, obviously also traveling in a southerly direction. It turned out to be a large communications vehicle of the German Air Force. The fellows stopped when they saw my signal, and asked where I was going. I told them in the direction of Hainfeld. Well, they were not going that far but they would give me a lift to a point as close as possible to this small town. But first they wanted to know what I had in the boxes.

"Radios. Table radios," I muttered.

"We think that the lift is worth one of the radios," said one of the Luftwaffe soldiers.

I did not agree with that, since they were driving in that direction anyway. But seeing that they themselves had filled the free spaces in their truck with goods of all sorts, I told them that I was willing to part with one of the radios - for a price.

We finally settled on a bottle of Schnapps. It wasn't that I had in mind to use the strong alcohol for myself, but besides cigarettes, which the Luftwaffe fellows did not have, Schnapps was one of the best things to barter. (A half century later I do not remember what I finally did with the hard liquor.)

Later, after being forced to walk again ever higher, and before I got in the vicinity of Hainfeld, I passed a road sign that pointed east and said, "Laaben 2 km". Years after the war I discovered that on that day the village Laaben had already been in Russian hands. How easily I could have become the victim of a Red Army patrol that undoubtedly reconnoitered the area. Long after this incident I found out that at the time the German defenses in this sector south of Vienna had totally collapsed.

Shortly before sunset I asked the owners of a single farm house high in the hills, a farm that was already filled with soldiers and refugees, whether they had room for one more. They pointed to the barn. But before I could bed down among the free running chickens, suddenly German (Army) military police appeared and checked the papers of all the soldiers, including mine. I had nothing to fear but I did notice that they took some of the soldiers with them. If one or the other had been found to be deserters, they faced a firing squad. In every village there were signs posted in prominent spots warning soldiers not to get caught away from their own units without proper papers. They had been signed by the new commander of the Southeastern front, Colonel-General Lothar Rendulic, one of the best known Generals of the *Wehrmacht* who came from the former Austrian army.

Of the refugees, probably Germans from Hungary or Yugoslavia, I remember seeing a column of them walking slowly and obviously totally downtrodden next to their horse-drawn wagons that were fully laden with household goods, and old people and children. An uncertain fate lay before them. Often they pulled cows and other animals along. Once I saw a heart-rending picture where a calf had not been able to keep pace with the wagon to which it was tied, and had fallen down. Seemingly nobody had noticed that the poor animal had expired and that its carcass was pulled through the ruts of the unpaved road, leaving a trace of blood and guts along the way.

Getting closer to my destination, I noticed, here and there, small tactical signs of the LAH. Then, near a road fork, I saw standing next to a very old, small house one of the VWs of my division. I had arrived!

Not knowing who was in the house but assuming that inside I could find the driver of the car, I walked through the low door, and suddenly found myself in front of an *Obersturmführer* who probably couldn't believe his eyes when he saw a soldier of the *Leibstandarte* entering the room leisurely carrying his rifle on his back, with a small carton filled with something fastened to the tip of the gun barrel. Due to this contraption I was unable to remove the rifle fast from my shoulder and position it properly, just as I had learned one does when standing at attention in front of an officer.

Explaining my entire situation and that I was returning unhealed from a bad injury to the division on my own initiative, the officer took my explanation about the radio with a grin, and then he made, by telephone, arrangements that I should be picked up by a driver from my regiment.

"You know," he said as I was leaving, "the First company doesn't exist anymore. It was totally wiped out in Hungary!" Then, as an afterthought he added: "You were very lucky!" I assumed he meant that I would probably be dead by now if I had not been wounded at the Gran bridgehead.

When I rejoined my comrades, the division and its regiments had, due to heavy losses and no replacements, shrunk so much that all remaining units fought these last weeks of the war under the designation *Kampfgruppe Peiper*, ie. Combat Team or Task Force Peiper, commanded by the legendary Waffen-SS hero Colonel Jochen Peiper.

At the time, the entire complement of the LAH consisted of 1,582 soldiers who were equipped with just 16 tanks. (Compare this to its full complement of about 18,000 men and more than 120 tanks. The entire 6th SS Panzer Army, then composed of four armored SS divisions (*Leibstandarte, Hitlerjugend, Das Reich, Totenkopf* plus one each of a *Panzerdivision*, and an infantry division of the regular army), and had shrunk to about 7,000 men and 45 battle-ready tanks.

The rear units of *Kampfgruppe Peiper* were located just west of Hainfeld in the small village of Rohrbach. With others I was quartered in a large hall that in better times was used for dancing or the showing of movies. Since the area still had electricity, I was able to plug in my little radio, and enjoy it.

Obviously I had expected to meet at least some of my buddies from the Battle of the Bulge and the Hungarian campaign, but except for the often-wounded platoon leader who had been injured by a Russian mortar round on the first day of the attack against the Soviet bridgehead over the Gran river, I never saw anybody from our old battalion again.

Although my right shoulder had not completely healed, I was immediately put into service as an instructor for a motley crew of soldiers who in these last minutes of the Reich had either been just drafted, or else who had spent most of the war years in cozy positions somewhere in the German realm. Some had in six years of war not heard a shot fired in anger, and most had forgotten how to even handle a 98k carbine.

To my knowledge (which was soon proven faulty) I was still without rank, although by then I had papers indicating that I was an officer's candidate. Yet I was again made the leader of a squad of nine men, among them two former staff sergeants of the German Air Force, much older than myself. The oldest soldier in my squad was an "old man" of 36, a railroader whose wife and five children lived near Burg not far from Magdeburg. I never did find out how he ended up fighting in Austria at his age. It just did not seem right. My youngest charge was a boy born in 1929.

Among others things, it was up to me to familiarize my squad with the *Panzerfaust* (a single-use rocket-propelled antitank grenade introduced a year or two before) and forge them in the shortest of time into a cohesive fighting force. There was very little emphasis on what I would call barracks drill, only field training, but every 24 hours we did at least once have to go on patrol into the surrounding hills, particularly toward the northeast where great uncertainties about the location of the enemy existed.

During the *Panzerfaust* training, I made a serious mistake when I forgot to put a fuse into the head of the weapon (similar to charging a hand grenade) before one of my soldiers launched it against a hard target. As a result, it did not explode. Thankfully, no officer was around, and so I merely told my group that, "Obviously, in a real combat situation you have to charge the *Panzerfaust* this way," and I showed them how to do that. I doubt that anybody noticed my ruse.

Once, two of my younger soldiers were missing for a day and a night, and just when I was going to report them as being AWOL, we found them hidden in a haystack with two refugee girls. In general, though, the discipline was amazingly good, considering that we all realized we were now fighting for a lost cause. As far as I know there were no desertions or mutinies. I did not have any difficulties in having my orders heeded by those soldiers who now wore their Air Force or Army rank insignia (as sergeants or corporals) on their Waffen-SS uniforms; in other words, by fellows who under normal circumstances would have been my superiors. Eventually, after we were all outfitted with brand new (?!?) camouflage smocks, the designations of rank became invisible anyway.

I spent about one week in the Hainfeld/Rohrbach area. There was no visible fighting nearby, and except for the refugee columns which still made their way west, one could have assumed that it was peace time and that we were just on maneuvers. Probably due to inclement weather there was no activity in the air, either from the Luftwaffe or by the enemy.

Still being weak from my six-weeks hospital stay, I tried to sleep in my spare time as much as I could. When I was neither in service nor sleeping, I listened to my little radio. Foremost though, I kept up with the news. Again I followed the advance of the American Army across Germany, and in the south from Italy. There was only sparse news about the location of the Red Army.

One day, a soldier from one of the *Leibstandarte*'s panzer units came to me, and asked whether I would like to trade my little radio for a much bigger, better and more expensive one. Tank crews suffer notoriously from the cramped space in their behemoths, and in the vehicle of this soldier there was no room for the large, beautiful "concert radio" he had been able to "liberate" from the warehouse of a radio manufacturer (in this case not from the Philips Corp.) near Vienna, before the Russians were able to loot it.

The radio which I was offered was absolutely stunning, with push keys instead of knobs, and with a backlit name screen listing almost all European and international broadcasting stations. It was made of shiny wood veneer and its design was so modern that it was to take another ten years before I saw something similar on the American market. Even so late in the war, the sound from two speakers produced music coming from somewhere of such a high tone quality that I thought I was sitting in a concert hall.

In spite of all this I wasn't certain whether I should trade my little radio for this wonderful piece of equipment. Somehow I lived with the unrealistic hope that I just might be able to end the war still in possession of the little set, and that I could take it home with me. But just when I was unable to make up my mind, an officer stepped into the hall where we were quartered and informed me that we would be going to the front in a day or two. That clinched it. I traded. And for the next couple of days I spent every free moment in front of my new possession, enjoying not only classical music but news from all over the world (even though it was strictly forbidden to listen to enemy stations, I rarely heeded this prohibition). I don't remember it but I am certain that I also listened to foreign stations playing the then-popular swing music, which in the Third Reich was not played by the nation's broadcasters.

On or about the 10th of April I heard Dr. Joseph Goebbels speak for the last time. He was as eloquent about the historical events unfolding about us and as sarcastic about our main enemies as ever. His command of the German language was extraordinary. It was a pleasure to listen to that man. I doubt that this particular speech of Goebbels' contained any words of hope for a possible reversal of our fortunes. At any rate, I do not remember anything of that sort. Only fifty years later did I discover that this speech was probably only a recording, broadcast from one of the Reich stations still operating. But in April of 1945 that didn't matter.

Once, still in Rohrbach, when we came back from a patrol, I had to report to a high-ranking officer who wore the Knights Cross with Oak Leaves and Swords around his neck, and was dressed in a black (submarine) leather jacket. I only knew that he was one of the top officers of the First SS Panzer Regiment. One of my comrades noticed that I was quite impressed by the soldierly appearance of this commander and he asked me whether I realized to whom I had just spoken. I could only say that I did not know. *"That was Peiper!"*

Few soldiers in the Waffen-SS did not know who this legendary Panzer officer was. He was one of the best, bravest, and most-liked heroes of Hitler's Praetorian guard. A few months later, Colonel Jochen Peiper would face American interrogators who were out to blemish the excellent wartime record of Adolf Hitler's *Leibstandarte* with the allegations of the so-called "Malmedy Massacre".

About a week after my arrival, I am assuming approximately on the 12th of April, we were loaded onto trucks and transported through the Triesting Valley about 30 km (20 miles) east to the front. Then, the rest of the way, we had to hike up toward the tops of the mountain range that towers over the Hungarian plains. To my regret, I had to leave the beautiful concert radio behind.

One of the units we replaced was led by a corporal who had been one of my class mates, so to say, at the noncommissioned officer's course at Breslau in the summer and fall of 1944. He was surprised to see me without the silver braids around the collar and on shoulder straps that in the German armed forces denoted a corporal. He told me that as of March 23rd, I had been on a list of newly named corporals, and that for December of 1945 we had been ordered to the SS-*Junkerschule* (military academy/officers school) at Bad Tölz in Bavaria. In normal times this would have been cause for a celebration but now, so late in the game, it didn't leave much of an impression on me.

The following seven days are only haphazardly in my mind. I do not remember what we ate and where we slept, or what we did most of the time. What I do still remember are some particular happenings.

SS Panzergrenadiers dressed for combat. Even in the worst of situations some of us did not lose their sense of humor.

Chapter 24

For reasons that are now unclear to me, I have only retained fragments of memories of the following days. I surmise this happened because I was still relatively weak after sustaining the shoulder wound during the battles in Hungary, and from the strain of constantly having to exert myself so close to the enemy lines. Additionally, for someone not used to mountain climbing and hiking up steep slopes, every day brought new challenges.

I do not remember even one skirmish with the Russians, although some fighting must have occurred, as can be seen by one particular incident I am still able to recall:

One night we made an especially difficult march from one mountain top to another. Some time after a desperately needed rest, and after we were again trudging along, I suddenly remembered that in the darkness (and as a result of being exhausted) I had forgotten to pick up a second rifle which I had been carrying. Naturally, I felt bad about this, but there was no chance of going back and retrieving the extra weapon.

As a rule, we collected the weapons of our dead or wounded comrades after a battle, and turned them over to a collection point of our unit when the opportunity arose. The fact that I had been carrying an extra rifle seems to indicate that we had had several losses: a squad leader generally did not have to carry extra equipment.

On another day I had my first serious breach of discipline to contend with: during a particularly arduous hike in the steep mountains, the 36-year old soldier from the vicinity of Magdeburg adamantly refused to carry the MG-42 when it was his turn to do so. And none of the others volunteered to assume the burden.

What was I supposed to do? Shoot the guy who was physically in worse shape than I was and according to his age could have been my father? Screaming and yelling wouldn't have helped either. Without ammunition the MG-42 weighed a little more than 25 lb., and to carry anything of the sort up and down the steep slopes took the last bit of energy out of any one of us. On the other hand, I could not lose face by letting this insubordination pass without notice.

I am not certain whether I did the right thing but first I arranged for a longer rest than had been planned at this location. Then I told the "old man" to lighten his own load by having the others carry his personal ammunition pack, his rifle, his canteen and even his knapsack. After that I ordered him once more to heave the machine gun on his shoulder, making certain that he cushioned the sharp metal with his blanket. Thankfully, this time he complied without complaining, but because of his insubordination, I demanded that he carry the weapon twice as long as was originally intended.

It must have been a day or two after the death of Franklin Delano Roosevelt (April 13th, 1945) when I was ordered to leave my squad for the day, hike down the mountains, and deliver something to a command post that was located near the small town of Pottenstein, southwest of the city of Baden near Vienna. I remember the name of Pottenstein because I saw a big sign pointing to a factory producing nails ("NAGELFABRIK POTTENSTEIN"), and I would really have liked to see the machinery used for making nails. I assume I had to bring reports from the various patrols which we had undertaken the day before to the command post. At this HQ I found everyone quite elated, and when I inquired why, I was told of the sudden demise of the American president. Knowing full well that militarily the war was irrevocably lost, many Germans, including the officers of this staff, expected and hoped for a miracle similar to the one that had saved the Prussian King Frederick the Great from certain defeat during the Seven Year's War, and FDR's timely death might just be this miracle.

(The Seven Year's War lasted from 1756 to 1763, and involved almost all great European nations then in existence, among them France, England, Russia and the two major German states, Austria and Prussia. It was also fought on American soil. At the end of the war's fifth year, in 1761, the Prussian forces under the command of King Frederick the Great were almost totally defeated. The king had not only lost most of his troops but also the larger part of his kingdom, which was occupied by the enemy. Then the miracle occurred: On the 5th of January 1762, an enemy of the Prussian king, the Russian empress Tsarina Elisabeth, died suddenly, and her nephew Peter ascended as Tsar Peter III to the throne of the Eastern empire. Peter was a great admirer of Frederick the Great, and almost immediately began withdrawing his soldiers from Prussian soil (even leaving 15,000 troops to fight under Frederick's command). This development enabled Frederick to regain the initiative, and when a peace treaty was signed by all warring factions a year later, Prussia emerged as one of the new superpowers of Europe. As such, the State of Prussia was to play an important role in Old Continent politics until it was eradicated from the map by American and British fiat in 1947.)

Having been told to await further orders, I remained at this command post for several hours, and was therefore able to watch the officers and their aides perform their duties. What impressed me most was their calm professionalism at this time of extreme hardships and seemingly constant emergencies, and their never-ending concern for the soldiers under their command.

I myself wasn't certain what to make of all the hopes for a miracle, although I also wished that the Americans would come to their senses and fight alongside us to get the Red Army out of Europe. At that time most of us would gladly have subordinated ourselves to American command and undertaken the long road back to Moscow, to free the Eastern peoples from Bolshevism. In 1945 I did not comprehend that the head of the hydra was really in New York or Washington. This realization would come decades later.

At about that time, our company commander, the platoon and squad leaders, and a few of the older and most trusted soldiers, including myself, sat together one evening, and decided what to do now that the end of the war was near, and while certain defeat was in the offing.

We agreed that it was our duty to fight to the bitter end, and not to permit the Russians to breach our lines or to conquer any territory which we were still able to defend. We realized that the leadership of our country needed more time to get as many refugees back within the Reich borders as possible, and this could only be done if we held the front.

No new horror stories were needed to convince us of the necessity of avoiding capture by the Communists. Far more often than it occurred in the West, the Russians immediately shot immediately captured Waffen-SS soldiers that fell into their hands. And even if we survived initial capture, a transport to Siberia and an uncertain fate would lie ahead for us. In other words, captivity in American hands seemed preferable to that by the Russians in spite of bitter experiences some of my comrades had with U.S. soldiers in the Battle of the Bulge.

After we had agreed to stick together to the last, and not to forget our duty to our people and the collapsing Reich, we made one further deal: if any one of us was going to be wounded, however slight, in the next few weeks, he could count on the combined efforts of the entire company (then still about 80 men strong) to get him out of the combat area, and on the road toward home. There was no hint that we would try to avoid battle, if necessary, in order to save our lives so close to the end of the hostilities.

Going on patrol and reconnoitering enemy positions was a never-ending chore. I especially remember one late afternoon: A mountainous, heavily forested area. The famous "Vienna forest". Across a valley a mountain was aflame. Incessant small arms fire could be heard in the distance, without doubt a serious skirmish was taking place. The smoke from the burning woods was mixed with the pungent smell of the cordite from discharged weapons. On this particular day we had been out in the forest in platoon strength but seemingly without enemy contact. As evening neared, we were tired, hungry, cold and also wet from the intermittent rain. Suddenly, a beautiful building, a small castle of some sort (the hunting lodge of a princeling, I discovered later) could be seen nearby, and we hurried toward it, seeking shelter and perhaps something to eat.

I stood next to my platoon leader, a nineteen-year-old *Fahnenjunker* (ensign), when he knocked on the heavy oak doors. An elderly servant in an elegant livree opened it. Seeing us in our mud-splattered camouflage smocks, with unshaven, gaunt faces, and muddy boots, the servant's face became haughty. Behind him I noticed a long, candle-lit corridor lined with large paintings, and with beautiful oriental carpets on shiny parquet floors.

"You can't come in here," we were told in a commanding voice. But if we would go behind the buildings and make ourselves comfortable in the stable, someone would bring us some food and apple juice. And so, after a frugal but healthy meal, we rested for a few hours in the warmth and on the straw of a stable, where, until a couple of weeks earlier, fine riding horses had been kept.

I didn't say anything to the *Fahnenjunker* but I was thinking that if had I been in his place, I would not have allowed the servant to send us to the stables (even though under the circumstances I felt more comfortable in the stables than I would have been in a more refined setting). I would have forced entry for my soldiers behind the barrel of a gun, just to make a point. I was sure that the Red Army soldiers certain to arrive soon were not going to be as polite, and would not be satisfied with staying in the stable.

Another incident I remember clearly shows my attitude toward money: My squad had received orders to prepare a strategically located building for defense. That meant we moved heavy furniture and mattresses as additional bullet deflectors near the windows, and cleared all passageways in case we had to move out fast.

In this case the building was a rather nice country inn with a restaurant, and a well stocked beer and wine cellar. Knowing that in the coming battle the entire building was almost surely going up in flames, (the Russians liked to use incendiary grenades, and the like,) I did not mind when my soldiers enjoyed the food and drink on the premises. I myself filled my flask (strictly against regulations!) with red wine.

Suddenly one of the soldiers found wedged between the bar and a wall a big wad of money, possibly as much as 2,000 Reichmarks. (At the time, a worker earned about 200 RM per month.) The soldier then began splitting the money into equal parts for everyone to have his share. Under normal circumstances I would have insisted that the money remain untouched, but with the house almost certainly going to be a loss, I saw no reason to object. As for myself, I did not accept any part of the loot. I never could give a coherent reason for this action on my part, (and I never regretted my decision,) but it just didn't feel right to take any of the bills.

Just about the same time we came upon a soon-to-be abandoned warehouse full of equipment of the German air force. The most wonderful items we all saw were almost knee-high, zippered pilot's boots of soft leather, with a lining of sheep's pelt. Many of the soldiers in our company thereupon exchanged their regulation boots for this wonderful piece of footwear. Weeks later these fellows would seriously regret their decision: as the fighting ranged ever higher into the mountains, the pelts of the air force boots became water-logged, and the soles were very slippery. Then, at the beginning of May, after I had been wounded once more and was gone, it turned icy cold again and our outfit had many losses as a result of frostbitten feet.

Although I also would have liked to have a pair of the pilot's boots, I was too well satisfied with my still nearly new Italian-made hiking shoes to get rid of them at this time.

On the morning of the 19th of April we suddenly received orders to withdraw from the front along the Eastern Austrian mountain range immediately and without replacement. An obvious sign that something serious must have occurred. In the valley below we boarded trucks and half-tracks and soon made our way, at high speed, west toward Hainfeld, the little town which we had left in near peacetime condition a week earlier.

We made one stop on the way, near the town of Altenmarkt, and very near a battery of field artillery of the 12th SS Panzerdivision *Hitlerjugend*. The HJ division artillery pieces, of the 105mm caliber, if I remember correctly, were firing furiously but, to my surprise, seemingly without leveling the guns after each barrage, as was customary. I walked over, and asked someone in charge what they were firing at.

"Just in the general vicinity where we assume the Russians are", was the answer. "We want to expend all our ammo before destroying these guns ourselves."

It was then that I was told that the Russians had managed to break through German lines SW of Vienna, and that the area where we were located now was already cut off from the German main force. It was going to be our duty to reopen the cauldron. (Years after the war I read that in this general area many young Waffen-SS soldiers of the *Hitlerjugend* division had been killed by the Russians after they had surrendered. I suppose they were from the same unit I had seen on that day.)

Re-boarding our vehicles, we were told to get ready for battle. Then we roared off: Nearly a week of vicious street battles lay just ahead.

More than three decades after the war, while I was living in Palm Springs, California, I once received the visit of an ex-G.I. whose unit had been fighting against mine in the Battle of the Bulge. The late former Staff Sergeant Ralph Van Landingham of the 35th Infantry Division (134th Infantry Regiment?) had been fighting near the Belgian village of Lutrebois in the first week of January 1945, when he was captured by my unit and shipped to a prison camp deep inside Germany. As we talked, we felt more like buddies than former enemies: We had both gone through the same ordeal, albeit on different sides of the front. Ralph had been slightly wounded, and for him, as for thousands of other GIs captured in the "Bulge," the trip from Bastogne to a POW camp in the center of Germany was an unmitigated nightmare. But of this we at the front couldn't know anything.

During our conversation Ralph asked me whether I had ever been in any street battles, to which I replied with a firm "no". Seemingly I had (by then) forgotten what had happened in and near Hainfeld in Austria in the week from the 19th to the 26th of April 1945. Only later, when my comrades compiled a division history from scratch (since the official war diaries were either destroyed or had ended up hidden in some Allied archives, as did most Third Reich documents), did I try to reconstruct what we had been doing on any given day, and this then awakened memories that had lain dormant for so long.

Chapter 25

On the 19th of April 1945, hours after we had been pulled out of our positions atop the eastern reaches of the Alps facing the Hungarian plains, without having been replaced by other German troops and thereby leaving the front wide open to the Russians, we arrived in the little farm and vacation town of Hainfeld, near where I had been stationed only a week earlier. In the meantime the approximately 5,000 inhabitants of Hainfeld had been evacuated, and both Germans and Russians vied for its possession.

Already from the distance, as our trucks and half-tracks were racing toward the town, we could see the smoke from burning houses and the flare-ups of exploding shells. As we got nearer we also heard the rapid fire of machine guns, and various other battle noise. The truck on which I had traveled stopped right in the middle of the small city, not far from where only a week before I had enjoyed a good beer in a sort of Rathskeller. I noticed that this very same building was aflame, and there was nobody to fight the fire.

The next scene that is imprinted in my mind is one that again shows the surrealism or incongruities of war: After we had disembarked from the vehicles, and while the violent battle noise was all about us, we stood leisurely around, waiting for further orders. We had quickly discovered that the Russians had occupied some of the hills to the north of Hainfeld, and from there they were firing, mostly with light infantry weapons (machine guns, rifles, light mortars, etc.), into the town below.

The German forces in Hainfeld must have been relatively weak, and there was no noticeable defense effort, except from one of Colonel Peiper's "*Panther*" (Mark V) tanks, and a four-barrel

20mm anti-aircraft gun on a tank chassis, a "*Wirbelwind*" weapon system, both of which were furiously firing into the heavily forested hills. And so it happened that for a while we newcomers stood in the safety behind the constantly firing tank (a 45-ton behemoth) and the anti-aircraft gun, some of my comrades smoking their cigarettes, and we all were conversing about rather mundane things, but likely not about what was going on around us. (Due to the irregular delivery of provisions, food was constantly on our minds, but talk about girl friends was also not rare.) In such situations the German soldiers were superb, "*sie waren die Ruhe selbst*" - -they exuded an aura of calm and self-assurance.

While we stood behind the Panther, I saw several hundred yards away, I guessed nearly a kilometer to the north, on a large clearing atop one of the hills, within easy view of us, droves of Russian soldiers coming over the crest of the mountain, and immediately being mowed down by the immense firepower of the *Vierlingsflak*, the rapid-firing anti-aircraft gun, each of which 20mm bullets exploded on impact. The carnage must have been horrible. The distance from where we stood to the clearing was too great to enable us to aim and fire either our carbines or submachine guns, or use any other weapons at our disposal at the moment. As it was, it would not have made much sense. The saving of ammunition was also a constant concern. We merely kept our weapons at the ready, and waited for further orders.

As usual in combat situations, few of us had any real idea of what had transpired, or how the Russians got in the back of us. It was clear, however, that with their intrusion into the Hainfeld area they had managed to close a major escape road to the west for my division. As a matter of fact, while we were being transported out of the front-line from the eastern mountain range to Hainfeld, we had passed the town of Weissenbach where the staff of the *Leibstandarte* was located (it could well have been at Weissenbach where I gave a report on our situation a day or two after the death of Franklin Delano Roosevelt.) With the Russians now in or near Hainfeld, the divisional HQ was trapped.

From later reports I know that we had successfully reopened the east-west route through Hainfeld for a short while, and some convoys of vehicles managed to make a break-through toward the west. However, the village of Rohrbach, where I had had to leave my beautiful “concert radio” a week earlier, was never free from Russian observation and infantry fire. As a matter of fact, our medical personnel had difficulties getting a number of wounded out who had probably been convalescing in the same building where I had been quartered after my return to the division. The LAH division staff eventually had to select an almost impassable logger’s road leading south into the higher elevations, in order to avoid capture by the Red Army.

Many years after the war I read in after-the-battle reports that in the six days from the 20th to the 25th of April, 1945, Hainfeld changed hands several times. Since I was there during that time, I must have taken part in these see-saw battles (I am certain I was not hiding in a cellar) but what I can recall are merely fragments of occurrences:

I distinctly remember being one of the last soldiers to abandon the northern bank of the Gölsen creek that runs through Hainfeld in a west-to-east direction. We managed to do this not far from a fought-over railroad station, in the middle of a very dark night so that the Russians did not notice us, and had to cross the cold water of the creek atop a weir in order to accomplish this.

A day or two later, I assume, I was positioned near the eastern end of Hainfeld where a road bridge crossed the very same creek. Soldiers of the German Luftwaffe had placed one or two large aerial bombs (of about 250 lb. each) atop the bridge to blow it up when the order to do so arrived.

Realizing that with the dynamiting of the bridge some of the nearby buildings were also going to be destroyed, I went into the house closest to the bridge which had an apartment on the second floor, and helped myself to a clean suit of underwear (of which I was in great need) and about a half dozen neatly folded handkerchiefs of good quality. I never felt good concerning this “theft”, and for decades after the war I had hopes to be able to return to Hainfeld someday, and recompense these people. Alas, when nearly a half century later I was able to return to the area I discovered that this particular building had never been rebuilt after the war, and nobody remembered who had lived there so long ago: the property of the destroyed house had been needed for a new and wider river crossing.

(I was finally able to visit Hainfeld in the fall 1994. While taking photographs of the very same spot where we had been standing and conversing behind the Panther tank in 1945, an eerie thing happened: Suddenly I heard a very familiar noise, and one of the new tanks of the Austrian Army, the soldiers sitting atop the steel monster dressed in Waffen-SS-like camouflage uniforms, drove by. They were just on maneuvers.)

There were days when the Russians and we occupied one half each of the same building. It was nerve-wracking. Then submachine guns and hand grenades had to be used to clear the enemy out. Neither side had a chance to shoot with machine guns like the MG-42, or mortars (one of the favorite weapons of the "Ivans").

One night, during one such occasion, we received orders to withdraw from a particular area near the Gölsen creek, and it was my duty to inform some of the nearby units of our retreat. I went into the basement of a large building near the railroad station where I knew that an *Obersturmführer* with the last name of Nikolai (or similar) had his command post. I knew that this officer was a German from Rumania, and it was said that he had been the commander of a Rumanian submarine in the Black Sea before he had joined the Waffen-SS.

The officer was all alone. He had probably given his men orders to leave earlier. I can still see him sitting in the dimly lit room behind a table, atop which he had a bottle of wine. Next to it lay a pistol. He was slightly inebriated. When I told him that it was time to abandon position, he merely waved the handgun at me:

"Schmidt, get out before the Russians catch you. For me it is all over. We both know that with the war being lost, I shall never see my family again."

Before I could say anything, he again waved me out, and added only:

"Gleich mache ich Schluss!" (Soon I'll end it all!)

I doubt that I heard the shot with which this officer ended his life (there was a lot of other shooting going at the same time) but there was never a question in my mind that he had committed suicide. At any rate, I never saw this officer again.

(Friends reading this chapter before publication asked me whether at the time I considered talking the officer out of this final act. The answer is no. I do not think that under the circumstances the thought even occurred to me. First of all, I was but a lowly corporal and much younger than this man. Furthermore, under the horrible circumstances surrounding us I did not consider suicide a dishonorable, immoral or unethical act. That was a decision everyone had to make for himself. The feeling of *Götterdämmerung* - The Twilight of the Gods - was all about us.)

A couple of days after Hitler's birthday (which was on April 20th) we had just occupied a row of buildings near the southern part of Hainfeld, when we each received a piece of by then extremely dry and hard *Streuselkuchen* (crumb cake) that had probably been baked in honor of the Führer's "56th". It was a welcome addition to our otherwise scarce and bland food.

Shortly thereafter I received orders to prepare the house we were in, formerly the home and office of a dentist, for defense. Having lost some of my soldiers during the past days' fighting, some wounded, some dead, I received two young soldiers in regular German Army uniforms armed with a MG-42, as replacement. Today I must assume that somehow they had been separated from their own unit, been "captured" by Waffen-SS MPs, and summarily assigned to us. Since we were in a combat situation there was not much time to lose on amities: I asked for their names, wrote them down, and then showed them a corner room, from the window of which we had an unobstructed view of a row of gardens just below us, and also the houses and the hills to the north. No sooner had I returned to the part of the house where I had positioned our other MG-42 when we heard a shell from either a tank or anti-tank gun crashing into the building. Returning to the room where I had just left the two young army soldiers, I found only shambles. It had been a direct hit, and both fellows had been killed instantaneously. There was not much left of them.

Here I must inject that several after-the-battle descriptions of the fighting for Hainfeld contain reports about a superbly led Russian anti-tank gun. It was so well camouflaged that we never discovered its position, and its gunner must have been so accurate that he never needed what artillery men call "shooting in" before striking the lethal blow. This was proved in my case with the young infantry soldiers: One single shot was sufficient to eliminate their machine-gun nest. I am convinced that I had warned the young soldiers of this potential Russian danger but somehow they must have drawn the attention of the Russian "Pak" (*Panzerabwehr-kanone - anti-tank gun*) to themselves, and paid with their lives.

On the 25th of April it was clear that we had to abandon our last foothold in the now severely destroyed town. We had heard that the armored units of the *LAH* had retreated to the area near Lilienfeld, about 15 km to the west, and for us there was but one way to safety, namely to reach the higher elevations south of Hainfeld. This meant hiking up to 3,000 feet mountain tops. To the best of our knowledge, the entire western part of the town was already in Russian hands. Myself being the leader of the first squad of the first platoon again, we prepared defense in the very last house on a narrow road leading past the church up into the mountains. (A half century later one can still see bullet holes on parts of this church.) It was our duty to hold out until every last German soldier was safely out of the city, and in the forested hills above us.

Now we did something which we had put off to the very last moment: We ate our so-called *Eiserne Ration*, the "Iron Ration" emergency food supply that every German infantry soldier was supposed to carry with him. My last bit of food for a while was a tin of *Schoko-Kola*, dark chocolate that contained caffeine to pep us up in emergencies. And somehow I had been able to replenish my water flask with red wine again, but I drank it only sparingly.

Having ascertained that the fighting had almost stopped, and that we were the last soldiers still in Hainfeld, I sent my remaining soldiers, one by one, up the few hundred feet of grassy slope that separated us from the rim of the forest covering the hills. All went well, except for the fact that our "old man", the 36-year old father of five children, seemed to be so afraid of crossing the open area that instead of leaving with the first escapees, as I had ordered, he let all the others go ahead. Finally there were only the two of us left, he and I. It took me some time to convince him to leave the relative safety of the house with me, and run in short spurts in the direction of the trees. For a single German soldier to be captured by the Russians at this time would almost certainly have meant immediate execution. A run toward the forest was our only chance for survival.

I noticed that the soldier was shaking with fright. There was no doubt in my mind that the Russians were intent on not letting any one of us get away, and we had clearly noticed the short staccato of their rifle or machine gun fire every time one of our comrades had made a run for it. But as far as I knew, all men of my squad had safely made it beyond the grassy expanse before us.

I had the "old" soldier run almost next to me in order to make sure that he acted exactly like we had been trained to do in such situations. For these few hundred feet we made use of every furrow and every knoll, never giving the Russians time to aim their weapons correctly. We were spurting forward like rabbits on the run, and had almost made it when, perhaps 15 or 20 feet from the tree line and some hastily dug fox holes of our comrades, I heard simultaneously the tac-tac-tac of a Soviet machine gun and saw the earth around us being churned by bullets. Miraculously I was not hit, but my comrade let out a short cry and then lay still. Others came running out of the safety of the forest and helped me carry the "old man" behind the tree line. Several bullets had entered his body in the upper torso, and I assume that he had died an instant death. There was nothing for us to do but to bury him on the spot.

While I do not know what had transpired at the western end of Hainfeld because I was not there, I am pretty certain that the Russians had in the meantime taken possession not only of this part of the town but of several miles of road leading west to the small city of Lilienfeld. This would make me the last German soldier to have left Hainfeld gun in hand, (ie. not as a prisoner of war), in World War II.

(Twenty or thirty years after the war I read in a German veterans magazine that in the general area where we had buried the man from Magdeburg, the skeleton of a German soldier had been found in a shallow grave. I wrote to the authorities mentioned and told them what I have just described, but never received an answer. I am still not certain whether the skeleton belonged to the soldier from my squad.

Tragically, an American MP removed all the personal papers I had carried in one of the chest pockets of my uniform after I had voluntarily entered American captivity, and then threw these papers onto a huge heap of similar items that were then burned. Among these papers were the lists of all my comrades that had lost their lives in battle since December 1944, among them the names of the 36-year-old soldier, and also of the two infantry soldiers who had been killed by the Russian Pak. Then, after I got home from the war, all the Allies [including the Americans and the French with whom I was mostly in contact] for years prevented the Germans from establishing central registries where returning soldiers could inform authorities of the fate of their comrades. One must wonder whether this was done in order to purposely increase the number of missing soldiers? For it is almost certain that neither the family of the old railroader nor the relatives of the fallen young Army infantrymen ever discovered what had happened to their loved ones.

Similarly it was with the Jews and others who had died in the concentration camps. The Germans, being meticulous record keepers, had kept lists of all the deaths in the camps, except of those in the very last months of the war, and to this day there is no reason for most Jews not to know exactly what happened to their family members. But after having been used at the Nuremberg trials, these German concentration camp doçuments were stamped top secret by both Russians and Americans, and hidden from the public for half a century. No doubt this was done maliciously and so that no correct count of human losses in the concentration camps could be established. Sometimes lies are elevated to state policy that may not be questioned - - - and certainly not with documented facts.)

My last memories of Hainfeld and its surroundings were a heavily destroyed small city where a couple of weeks before not even a window pane had been broken through war causes. Just before we reassembled for our hike to higher elevations, there was a verbal altercation between one of our commanding officers and several members of the Luftwaffe crew of the *Vierlingsflak* that had supported our battles so courageously. It seems that the air force soldiers had to abandon their tracked vehicle in a hurry, and had been unable to destroy it completely. Thereupon one of the Waffen-SS officers wanted to order the *Luftwaffe* men, one of them a lieutenant if I remember correctly, to slip into town after dark and use a *Panzerfaust* to finish the work. The air men merely told our officer that he could not order them around, and left on their own shortly thereafter. My sympathies had in this matter been with them. It would have been suicide to try to sneak back into the city.

We, the remnants of the 2nd battalion, had no choice but to begin a long hike toward south, ever higher into the hills, while the Russians were following us with their tanks in the valleys below...

Regarding the fighting in and around Hainfeld there was little hand-to-hand combat at closest range, except during the couple of times when we practically occupied the same buildings. It was always our aim to keep the Russians at a distance, and it may well be that they, so close to the obvious end of the war, also did not want to risk their lives unnecessarily. I do not remember even once receiving or giving the order to place the bayonet on our rifles. As a rule we used a tactic that had enabled the German defenders of Stalingrad to hold out for so long: Machine gun positions became the pillars of defense, and it became the duty of every member of the squad to both safeguard the machine gun position and to keep this rapid-firing weapon supplied with ammunition.

The question must be asked whether the battle for Hainfeld was, at this late stage of the war, necessary, for it cost the lives of many soldiers and caused great destruction. My answer is this: In the larger scheme of things it was the duty of all German soldiers of the Eastern front, from the Baltic to the Adriatic seas, to prevent the Red Army from advancing too rapidly into the center of the Reich, and therefore also into the heart of Europe. There was also the concern for the millions of East German refugees who were ever so slowly making their way toward the west, for it had by now become known (at least to the higher staffs) that the Allies intended to depopulate a quarter of Germany, namely all of its Eastern provinces, from their purely German inhabitants, and resettle these areas with other peoples. At Hainfeld we assisted in preventing the complete collapse of the German front in Austria, and thereby assured that not only hundreds of thousands of South East European refugees but also great numbers of the brave soldiers from the Eastern front were eventually able to reach what they considered the safety of the American lines. That many of them were subsequently delivered to the Russians by the Western Allies, and thereby to almost certain death, or that many others would suffer and die later in Eisenhower's *Rheinwiesen* stockades and similar enclosures, could from our vantagepoint in Austria not be anticipated in April of 1945.

Passing a lone farm house atop the hills, in front of which stood, abandoned, a *Kettenkrad* (half-track motorcycle), I was wondering how on earth this vehicle ever got up so high. It may also have been at this farm house where one of the women asked us whether we were German or Russian soldiers. We could only tell them to get away from here fast because of the treatment women received by the soldiers of the Red Army.

It was not surprising that civilians were frequently unable to discern the nationality of the soldiers which they encountered in a battle situation. Although I had been interested in military matters since my childhood, I had never seen a Waffen-SS camouflage outfit before I joined this elite corps, and since the newsreels of the time were only in black-and-white, they did not provide a true picture. In or near Saarbrücken there were no Waffen-SS barracks, which further prevented my becoming familiar with the uniform I was ultimately wearing. Besides, by the end of the war, soldiers from all combating nations often wore not only different uniforms even in the same company, but had taken to individualizing their outfits with scarves or other apparel. During the Battle of the Bulge it was even worse, when both Germans and Americans froze equally badly in the cruel winter weather of the Ardennes; we (all) wore anything, and I mean anything, that kept us warm. Frequently parkas, gloves and wool sweaters scrounged from enemy vehicles. There were occasions when in a snowstorm German and American units walked past each other without recognizing the others as the enemy. Or some soldiers who realized the truth kept their mouths shut, because recognition would mean shooting, and hence possible death.

It must have been near this farm house, in a dense forest that covered a steep downslope just behind it, that we made our first major rest stop since getting out of Hainfeld. By then it was evening, and our officers decided not to go any further. It is possible that we received some warm food from the people at the farm before they heeded our warnings and joined the millions of other refugees then clogging the roads of Central Europe.

As usual, that close to the enemy, and while no fortifications of any kind could be erected, we took turns in taking short naps. While half the soldiers were on guard, the other half were allowed to sleep a bit. It must have been after midnight, at a time when it was my turn to rest, that I was suddenly awakened by an infernal noise: Shooting, screaming, yelling, explosions of hand grenades and the thumping sound of many men running here and there in the darkness.

I could not see anything. But before lying down I had unfastened my belt buckle, and slipped out of the shoulder straps, leaving everything that was connected to belt and straps close to my body. Not having time to come to my senses, I automatically grabbed only my rifle when the shooting started, and ran several hundred feet downhill toward a spot where we had earlier agreed upon to meet in an emergency, leaving the belt and all behind. Soon, however, one by one all of the soldiers of the platoon, which was now down to two squads, arrived. Not only was nobody killed but not even one of my comrades had been wounded. It seems that a Russian patrol had walked right into our position, and this patrol, probably consisting of only a few men (and not knowing our strength), used an old infantry ruse of creating as much battle noise as possible to extricate itself from a seemingly dangerous situation. We never did find out whether the Soviets had any casualties either.

As dawn broke, we cautiously went back to where I had rested. There I found my belt and shoulder straps, along with the pistol, bayonet, knapsack and flask, ammo pouches, map container, hand grenades, blanket and poncho, spade, and the gas mask container filled with things other than the gas mask, just as I had left it. It was obvious that the comrades who should have been watching had not done their duty. But what were we, the non-commissioned officers, going to say that would leave a deeper impression than the scare we had all just experienced? In the following night, the increased watchfulness of my soldiers would have other consequences.

It is obvious that this incident could have been much more serious, and possibly even cost the lives of some of us. If, for instance, the Russians had infiltrated our position in greater strength, and had been intent on killing as many of us as possible, who knows what would have happened. Had I been killed, I might have ended up one of the more than a million German World War II soldiers still missing today, for as a result of my having been wounded in Hungary, I had since February 18th been without my dog tag. It seems that the shrapnel which went into my right shoulder had also cut the string of the dog tag, and it was subsequently lost. There is also a possibility that a medic had thought I was "a goner" at the time when I was placed on that large table next to a dead soldier in the First Aid station of the Hungarian village, and had, for one reason or another, removed the entire dog tag from my body.

The presence of some civilians in the battle area of the lower Alps led to some unfortunate incidents, one of which is clearly in my mind:

Trudging from one range of hills toward another, we had to hike down into a narrow valley where we passed a small, still inhabited cottage before climbing up the steep slopes of the next range. Once we had reached the crest, we took positions toward the direction where we expected the Russians. A few hundred feet below us, clearly visible, was the cottage which we had passed earlier. After a few hours we heard the familiar sound of approaching tanks, and eventually the first of the enemy vehicles, a T-34 surrounded by a crowd of Soviet infantry, came into sight just about where the little house was located.

The T-34 stopped, and I saw from the distance, about 300 meters (900 feet) or somewhat more away, one of the Russians, obviously an officer, judging by the type of coat he wore, going into the cottage, and soon coming out again dragging an Austrian woman with him who then pointed in the direction where we were positioned.

I was lying next to our machine gun and was watching the situation through a pair of binoculars. Also seeing what was happening, the machine gunner lifted the weapon and would have fired, killing both the officer and the woman, if I had not pressed the barrel of the gun down, preventing my comrade from shooting. Unlike the finer-machined MG-34, the faster and more crudely manufactured MG-42 could not be used for single-shot firing. The least amount of shooting one could do with the MG-42 was a volley of about 20 or 30 shots. To me it was clear that even a small burst from this gun would also have killed the woman. And I saw no need for that. Even without the woman's pointing in our direction the Russians must have known approximately where we were. There simply was no other way to go. Killing just the officer, if that had been possible, would probably have had little effect on the battle effectiveness of our enemies, but *any* action on our part would have shown the Russians exactly where we were located. After the incident with the woman, the "Ivans", as we called them, continued their advance on the narrow mountain road, and except for the lead tank once pointing its 75mm gun menacingly at us, nothing further happened. By 1945 all armies had a sufficient number of experienced non-coms who could take over in emergency when their commanding officers became incapacitated. There were two other reasons why at that moment I prevented my gunner from firing: we had orders to fire only in defense, and, considering our general situation, it was wise to conserve ammunition.

Lest I am being misunderstood, I would like to make it clear that at no time were we a small band of lost soldiers trying to get back to the German "HKL" (*Hauptkampflinie),* the main battle line. We were the HKL. We had never lost contact with our higher staffs, and although at times we had trouble in getting supplies, this was more often the result of equipment failures or lack of fuel for transport vehicles than the unavailability of food or ammunition. At all times were we able to get our wounded first to a First Aid station and then to a regimental *Verbandsplatz* (regimental aid station), from where they usually were transported by half-track or a *Sanka* (*Sanitätskraftwagen*) ambulance to a field hospital. Whenever possible, our battalion slowed the Russians down, either through a serious defense at crucial spots or merely by having single soldiers destroying one of the leading Russian tanks with a *Panzerfaust.* This latter tactic was quite hazardous due to the Russian method of having their lead tanks surrounded by squads of infantrymen, and in the steep valleys it was very difficult for single *Panzerknackers* (infantrymen who used the *Panzerfaust* to destroy tanks) to make a quick get-away. However, after Hainfeld, my own platoon, or even the entire company, did not see any further serious action until I was once more wounded on the morning of the 28th of April.

I mentioned earlier how difficult it was for men and boys who are not used to mountain climbing or hiking to climb up the steep slopes of the Austrian mountains fully laden with weapons, ammunition and other necessities. Apart from the tremendous fatigue and the aching muscles, the constant thirst left our throats dry. The fact that for days I had kept my flask filled with red wine (which I always knew where to find,) ironically saved me from a misfortune that befell many of my comrades at this time.

After a long uphill hike without a stop we finally heard the murmur of a mountain creek in the distance, and almost everybody ran toward it to fill themselves and their flasks with clean, clear mountain water - or so they thought. I was not so much in a hurry as most of the others since I just had a small sip of wine (I rarely drank more at one time) and therefore was not in such a bad shape. There could have been another reason why I did not drink from this creek but by now I have forgotten it. Soon, however, I was glad I had not done so. Not more than 50 feet upstream we discovered the bloated corpse of a dead Russian soldier lying clear across the creek. There was no doubt in my mind that the water had been badly contaminated. (I do remember wondering how this Red Army soldier could have died so far in the rear of us. How did he get there? I never found out.)

In the following days many of our soldiers (not only from my squad) came down with awful dysentery. Their excrement was a bright yellow in color, and our numbers dwindled considerably as we had to send one comrade after another to the First Aid station and from there to a field hospital. One medical report of the time, published in one of the volumes of the history of the *Leibstandarte*, mentions one "death by malnutrition" at about this time. I assume that one of our soldiers was misdiagnosed; he had probably died from dysentery contracted after he drank the poisoned water.

April 27th, 1945, my 18th birthday, I "celebrated" without a platoon leader. This came about this way:

As a result of the previous night's fiasco, when the Soviet patrol stumbled into our position, I impressed on all the soldiers of my squad that henceforth it was in all our interests to remain fully awake and alert when on guard duty. I especially mentioned that they should never lose contact with our neighboring units, since I considered it important that a continuous line prevented the Russians from making a break-through.

The following night, after we had rested for several hours, suddenly one of the soldiers on guard duty crept up to where I was lying and told me that he had heard some strange noises coming from the position of the second platoon that had been next to us.

When I went there to investigate, I discovered that they were gone. What to do?

Informing my platoon leader, the 19-year-old *Fahnenjunker*, we both contemplated our next steps. Considering the events of the previous night, and the increased activities of the Russians on the previous day (we had heard considerable battle noise in the distance), and remembering also the dead Soviet soldier in the creek, I suggested that the Russians might have infiltrated and had caught the runner who was supposed to notify us of orders for retreat. If this had happened, it would take time for our other units to miss us, and if "*der Ivan*" was now between us and the others, it was unlikely that anyone could get through alive.

For the young platoon leader it was not an easy decision to make, but eventually he gave orders for all to get up and begin the single-file hike in a southerly direction, where we assumed the *Leibstandarte* was now located. It was our aim to try to find the rest of the company, no easy matter considering that it was so dark that we practically had to keep physical contact with each other in order not to lose the men in front of us. Due to the terrain we had no choice but to hike downhill. After a few hours of tortuous marching we were almost on flat ground in a valley, when contact was made. Finally, in the grayness of the early morning hours, I saw that the remnant of the battalion, or even a larger unit, was already assembled in the courtyard of a larger farm. One by one the arriving company and platoon leaders reported their unit's presence to a high officer standing in the center. Everything was done quietly and professionally, yet not with the stiffness of a barracks' drill. When my young superior reported the 1st platoon of the 5th Company present, I heard some very sharp words. The *Fahnenjunker* was dressed down for leaving his post without orders, immediately relieved of command, and on the spot demoted to private.

Later, while it was still somewhat dark, I saw him standing all by himself in a corner of the courtyard and crying. Feeling sorry for him (after all, I was partly responsible for his misfortune) I went to him and merely said, "Remember, it is better to be a live private than a dead *Fahnenjunker.*"

I was almost certain that the Russians would have cut us off and eliminated us totally, once they had noticed a gap between us and the German main force. I do remember that when we left without orders for fear of having been separated from our main force, we had been located in a position that was in a strategically excellent location, and, chosen for defense. Obviously, I never did find out what had been the plans of one our commanders before our unexpected arrival. Had we earlier been declared expendable?

After the early morning excitement, we continued our hike back up the mountains, always avoiding roads and age-old foot paths. Although I always tried to keep track of the days, and I knew that it was my birthday, there was nothing to celebrate. I doubt that I even mentioned it to anyone.

It was about at this time that I had a short meeting with my one-eyed platoon leader from the 1st Company, who had been wounded for the 17th time in this war (on the 17th of February) while I was moving forward right next to him as we broke through the Russian lines in the Gran bridgehead. He seemed all right, and had not lost his calm professionalism as a soldier that was the hallmark of so many German *Ostfrontkämpfer*.

On the evening of the 27th, we were in the hills above a village named Kleinzell, about 10 km south of Hainfeld, on the property of a farm with the quaint name *Kaiserhof* (if I remember correctly), when we were finally able to rest and lie down with thc conviction that the Red Army was still several kilometers away. True enough, the night was quiet, and to this day I am fairly certain that there had not been any shooting near or far. Still, we had received orders to dig fox holes, one of the ubiquitous and perennial tasks of infantry soldiers.

We had dug our fox holes next to a field road that traversed from the *Kaiserhof* along a mountain ridge. In front of us there was a steep slope going several hundred feet down to a beautiful valley. The opposite side of the ravine seemed equally steep and was also heavily forested. We were again in a good defensive position.

The early rays of the morning sun bathed the countryside with their golden hue when I awoke after a restful but cold night. I decided to "inspect my troops" before having anything to eat and drink. Since there was absolutely no indication of danger, I did not put on my helmet, nor did I crawl past the fox holes of my comrades in a crouched position as one does at the front; I walked nearly upright from one soldier to the other, probably talking to each of them. That was my undoing:

Suddenly I felt as if someone had hit me on my forehead with a hammer, and losing consciousness I fell down. When I came to, I tried to open my eyes but was unable to do so. My comrades had immediately come to my assistance. When they asked me how I felt, I distinctly remember telling them that I was blinded.

They laughed. While one of them washed the blood that had prevented my eyelids from opening from my face, another said only the word "*Masche*". Masche translated into English means stitch or trick. At the time it was in common usage, probably by German soldiers more than by civilians, as an expression for "being able to slip through", or "getting by with things". In my case it meant that this was the wound which was going to get me out of the war.

To this day I do not exactly know what hit me on the morning of the 28th of April 1945. When I could see myself in a mirror a few days after the incident, I saw an inch-long deep cut just above my left eye (depending on the weather, and when I touch it, I still feel slight pain on the bone about an eighth of an inch above the left eye socket). On one of the documents still in my possession, a doctor had written, "wounded by a shrapnel". However, I beg to differ with this diagnosis since a shrapnel has to come from somewhere, and there were definitely no explosions of any shells before or after my being wounded. I believe that I was hit by a rifle bullet, possibly fired by a Russian sniper over too great a distance so that it had lost some of its power. The fact that for days I had a large shiner and also suffered from a concussion seems to confirm my assessment. But it deserves remembering that this was the only bullet (or whatever...) fired at our positions during these morning hours while I was at this location.

Once I felt a little better, and was able to talk to my company commander, I prepared for my departure. I must not forget to mention that all of my comrades from the company commander on down were not only very helpful but sincerely glad that for me the war was seemingly over. Some of the things that I felt I would not need anymore, I left with my soldiers: the Polish-made, nearly new "Radom" pistol; the binoculars; some food; a map; and the U.S.Army-issue compass that had been given to me by one of the American POWs our battalion had captured near Bastogne during the Battle of the Bulge and whom I and another German soldier had taken back to the rear, and therefore to safety, under most difficult conditions.

Our First Aid station was located in the *Kaiserhof.* I was taken care of by a medic not much older than myself. He washed the still-bleeding wound, put a thick bandage around my head, and then told me to go back to the company. The soldier of my squad who had brought me downhill, one of the older ex-Luftwaffe sergeants, protested that I obviously had suffered a concussion, and was unable to take care of myself (I was unsteady on my feet, and couldn't see straight, albeit the loss of blood did not seem not serious.) The sergeant also pointed out that the company was so short-changed of men that nobody could be assigned to take care of me should another hike up and down the mountains be in the offing. But the medic remained adamant. It seemed that he had orders to send all walking wounded back to their units.

Without further ado, the ex-Luftwaffe sergeant led me further downhill into the valley until he was able to elicit from another soldier the location of the Regimental Aid Station, which was not very far away. Once we were close, he bid me good-bye and went back to the company. I walked by myself a couple of hundred feet to a building in front of which I saw a few ambulances and trucks marked with a Red Cross flag, only to discover that everyone was getting ready for a hurried departure. I was immediately supplied with an injury ticket, (similar to the large baggage ticket one used to hang on airplane luggage with a string,) assigned a seat in a truck full of other wounded, and a couple of minutes later we were racing further south and uphill, then on steep, serpentine roads over a mountain pass, and to the small town of Hohenberg about 20 km distant, where the center of operations of the *Leibstandarte* was located by then.

Chapter 26

Within an hour after arriving at a *Leibstandarte* hospital at Hohenberg I was aboard a small mountain train, sitting between other wounded and a number stretcher of cases, and assisting the medics as much as I could, traveling further east to the small town of Türnitz, the last stop on the other side of a 4000 foot high mountain, where we disembarked.

What happened next, I don't remember. I now believe that I had passed out, perhaps in a belated reaction to the rather violent blow to my head. For certain I must have been loaded aboard a truck or Sanka (*Sanitätskraftwagen* - ambulance), and transported further west toward the Reich, and consequently toward the American lines. All I do remember is finding myself later about a half day's trip away in a field hospital of the German air force in the village of Weyer, not far from the city of Steyr. The *Luftwaffe* doctors gave me a thorough check-up and told me that I should have no serious after-effects from my wound.

When the doctor in charge returned my papers and gave me some pills to take for my aching head, he mentioned, as if in passing, "I have assigned you to a convalescence hospital in Waidhofen for the next two weeks. By then everything should be over, I assume." Obviously he had meant the war.

In this connection I would like to point to the tremendous order and discipline all these Germans and other Europeans showed in the face of certain defeat and the great uncertainties that lay ahead for all of us. There was no panic; there was no feeling sorry for ourselves; and there were few attempts by individuals to abscond from their duties and leave their comrades to their fate. Even those still battling the Russians (or being too close to the Russian lines for other reasons) who might face many years of imprisonment or even certain death in the depths of the Bolshevist empire, kept their calm and often even their good humor to the very last.

(A prime example of this kind of heroism is my German lawyer, Hajo Herrmann, who was then a very highly decorated Luftwaffe pilot and the commander of two large units of fighter planes. After the fighting had ended, he had sent some of his men by plane on a reconnaissance mission into Hungary. When they did not return in time, he himself flew behind the Russian lines to effect their release, and made contact with the Soviet Air Force. Although Hajo Herrmann's main battles had been fought against the bombers of the Western Allies, the Russians kept him for 10 years in the ignominious GULAG.)

From Weyer to Waidhofen "*an der Ybbs*" (on the mountain stream named Ybbs) it was only a short ride by truck. When I arrived there, I was assigned to a small room on the first story of a country inn/restaurant that was now bereft of any furniture except many straw mattresses which covered every square inch of the floor. And most of the mattresses were occupied by wounded soldiers of every branch of the German armed forces, *Heer, Kriegsmarine, Luftwaffe* and *Waffen-SS,* and also of the *Arbeitsfront* and the *Organisation Todt* (the latter comparable to the American Seabees).

I quickly became acquainted with some Waffen-SS non-commissioned officers (sergeants and corporals) who for most of the war had been German air force soldiers, and who, like those Luftwaffe-*Hauptfeldwebel* I commanded in my squad, had been assigned to the Waffen-SS only recently. They, like all the others, were either only slightly wounded or on the way toward full recuperation after a more serious injury. Waiting for the war to end, they whiled the time away by playing cards, or just sleeping, making up for the exertions of the last few months.

Unlike all others, I did not spend much time at the inn. I felt that I had to know what was transpiring in the world around us, and since we had neither radio nor newspapers, I had to look to other means to get information. With my head still heavily bandaged, and also having the injury ticket dangling from my uniform, I was not fearful of being accosted as a deserter by the

MPs of Army and Waffen-SS doing their duty. On the other hand, I also did not venture too far from my assigned domicile.

I am fairly certain that it was on the 2nd of May 1945 when I discovered the display case of a local newspaper beneath a medieval gate. The headline was simple: *"Adolf Hitler gefallen!"* (Hitler dead in combat!) The accompanying article stated that on the day before, the German radio had reported that Adolf Hitler, "our beloved Führer and Reichskanzler", had personally joined the battle for Berlin, during which he had received fatal wounds. The article also mentioned that *Grossadmiral* Dönitz, the head of the German navy, had assumed the post of the German head of state.

Was I shocked to read this news? No! I clearly remember that I watched my own reaction: There was neither surprise nor sorrow. In my innermost being I had known that "Adolf" could not survive the defeat and destruction of his Reich. (For this very reason, in later years, I never gave credence to reports of Hitler's survival, or that he somehow had ended up in South America to continue the battle from there.)

Things happened as, under the circumstances, they had to happen. Lamentations were not going to alter the dismal facts we all had to face.

When I went to the inn to tell the others of Hitler's death, their reaction was similar to mine, or, perhaps better described, there was no reaction at all. Those who played cards continued with their games; those who had been dozing off, also continued to do so. Neither on this day nor on any of the few next days thereafter, while I was still with these soldiers at the inn, was Hitler's name ever mentioned again.

As fate had decreed it, I heard of Hitler's death in what National Socialists call "the Austrian Hitler country"; this was the area not far from where he grew up; a region which he considered his *Heimat.* In a still surviving Hitler painting of Waidhofen, painted about 1910, the very building is shown where I read of his demise some 35 years after he had painted the scene.

It was on the 6th of May when on my early morning expedition I noticed more than the usual activity in the small city. I decided to stay outdoors most of the day. Clearly something important was happening. Soon I saw, on a road in the distance and across the Ybbs river, a German staff car occupied by several officers, and bedecked with a white flag, driving at great speed. Then, a few hours later, a *Fieseler Storch*, one of the famous German spotter planes that was able to land even on a short potato field, made several low passes over the town. The plane still had the swastika and *Balkenkreuz* markings of the Luftwaffe, but for one reason or another I assumed then that the occupants were Americans using a captured plane for reconnaissance. I was probably wrong. But this was the last time I was going to see a plane with the swastika on the tail assembly, until not too many years ago I went to an air show in California, where an ME-109 of the Texan "Confederate Air Force" was one of the major attractions.

A view of Waidhofen "an der Ybbs", painted by Adolf Hitler about 1910-12. It is entirely possible that at that time the young Hitler stayed at the very same inn where I convalesced in May of 1945. This reproduction is from the book, "Adolf Hitler, The Unknown Artist" by Billy F. Price. Price Publishing Co., Houston, TX 1984

(Years after the war, when I was already living in America, I discovered that in April and the beginning of May 1945, Waidhofen had been the very last headquarters of the entire German front in SE Europe, the *Heeresgruppe Ostmark*, under the command of Colonel-General [*Generaloberst*] Rendulic.)

The city of Steyr, by air only about 15 miles to the west, had been occupied by American troops of the 71st Infantry Division on May 5th. On the following day, when I saw the staff car with the white flag, a small detachment of the U.S. Army tried to reach Waidhofen but couldn't get through to the high German headquarters because the roads were all clogged by German units streaming west, trying to avoid capture by the Russians.

It did not take me long to run back to the inn to tell the other soldiers what I had seen. I also had heard rumors that some units of the Red Army had bypassed Waidhofen on their march west, and that in some places it had already come to clashes between Russian and American troops, something we wanted to hear. (The rumors about some skirmishes between Russians and Americans were true, but I know now that at the time the Soviets had not yet bypassed Waidhofen.)

Now I realized that the time had come for all of us to take our lives into our own hands, and I said so to the others. As for myself, I had decided to try to reach the American lines, come what may, as soon as possible.

Having studied a map of the area, and being mindful that the Russians would most certainly advance on the better roads, I knew that I had to hike on a little-traveled logging road over a 3000 foot pass to near where I expected the U.S. Army to be. (I assume that by then I had heard of the American occupation of Steyr.)

Up to that day I had worn my Waffen-SS uniform with pride. But realizing that the end was near, and since the Battle of the Bulge being conscious of the fact that enemy propaganda had depicted especially the soldiers of the Waffen-SS as bloodthirsty monsters, criminals, and worse, I knew that it would not be wise to go into captivity wearing a uniform with the two SS runes on the collar, and the German eagle on the left sleeve of my tunic rather than over the right breast pocket as was customary on Army uniforms. I went to a nearby *Kleiderkammer* (uniform outfitter) which was part of the string of convalescence hospitals in town, and there selected the most simple uniform jacket of the German Army (*Heer*) that fitted me. (The pants were all the same.) The tunic was used, but not overly so, and there were no indications of the former owner either having had any kind of rank or having received any medals: exactly what I wanted. I really regretted having to throw my Waffen-SS uniforms, both the field gray jacket and the camouflage smock, into a huge container originally destined for the cleaners, but I knew it was the smartest thing to do. I probably also exchanged my belt buckle reading *"Meine Ehre heisst Treue"* (LOYALTY IS MY HONOR) to an Army issue with *"Gott mit uns"* (GOD IS WITH US), but I can't be certain.

Fifty-six years later I am still in possession of one piece of paper that shows I must then have gone to the doctor or medic in charge of this convalescent unit, and ask for a discharge or document showing that I had been in the hospital.

Thus newly outfitted, I now approached the other soldiers and asked them to hike with me to the Americans. Alas, not one of the approximately 20 men and boys wanted to take "the risk" of venturing out of what they considered a safe area. And the former non-commissioned officers of the *Luftwaffe,* especially some older staff sergeants among them, didn't even heed my suggestion that at least they get rid of their SS-uniforms. "I last fought honorably in this uniform, and I see no reason to wear another one when we all go into captivity," said one. With these men being in their late twenties, or older, I thought they would have more sense than that.

All of the men in that room believed the assurances of our enemies east and west, that we were going to be discharged and sent home as soon as the hostilities had ended. These assurances had bccn printed on the zillions of propaganda leaflets that in the past couple of years had been raining down on German lines, usually dropped at night from enemy planes. I had read the stuff with derision: Because of the experience I had gained throughout the war in dealing with Allied propaganda, I didn't believe one word that came from Germany's enemies. In addition, I had never forgotten the admonitions of my mother's uncle Jakob, a German World War I infantryman, who had in 1918 believed similar promises given by the French military, and as a result was kept until 1921 as a slave laborer.

The only fellow who walked with me part of the way was a young recruit from the German Labor Service, the *Arbeitsdienst,* a boy of about sixteen. But halfway up the steep mountain road he suddenly got cold feet and decided to turn back. Either he had gotten tired too soon, or else some shooting in the far distance had awakened him to the fact that the war was still on and that danger could be lurking around every corner.

Undeterred, I continued on my way to the Americans, and into voluntary captivity. Unlike my older brother Richard, I had at no

Formblatt 6
zu H. Dv. 193/8 Z. 49.

Schmidt Hans Gr. 1. L.A.H. 18 Jahre, 1.80 cm
(Name) (Dienstgrad) (Truppenteil) (Alter) (Größe)

zugegangen am: 1.5.45
(Tag, Monat, Jahr) (Lazarett und Kranken-Abt. oder Krankenrevier, Schiffslazarett)

Monatstag

Krankheitstag

Verordnungen (Kost, Arzneien, physikalische Behandlung usw.)

A	P	K
70	180	41,0
60	160	40,0
50	140	39,0
40	120	38,0
30	100	37,0
20	80	36,0
10	60	35,0

Vorgeschichte: Am 28.4.45 bei Klein-Zell verwundet. Ueber H.V.Pl. hier eingeliefert. Tetanus erhalten bereits im Februar anlässlich der ersten Verwundung.

Befund: Es handelt sich um eine ca. 2 cm grosse Wunde am li. Auge.
Behandlung: Schutzverband.

6.5.45: Patient wird in das rückwärtige Luftwaffenlazarett Weyer verlegt.

Bisherige Befunde Untersuchungen: Blutbilder, Senkungen, Wa. R., Harnstoff usw.; sonstige Untersuchungsergebnisse

A = Atmung: blau --×--, P = Puls: rot -.-, K = Körperwärme: schwarz —●— axillare —○— rektale Messung
Stuhl: geformt |, breiig /, Durchfälle -

W.-Form. 328. — Carl Ueberreuter'sche Buchdruckerei in Wien.

This is my fever chart from the convalescent hospital in Waidhofen/Ybbs in Austria. Today I can only assume that on the day when I decided "to leave the war", namely on May 6th, 1945, I went to the intern (Dr. H..) in charge and asked him to sign it so that I could use it instead of discharge papers. The text from the backside of the chart, shown at the bottom, is as follows:

"(Patient was) wounded at Kleinzell on April 28. He was sent here from the main field hospital. A tetanus inoculation was administered in February after the first injury.

The injury is from a two centimeter long cut above the left eye. Normal treatment is recommended.

6 May 1945: The patient is being transfered to the *Luftwaffe* hospital at Weyer."

This last sentence was false, possibly written by myself to have an excuse to hike in a westerly direction.

time considered the possibility that I could reach my home in the Saarland, on the opposite end of Germany, without being apprehended by some of the enemy troops.

I hoped to reach American lines sometime the following day. Soon after the young *Arbeitsdienst* recruit had turned back, I was totally by myself. Not having to watch for traffic of any kind on the little-used (and unpaved) logging road I had selected as the safest route, I made good progress, and reached the crest of the nearly 3000 foot high pass after a few hours.

Sitting down on a boulder to take a well-needed rest near a spot where two logging roads converged, I suddenly heard the familiar noise of a German half-track personnel carrier coming from a northerly direction. The vehicle, by its markings clearly recognizable as belonging to the Waffen-SS division *Wiking*, stopped right in front of me, and a young lieutenant, probably only a couple of years older than I, approached me with a map to inquire about which road to take.

I answered all questions as well as I could, but then asked in return what the *Untersturmführer* and his crew of about a dozen soldiers were going to accomplish this late in the war. The officer was obviously surprised that a lowly private of the Army infantry would talk to him almost on an equal basis, but then I quickly explained what my real unit and rank was, and that I was on the way to the Americans. Undoubtedly, the bandages around my head, and the worn *Verwundetenabzeichen* and the faded ribbon of the Iron Cross which I had wisely stuck on the infantry uniform, helped convince him of my story, but only after I had shown the lieutenant my Waffen-SS paybook with a photograph and all pertinent information did he provide the information that he and his men had orders to blow up a nearby viaduct crossing both a mountain river and railroad tracks.

It was my opinion that the destruction of such a bridge that close to the end of the war was not warranted, and I said so to the lieutenant. I also told him, quite convincingly I am sure, that earlier in the day I had seen German *Parlamentäre* (bearers of a flag of truce) with white flag-bedecked staff cars driving near Waidhofen.

After having heard my argument against the ordered, totally unnecessary destruction of the bridge, the young *Untersturmführer* conferred with some of his soldiers who seemingly had also not liked this task. Then, after eliciting a few more bits of information from me, he suddenly boarded his half-track, waved good-bye, and gave the order to the driver to take the same road back where they had come from. I assume that subsequently the bridge was not blown up.

(Here I would like to explain that according to my memory I "saw" the soldiers of the SPW unload the bomb they had aboard the vehicle, and throw it in the river, rather than destroy the viaduct as they had been ordered to do. Today I believe that the bridge/viaduct was near Weyer, where the air force doctors had examined me, and it is possible that I had seen this spot earlier in the week, merely imagining what could happen as the lieutenant and I spoke. I mention this to show what tricks our memories can play. The fact is that on the road from Waidhofen to the village where I went into captivity, I traversed only high mountain roads, and saw neither a railroad nor a river or major creek.)

Shortly after the "Wiking" soldiers had driven off, I went on my merry way. From now on the going was easier, mostly downhill.

To this day I remember a road sign showing a 10 percent downhill-grade just ahead, when behind me I heard the noise of an approaching vehicle. From the distance I could see that it was a tarpaulin-covered truck of the Waffen-SS. By now getting tired of walking, I gave the *"Anhalter"* sign (a sign used by hitchhikers to ask for a ride) and I was very happy when the truck stopped and the officer sitting next to the driver in the truck's cab asked me where I was going. *"Zu den Amis!"* ("To the Americans!") was my answer.

The officer motioned me to climb in the back of the truck where, to my great surprise, I was received by officers and non-commissioned officers of my division. They had been the Waffen-SS liaison to some high headquarters (which today I assume to have been General Rendulic's command post) and only an hour before stopping for me they had been ordered to evacuate west so that they would not be captured by the Russians, who were dangerously close to Waidhofen.

After having made myself comfortable in the back of the truck, I was naturally asked where I was going, what I had seen, and what was my unit. When I told the officers that I was also from the LAH, there was general laughter. None of them minded that I had already exchanged the Waffen-SS uniform for a less conspicuous outfit. The fact that I had been wounded twice in combat (three times if one counts the badly frostbitten feet of the Battle of the Bulge) obviously proved to the officers that I was not a shirker or deserter.

We had not driven downhill very long, probably less than a quarter of an hour, when the truck made a sudden stop and I heard some strange noises. An American soldier, his rifle at ready, ordered all of us to jump out of the vehicle and position ourselves in front of it. Another GI was crouching in a clump of bushes on the side of the road, his weapon trained on us. One could see that the GIs were getting nervous, suddenly facing so many battle-hardened soldiers of the feared Waffen-SS. One by one we jumped from the truck, and, as ordered by the GI closest to us, my comrades immediately placed their pistols, MPs and other weapons on the ground. I had obviously been unarmed all along. After we had all exited the truck, I saw a highly-decorated one-armed Waffen-SS first lieutenant throwing up on the side of the road as he had to place his arms in front of the enemy. The emotional impact of the moment had been too much for him. I felt sorry for him.

Not very far away, still further downhill, I saw the first houses of an Austrian village. I also noticed that this little-traveled road had been guarded by only two GIs. No wonder they had been getting increasingly anxious as one SS-officer after another jumped down from the truck. Excluding me, there were 17 of them, including the driver, and all still had their handguns in their holsters as we left the vehicle. It would have been easy to overwhelm the Americans.

One of the first things the American in charge did after our surrender was to order that we had to raise our arms over our heads, and walk or march in twos in front of the truck toward the village. The other GI stayed at his post near the road, while the one with a seemingly higher rank stood triumphantly on the truck's running board, next to the driver, and brought "his" prisoners in. I can still see him today, with not just one but two newly "liberated" binoculars dangling from his neck and a couple of German pistols (P-38s) stuck in his belt.

(Here a comment is in order about the Allied method of having POWs marching often for hours on end with their hands raised above their heads. This was certainly called for in an immediate combat situation, but not, as in our case, when we obviously had voluntarily gone into captivity, or were otherwise incapacitated. I considered the behavior of the GI who brought us to the stockade nothing but grand-standing.

But perhaps I shouldn't complain: in modern allied armies *of the present* it now seems customary to even handcuff captured enemy soldiers after battle, a custom the great Prussian soldier king Frederic the Great had already frowned upon. We surely made progress, didn't we? The reason for this change in attitude can be found in the fact that concepts like honor, loyalty and chivalry have been eliminated from Western civilization by Bolshevism and Western 'Liberalism'.)

While being marched through the village, I do not recall seeing any Austrian civilians, but I clearly do remember my disdain when I saw next to the white flags (bed sheets), with which most houses had been bedecked as a sign of surrender, a few red-white-red flags of the post-World War I Austrian republic, which had existed until Austria was reunited with the Reich in March of 1938. Now, more than fifty years later, I view this quick action by some of the Austrians more benignly: Some older people surely knew that the destruction of the united German Reich (Hitler's *Grossdeutschland*) had been one of the main aims of Germany's worst enemies, and these Austrians had merely been more expeditious than others to adjust to new realities.

The village was small. At its far end we soon saw a large lumberyard, probably a collection place for trees that had been cut in the nearby forests, totally surrounded by barbed wire. Within this encampment I noticed a separate, more fortified barbed wire enclosure. Perhaps as many as 1000 German soldiers, now POWs of the Americans, were milling about beyond the barbed wire, waiting for things to come.

The Americans had placed heavy machine guns at strategic locations outside of the perimeter of the stockade, but I saw no tanks or armored personnel carriers that could have prevented a mass break-out if such had been planned. In other words, most if not all of the POWs had capitulated to the Americans on their own free will. Just as we did.

Just as we were marched past the skimpily constructed gate of the stockade, I noticed a group of four or five American officers standing in the midst of the clearing and talking intently to another officer who wore an Italian uniform and who was still carrying his sidearm; the man obviously belonged to the "Badoglio"-Italians who had switched sides in 1943, and since then had fought against Germany.

Our arrival generated quite some interest among other POWs and the Americans. Even the group of officers had interrupted their conversation and were staring at us. "Everybody" now watched the unfolding spectacle.

The group of Waffen-SS officers and non-coms with whom I had arrived, and among whom were quite a few men with very high decorations, including the famed *"Ritterkreuz"* they had received for bravery in battle, had been ordered to stop in the middle of the square, stand in single file next to each other, and were then each individually frisked, and at the same time asked by an American soldier with some stripes on his sleeves, "You SS?", "You SS?", "You SS?", and so on, to which they all obviously answered in the affirmative.

It was during this frisking that the American sergeant, or whatever he was, and who clearly belonged to the MPs (military police) removed the list of the names and addresses of my fallen comrades from my breast pocket and threw it on a pile of other things to be burned. If my memory is correct then it was also at this time when my officer comrades were "liberated" from their Iron Crosses and other medals which they had earned in nearly six years of war.

I quite naturally had placed myself on the very end of the line, and I do recall hearing the Waffen-SS officer next to me telling me to say "no" to the American's question when it was my turn to be asked whether I was "SS". But how could I say no? Standing next to these fine soldiers, how could I deny that I had belonged to the same proud unit? That I was part of them. I did not feel bad to have changed my uniform early in the day, but now that fate had again placed me among my comrades, I would have felt that I was betraying them if I denied my association with them.

I said "Yes", I was a soldier of the Waffen-SS, when asked by the American MP. Thereupon we were all ordered to make a right-turn, and march still single-file toward the separate enclosure in the corner of the yard, a sort of cage obviously constructed for the "bad guys", the soldiers of the Waffen-SS.

It was at this moment when the Italian officer stepped forward and ordered all of us to stop. Then he walked over to me, while at the same time calling the American with the stripes on his sleeves to his side. Pointing at my collar without the SS insignia, and comparing it to the "lightning bolts" on the tunics of the officers next to me, he made clear to the GI and other Americans standing around that I had obviously misunderstood the question; that I was a soldier of the German Army, and not of the Waffen-SS. Then, without much ado, the Italian pulled me away from my *Leibstandarte* comrades, and pushed me toward the many other German soldiers standing around, most of whom were from the regular Army. While he did this, he gave me a kick in the pants, at the same time whispering in good German: *"Das nächste Mal halte das Maul!"* ("The next time keep your mouth shut!")

Thus I had joined the army of millions of Germans who at war's end had found themselves behind barbed wire of the enemy.

This photograph shows a modern tank of the Austrian Army traveling through Hainfeld in Austria, during maneuvers in November of 1994. The large building to the left is possibly the very building in which the SS-lieutenant from Rumania committed suicide in April of 1945. The truck to the left occupies the spot where the "Panther" tank was firing from at the Russians on top of the hills (which were then not so forested).

Chapter 27

I considered the open field, now a barbed wire-enclosed stockade, where we were being held an obvious "end of the war"-situation. Everything was in great flux, and I made no attempt to make acquaintance with any of the other POWs: to make friends now could be a hindrance later. Rather, I began watching the Americans; their behavior, their equipment, and their ways treating the helpless soldiers in their hands.

Soon after we had arrived, I had placed myself at the highest ground within the stockade, and from there kept track of the comings and goings. After a while, the gate of the barbed wire enclosure opened again, and an entire company of very young boys (15 to 16 year olds) of the *Arbeitsdienst,* the German Labor Service, came marching in, properly led by their officers. I marveled at their good (spotless) uniforms, and the other equipment, including properly packed backpacks they carried, and their discipline. They were not armed.

The officer in charge of the *Arbeitsdienst* unit reported, immediately after all his "men" were inside the stockade, quite properly, and with the right arm raised for the German salute, to the American officers in charge. Immediately, the German was told to order his company to assume a spread-out formation of three rows, so that the MPs (and other American soldiers?) could check each of the boys individually. It was then that I saw watches, fountain pens and other personal effects being stolen. One American soldier had at least ten wrist watches on one arm, but none of the U.S. officers viewing the entire spectacle seemed to see anything wrong with that (something like that would have been impossible in the German Armed Forces, and especially in the Waffen-SS).

After the American soldiers had satisfied their greed (or whatever one could call it), suddenly, out of nowhere, came a group of former concentration camp inmates in their striped uniforms, and began ripping the backpacks and other possessions of the Labor Service boys apart, seemingly searching for valuables that were not there. I saw some of the boys crying as they had to watch photographs of their loved ones, perhaps those of family members that had been killed in the Allied terror bombing, and other personal effects, such as a shawl knitted by their mother, being thrown into the mud and maliciously being stepped. If these former concentration camp inmates had been suffering from malnutrition before their liberation a few days earlier, I certainly would have noticed it. They did not look skinnier or worse than most of us German soldiers.

As all this happened, I stood apart from the others, watching the dismal scene with obvious contempt showing in my face. Not far from me stood a young, unarmed American soldier who must have felt as I did, for when our eyes met for just a moment he merely answered with a hand movement showing that he too was helpless, and couldn't do anything about this shameful spectacle.

Shortly before, when I was a hitchhiker aboard a truck occupied by Waffen-SS officers and non-coms who were also going voluntarily into American captivity, I had shown these comrades my *SS-Soldbuch* (soldier's pass) upon request. Then I was told that it wouldn't be a good idea if I continued to carry this document in one of the pockets of the Army uniform jacket I wore illicitly. It could be easily discovered by an American soldier, who would then also realize that I had been a member of the Waffen-SS and not of the Army, as I had pretended.

As a result, I had stuck my *Soldbuch* deep into my underwear, still hoping to get it safely home from the war. But after the sorry incident with the Labor Service boys, I had lost all hope that any of us could receive fair and decent treatment by the Americans.

What bothered me most was the fact that not one of the American officers had stopped the thievery. I could only guess how my Waffen-SS comrades were going to be treated. I decided that it was wise to get rid of the *Soldbuch* and other "incriminating" papers. In an unguarded moment I hid the stuff deep in a pile of cut logs. (To this day I still wonder what the lumberyard worker or farmer who eventually must have found these documents did with them.)

It seems that I spent only a few hours in this encampment. Today I know that it was located in an area which was soon (practically within hours) going to be occupied by the Russians. It was on the Soviet side of the demarcation line which the victorious Allies had agreed upon months earlier, possibly at Yalta.

Suddenly I saw a long line of U.S. Army 10-wheel trucks arrive at the stockade, and almost immediately the POWs started to board them in a rather undisciplined fashion. There was a lot of pushing and shoving, and I even noticed some fisticuffs. (This proved to me that most of the German soldiers in this encampment did not belong to a larger, still cohesive unit.) It is entirely possible that by then many of the Germans knew that the nearby Enns river, less than 15 kilometers (about 10 miles) away, was going to be the border between American and Russian troops. But I didn't know that, and I did not join the fracas to get aboard the trucks. I was of the opinion that the Americans were going to transport all of us to a more permanent POW camp.

It was the young American soldier who earlier seemed ashamed of his comrades' dishonest behavior, who came out of nowhere and ordered the other Germans to make room for me. I was the last man to board this particular vehicle, and no sooner had I taken a seat on one of the side benches (which the American soldier had insisted on, probably because he saw that I had been wounded) when we drove off at a speed that soon became the hallmark of all truck drivers of the American occupation army in Germany.

Our trip did not last long. Within sight of the city of Steyr, where one especially good type of "*LKW*" (truck) that was often used as a towing vehicle for artillery pieces had been manufactured for the *Wehrmacht*, we crossed the Enns river. Then, only a few hundred yards to the south, still within sight of the waterway, we found ourselves in a much larger stockade, this one holding several thousand German soldiers of all branches and units.

As before, there were no buildings or shelters of any kind should it rain, and once inside the barbed wire enclosure most German POWs were left to their own devices. The majority of them were lying on the grass, doing nothing. Not very far away I noticed now empty factory buildings which in my opinion could have been used to house these POWs temporarily and more properly, but then again it would have been more difficult for the Americans to keep an eye on the prisoners.

This stockade (that's all one can call these camps) did not have a separate enclosure for Waffen-SS soldiers. I assume that, officially at least, none were brought here. However, after the truck on which I had been transported had arrived at this place and disgorged us, we first had to stand in line and give our name and unit. (I probably acted dumb and couldn't remember a unit larger than some infantry company.) Then we were told to remove the clothes from our upper body, and lift our arms high. Thereupon each one of us was carefully inspected for the blood type tattoo on the inside of the left upper arm that was standard with soldiers of the Waffen-SS but not of the other services of the German armed forces. Thus it was a simple procedure for the Allies to separate the wheat from the chaff, so to say.

It then dawned on me how lucky I had been in late 1944 when, because of my perennial attempts to break the rules, I had arrived in Breslau too late from my self-prolonged furlough to have my arm tattooed. On the other hand, the loss of my dog tag as a result of my shoulder wound in Hungary proved the soundness of the SS-hierarchy in introducing this type of life-saving tattoo.

In Steyr I did notice that *in general* the officers were separated from the soldiers and non-commissioned officers, and this was possibly done purposely to create a mass of more easily-to-manage prisoners. Without unit cohesion, discipline was fast breaking down. Some American soldiers outside the barbed wire had their fun by smoking their cigarettes only about half-way, and then throwing the large butts across the wire between the POWs. It never failed that a whole bunch of the nicotine-starved German soldiers threw themselves like a pack of wolves on the spot where the single butt had landed, and the "victor" of this ignominious game usually walked away with a smile as if he had won a battle. A young ensign of the German Army and myself hated to see brave German soldiers demeaning themselves in such a way, and we decided to put a stop to it. When we noticed some Americans getting ready for their fun, both of us immediately waded among the throng of soldiers and bawled them out in no uncertain terms for dishonoring their uniforms and, *ipso facto*, their fallen comrades. It worked. Myself not wearing any insignia of rank at all, I was surprised that the soldiers took heed. Perhaps my head bandage made a difference.

At one time while I was in this *Lager*, I saw a group of officers from the German Army arrive who almost surely had been part of some higher staff or headquarters. They all wore immaculate uniforms, and many of them carried not only their military backpacks but suitcases as well. Most were well fed and not fit for combat. In retrospect I wonder how long they were able to keep all their possessions, with some of the GIs being as rapacious here as I had experienced earlier in the day in the other stockade.

Not far from where I had placed myself (again at a high point) I noticed a high officer of a German elite parachute regiment, a Colonel if my memory is correct, resting all by himself. I could see that this man was also a *Frontschwein* (a combat swine), a designation which in such a case was used as a sign of respect. It was obvious that this officer, according to still recognizable tell-tale signs on his uniform, had been highly decorated for bravery. No wonder he did not want to associate with the other officers who probably had not heard a shot fired in anger in years. I was surprised that the Americans permitted this Colonel to remain among the lower grades.

Some German units (albeit only small ones) drove into this encampment with their vehicles. Once I even a saw a prewar-type Sd Kfz 232 reconnaissance vehicle equipped with a short, prewar, 20mm cannon enter. I wondered if it still had ammunition on board.

At the time I didn't know anything of the non-fraternization policy which the Allies had instituted for their soldiers. According to this nonsensical order emanating over General Eisenhower's signature, none of the conquering soldiers was supposed to privately talk to or just be nice and helpful to <u>any</u> Germans, and this included German children, or, if the American soldiers had been born in Germany as was the case with many, to contact their closest family. Obviously, many GIs in such a situation didn't give a hoot about such insane Eisenhower orders.

While most German soldiers still regarded the GIs as enemies and did not want to have anything to do with them, I myself was very curious about them, and I was greatly interested in talking to an American soldier about the historical events occurring just then, in other words, about politics. Here I must reiterate that German soldiers, and particularly those in the Waffen-SS, were much more interested in the political events of the time than are young Americans of the present. I still remember how we frequently considered the future not only of Germany and Europe, but the entire world, and how we, in our minds, recreated Europe according to our *Weltanschauung.*

Having selected a resting place near the barbed wire in the upper right corner of the camp, I noticed, on the second day of my stay in this stockade, after spending a night on the cold, wet grass, a GI standing guard nearby who, judging by the stripes on his sleeves, must have been a corporal. I also saw that he had carved some notches in the butt of his rifle, something unheard of in the German armed forces; it would have been considered damaging Reich property.

Since this was not a regular POW camp but (probably) merely a holding pen, and all that kept us from walking away were some thin strands of barbed wire, I walked over to the GI, pointed at his rifle, and told him in German (since I didn't know any English then) that if the custom of notching one's gun had been permitted in the German Army, my weapon would have looked like a crocodile (I was purposely exaggerating). The American laughed, and a lively conversation began that lasted many hours.

As it turned out, Corporal John Shoemaker (I am almost certain that this was his name), age 19, was a philology student from the American East Coast, and spoke German fairly well. I found out that one of his grandfathers or ancestors had been a mayor of Hamburg, and, like myself, this American was very much interested in talking to the other side. If my recollections are correct, he was from New York or New Jersey.

But first, the corporal told me not to look directly at him when talking, that was *verboten*. Nobody was supposed to know that we conversed with each other. (It was then that I first heard of the insane Allied non-fraternization order.) So we stood on that hill, separated by the barbed wire, he looking into one direction and I in the other, and we delved into the momentous events of our era.

Shoemaker wanted to know how I felt about Hitler's death, and I asked him the same question about Roosevelt. Neither one of us could guess what was going to happen to Germany now. But the GI was adamant in believing that American troops could not be kept in Germany more than a couple of years at most: Everybody was sick of the war, and wanted to go home.

A while later, after the American had been relieved for several hours, he came back with a bunch of now well-known "concentration camp pictures", seemingly from the American capture of the Dachau and Buchenwald concentration camps weeks before. Shoemaker studied me closely as I looked at the photographs of emaciated bodies, stacks of corpses, and even a door marked as a gas chamber entrance. My reaction was not unlike that of today when viewing the same: I shrugged my shoulders. It left me absolutely cold. I didn't take it seriously. Thanks to my breaking the law throughout the war, and listening often, with my older brother, to enemy broadcasting stations and reading all the enemy propaganda leaflets I could get hold of, I was immune against such nonsense. It was not unlike today when American and German school children are being inundated with Holocaust propaganda that may, in the U.S. by psychological pressure and in Germany by law, not be questioned: The more astute of the students will soon notice that something about the tale is not quite kosher, and they will remain skeptical. Seemingly only the truth can stand on its own without having to be supported by unenforceable laws.

I knew the GI expected that I ought to be horrified about what the Germans had (allegedly) done, but when I asked him if he knew of the World War I propaganda by the Allies accusing the German Army then of raping Belgian women, hacking the hands off their babies, and other similar nonsense, he had to admit that he didn't know any of this. But I remembered having read about it before *our* war in my father's well-stocked library, and I placed the concentration camp pictures of 1945 in the very same category. Regretfully, some weeks before, I had used up the soap with the RIF embossed into it, which I had received from the Judenau hospital when I left there. Shoemaker might have been aghast to see that I was using soap allegedly manufactured from Jewish cadavers, as the Allies then claimed. The victors had made an RJF out of the three initials, and that was then supposed to mean "(manufactured from) Pure Jewish Fat"! Actually, RIF stands for *Reichsstelle für Industrielle Fettversorgung,* namely, Reich Office for Industrial Fat Supplies. But thus legends are born.

Fortunately, I was able to tell this American soldier as much as I knew about Germany and the Third Reich, and why, in my opinion, we had been the true defenders in the war which we had just lost.

I ought not to forget to mention that the young corporal was standing guard at the POW encampment as a form of punishment for insubordination. He was obviously the kind of fellow who had not lost his individuality when he joined the U.S. Army.

The night following my arrival at the American POW stockade at Steyr, Austria, ie. the night of the 7th to the 8th of May 1945, was quite cold, and there was not much of a chance to sleep on the wet grass. Nevertheless, I must have dozed off near where I had talked to the young American, when I suddenly heard some unusual noise. It was the corporal. He quietly called me over to a spot nearer the barbed wire. When in the darkness he was certain that I was close, he began shoving several cartons full of canned goods, some containers opened and half consumed and others still factory-closed, underneath the fence, and mentioned that this was for me and my comrades. I thanked him and, taking only very little of these goodies for myself, had other soldiers carry all the boxes to the *Fallschirmjäger* colonel so that this officer could distribute the welcome nourishment as he saw fit. I distinctly remember the American corporal telling me that he and his comrades had been strictly forbidden to give any foodstuffs, even opened cans that would otherwise end up on a trash heap, to us German POWs. Under no circumstances were we to tell anyone where we got the food.

Corporal Shoemaker and I continued our conversation on the following morning, May 8th, 1945. Neither of us knew that this was going to be the day the German *Wehrmacht* capitulated to its enemies, thereby (officially anyway) ending the hostilities in Europe. Instead, we continued our talk of the previous day, leaving no major subject matter of the era untouched. Once, just as the American again brought up the matter of alleged German atrocities in concentration camps (of which he had seen as much as I did, namely, nothing) and I reminded him again of the anti-German hate propaganda of the Allies during and after World War I, we suddenly noticed a commotion near the barbed wire gate of the stockade, next to which stood a couple of tents, one obviously for the American guards and the other possibly a sort of sick bay. In plain view of all of us, four stocky GIs brought a German girl in the uniform of a *Nachrichtenhelferin* (similar to American WACs) into the camp and carried her into one of the tents, each of the GIs holding an arm or a leg and the girl screaming as loud as she could. I noticed some of the guards (but not Shoemaker) around the perimeter of the stockade getting nervous, and cocking their rifles. They were afraid of a reaction by the thousands of German soldiers milling about. But nothing happened.

I never found out what was the matter with the girl. It is possible that she had been raped by American soldiers (not quite as rare an occurrence as some ex-GIs now seem to believe) or else she was from near Steyr and had been snatched from her home because she did not have proper discharge papers. But I took the opportunity to mention to my American conversation partner what one could make out of this incident (even without knowing further facts) if one wanted to harm the reputation of the American Army.

After our morning talk Shoemaker went back to his quarters, promising me that he was going to collect more food throughout the day so that I could distribute it after darkness among the other POWs. I really did appreciate the kindness of this American soldier. Incidentally, I still remember vividly that the corporal had earned several medals, and he wore the close combat badge on his uniform.

It must have been near midday when Shoemaker suddenly appeared at the spot of the barbed wire near where we had spoken before, and motioned me to come close. He seemed agitated.

"You have to get out of here!" he said, almost as if he was in a hurry. I on the other hand had gotten used to the fact that really nothing was happening with us anytime soon and seemed unimpressed. I remember shrugging my shoulders, and mentioning only that during the following night it would present no problem to crawl underneath the barbed wire and make my way out of the camp. This was not without risk, but not as difficult as it may seem today. After all, I had been an infantry soldier, I knew how to overcome obstacles.

Shoemaker wanted to hear nothing of this. He was adamant: "You have to get out of here now, and fast!" When I wanted to know why, he merely said that was none of my business. Then he told me that as a wounded soldier with a still-bloodied bandage around my head, I was, according to the Geneva Conventions, entitled to be taken care of in a hospital.

"Don't waste any time. Go right now, *schnell,* immediately, to the officer in charge whom you will find in the tent next to the gate, and demand that according to the Geneva Conventions you ought to be in a hospital. Don't let the American soldiers or some of their German helpers milling about keep you out of the officer's tent. If necessary, scream your head off!" Having said that, the corporal said good-bye, and left.

(All my attempts to discover and meet this "angel" again later, when I was settled in the United States, came to naught. Now, with millions of names and addresses in home computers, this might be easier, but years ago finding a single person in this huge country was no simple task. After all, I had no date of birth for John Shoemaker, and no idea what his hometown was. And the U.S. Army was not very helpful either. By now most GIs from World War II have passed away.)

I followed Shoemaker's advice and walked to the tent near the gate. I did not have to scream or otherwise make a commotion, although there was some trouble with German soldiers serving now as flunkies of the Americans. But I did tell the man in charge that, due to my wound, I was just about ready to keel over. Having lost quite a bit of weight during the previous weeks of fighting as a result of the worsening war situation, I must have looked the part. Ten minutes later I was sitting in a type of American staff car, somewhat larger than a Jeep, and was being driven further west to the famous spa of Bad Hall in the lower Alps, a town still totally in German hands.

(More than 4 decades after the war I finally received confirmation of what I had merely guessed for years after the incident: Corporal Shoemaker's reason for wanting me out of the Steyr stockade fast was because he must have heard that on this very day all German POWs in this stockade were going to be delivered to the Soviets who were by then just across the nearby Enns river. A former German soldier (not Waffen-SS) who had spent years in a Russian POW camp after the German capitulation had also been in the Steyr stockade on May 8th, and it was he who told me that, yes, in the afternoon of that day all or most of the German POWs there had been driven across the Enns river bridge, and turned over to the Soviets. Without Shoemaker's intercession, this would also have been my fate.

It bears mentioning that in the mind-set of the average German soldiers of World War II, such Allied transgressions as "Operation Keelhaul", when millions of European soldiers were turned over to the murderous Bolshevist system and certain death, were inconceivable. We believed that we had fought a fair war for six long years, and now that fate had decided against us we felt no rancor against any of our enemies. Most of us sincerely believed that now that the fighting was over, a more just world than after 1918 could be created. Many, if not most Germans held the opinion that it had been the French and British who had to be faulted for the Versailles "dictate" of 1919 that seemed to have been the major cause for World War II. This type of thinking led to the erroneous assumption that the Americans would do better this time. Few Europeans realized that the major war mongers and German-haters, people like Dwight D. Eisenhower, could now be found across the Atlantic.)

Having been a member of the Waffen-SS, I am obviously concentrating on this elite unit when telling of my war experiences. In doing so I am inadvertently short-changing the millions of German soldiers who served in the *Heer,* the regular German Army. It was mainly common soldiers of the Army who from 1941 to 1945 held the 1000-mile front from the Baltic to the Black Sea and thereby prevented the Bolshevists from overrunning Europe. Without the sacrifice of these brave men, Europe, the cradle of Western Civilization, would by now have descended into total darkness. It is doubtful whether the United States could have withstood the succeeding assault.

Chapter 28

To the best of my recollection, I arrived at Bad Hall, a little more than 15 km west of Steyr, in the early afternoon of May 8, 1945. Bad Hall in Austria, a small, famous spa about 30 km by air due south of Linz, Austria's second largest city, had for centuries been known as a place for curing mankind's ailments. The Tassilo fountain at Bad Hall was first mentioned in 777 AD. Since the middle of the last century, European royalty had regularly met at Bad Hall to recuperate from the strenuous duties of ruling often dissatisfied peoples.

The GI driver of the American staff car drove me to what must have been the office of the (German) commanding medical officer of Bad Hall, one of the many European spas which had been turned into hospital towns. I remember seeing Red Cross markings on the roofs of many of the buildings. Having been brought to Bad Hall by the Americans assured that I was properly received, and I was soon assigned to a nice, clean bed in the dining room of one of the larger hotels which had now been turned into a convalescing ward. I was surprised to note that Bad Hall seemed to be still totally in German hands, there was not even one American soldier to be seen.

Shortly after I had arrived at Bad Hall, I had somewhat of a scare. Walking with a medical officer in German Army uniform along the corridor of a large building that had also been turned into sleeping quarters for wounded soldiers, to an examination room, I suddenly heard someone call me by my Waffen-SS rank: the caller was the youngest soldier (born 1929) from my squad of the 5th Company. I pretended not to hear him, and walked on with the officer. But later, when I was settled and able to move about, I went back to the boy and explained to him why I had discarded my Waffen-SS uniform and was now simply an Army private. He understood.

It was this comrade who informed me of the losses through frostbite (the very reason why he had ended up in Bad Hall) which my outfit had incurred a few days after I had been wounded on the 28th of April. Around the first of May it had been snowing again at the higher elevations, and none of my comrades was prepared for this change in the weather. The beautiful sheepskin-lined pilots' boots, which many of my buddies had 'liberated' from a German *Luftwaffe* warehouse in early April, had by the end of that month been totally water-logged, and it took but a few hours of subzero temperatures in the high mountains to create havoc among the troops. I was glad that this had been the young boy's chance to get out of the war.

Once I was somewhat settled in the Bad Hall *Hotel zur Post*, I realized that this was but an intermediate stop on my way home from the war. I did not intend to stay long, but having a nice clean bed, and being able to take a bath again, I was in no hurry to continue on my way. Besides, the food in Bad Hall was good and sufficient, and I took advantage of the situation to strengthen my body for exertions sure to come.

Again I looked for every opportunity to discover what was happening in the world about us. But now that all the German broadcasting stations had been silenced, and no newspapers were available, we (Germans) had to rely on Allied information, most of which was obviously slanted. Rumors abounded. The truth was hard to come by.

I assumed that my father was still assigned as an occupation soldier in Norway; and that my mother, sister and three little brothers were with relatives in Northern Germany, after having been evacuated from our home for the second time in the war. I also hoped that my brother Richard, who since 1943 had been with the German Navy, and who was last posted in Greece, had somehow made his way up through the Balkan peninsula back to the Reich. (Ironically, at the exact time while I was at Bad Hall, Richard, who had escaped from the murderous Tito partisans, was hiking across Austria only a hundred miles or less to the west, as we discovered later.)

There was (obviously) also no news about our home in the Saarland which had been in a major battle zone from early December 1944 to the end of March 1945, when the American Army conquered Saarbrücken. For me there existed the great likelihood that our house had been destroyed, but, come what may, I wanted to get back home. Interestingly, the very U.S. division, the 71st Infantry, to which I had capitulated, had fought in the same sector in front of the *Westwall* (the Siegfried Line) as was my home town.

I soon discovered that the German Army authorities in Bad Hall were not entitled to officially discharge any of the soldiers in their care, not even amputees. It became clear that the Americans were not recognizing German discharge papers that had been executed in the last year of the war. Already in the Steyr stockade I had spoken to Austrians who had served in the *Wehrmacht*, and had, due to wounds or for other reasons, been properly discharged as early as 1943. They had been picked up at their homes by American MPs almost immediately after the arrival of the U.S. Army, and were 'interned' for the simple reason that they had been men of military age, at that time anywhere from 16 to 60 or more. One such inhuman incarceration to which I can personally attest happened to a former Army private who had lost both legs in combat on the Eastern front and who was convalescing in his parents' home where he was arrested. The mere service in the Armed forces had been sufficient cause for bringing this man to a stockade. I must mention, however, that there were tremendous differences regarding this type of actions among the various units of the U.S. Army. It probably depended on the mind-set of the commanding officer. In many instances, the body count of "captured" German soldiers seemed to have been playing a role: The more POWs a unit could show on its "heroic" roster, the more likely was a unit citation and a medal for the General.

I rested in Bad Hall until May 13th, when I got tired of waiting for the unknown to happen. There was no protest by the medical staff when I told them that I was leaving the following morning. After a good night's sleep, I first went to the very office where the American GI had let me off nearly a week earlier, and asked for some kind of paper which I could use as an identification card, should I be stopped at check points. In the absence of my *Soldbuch* I was issued the document reproduced on the next page.

While I was asking for the ID paper, a funny situation developed, for the German Army sergeant in charge who typed the document (actually only a medical patient's record, a *Krankenblatt)* couldn't believe that someone could be as stupid as I (purposely) presented myself:

He: "What was your unit?"

I: "Kampfgruppe Leutnant Sporn (a name I had invented on the spur of the moment)."

He: "To which division did this Kampfgruppe (*task force)* belong?"

I: "Division?"

He: "Yes, division. A *Kampfgruppe* is always formed from a larger unit when the situation demands it. So, which larger outfit did your *Kampfgruppe* belong to?"

I: "How would I know? I never asked!"

He (exasperated): "Would you at least know where you had your basic training?"

I: "Yeah, in Landau in the Pfalz (the Palatinate,) with the *Panzergrenadiere*." (I have previously mentioned that, while in the Hitler Youth I had visited there in 1943. In 1945 still knew that unit's designation.)

He: "Well, we are finally getting somewhere. Where did you get wounded?"

I: "Near Vienna!"

He: "Where near Vienna, how close to it? Near what smaller town?"

I: "No idea!"

He: "What do you mean, you have no idea where you were, you must have seen something!"

I: "Nope, I didn't. We arrived in the combat area at night, I got wounded while it was still dark, and later I couldn't see anything because my head and face were bandaged!"

It was then that he gave up. And as soon he had the document signed by two doctors in charge, he handed it to me with a look in his eyes that showed both disdain and exasperation. It bears remembering that at the time I was barely 18 years of age, and I looked it. The sergeant who interviewed me had no reason to doubt my feigned ignorance. Having heard rumors in the Steyr stockade that the Saarland had been occupied by the French, I named Bad Bertrich near the Moselle river, where relatives lived, and not my hometown, as my final destination.

An Personaldokumenten vorhanden: kein Soldbuch

Reserve-Lazarett Bad Hall
Teillaz.Hotel zur Post.

den, 14. 5. 1945.

Krankenblatt

Dienstgrad: Gren.
Vorname: Hans
Zuname: Schmidt
Truppenteil: Kampfgruppe Ltn.Sporn
Geboren am: 27. 4. 27. in: Luisenthal/Saar
Zugang woher: Truppe Abgang wohin: Bad Bertrich/Mosel
verwund.o.erkrankt am: 28. 4. 45.
Diagnose:
Granatsplitterverletzung über dem li.Auge.

Decursus:
Wunde gut zugeheilt.Keine Augensymthome.Entl.fähig.

Oberstabsarzt u.Chefarzt Oberstabsarzt u.Abt.Arzt.

Having looked at a map of Austria, I decided to walk from Bad Hall in a northwesterly direction toward the city of Wels, perhaps only a half day's hike away, and from there always due west via Braunau on the Inn, where Hitler had been born, into Germany proper, and then home. From Bad Hall to Luisenthal it is about 350 miles as the crow flies, and I figured I could walk the distance in about a month, considering that I had to stay off the main roads, and cross rivers by avoiding guarded bridges.

It bothered me that I had neither money nor any food in my knapsack and pockets. Therefore I decided to keep off the beaten track as much as possible, and stop only at small hamlets or single farms for food and rest. With all major roads of Central Europe clogged with discharged soldiers, foreign ex-prisoners of war and millions of refugees, I was more likely to receive hospitality outside of the main routes.

I was still dressed just as I had left Waidhofen, namely with a field-gray infantry soldier's uniform, wearing an extra pair of pants, probably fatigues from the Italian Army, on top of those of my regular outfit. Also of Italian origin was my fine pair of hiking boots. Having experienced the cold ground in the Steyr stockade, I had asked for and received a woolen blanket from German Army stock in the Bad Hall hospital. And since I did not have a bayonet anymore, I had 'liberated' a normal dinner knife from the hotel where I had just convalesced. I still wore the plain field cap of the Waffen-SS, with the skull insignia quite noticeable, and wore it most of the time. (In retrospect I have to admit that this was a very stupid thing to do under the circumstances.)

Only about an hour out of Bad Hall I suddenly came upon a small town or village where a prominent sign **ORTSKOMMANDANTUR** (local headquarters of the German Army) pointed to a house near which, incongruously, a swastika flag was still fluttering in the wind. I went there, knocked on the door, and was greeted by an older, jovial master sergeant of the German Army who was sitting behind a desk, keeping everything in order. Asking me what I wanted, I told him that I was on my way home and that I did not have any money or food ration coupons, at the same time showing him the Bad Hall document. Thereupon he opened some kind of safe, and gave me both the food ration coupons for four days for a soldier on furlough shown on the next page, and one nice, new, crisp 20 Reichsmark bill, for which I had to sign a proper receipt.

4 Tage

Reichskarte für Urlauber

Gültig im deutschen Reichsgebiet 5. Ausgabe

Diese Karte enthält Einzelabschnitte über insgesamt:
1280 g Brot, davon 900 g R-Brot
150 g Fleisch
85 g Butter
40 g Margarine
100 g Marmelade
100 g Zucker
75 g Nährmittel
25 g Kaffee-Ersatz
30 g Käse

Ausgabestelle EA: Kremsmünster/Od

Name: ....

Wohnort: ....

Straße: ....

Ohne Namenseintragung ungültig! Nicht übertragbar! Sorgfältig aufbewahren! — Abtrennen der Einzelabschnitte nur durch Kleinverteiler, Gaststätten usw.

Urlauber 50g R-Brot | Urlauber 50g R-Brot | Urlauber 50g R-Brot | Urlauber 50g R-Brot | Urlauber 50g R-Brot | Urlauber 50g R-Brot | Urlauber 30g Käse | Urlauber 50g Zucker | Urlauber 25g Marmelade | Urlauber 25g Marmelade | Urlauber 25g Marmelade

Urlauber 50g R-Brot | Urlauber 50g R-Brot | Urlauber 50g R-Brot | Urlauber 50g R-Brot | Urlauber 50g R-Brot | Urlauber 50g R-Brot | Urlauber 25g Kaffee-Ersatz | Urlauber 50g Zucker | Urlauber 25g Marmelade | Urlauber T 25g Nährmittel | Urlauber T 25g Nährmittel

Urlauber 50g R-Brot | Urlauber 50g R-Brot | 10g Brot | 10g Brot | Urlauber T 25g Nährmittel | Urlauber 50g Fleisch

Urlauber 50g R-Brot | Urlauber 50g R-Brot | 10g Brot | 10g Brot | Urlauber 50g Fleisch | Urlauber 50g Fleisch

Urlauber 50g R-Brot | Urlauber 50g R-Brot | 10g Brot | 10g Brot | 10g Brot | 10g Brot | Urlauber 5g Margarine | Urlauber 5g Margarine

Urlauber 50g Brot | Urlauber 50g Brot | Urlauber 50g Brot | Urlauber 5g Butter | Urlauber 5g Butter | Urlauber 10g Butter | Urlauber 10g Butter | Urlauber 10g Butter | Urlauber 5g Margarine | Urlauber 5g Margarine | Urlauber 5g Margarine

Urlauber 50g Brot | Urlauber 50g Brot | Urlauber 50g Brot | Urlauber 5g Butter | Urlauber 10g Butter | Urlauber 10g Butter | Urlauber 10g Butter | Urlauber 10g Butter | Urlauber 5g Margarine | Urlauber 5g Margarine | Urlauber 5g Margarine

Interestingly, I was never able to use these ration coupons since in the meantime the issuer, namely the Reich, had ceased to exist.

After having this business taken care of, I asked the sergeant how come he was still at his post. Didn't he know that the war had been over for nearly a week?

Yes, he answered, certainly he knew. All his comrades had already left on their own. But so far nobody had told him to pack up or abandon his post, and as long as nobody told him to do so, he intended to keep the *Ortskommandantur* open. He did not mind raising the swastika flag every morning, there was not much else to do anyway.

I am convinced that this brave German was not the only one staying at his post in these uncertain times. People like him were the very ones which kept the German fronts from collapsing during the war even under the worst of circumstances (on the Eastern front German soldiers frequently had to fight against a 10 to 1 enemy superiority in men and tanks.) On the other hand, it also happened that the inflexibility of this type of German could create problems for everyone who had to deal with them.

I was never able to use the 4-day food ration coupon, and subsequently kept it as a souvenir. The 20.00 Reichsmark came in handy once I got home three weeks later. Before that I had no opportunity to use it.

Leaving the *Ortskommandantur* and bypassing the nearby town of Kremsmünster, also of medieval fame, I was soon on my merry way west again. Getting tired of walking, I asked a passing farmer, with a single horse pulling his hay wagon, whether I could ride with him, to which he readily assented. He also gave me some homemade apple juice to drink. From the farmer I heard that he was on the way to a large POW camp near Lambach, where the Americans were holding one of his sons. He hoped to get him out of the camp and back home since he needed the boy on the farm.

The horse had been trotting along slowly for some time, when in the distance I saw, near a narrow bridge, an American road block, next to which stood a group of German soldiers who had obviously been retained due to faulty or non-existent papers. I could have jumped off the wagon and lost myself in the nearby fields but had I done that I would never have discovered whether there was any chance to get home with the Bad Hall document. So

I kept my place next to the farmer, sitting high on the bench behind the harnessed horse.

A GI took my paper, studied it with feigned interest, and then motioned me to get down from the wagon, while telling the farmer to go on. I was a POW again.

The Benedictine Abbey of Lambach in Austria where Hitler went to school, and where he saw the "Sonnenzeichen", namely, the swastika, for the first time.

Chapter 29

I remember some of the other Germans admiring my cool demeanor when I was dealing with the GIs. I myself didn't think that what I did was anything unusual. I didn't take the Americans quite as seriously as they themselves and most of the other German soldiers did.

Before the sun had set on this May 14th, 1945, I had again entered an American stockade, this time aboard a U.S. Army truck built by the Studebaker Corporation (it is odd how such details can be retained in one's memory). The "camp" was near the small city of Lambach, the very town where Adolf Hitler went to school, and where he allegedly had first become aware of the significance of the swastika. I was told that it is still emblazoned in a stone frieze at the Lambach abbey, one of the most famous convents in the German lands.

The encampment at Lambach was again just an open field without tents or any other sort of shelter surrounded by barbed wire. It was just like a stockade in one of the American western states after a cattle round-up. Except that for the cattle the farmers usually have enough troughs so that the animals do not die of thirst, something that was not the case in the American POW enclosures.

This “camp” was truly huge. A later report stated that as many as 40,000 German soldiers were kept there at one time, and that there were three separate encampments in all; one for common soldiers, one for officers, and the other for the Waffen-SS. As at Steyr, there were only a few tents for the American guards, while most of the Germans were lying on the often wet, cold earth or grass, merely covered with a blanket or a tent half (a poncho), if they owned one. Cardboard boxes were also in demand but hard to come by.

Upon arrival, newcomers were assigned a piece of ground that was supposed to be large enough for one hundred men. This area was somewhat marked, and after the number hundred was reached, which was soon, since new POWs were constantly brought into the “lager”, the next newly arrived officer was assigned to take command of this group. *The Americans made no attempts to register us by name or take other personal data.*

Again I was extremely lucky. The officer who took charge of our motley crew and the area assigned to it was a young *Oberleutnant* (First lieutenant) of the German *Luftwaffe*, an intelligent, affable man, who had an excellent command of the English language. He called us all together, and then brought some discipline into the group by insisting that military procedures were still to be followed. Then he asked us if we wanted to live like the other POWs surrounding us, most of whom were lethargically lying on the ground, and were whiling their time away with doing nothing, or if we wanted to make the best of a bad situation.

Obviously, we didn’t like what we saw, and we quite willingly followed the officer’s orders: First, we made an inventory of what we all still possessed: How many blankets there were, how many tent halves we owned, and how many mess kits and eating utensils were still in our possession. We also had to report whether we owned long coats or not. The *Oberleutnant* also insisted that we mark “our” rectangular territory with rocks, and keep it clean. Soon we had the best-organized POW-unit among the hundreds that were within our sight.

From other POWs we heard that the food situation at Lambach was catastrophic, and that some of the first arrivals at this camp, those that had been there for about ten days, were on the verge of starvation. It seems that the Americans were feeding the multitudes from German Army stocks only, and in this case there was nothing provided daily but a handful of uncooked legumes (peas, beans or lentils) which the POWs were supposed to chew with the cup full of water also given out. There were no trees on the plain to chop down, or ruined buildings, from where firewood for makeshift stoves could be garnered.

As everywhere across Germany at that time, civilians or civilian services like the Red Cross were not allowed in or near the stockade. The American guards had orders to shoot anybody nearing the barbed fence, whether from inside the camp, or from the outside. And this included women and children of Austrians who were held in the stockade.

Our *Luftwaffe* officer knew how (generally well) the German Government had treated the nearly 100,000 Allied air men which had been captured by the *Wehrmacht* during the war - fewer than one percent died in German captivity -, and this knowledge gave him the strength to seek out American officers who once in a while ventured into the area, and demand better treatment. Coming back from his talks, the *Oberleutnant* told us of his encounters with the Americans, and how one ought to approach them: Never be submissive, always remain proud German soldiers who had withstood almost the entire world for six long years. Somehow this officer had guessed that I was from the Waffen-SS even though by then I had removed the skull insignia from the field cap I wore, for there were times when he alluded to this or that situation which seemed to give an indication of his assumption. At any rate, both of us got along fine, having both served in elite units.

Once, when an American officer wanted to impress our First lieutenant with photographs of the horrors of the concentration camps and the ubiquitous walking skeletons, the German merely retorted that he wished he could transport the POWs in his care to the well-built Dachau barracks one was able to see in the background of one of the photographs (barracks which were certainly an improvement over sleeping out in the open for weeks or months) and he did not forget to mention that in his estimate none of the German POWs at Lambach could survive imprisonment for five or more years, as was claimed by many of the Dachau concentration camp inmates interviewed by their liberators.

Dried peas, chewed in one's mouth with a little water to a swallowable mush, taste horrible. Beans and lentils are not any better. And it seemed that the Americans made no attempt to change this diet for us. We had to find a way to get better food. Today I have forgotten which of us had seen on the way into the stockade, somewhere not far from Lambach a wheel-less, abandoned German *Feldküche* (field kitchen: a type of movable stove on two wheels that can be pulled by a light truck or a team of horses). One day, soon after I had arrived at the camp, the *Oberleutnant* asked for volunteers to drive with him to where the field kitchen was located, and "capture" the thing for us. He cajoled the Americans to provide a truck and some guards for the trip. As always, I volunteered, and soon we had the *Feldküche*, without the wheels, both of which had probably ended up on a farmer's wagon, aboard the truck, and brought it back to our area of the encampment. I am sure we also loaded some firewood on the way, and somehow the officer was also able to get some salt somewhere, an addition which made the watery pea soup which we soon cooked for our hundred men, edible.

On this and a couple of other scrounging trips which I made with the *Oberleutnant*, I watched very carefully how the Americans were behaving and operating, and what outward signs they used to differentiate between prisoners still in the camp, and soldiers who had been discharged. After six years of war few German men still owned any decent civilian clothes, and most were by necessity forced to continue to wear their uniforms even after their discharge from captivity. While we never traveled through the town of Lambach (I do not recall ever having seen the famous Abbey nearby), I noticed some farmers working in their fields wearing their old uniforms but with some kind of colored dot, about the size of a silver dollar, painted on the outside of their lower pant legs. Most of these dots were white. I also noticed that American soldiers were more interested in playing an odd game called baseball than taking care of their soldierly duties. I was certain that I would not have been recaptured on the morning of the 14th of May if I had had a white dot painted on my pants leg. One more thing was soon obvious: The Americans at the gate of the encampment did not keep a written record of incoming or outgoing POWs who passed the gate on what I would call official business.

There were times when they did not even count us. An escape would be relatively easy, but not, however, across the adjoining Traun river that was swollen with run-off from the Alpine mountains.

The distribution of the food (the dried legumes) was in the hands of other German POWs, and even though we of the *Oberleutnant's* group cooked our peas together in the field kitchen, we received them first individually, and then poured all of them into the big pot. We did likewise with our ration of drinking water (the amount of which changed from one day to the next, probably depending on which one of the American officers was in charge.)

If one considers that at the time I was imprisoned at Lambach at least 20,000 "common soldier" POWs had been held there, this means that 200 groups of one hundred men had existed. While I was never able to walk through the entire camp, I doubt that any other group owned a workable field kitchen, although I did see numerous soldiers boiling their legumes in mess kits over small fires. I still wonder where they could have obtained their firewood. In other words, we were probably better off than most of the others.

I also noticed that some of the neighboring soldiers were unable to eat all the peas they received daily uncooked, since the chewing was difficult, and the stomach could only take so much of this cruel stew, or whatever one could call it. On the other hand, our cooked pea soup seasoned just with salt didn't taste too bad.

This gave me an idea: For my planned escape I needed food to take along. Dried peas would just do fine. What if every day I ate only half my pea soup, and traded the other half for as many dried peas I could get from those who couldn't chew their legumes anymore? Due to my week's stay at Bad Hall I was in a good physical condition, and for a little while at least I could get by with eating just part of my ration. The POWs from the other groups were very grateful when I made them the offer, and since some of them had saved most of their peas (beans and lentils had only been given out on the first few days) the gas mask container which I used for the storage of my peas was filling up rapidly. Little did I think that I would be eating that chow for many more days, and even after I got home to the Saarland in the following month.

Apart from the pea soup matter, I don't remember very much about my stay at the Lambach stockade, except that the nights were cold, long and uncomfortable.

Every day I saw some units of the Waffen-SS soldiers marching in formation from their separate barbed wire enclosure down to the river for washing. They were very disciplined and orderly. Their uniforms were kept neat. While marching, they were sung our old marching songs. Although I was in a better position than they, I envied them. I belonged with them, and not with the odd amalgam of soldiers lying around me. It is embedded in my mind that most of the Waffen-SS soldiers were from the "Wiking" division, but I could be wrong.

During one of the forays for firewood, we drove alongside a railroad track leading out of Lambach where an entire train with box cars, regular freight wagons of the *Reichsbahn,* had been parked on a siding. There was clear evidence that the boxcars had been opened and plundered. I noticed hundreds of fine quality hats and caps, among them a great number of expensive, black, peaked caps for SS-officers, lying around. At the time few people considered that someday such caps would bring high prices in the American militaria market.

There were some rare times when our group was able to go down to the river for washing. We didn't march though. It seems that sometimes we had enough time to mill around a bit. The few trees still standing near the water line (where nobody could miss seeing them) had been plastered with signs and scraps of paper, like calling cards and larger: soldiers looking for other soldiers, fathers for their sons, brother for brother, etc. There were also calls for men from particular units to meet at a given spot at this or that time, and one could also discover signs from the many German provinces where POWs had signed off with their names and, "*Ich bin am Leben*" - - - I am alive! - - - and requests for information about their home towns or even their families.

One day I even met a soldier from Luisenthal who throughout the war had fought with the infantry on the Eastern front. However, he was quite a bit older than I, and from exactly the opposite end of the town. I knew neither his name nor his family. But he knew who I was. I think he returned home from the POW stockades, and therefore from the war, about two years after I did.

In the memories of my POW days I remember but one dead: One evening I talked to an older soldier of about 45 years of age who was lying nearby on the cold, wet grass. He was a nice man, a fatherly type, but under the circumstances fraught with extreme pessimism. I tried to raise his mood, but to no avail. During the following night we were all shivering from the cold but finally, some hours before dawn, I did fall asleep. When I awoke, I wanted to talk to the old soldier again, but I soon noticed that he had died in the darkness; his empty eyes were now staring into nothingness.

I felt sorry that the man had died now that the shooting had stopped. The family he so desperately wanted to see again was going to wait in vain for a father never to return. And, knowing now how the Americans and their allies operated at the time, it is entirely possible that the family of this soldier was never notified that he had died in an American stockade in May of 1945. Possibly, even likely, he was kept on the missing lists for years, the wife and children hoping against hope that one day he would return.

It was still very early in the morning when the "body snatchers," German POWs assisting the Americans, came and took the corpse of this soldier away to an unknown destination. Knowing what I do now, he is probably still lying in an unknown mass grave that was soon covered by freshly planted trees. (A method the Americans probably had learned from the Soviets who were masters in mass murder.)

Every day soldiers in my immediate surroundings would get desperately ill from one thing or another, and be taken away by German medics. I do not remember where they were taken, and I am certain that none returned to our group. Slowly but surely, our ranks were thinning.

I waited for the right opportunity to take my fate in my own hands, and, come what may, get out of this hell hole. There were some discharges, probably Austrians who lived nearby (and had somehow been able to see to it that their relatives were informed of their whereabouts), and others who suddenly discovered that they were Frenchmen, Poles, Czechs or the like, who now claimed that they had been forcibly impressed into the *Wehrmacht.* I myself didn't trust Allied assurances that we would *all* be sent home soon. As a matter of fact, the situation in Lambach confirmed my worst expectations.

At Lambach a few lean-tos provided shelter for some of the POWs. Since I was without a poncho (tent triangle), I had to lie in the open.

When I voluntarily entered American captivity on May 6th, 1945, I never could have imagined that I would end up a week later in one of those U.S. Army stockades (open pastures without shelter of any kind) that James Bacque, the Canadian author, calls in his book "Other Losses" (Stoddart Publishing Co., Toronto, Canada, 1989) one of "Eisenhower's death camps." Bacque states that as a result of such "camps" and other immoral actions by the U.S. high command, about one million German soldiers died *after* the cessation of hostilities. While I personally doubt that the number of deaths was that high, it likely was in the hundreds of thousands.

In the book "The Interrogator" by Ray Toliver and Hanss Scharff (Schiffer Publishing Co., Atglen, PA, 1997), the latter described his experiences in the horror camp at Bad Kreuznach that was first established by the Americans and then turned over to the French Army. Unknown thousands of German POWs died there, some within sight of their homes.

Another book where the horrible conditions in an American POW camp in 1945 are described, a camp the name of which became *clandestinely*[31] known in Germany already in the immediate

[31] For many years after the war it was forbidden, by Allied law, for the Germans to criticize, question or belittle the Allies. From the era of the Nuremberg trials

postwar years, has the title "Marseille 404" (VGB, 1999). To the best of my knowledge it is only available in the German language. The author is Paul F. Wagner, who wrote a diary about his experiences.

Exact numbers and other facts about the Lambach POW "camp" are impossible to obtain because U.S. authorities (ie. "Washington") have in time-tested fashion the habit of destroying incriminating evidence of their criminal conduct after all their wars, even though in modern times and before the advent of computers originally all documents had to be typed or written with 3, 4, 5 or even six copies. Not very long ago I read that during negotiations between the Americans and the Vietnamese the latter asked Washington for the lists showing the grave sites of nearly a million Vietnamese soldiers still missing from that war. It was known and acknowledged by the U.S. that these lists had in 1975 been in American care but somehow they cannot be found anymore. That is par for the course.

Now, nearly fifty-five years after the Second World War, it is easier to get accurate POW records from Russia than from the United States. And it deserves mention that in 1944 and 1945 Russia (the Soviet Union) was not only largely destroyed but also totally impoverished, whereas the United States mainland had been untouched by war.

The following will mainly consist of translations of other reports than mine about the Lambach stockade. I am reprinting these not to generate sympathy or pity for myself (at the time I took all hardships in stride) but because so far, in more than half a century, no member of the allegedly free American media has had the courage to publish these dismal facts and criticize the U.S. behavior. As a rule, when the U.S. media now publishes stories about such occurrences during and after World War II, they are often attempts at whitewashing. For instance, only recently the History Channel brought a report on the massacre of German medical personnel and others that happened on the day the inmates

(1945-1948) of the German leaders, not a single published document can be found in German archives where a German was permitted to publicly question the legality of this judicial charade. Had a German done so, a trial and incarceration would have followed.

of the Dachau concentration camp were liberated by elements of two American infantry divisions (the 42nd and the 45th). While the History Channel report was essentially correct, the number of unarmed Germans murdered was reduced to 17, whereas an American medical officer who was there, Colonel Howard A. Buechner, mentioned a total of 520 Germans executed on that day. See his book, "Dachau, The Hour of the Avenger" (Thunderbird Press, Metairie, 1986). Incidentally, the killings at Dachau by Americans were the greatest massacre of unarmed soldiers, among them doctors and nurses, that occurred on the Western front in World War II.

There were times in the past when I spoke to American World War II veterans about these occurrences, and, like most common soldiers, few of them had any inkling as to what had really transpired. In an army (*any* army) and during wartime, the individual soldier often exists as if in a cocoon, knowing only what he needs to know about his very own survival and existence. Even if an individual sees things that are wrong and immoral, he seldom has a chance to do anything about them for the simple reason that in a hierarchical system such as all armies are, neither dissent nor protest is really permitted and rarely possible.

If so many German soldiers succumbed in the POW stockades of the Western Allies (mainly of the U.S. Army and the French), where are their bodies? So far we have never heard or read of mass graves of German soldiers being found that had been hidden and later accidentally discovered in those parts of the German *Bundesrepublik* still - in 2001 -occupied by the Western powers..

The answer can be partly discovered if we realize that the Bolshevist mass graves of the immediate postwar period on the territory of what was until 1990 the East German "DDR" were only dug up after the collapse of Communism, and after a search for such burial grounds was allowed. *And in almost every single instance such discoveries were made in large, enclosed areas that hitherto had been military installations of the Soviet Army or, like at Bautzen, prisons of the East German vassal regime.* In other words, the mass graves were in areas that had been off-limits to the general population.

In the Western part of Germany, the authorities use spurious excuses, such as "it is against human dignity to disturb the resting places of the dead", to prevent the discovery of the truth, as happened at the burial place of the aforementioned former POW stockade at Bad Kreuznach, and at Dachau.

We can almost be certain that undiscovered mass graves of missing German soldiers could be found on the grounds of facilities in the *Bundesrepublik* currently still occupied by U.S. Armed Forces; graves, of the existence of which young American soldiers of today have as little knowledge (meaning none) as had young Russian soldiers stationed in Germany until 1993.

The following report relating to this problem was printed in the September 1997 issue of *Der Freiwillige*, the monthly magazine of the veterans of the Waffen-SS:

"On June 6th, 1997, a memorial plaque was unveiled in memory of those of our comrades who succumbed in May and June 1945 in the former death camp of the United States Army at Aigen-Schlägl. This town is called the door to the Bohemian Forest, and is located near the Czech border.

Our comrade Werner Barmann, then an 18-year-old private, had entered this camp on May 18, 1945. He and two others of his SS-cavalry squadron, along with other POWs, survived the privations of this stockade.

For many years after the war Barmann tried to discover, without success, what had happened to the remains of those of his comrades whom he saw die in those fateful months. In spite of intensive research, and after reviewing all available records of all World War II soldiers buried in Upper Austria, not a single grave could be found of those who succumbed at the Aigen-Schlägl camp. They remain on the lists of the missing to this day.

Finally, in 1996, other witnesses came forward who were able to confirm Barmann's recollections. They agreed that between the 8 of May and about the 10th of July, 1945, somewhere from 500 to 1,000 German soldiers died at this stockade, and that their remains were taken away by U.S. Army trucks to an unknown destination. They were obviously buried in mass graves that to this day could not be discovered. Incidentally it is known that in the area of the open pit latrine of the stockade a number of POWs had been killed by the guards. No trace of their remains could be found either. Altogether about 7,000 to 8,000 POWs had been held at Aigen-Schlägl.

At the end of June 1945, about 10,000 POWs from a nearby stockade for soldiers of the regular German Army were delivered by the Americans across the Czech border to the Communists, and of those about 50 percent died in captivity."

So far the report from *Der Freiwillige.* The tragedy of the whole matter is that even now, so long after the fighting, neither the American Army nor the German vassal government is making any attempts to assist in such endeavors as was undertaken by Werner Barmann, and thereby bring closure to a sad chapter in European history.

As a matter of fact, if there is the "danger" that the truth might come out, then doubts are immediately planted into the public's minds by the behind-the-scenes masters who are also experts at obfuscation. I assume that these people do know the truth, and are only concerned about their own dead that were allegedly the victims of a "singular" crime. I also would venture to guess that they really deem it in the Jewish interest not to permit the mass graves of German postwar casualties to be discovered and registered.

In this context I would like to compare the American treatment of German POWs with that of the German treatment of the American air crews which devastated the 1000-year-old German culture, who (along with the British) killed about one million civilians, mostly women and children,[32] and in doing so fell into German hands: only about 1 percent of these American POWs did not survive the war.

Most Americans have watched STALAG 17 in the movies or on TV. I am certain they enjoyed the antics of the German Colonel Klink and his sidekick Sergeant Schulz, and how both were always outsmarted by the wiliness of a high-ranking American officer assigned to deal with the Germans. Well, in 1945 the U.S. Army had no problems with something like that. In *none* of their

---

[32] Until recently this civilian German casualty figure was always given as "600,000", but on Nov. 19, 1998, Col. Harry G. Summers, a former professor at the U.S. War College, stated in an article in the Washington Times the more accurate figure of one million figure for the first time. It took "only" 53 years for a courageous American officer to come closer to the truth. One compare the million figure with the six civilian war dead on the U.S. mainland in WWII.

stockades did the Americans permit the German POWs to be represented by an officer or by a spokesman from the ranks. Not at Lambach, not at Steyr (where I also was) and certainly not at Bad Kreuznach, to name but these few camps.

To me it seems that the major lessons regarding the treatment of prisoners, and how to deal with "enemy" populations, lessons that seem ingrained in the psyche of the U.S. Armed Forces (and other Washington authorities) stem from the American War between the States. A direct line of "Washington"-behavior runs from the battlefields of Antietam and Atlanta to Germany and Vietnam, and now, to places like Waco, Whidbey Island and Ruby Ridge. Already in 1865 they hung hapless Swiss-born Confederate Captain Heinrich Wirz for his "crimes" at Andersonville, forgetting to even reprimand the Northern jailers who together caused many more deaths of Confederate POWs than he was accused of. As long as the bones of the victims remain hidden, no account is needed or desired by the U.S. political system. When fifty or a hundred years after the fact the truth comes out, such as happened in regard to the Indian wars and slavery, the individual culprits are usually dead, and the system is ready for the next charade as savior of mankind. The American Government could not very well play the moral arbiter in such places as the Middle East, Kosovo, Macedonia and Latin America if the whole truth about "USA"-behavior in wars and after wars became generally known. Unfortunately, the American people knows very little of such dismal facts, and the head honchos of the Establishment see to it that information regarding such transgressions against human decency are published only in a sanitized form, if at all.

The following are excerpts of stories about the cruel and inhuman treatment that was endemic in American and French stockades for up to two years after the end of the war. These stories are taken from various postwar sources, among them a magazine called *Eurojournal* (2/1996), and from a local Austrian postwar newspaper. Please note that it was at the Lambach "camp" were I was held from May 14th, 1945 to one of the first days of June:

"The first American soldiers entered Lambach, which in the meantime had been declared a hospital town, on the 4th of May 1945. They were from the 71st U.S. Infantry Division. Immediately

after their arrival, the Americans arrested the mayor and the city councilmen, and demanded that persons without "Nazi" political affiliations assume the administration of the town.

(This was the normal procedure of the Americans whenever they conquered a town in the Reich. More often than not the new people chosen as administrators were known Communists. HS)

"Within hours, some parts of the population had heard of the existence of a food depot at the brewery of the abbey, and soon this depot and a warehouse of the Wehrmacht at the railroad station were being plundered. American soldiers with drawn weapons had to end these wanton acts.

"Also on the 4th of May, units of the 71st Infantry Division liberated the concentration camp at Gunskirchen (only a few miles to the north, HS). They were shocked by what they saw: Tens of thousands of concentration camp inmates stood between the primitive wooden barracks (prefabricated buildings, HS) behind the barbed wire. Many were weak from hunger, others were walking around looking like the many dead that were lying between the buildings.

"The combat units of the U.S. Army were in no position to take care of these unfortunates. Therefore, they simply opened the gates of the camp, and permitted the prisoners to go where they wanted to go.

"Soon the townspeople of Lambach heard of the first attacks of concentration camp inmates on the population, and for a few days it was wise for Austrians to barricade themselves in their houses. Many of the concentration camp inmates, who were simply called "the Jews" by the citizens, were suffering from typhus, and there was the fear that an epidemic would break out. Thankfully, the large part of the population was spared from this scourge, and there were only a few casualties.

"Almost unnoticed by the people of Lambach, the Americans began creating a collection point for German POWs at the open meadows near the Traun river called the Hofau. Soon it became obvious that this was not going to be a normal POW camp: nobody was being discharged or sent somewhere else, and the meadow began filling up fast with disarmed German soldiers. ***The POWs were not registered, nor had they to undergo admission formalities.*** *They were simply placed out in the open grasslands,*

behind the barbed wire, and left to their fate. It is now estimated that the number of German POWs at the Lambach stockade reached as high twenty or thirty thousand. To the citizens of Lambach it looked as if there was not even enough room for all the POWs to lie down.

"The food supply for so many German POWs had broken down. Those soldiers who still had some of their Iron ration in their mess kits were lucky. The others had to depend on the little food, mostly legumes and some bread in extremely small amounts, given to them by the Americans. Some of the German POWs began eating grass and dandelions. While in the beginning there were still some bushes near the river that could be used for firewood, this was soon gone also. As a result, the untreated water from the river could not be boiled, and this caused sickness and death. ***There was no medical care for the POWs.***

"Today nobody knows how many German POWs died in these couple of months at the Lambach stockade. A comparison with the infamous Rheinwiesenlager near Remagen cannot be denied. The dead were collected by their comrades and then taken away to an unknown place, often in American Army ambulances. Today nobody knows where they are buried, and how many there were.

"POWs in the separate Waffen-SS camp fared worst. The Americans still had the horrors of the Gunskirchen concentration camp in mind, and held the entire SS responsible for this atrocity.

"Eventually, the American combat troops were replaced by administrators who were trained to deal with POWs, and their task was to send the "innocent" (unincriminated) POWs home. This was none too soon because there was the real danger of an unimaginable catastrophe in the form of the starvation, and an infectious disease epidemic was going to break out.

"Many of the newly arrived American soldiers who interrogated the POWs spoke German because they had emigrated to America when Hitler took power. Some of them even were from Austria.

"In the middle of June, there were still 11,000 POWs in the stockade. This figure is known because it seems to have been the first counting of the POWs that had taken place since the end of

the war. It had been undertaken by soldiers of the 65th U.S. Infantry Division which had arrived as occupiers.

"Similar encampments such as at Lambach could be found in the nearby area at Steyr, Ebensee, Mauerkirchen, Wegscheid and Freistadt. In the beginning of August the number of POWs in Lambach again increased by thousands when many former German soldiers who had not been properly discharged by the Allies were re-arrested, and brought into the camp. By then, however, the situation was not as bad as it had been before. This action was undertaken by the U.S. 26th Infantry Division, parts of the permanent occupation army.

"Finally, at the end of August it was possible for relatives to supply food and other items to the POWs inside the camp, and even a few visitors were allowed. As the winter approached, the Lambach stockade was dissolved, and the remaining POWs were taken somewhere else. Soon nothing reminded of the tragedy that had taken place in the Hofau meadow."

Before I am going to make a final comment on the Lambach stockade, I will reprint below some excerpts from the report of a young Austrian boy who had been a German soldier for all of two months at the end of the war, and who was taken to this "camp" in mid-August, seemingly at the time when the 26th Infantry Division had been assigned to the area. More than fifty years later I am still surprised by the callousness and the cruelty so many GIs showed at the time. Most American soldiers were indifferent, an attitude one can ascribe to immaturity and the lack of education but more of the bad guys than good ones stood out. I personally was more than lucky to encounter such fine men as John Shoemaker, the GI at the first small stockade on May 6th and, later, Captain Frye. Since Americans are, as a rule, people with strong Christian beliefs, and it is known that they are diligent churchgoers, one must wonder what happened to some of them with their Christian charity once they stepped onto European soil. Well, perhaps it was only heathens that guarded the Eisenhower stockades.

"We were six young boys from Waizenkirchen whom the American soldiers sent to the Lambach camp. I was 15 years old at the time, two of the others were even younger than myself. Once in the stockade we received neither food nor water from the

Americans, and otherwise there was only a small plot of God's nature to lie on.

"I was lucky, an older German soldier who was going to be discharged the same day left me with the hole in the ground he had dug himself, and where he had slept on a piece of rubber mat about 24" by 30" in size. I have kept this mat to this day.

"As I said, we didn't get anything to eat, and those that had been at Lambach before us had eaten all the grass including the roots. We drank the unfiltered water from the Traun river.

"I was only two or three weeks in the camp. Once when I was lying in my hole in the ground someone called me by my name, but I didn't recognize who it was. When he told me, I could hardly believe it, he was an old acquaintance but now he was only bones and skin. ***I did not see any dead soldiers, their bodies were taken away by night.***

"There is no doubt in my mind that it was the intention of the Americans to kill as many of us as possible by starvation.

"The nearby SS-encampment was much more closely guarded than our area. There were machine gun nests all around it. Many of the POWs there were from our area, but their relatives were only allowed to throw food-packages to them across the barbed wire. If one of the packages fell short and a POW tried to retrieve it anyway, he was shot to death. Only once in a while it happened that a gallant American soldier saw to it that the package was pushed underneath the barbed wire to the POW.

"Black American soldiers were nicer to us than were the white ones. Most of the white Americans with whom I had to deal were oafs.

"After a couple of weeks we suddenly were fed, and there were rumors that former German soldiers might be used in a war against the Russians. But eventually this proved not to be true, and I was discharged home."

It bears remembering that this boy was only sixteen years of age, and he was "captured" more than three months after the shooting had stopped. I also can state unequivocally that there was no German underground operating. In other words, this excuse for incarcerating sixteen year-olds never had any validity. Attacks against Allied soldiers were almost unheard of. Luckily for the Allies they did not get back any of the "partisan" (in 2001 "terrorist") medicine they had prescribed for the Germans almost since the beginning of the war.

As I was writing these memoirs, I came into possession of a bilingual brochure titled "War memoirs, February 17, 1943 to December 14, 1949", the remembrances of a former German soldier Georg Karl Rings. (Published in a small quantity by Leo R. Wastler, 29 Heron Rd., Lititz, PA, 17543, and available for $20.00.) What stands out in this booklet was the extremely cruel treatment Rings received at the hands of the Poles, by whom he was forced to do slave labor under extremely harsh conditions in a coal mine (without pay!) from 1945 to 1949, and the fact that the Poles, like the U.S. Army, had prohibited the International Red Cross to visit the Germans in their camps. Compare this to the fair treatment tens of thousands of Polish officers and hundreds of thousands of their soldiers received in German camps. Tragically, even the Red Cross was amiss when it did not officially notify Rings' parents of his survival. And this happened two years after the war had ended, and in spite of the fact that he was first mentioned on a list of German soldiers still in Polish hands six months earlier. Geneva is but a couple of hundred miles from the Palatinate where Rings came from and still lives today. Coming from a German coal mining region (our home is only a few hundred feet from the shafts of the mine) I can vouch for the fact that in the large Luisenthal mine during the war foreign miners, of whatever nationality were <u>not</u> mistreated.

Reading this sad, very small chapter of World War II, a number of things become apparent. First of all I would like to state that the Lambach "camp" was no exception. There were hundreds of similar stockades for German POWs all across Europe, and the conditions in them varied only slightly. James Bacque was right when he wrote that the wholesale starvation in the camps was pre-planned and pre-determined. Seemingly, according to the thinking of the Allied high command, the German armed forces had not incurred enough battle casualties in six years of war, and this deficiency had to be belatedly corrected. The major responsibility for this war crime can be squarely laid at the feet of then General Dwight D. Eisenhower, the Allied Supreme Commander in Europe who, according to his own words, hated the Germans with a passion. Eisenhower removed the POW status from most German prisoners of war near the end of the hostilities illegally, and definitely against the international laws that had also been signed by the United States. Thereby he prevented inspections of the "Eisenhower death camps" by the Red Cross, and also prevented fair treatment for the POWs. Personally, I consider it an act of cowardice to vent revenge against people who cannot defend themselves anymore.

Americans who were born long after World War II may wonder why most of these unfortunate German soldiers did not take their fate in their own hands in the face of almost certain death by starvation. Certainly the U.S. Army could not have stopped a mass break-out from the camp by the tens of thousands of POW at Lambach if such an escape had been attempted.

The primary reason for such a life-threatening failure by the very soldiers who had proven their personal courage in a war that had brought them to the center of Stalingrad, to the city of Narvik near the Arctic circle, to the hot deserts of Libya, and even to the shores of the United States in their U-Boats, can be found in the different codes of honor and chivalry that existed between the German *Wehrmacht* and the Allied armies; between the victors and the vanquished. How else can one explain the incident near the entrance to the Dachau concentration camp in late April 1945, when a young, highly decorated Waffen-SS first lieutenant approached, seemingly without any trepidation, the ranking officer of the first American column nearing the gates, and tried to turn over the camp according to international standards. The American officer, seemingly incensed because the German had greeted him with the raised right arm, just as Roman soldiers had greeted Emperor Augustus, promptly lifted his machine gun and shot the German dead. The saddest part of the story is the fact that this young Waffen-SS officer was a combat officer who, with his soldiers, had been ordered to guard the inmates of the Dachau camp after the regular concentration camp guards had run away.

For most Germans it was inconceivable that now that the war was over, the Allies were going to continue the war by other means, and, as we have seen so far, even into the Twenty-first Century. Already during the fighting the Germans could not envision why personal rancor and hate should exist among common soldiers. The 'grunts' of both sides were all merely doing their duty. Once the shooting was over, most German soldiers laid down their arms, and marched willingly into Allied captivity. With few exceptions, like myself, they believed the assurances of the victors that after some screening they would be sent home to their loved ones soon and begin rebuilding their lives and towns. At the time most of them were convinced that the starvation in stockades like at Lambach was due to the fact that the American supply system had broken down. And while they slowly starved to death, they were hoping, day by day, that the following morning would bring relief from hunger, and speedy discharge. That is why they made no attempt to get away on their own.

German soldiers did not view World War II as a war between "good and evil", or black and white. They knew that wars are the bane of mankind, and that when one side wins, the other loses. Even while victorious in the first years of the war, they did not ascribe to themselves a moral superiority, and this is proven by their exemplary behavior in such countries like France and Denmark, and others. No doubt the German population supported the Hitler Government in its *justified* quest to rectify the obvious injustices and insanity of the Versailles Treaty, and when the Polish atrocities at Bromberg became known in September of 1939, where many thousands of German civilians had been murdered by Polish thugs, emotions ran high. But this did little to affect the discipline prevailing in the German armed forces.

American soldiers were much more imbued with hate against the unknown enemy as can still be seen in the hundreds of anti-German movies of the war and pre-war years shown on television. The American illusion of fighting for "democracy" remains just that, an illusion, as the political conditions in present-day Germany prove. If put to test, few GIs could have explained how a so-called democratic world should look, and who would eventually be the real (behind-the-scenes) rulers.

On September 9, 2001 the HBO TV channel began showing the first segment of an expensive twelve part series that is based on the book "Band of Brothers" by the current U.S. court historian Stephen E. Ambrose. The series deals with a group of U.S. parachutists who fight their way from the D-Day through France, get stuck in Bastogne, and eventually reach Adolf Hitler's alpine redoubt near Berchtesgaden. I have not read the book but the story is obviously about the war experiences of soldiers of the 101st Airborne Division, the Screaming Eagles.

In the NYT write-up about the TV-series written by Caryn James, I discovered this sentence: *"By Episode 9 (---) Easy Company discovers a concentration camp. The camera focuses on the emaciated bodies and those inside and also on the shocked faces of the American soldiers we have followed. The installment called "Why We Fight," is undeniably forceful and (---) comes late in the series. But from a viewer's perspective, (it) comes (too) late."*

I wonder what the American leadership would have done if Germany had been defeated by fall of 1944, and if the U.S. and British air fleets would not have had a chance - - exploited to its limits in 1945 - - to destroy the German transport system that, among other things, previously had brought food and medicine to the concentration camps. Would it have meant "no emaciated bodies, few deaths, hence no German guilt?" It must be remembered that in the first exuberance after the German defeat the Allies couldn't even get their act together as to what had (allegedly) happened at camps like Auschwitz. I still recommend the 1944 book "The Story of a Secret State" by the late Polish agent Jan Karski as a prime example of crude Allied propaganda that consists not only of phony but really stupid anti-German accusations. Alas, these accusations were obviously not so stupid that many Americans did not believe them at first sight.

As I am writing this, the "Band of Brothers" series is still being shown for the first time. I doubt, however, that it will depict, at its very end, the POW cages holding tens of thousands of German POWs, and their slow dying off under circumstances that were much worse than anything experienced in the concentration camps, something the soldiers of the 101st Airborne Division must also have seen.

Mr. Ambrose's version of history could also be found in an article titled "GI Joe: Person of the 20th Century" that was printed in the September 2001 American Legion magazine.

First I have to take issue with Stephen E. Ambrose's statement that "GI Joe" was <u>the</u> "Person of the 20th Century". Unhesitatingly I would give this title to the German *Landser* (Army infantry soldier) of the Eastern front. No allied soldier had to go through and fight for four years against such overwhelming enemy superiority in numbers and material as these soldiers had encountered. Had they not stopped Stalin's hordes weeks before their planned onslaught, European civilization would really have been destroyed. Unfortunately, very few of the *Landsers* survived the Eastern front ordeal, Eisenhower's death camps or Soviet captivity.

There is no doubt that Mr. Ambrose is a good propagandist. At this time of reawakening, and purposely generated, American patriotism, his many books and articles seem to hit the right chord. Unfortunately, this historian does it at the expense of others; at times of brave German soldiers. In the above-mentioned American Legion magazine article, for instance, Ambrose wrote the following:

"(An ex-GI) said, 'Listen, Steve, I was 18 years old. I had my whole life ahead of me. I knew the difference between right and wrong, and I did not want to live in a world in which wrong prevailed, so I fought.'

To this I only have to ask the question where this young American learned the difference between right and wrong? From the hundreds of anti-German movies produced in Hollywood studies, and writers like Theodore Kaufman ("Germany must perish!") and Walter Winchell?

Ambrose continued:

"Right here is the hallmark of GI Joe. In the first decades of the bloodiest century ever, German, Japanese and Russian boys were brought up not to know the difference between right and wrong."

"It's impossible for me to imagine American teenage soldiers doing to defenseless civilians what Serbian troops did in Kosovo, - - - and what the German boys did wherever they went during World War II."

In this context one must remember that Ambrose denigrates with such words the soldiers of the most disciplined Army of World War II. It was the (combined) Allied armies who raped millions of women, killing hundreds of thousands of them in the process, it was they who refined the art of looting to the point that in all of Germany not a single safe deposit box had been left untouched, and who introduced the black market, drug trade and prostitution wherever they went. And, must I (again) mention Dresden and

Pforzheim and Würzburg, and all the other non-industrial cities that were laid to waste "by boys who knew right from wrong" because of the Allied overabundance of bombs, or lust for unwarranted revenge?

I have mentioned earlier in these recollections that my own disbelief in Allied assurances and integrity stemmed mostly, from the bad experiences my mother's uncle Jakob had with the French after the First World War. In spite of having been one of the German infantry soldiers who had been buried in the trenches of Verdun after an enemy artillery barrage, and from which he had suffered permanent damage, he had been kept a slave laborer in France for more than three years. Uncle Jakob had warned me never to trust the promises of either the French or any of the other Allies.

Another reason for my distrust in anything that came from the victors could be found in my intensive reading of Allied propaganda leaflets, and my officially forbidden listening to enemy broadcasts on the radio. Far too often I had discovered flagrant lies in the Allied claims. For instance, at war's end I still remembered reading Thomas Mann's, the exiled famous German writer's, 1942 message to the German nation wherein he had stated that in a 1940 air raid on Rotterdam, the *Luftwaffe* had killed 30,000 Hollanders, while one of the Dutch "slave laborers" (modern nomenclature) whom I had befriended in Luisenthal, told me about the same time that there had been fewer than one thousand unfortunate victims of the German air attack against Dutch forces.

By the end of May 1945 I had been an American POW for more than two weeks, and I did not like it. During this time I was obviously unbeknownst to me one of the millions of former German soldiers who, on orders of Dwight D. Eisenhower, had been criminally classified DEF (disarmed enemy forces), and thus were removed from the oversight of the International Red Cross that *during the war* had at all times the opportunity to inspect the German camps where, for instance, American POWs were kept. As a result of Eisenhower's action we were practically starved to death in open air-stockades where there was no shelter of any kind.

In the spring of 2001 stories about a so-called German concentration camp at "Berga" appeared in the American media where former American ex-POWs, among them a number of Jews, claimed to have been awfully mistreated. The slant of these stories was that especially the Jews among these POWs had been selected because they were Jews, and therefore ended up outside of the Red Cross-inspected normal POW camps. Available statistics disprove these allegations. To anybody knowledgeable in these matters, the claims seemed phony from the start. However, on the other hand, there is some truth in the saying "where there is smoke, there is fire". Therefore, my assumption must be explained:

There is little doubt that in *all* German camps where foreign POWs were held, there existed some serious troublemakers. We can also assume that efforts were made to separate these troublemakers from the general population of POWs, and this is where the camp at Berga could come in. We may also assume that Berga, if it was a camp for troublemakers, had harsher conditions than was true in a regular POW camp. If there were more than the average number of Jews at Berga then this can be explained by pointing to the proclivity of Jews for being troublemakers (Jews in the forefront of Vietnam War anti-war protesters; Jews as premier fighters during the battles of the Civil Rights era; Jews as the major agitators for socialist [Communist] causes; Jews who supplied most of the soldiers of the International [Communist] brigades during the Spanish Civil War; Jewish children complaining in schools attended mostly by Christian children when at Christmas time Christian chorals are sung, etc. etc.).

The Lambach "camp" in Austria contained at one time about 30,000 to 40,000 German POWs, and every day a number of them died, with their emaciated bodies being stripped of everything in the dark of the night, and then unceremoniously dumped in places where to this day they cannot be found. These dead heroes are still part of the 1.2 million German soldiers missing from World War II 56 years later. (A reminder: The Armed Forces of the United States officially lost 407,316 men and women between 1941 and 1945, about a third the number of *missing* German soldiers. Can anyone imagine the heartbreak that lies in these numbers?) In 1939 the U.S. population stood at about 145 million, Germany's at about 80 million. For many decades after 1945 the parents, children and siblings waited in vain for the return of these German servicemen and women. Part of the reason for many German families never giving up hope was the Allied policy of not permitting German

POWs to write home for extended periods of time. Some Germans held in the Soviet Union returned ten years after the war without ever having had the opportunity to contact their families. (Is that what American soldiers had fought for? After all, the Soviets were America's ally in this so-called "good" war.)

The Gunskirchen concentration camp story that was years later printed in the *Eurokurier* must be viewed in the proper context, and cannot be compared to the mistreatment of the POWs: Gunskirchen was originally probably a work camp belonging to the nearby Mauthausen concentration camp complex (where, incidentally, many captured Polish insurgents of the 1944 Warsaw uprising were kept). As the Germans retreated from the east, many concentration camp inmates were brought deeper inside the Reich from areas now under Russian control, and existing housing in the concentration camps became overfilled with internees who were weak and sick from the deprivations of long marches. In addition, the lice-infestation in all of Eastern Europe was incredible, as was the bad personal hygiene of concentration camp inmates fresh out of the ghettos. (This latter point is proven by the fact that few typhus outbreaks occurred in camps filled with starving German POWs, while such epidemics were responsible for the high death rates at, for instance, the Bergen-Belsen concentration camp where Anne Frank died.)

We can be certain that the Germans in charge of the concentration camps at the end of the war made every effort to feed their charges to the best of their abilitiy, even if these rations were by then only so-called hunger rations. The incessant bombing and strafing by Allied planes of everything that moved inside the German realm prevented an orderly distribution of food and medicines. (Was this also intended?) In addition, I would like to point to the previously reprinted sentence from the *Eurokurier* article where it says that the concentration camp inmates "stood between the barracks at Gunskirchen", proving the fact that these internees had been able to sleep inside a reasonable shelter, something every German POW at Lambach would have wished for.

The purposeful hiding of the bodies of German POWs that had died in these death camps proves, in my opinion, the fiendishness of the American ruling clique. It has nothing to do with the general goodheartedness of the population of the United States. It is comparable to the abandonment of American POWs by this satanic system after World War II, the Korean War and in Vietnam.

A "timely" addendum to the Lambach story: In the winter of 1996, workers preparing the so-called Lambach Hofau (meadows) for the building of a dam across the Traun river, discovered a mass grave with skeletons of fifteen mostly young men. A former POW who was called in as an expert stated that these were probably the remains of some of the dead German POWs of the Lambach stockade of 1945. But almost immediately a Jewish expert was sent from Vienna who claimed that these skeletons might be those of Jews who had been killed at the end of the war. This Jewish expert then prohibited further disturbance of the mass grave since Jewish graves may not be disturbed. Another expert countered that the skeletons could not have belonged to Jews because the teeth and bones were in good shape, such as had been the norm in the German armed forces. This statement was immediately rebuked as an expression of anti-Semitism, with no further comment permitted.

To make a long story short, eventually all sides agreed that the bones were probably those of rebels killed in a battle in 1626, and are therefore 370 years old. But in order not to harm Jewish sensitivities no further testing of this allegation was permitted.

My opinion: Just like at Bad Kreuznach and other places where mass graves of American origin might be discovered, a well-oiled machinery comes into play to kill the story through obfuscation or tall tales, or else the present "authorities" prohibit further searches with spurious arguments. The people currently in power in Europe know who butters their bread. It is also not surprising that "a Jewish representative from Vienna" arrived so fast. Perhaps this points to the real culprits for the 1945 policy of burying the dead German POWs in hidden mass graves.

Even if it is true that the fifteen skeletons found at Lambach belonged to victims of a long-ago war, there is no reason why one should not probe further. In spite of all the talk, and all the newsprint that was wasted in the spring of 1996 in Upper Austria after the discovery of this mass grave, the question still remains where are the skeletons of those German POWs that died while in American custody at Lambach? And why is no effort being made to provide these unfortunates, whose number will never be known, with a decent, Christian burial? Whatever happened to the Christian values Americans pride themselves on?

In his book CRIMES AND MERCIES, published by Warner Books, London, in 1997, the previously mentioned Canadian writer James Bacque, who did such yeoman work in bringing out the truth about what had happened in Central Europe after the defeat of Germany in 1945, wrote the following about the Lambach POW camp:

"At Lambach in Austria, early in 1996, during excavations for a new power plant, a mass grave was opened on an 80m square site near the river Traun. One theory is that these were bodies of Jews who died during transport, but the evidence suggests strongly that these were German prisoners of the Americans. In 1945 there were three American-run POW camps in the region. Horst Littmann, an expert recommended by the Austrian Ministry of the Interior, concluded that the bodies were the dead prisoners from these American camps, men between the ages of nineteen and twenty-two, judging from the good condition of their teeth, the shape of their heads and other evidence."

Bacque then uses the fact that the Austrian Government had sent an expert for the Lambach investigation as an example of how differently such matters are handled in Germany, where usually the whitewash of Allied crimes begins at the local level. With myself having been a POW at Lambach, however, the story reads (now, with new facts) differently: After hearing of the Lambach discovery, I immediately contacted the Austrian authorities in charge of the investigation and offered my help. I also described in detail where I had been in 1945, and what I had experienced. I never heard from them. In fact, I did not even receive an acknowledgment of my letter. Later I found out that the Austrians had (in the meantime) contacted the *Oberjuden* in Vienna, who desperately needed some bodies for their Holocaust allegations. When it appeared that the bones were really parts of the skeletons of German POWs who had died in American hands (and that this could be proven through people like me who had been there in 1945) the story was totally altered: A month after the matter had made news, the Austrian press reported that the remains had in fact been those people who had died 300 or 400 years ago in the *Bauernkriege*, the farmer's uprisings that had been fought in the area. A commission of (court) historians hastily called together by the Austrian Government allegedly also did not find proof that in 1945 German soldiers had been buried in the area, thereby giving the power company a go-ahead with plans to build a reservoir on the spot. This was done in spite of the fact that the Lambach registrar of births and deaths had in 1945 registered the names of about 450 German POWs who died in a short time in the American camp from various causes, but whose remains were never found, since the U.S. Army was quite adept at getting rid of unwanted bodies. Furthermore, the Government commission totally disregarded the eyewitness accounts of Austrian witnesses who in 1945 had been held at the Lambach stockade, at least one of whom who had been with the burial detail.

As was to be expected, James Bacque's two books on the criminal mistreatment of German POWs by the victorious Allies never generated a reasonable response from the wrongdoers. Stephen E. Ambrose, the current major U.S. military writer, tried to whitewash Eisenhower in cooperation with a German renegade but failed miserably in doing so.

I had no intention of becoming a nameless American statistic, anonymously being buried in a mass grave. After having been kept in the open field of the Lambach stockade for more than two weeks without shelter of any kind, and very little food, I decided to take my fate in my own hands again. I therefore seriously contemplated escaping through the barbed wire fence, accepting the risk of being shot by trigger-happy GIs. But again fate intervened.

On one of the very first days of June, 1945, when our young *Luftwaffe* officer asked for a handful of volunteers for an *Arbeitskommando* (work detail) the Americans had requested, I was one of the first ones he asked, and without hesitation I said yes.

Aside from the fact that men who performed some duties for the Americans had a chance to get some extra food, I used such opportunities to case the surroundings for possible escape routes, and other facts that might come in handy when I was ready to leave the "camp".

Chapter 30

As usual, I had all my possessions, including my blanket and the gas mask container nearly filled with dried peas, with me when we boarded a U.S. Army truck. There was always a chance that these things would get stolen in my absence. Also as usual, the Americans made no attempt to write down our names when we left the stockade aboard one of their ten-wheelers. I doubt if they even counted us.

Our work consisted of unloading full gasoline canisters (Jerry cans) and crates with C-rations from huge trucks with trailers, and stacking them alongside rows upon rows of similar supplies in the open, and then pulling large tarpaulins over the perishables. While we were doing this, we were constantly guarded, and there was no chance to "liberate" any of the foodstuffs.

It must have been in the afternoon, and after we had been fed by the Americans, when I noticed several U.S. Army trucks with a greater number of German POWs arrive from the west, from the direction of my home. They too were put to work, but in another corner of this huge open air supply depot of the U.S. Army.

Since it was my aim to get out of the Lambach death camp as fast as possible, *and* to work my way west, home toward the Saarland, come what may, it did not take me long to look for an opportunity to join the other group of POWs, assuming of course that after completion of their work they would be driven back to the other camp in the direction from which they had come. In addition, it was my assumption that nothing could be worse than the conditions at the Lambach stockade. - I could not envision that such situations existed in U.S. and French Army stockades all over the Western part of Europe.

The open air latrine, a long ditch in the ground, in front of which a couple of tree trunks had been placed whereon to sit, provided me with the opportunity to switch sides. I had noticed that all POWs performing work for the Americans used the latrine, and there was no GI nearby to watch that the prisoners went back to "their" group. The horrible stench of human excrement made certain that no GI came close. At an opportune moment I went to the "open air" latrine when at least twenty of the Germans were sitting peacefully next to each other doing their business. Then I walked back with some guys from the other group, and nonchalantly helped them unload artillery shells and stack them neatly on the ground.

To my surprise this work was finished much sooner than I had anticipated, and within an hour I was aboard a truck in a small convoy not being driven to the west, as I had expected, but in a northwesterly direction - toward Germany. I wished I could have said goodbye to the *Luftwaffe* officer, but under the circumstances I realized this might not have been a good thing to do. Driving away from the supply depot, I saw the Lambach POWs still hard at work. For a while I was afraid someone aboard the truck might discover that I really did not belong to this group of POWs, and I therefore kept to myself and also my mouth shut. But my fear was unwarranted: this crowd of POWs was just as motley a crew as were the hundred guys at Lambach under the *Oberleutnant's* command. At the end of hostilities they had all been stragglers like myself, removed from their original units of the German Armed Forces, and even on this transport they did not belong to any particular group of POWs except that for some unknown reason they had been put aboard the same truck. I also noticed that almost all of these men were considerably older than myself, 25 years of age and up. But beyond that I didn't give it any thought. Shortly after climbing aboard the truck I had discovered that this was a *Verlegung,* a transport of POWs from one camp to another, and nobody knew the destination nor the reason.

Of this trip, which lasted quite a few hours, I remember but two things: soon after we had left Austria, and as we were still being driven in a northwesterly direction, I saw several rows of American fighter planes, either P-47s or P-51s, to the west of the road where we traveled, on the tarmac of a partially destroyed large airfield of the *Luftwaffe*. It was an impressive sight. The planes had their noses painted bright red, and probably were from the same squadron that had given us such a hard time in the Battle of the Bulge.

I also cannot forget the abandon with which American truck drivers raced through the extremely narrow streets of quaint old German towns with their many half-timbered houses and imposing churches. More than once I saw German civilians, children among them, jump aside in fright when the U.S. Army vehicles passed at full speed through streets that were almost too narrow for any motor vehicle.

In the evening we arrived in a mid-sized Bavarian city with a distinct medieval look. By then I was so tired, and probably so weak, that I didn't even care what the name of this town was. But I do recall that we were placed in a large old equipment hall of a former German artillery barracks, with the architecture pointing to the Kaiser's era, and for the first time since I had left the hospital at Bad Hall I was able to sleep indoors.

The following morning we received some food, and then we had to stand in line in front of a row of American Army tents that were marked with letters of the alphabet. Schmidt, for instance, had to stand in front of the tent marked (something like) "R to Z". Seemingly we were being processed for discharge!

Looking at the document that I received at this place, and which is still in my possession, I know that we were examined by German POW doctors, but I have no recollection of this at all. However, I do remember the moment I stepped inside the "R to Z" tent and faced a young officer of the U.S. Army. Captain J.B. Frye of the 22nd Infantry Regiment, 4th U.S. Infantry Division, III Corps, smiled when I stepped in front of him, probably because I greeted him quite snappily with the raised right arm, just as we had been taught in the Waffen-SS. I could see the horrified faces of the few German POW orderlies that scurried about, shuffling papers and seeing to it that everything was in order. (I assume these were the same guys which only a month earlier had told fifteen year-old boys that we were still going to win the war.)

At any rate, after Captain Frye had asked my name and rank in fairly good German, and after I had told him that I was a private, he began searching for "Hans Schmidt" in a book in front of him that was thicker than the Chicago telephone book (years later I found out that it contained about 300,000 names of "suspect" Germans). Personally I thought the situation funny, and, being certain that I was not listed, I went closer to the table behind which the Captain was sitting, and at a glance I could see that there were about 17 Hans Schmidts mentioned in the book. Thereupon I told the Captain kiddingly that I could provide him with a reasonable number of additional Hans Schmidts since this is just about the most common name in *Deutschland.* The Captain laughed, and after that we had a pleasant conversation about my combat experience (I was still wearing the *Verwundetenabzeichen*/Purple Heart which I had stuck on my "false" Army infantry uniform, but my Iron Cross ribbon was gone by then.) The American had also fought in the Battle of the Bulge, and we discovered that on some days in the winter of 1945 we had not been far apart from each other, albeit on different sides of the front.

German POWs being interrogated by GIs.

Today I am certain that Captain Frye knew that I was a Waffen-SS soldier, even though I had stuck to my story of being a private from a *Kampfgruppe Lt. Sporn* of the Army infantry. He was, after all, a decorated combat officer who must have been familiar with the campaigns of the German elite divisions at the end of the war, and I was truthful as far as my battle experience was concerned. But on the following day, according to the discharge document on the 4th of June 1945, when I walked out of the Captain's tent I had papers in my hand declaring that I had been a soldier in the German army. Frye had also suggested that I do state Luisenthal as my home town since this would enable me to get home directly, and not via Bad Bertrich. The Captain assured me that Saarbrücken was occupied by American and not by French soldiers. My early discharge was largely the result of the need for coal miners that were necessary to get the Saar coal mines operating again. There was the assumption that I would volunteer to work underground, digging coal.

For several decades after the war I was not certain where the German barracks in that medieval city in Bavaria, where I had met Captain Frye, was located. I assumed that it might have been in Ansbach or Amberg, or a town with a similar name. But the truth, discovered not very long ago, is even more interesting: When I surreptitiously joined that other group of German POWs at the U.S. Army Supply Depot near Lambach, I unwittingly had joined a unit of German POWs whom the Americans thought to be in need of further investigation either as "war criminals" or because they were "suspected Nazis". They, and therefore also I, were driven to the city of Bamberg, about 250 kilometers to the north, where the U.S. Army had a special interrogation center. And, seemingly due to his knowledge of the German language, Captain Frye was one of the interrogators.

Attempts by myself to get in contact with this decent American officer years later, after I had immigrated to the United States, failed since I had no idea where this good man came from. There were any number of J.B. Fryes in various telephone books, but without the proper first name and the town, finding Frye was almost impossible. In retrospect it is amazing to note how often in my life I was rescued from bad situations by angels such as this officer, and the GI corporal who saved me from delivery to the Russians.

A half century later I assume that within a day or two after I had received the discharge paper signed by Captain Frye on the 4th of June, 1945, a transport of former German soldiers, now freed from captivity, was organized at Bamberg, and put on a train composed of freight cars using the railroad route that meandered along the Main River toward the west. Of this train trip, during which I stood for hours on end at the open sliding door viewing the still-beautiful German landscape, but also feeling deeply hurt when seeing the formerly beautiful and now destroyed cities and towns, I vividly remember seeing somewhere a huge pile of smashed aluminum: the remnants of Allied bombing planes shot down over Germany. During this trip we were not guarded anymore, but still under American supervision. This prevented us from having to show our new documents at the numerous check points which the victors had established ever so often. Some of the German ex-soldiers were sitting at the open door of the wagon, with their legs dangling on the outside. A GI came by and warned them not to do that since it had happened already that some ex-POWs' legs had been torn off when trains were traveling over one of the many extremely narrow emergency spans that had been built by U.S. Army engineers when they repaired the bridges.

The night from June 6th to the 7th we were put up in a building that was part of a German Air Force barracks near Mainz. The walls of the huge hall where we slept still showed nicely executed *Durchhalteparolen,* propaganda slogans extolling the German soldiers to fight on to final victory. It was probably then that I discovered why the U.S. Army was so kind, and was even willing to drive us home to the Saarland: at the end of the war it was every GI's dream to visit Paris and have a good time. But one had to have a good reason for traveling in the direction of the French capital, and not get caught by the Military Police that was particularly nasty and effective in occupied Germany, and very efficient at all Rhine crossings. The opportunity to transport "in emergency" a number of discharged German soldiers to the coal mines of the Saar, where they were desperately needed, was too good a chance to miss. After all, Saarbrücken lies directly on the French border, across which the controls were not as stringent as in occupied Germany, *and* Saarbrücken was only 400 kilometers, or about 250 miles, from Paris. It so happened that a number of GIs of various ranks stationed in Bamberg had some leave coming, and probably with the connivance of their officers, but against higher orders, they escorted us home. This became especially apparent when on the morning of the 7th of June 1945, exactly a month after I had surrendered to the Americans, we boarded trucks in Mainz belonging to Captain Frye's unit, and thus we were driven across the Palatinate to the Saarland.

As on the days before, the drivers of U.S. Army vehicles drove way too fast for comfort. They seemed to enjoy scaring hapless civilians. I also noticed that in some small cities and villages along the route the Americans had established new roads around the center of the medieval towns by simply driving through the private gardens behind or between the houses, thereby destroying all the fruit trees and vegetable beds the German burghers had planted so diligently.

Being driven through Kaiserslautern, soon to become a major American Army base, the famous "K-town", we noticed with satisfaction that the German population there still cared for its soldiers: women and girls encircled the few trucks of our transport when the going was slow due to road damage, and gave us bread and flowers.

But a half an hour later in St. Ingbert, one of the first major cities of the Saarland we passed, I had a scare when I noticed a tricolor, the flag of France, hanging from a civic building, and French soldiers milling about. I wondered whether Captain Frye had been mistaken about the Saarland still being in American hands. I knew that it was the U.S. Seventh Army that had occupied the Saar area in March of 1945, but I also guessed, correctly as I discovered later, that the French Government had not given up on its plans to pocket the entire Saarland again, just as they had done after World War I. That in 1935 almost all of the adult the Saarlanders had, in an internationally supervised plebiscite, voted against being tied to France did not seem to matter anymore ten years later.

Suddenly, after slowly driving through street after street of rubble and bomb craters, we were in the center of Saarbrücken, and our row of trucks stopped right in front of the partially destroyed *Rathaus* (City Hall) where Adolf Hitler had accepted the return of the Saar to Germany on March 1, 1935. In a small office inside we were issued papers allowing us to return home. This was still done under the supposition that we all were going to volunteer to work in the coal mines, something I had no intention of doing. A fat little

German, judging by his talk and demeanor a former concentration camp inmate, and, judging by his lapel pin, also a Communist, made a short speech telling us that now the time of *"Nichtstun"* (doing nothing), as he called the service in the Armed Forces, was over, and that we ought to prepare ourselves to make amends through hard work for what we had done to the world. I personally didn't even get upset by this nonsense, but some of the older soldiers next to me had a hard time to control their emotions. If it hadn't been for a GI who watched the spectacle from the side lines and who urged my comrades to stay calm, it would have come to a serious altercation that might have ended in some of the poor fellows found themselves locked up again instead of being at home with their families.

After this "ceremony" we boarded "our" trucks again. Looking around me, I noticed that Saarbrücken was even more destroyed than it had been seven months earlier. On January 13th, 1945, exactly on the tenth anniversary of the Saar plebiscite of 1935, when more than 90 percent of the Saarlanders had opted for Germany and, *ipso facto,* also for Hitler and a better future, a British air armada had attacked the city, by then undefended and emptied of its inhabitants, and caused great damage. One can assume that someone belonging to the "never forget, never forgive" crowd had assisted the British or Americans in selecting Saarbrücken as a target on this very day. Some people on the Allied side got a kick out of such small-minded acts of revenge.

The January 13th, 1945, air attack on depopulated and undefended Saarbrücken deserves a detailed accounting because it proves the satanic mind-set of some of the 1945 victors, and because we may assume that these facts will never be printed in another American work about World War II:

The industrial city of a normal population of 132,000 had been evacuated since early December 1944, when it came within range of American artillery advancing from Lorraine. At the beginning of 1945, only about 600 civilians, mostly elderly men and a few women, were left, and without exception they belonged to essential services such as the utilitity companies, the water works and some medical personnel. Most of the German troops had also been withdrawn, except for those holding the thinly manned frontline in the *Westwall* bunkers along the French border, only a few kilometers to the south. On the day of the air raid, exactly one single battery of four anti-aircraft guns, probably of the famous 88mm caliber, was still in firing position. To place the matter into context we must remember that on this very day Hitler had realized that he had lost the *Ardennenoffensive* (Battle of the Bulge) gamble, and he had already ordered the withdrawal of the elite divisions from that front. It was also clear that the Allied forces would use the troops amassed against the German December assault in the German/Belgian/Luxembourg triangle to launch their next major attack from there. The Saar area had now become a secondary theater of war.

In this very first *daylight* attack on the city during the entire war (!), more than 150 four-engine British Lancaster bombers dropped more than 1,000 tons of bombs on Saarbrücken, doing considerable damage.

In the evening of the same day, about 250 planes, most of them Halifax bombers, unloaded an additional 1,500 tons on the empty ruins of the city. About 20 people were killed.

The British still claim that these air raids on Saarbrücken were undertaken because its railroad marshall yards were an important target. The fact is that by then the railroad tracks were so close to the front as to be *totally* useless for the German war effort. In addition one ought to remember that it was the British and not the Americans which attacked a city so close to the American front lines that some GIs could have easily been killed by errant British bombs. I stand by my allegation that Saarbrücken was attacked on the 10th anniversary of the Saar plebiscite of 1935 because some "German" emigrant assisting the Royal Air Force with the selection of targets could not tame his hate.

I cannot miss the opportunity to mention that the person or persons responsible for this wholly unnecessary act of war likely belonged to the same tribe that is constantly harping about the "hate" others allegedly are imbued with. As if their "Never forget, never forgive"-mentality were not the real and most fertile breeding ground for hate.

After what seemed to me only a few of minutes of driving but really took much longer due to the horrible condition of all the roads leading into and out of Saarbrücken, I suddenly saw the first houses of Luisenthal from atop the driver's cabin of the American vehicle. I immediately started banging on the roof of the cabin, but due to the great speed of the vehicle it needed time to stop. The American truck needed but a split second to pass an entrance to the coal mine near our house, the exact same view from the main street of which that is pictured in an American geography textbook of 1938, and reproduced below.

Finally, just about in front of *Kaufhaus Kleber,* the department store, the truck came to a halt, and I was able to jump off, and wave good-bye to the GIs who immediately drove on in the direction of Völkingen - - - and on to Paris. **For me the war was over.**

(Or, in the light of what has been happening ever since 1945, was it?)

As one could expect, I ran the couple of hundred feet back to our home as fast as possible. Seconds before, when the truck drove past our side street, I had seen at a glance that the old house was still standing. But in front of the now shuttered *Konsum* grocery, an old man whom I had known ever since I was a child and who had seen me jump from the U.S. Army truck greeted me in a friendly and asked somewhat incredulously: “Hans, you are home already. Didn’t I see you only a half year ago in an SS uniform?” That was all I needed at this moment. I laughed and answered only, “Herr Scherer, I notice that you are getting old. Your memory seems to be leaving you already.” Which left him dumbfounded.

From the corner of our garden and the old *Kaiser Strasse* (the major road where we had traveled from Saarbrücken,) I could see that our home was not in a bad shape. It was dark, dirty and gray, as one could expect after six years of war and neglect, and it had a large shell hole in the front side, but the roof seemed all right, meaning of course that the house was inhabitable. The building had obviously been hit by an artillery shell that had left its mark on the sandstone rim of a window on the second floor, and a big hole on the wall next to it. Getting closer, I noticed that the front door was wide open, as if inviting everybody to come in and plunder, and numerous windows and shutters had been smashed when the enemy projectile had exploded deep inside the building.

The wide-open door was the result of scattered debris in the hallway from the explosion of the shell. It also proved to me even before I entered the house that nobody of our family was as yet at home. At that moment I had no idea whether we all or only some of us had survived the war. Knowing of course that almost every German family had lost at least one family member due to war action, the chances were that not all of us, our parents and their six children, had survived.

An inside inspection of the old house showed that an American artillery shell, probably a 105 mm projectile with a delayed fuse, had been fired from a position in nearby Lorraine, smashed part of the sandstone rim of a window and part of the thick outer wall on the second floor, and then exploded right in the middle of the building, creating considerable damage between the first and the second stories. There was a gaping hole in our first floor living room, and greater damage to several rooms on the second floor that had since the beginning of the war, when my grandmother moved to Bad Bertrich, been rented out. All in all, the building had withstood the blast well, there did not seem to be any structural damage. Any American house of similar size, and constructed with a wood frame, could not have withstood an explosion so deep in its innards. It would likely have totally collapsed. But the Schmidt mansion, by then more than 70 years old, was built like a fortress, and it was none the worse.

Within an hour I had begun removing the debris first from our living room and then from the hallway. The kitchen was totally undamaged and had even all its windows intact. The upstairs bedrooms, however, needed to be shored up so that when it rained the water did not seep in as long as the window panes could not be replaced. Once this was done, I began immediately and in the following days to use wooden braces, tar paper and cardboard to close the gaping hole in the living room ceiling. I did this well enough for it to last for the rest of the year.

Then I settled down to wait for the rest of my family, of whom I had not heard anything for more than half a year.

The first to arrive, exactly a month after my homecoming, was brother Richard. He had escaped from Yugoslav partisans on the Balkan peninsula, and had been careful not to be captured by the Allies. An additional two weeks later, my mother arrived with my sister and the three little boys from Northern Germany. And finally, in the middle of August of 1945, our father walked into the house in his dilapidated Army uniform, skinny and sick from maltreatment. As I had predicted earlier in the year, all our family had survived the fighting, and we were able to face the difficult times that lie ahead together. A new life lay before us.

Amazingly, our house seemed not to have been plundered on a large scale. Later, my mother lamented forever the loss of some comforters, suspecting a neighbor woman who might have taken them, and I personally regretted the loss of all of our antique weapons (muzzle loaders, sabers, uniforms and the like,) and similar ancient paraphernalia that had been hidden in Richard's and my bedroom. But all the fine dishes and linens, and other beautiful things that filled my mother's china cabinet seemed to be still in their place even though the china cabinet showed some damage from shrapnel of the artillery shell.

As far as plundering was concerned, be it by German civilians, French civilians from across the border, or American soldiers, Luisenthal had been extremely lucky. The fact that the Luisenthal bridge, then only 8 years old, had been dynamited by German engineers in the first week of December of 1944 made it impossible for thieves from Lorraine to cross the Saar river and steal everything from unoccupied houses that was not nailed down..On the other side of the river, in Ottenhausen, Klarenthal, Gersweiler, Fenne, Fürstenhausen and the other towns in that stretch of the Saarland, many evacuees found their homes cleaned out of everything moveable. Houses in the evacuation zone on our side of the Saar however, but closer to the area where the population had remained at home throughout the nearly four months while my homeland had been a battle zone, fared better. Except in rare instances there was no wholesale thievery. The behavior of American troops depended very much on the attitude of their officers. Some units acted like marauders from the Thirty Years' War, others had a strict discipline similar to that existing in *Wehrmacht* and Waffen-SS. Professional thieves among the Americans obviously had an eye on houses in upscale neighborhoods where the best booty could be found, and in both Saarbrücken and Völklingen the pickings in this regard where far better than in gray, dirty and dark Luisenthal, a little industrial suburb overshadowed by its numerous smokestacks and the elevator towers of the coal mine.

The day following my homecoming I ventured outside, taking care to have my American discharge papers with me at all times for fear of being picked up again as a POW. The weather was nice as I walked the familiar streets. But something was eerily unfamiliar. Then it dawned on me: Although I had grown up in this village, I had never, ever before seen it with an azure blue sky unsullied by smoke and smog from the hundreds of smokestacks and furnaces in the area. It must also have rained some days before, and the streets were clean of soot and grime. And, except for an occasional vehicle of the U.S. Army racing through along the old Kaiser Strasse, nary a soul was to be seen in all of Luisenthal. I must have been one of the first couple of hundred people to return. Most of the inhabitants were still stuck in the center of Germany, whereto they had been evacuated in the previous December, and the Allies were very reluctant to provide travel papers to German civilians who had been displaced by the war.

It was also nice to be walking the streets without fear of being shot at by American *Jabos*, and without having to expect an air raid alarm. Peace had arrived. Now the time for rebuilding and contemplation was here.

Sommer and fall 1945, life begins anew in the ruins of Saarbrücken and the other destroyed cities and villages in Germany. Here we can see one of the bridges spanning the Saar river. It had been dynamited, probably by German troops, and is as yet only fixed with a temporary span. Before the war this had been one of the most beautiful spots of the city, the picture having been taken from the former veranda of a famous Café that once occupied this spot. In the background are some of the houses of *Alt-Saarbrücken,* the district that was nearly 100 percent destroyed. Note the small steam engine on the bridge, these locomotives were then extensively used for the removal of the debris from the extensive ruins, and to pull the electric trams since almost all the electrical overhead wires had been stolen because of their metal.

EPILOGUE

Considering the long time span during which our town had been within reach of the U.S. artillery, and comparing it to the tremendous American artillery barrages I had experienced in the Battle of the Bulge, the war damage to Luisenthal was relatively light. Out of several hundred buildings in the town, perhaps fewer than 10 had been totally destroyed, among them the post office, the combined store and apartment building belonging to our family next door to the post office, and a few other homes. The railroad station showed considerable damage but was usable. None of the industrial buildings were destroyed. In the nearby city of Völklingen, with the huge steel mill, the situation was similar: the iron works were kept busy until the American troops were within shooting range, or even longer, and I know of no attempt to destroy the plant. Civilian human losses in Luisenthal were also not great, I doubt that they exceeded more than 20 out of a population of 2,000. The death toll of soldiers could in 1945 only be guessed at. But I do know that ours was the only family with three (or more) men in the services where every soldier eventually came home.

Contrary to what I had experienced in the Lambach stockade only a week earlier, I was not hungry when I got home because the Americans who had transported us into the Saarland had fed us well. In addition, I had been able to fill my knapsack with bread thrown to us by the good women in Kaiserslautern. And I had my gas mask container nearly filled with the dried peas from the Lambach stockade. During an inspection of our cellar, where my mother had kept all the canned goods, I did not discover much of anything to eat. Even the big earthenware container in which the sauerkraut was kept was empty. I surmised that during the months while the area was officially evacuated, some people had remained there against orders, and that they had systematically searched all the houses for edibles since, obviously, no grocery was open in the deserted towns. The real hunger times for all of the Saarlanders would come later, in 1946 and 1947, when the French government tried to starve the population into submission in order to reach the goal, namely annexation to France, that was thwarted by the 1935 plebiscite.

In spite of the immediate postwar chaos all around me, I was, in June of 1945, not worried about the food situation. We had two large gardens, one in front of the house and another one in the back of the now ruined apartment building a few hundred yards down the main street, and although nothing was newly planted in the spring of that year, there were fruits and vegetables I could harvest as the summer approached. Problems arose with other things that I had not counted on. For instance, there was no water, gas and electricity. Not having candles, flashlights or other fixtures to provide light with, I had no choice but to go to bed early in the evening (after I had removed "a ton" of plaster, dirt and dust from beds and bedrooms). The water problem was solved when older Luisenthalers returned from evacuation (they trickled back on a daily basis now) and someone remembered an ancient cistern in the garden of the neighbors that had been covered ages ago. Removing the cover we found that the water inside was clean and of excellent quality. Under normal circumstances there would have been no problem with the cooking: At the time all houses still had coal and wood-fired kitchen stoves which in turn were connected to the chimneys without which no house then existing had been built.

Due to the fact that Luisenthal had a large coal mine we also had sufficient fuel - - - even if one had to steal the coal from the mine property. Having some food, water and the coal in place, however, one still needed to light a stove, oven or furnace, and that was difficult without matches. I had neither matches nor a cigarette lighter, and I was certainly not in the mood to twirl wooden sticks until they glowed, as we had learned in the Hitler Youth. There were days when I got up especially early in the morning, long before six o'clock, to ask a smoking miner on his way to work - - the coal mine was preparing to reopen - - to light a piece of paper I had brought out. Then I ran quickly into the house and hoped that one try at lighting the kitchen stove would do the trick. Another time, an American tank with engine troubles had been forced to halt just around the corner, and the American soldiers aboard did not only give me a light but also a whole packet of matches. Incidentally, the tank was of a new and better kind than the many "Shermans" I had seen in action in the Battle of the Bulge haad been. It was probably a M47 "Pershing" tank, a behemoth the size of our Panther. Some of these M47s still saw action in the last months of World War II. When I asked the GIs whether I could look inside their tank, they absolutely refused, but I couldn't help telling them that our Panther tanks were better. (A year later I stood on a platform of the Saarbrücken station when a train loaded with Panthers now belonging to the French Army made its way east. Ironically, a number of the French soldiers I spoke to had served in the German Armed Forces during the war, some of them even in the Waffen-SS. They had been inhabitants of Alsace-Lorraine who had been drafted by the Germans, and were now draftees of the French.)

The Americans arriving in Germany now were new recruits fresh from the United States, and as a rule not much older than myself. Still, they were all interested in war souvenirs, particularly in items showing the swastika. This enabled me to overcome the fact that there was still no store open where I could purchase, with the few marks I had, some of the necessities such as soap, tooth paste, salt and pepper, items I was in desperate need of. I quickly discovered that I was able to trade with the Americans almost anything I could find in the house with the swastika on it, be it a Hitler Youth arm band, a "Nazi" badge of one kind or other, or a booklet or magazine with many pictures of Hitler and his entourage.

Ironically, throughout the first few weeks after my homecoming, and possibly even as long as a month thereafter, a slightly damaged German *Sturmgewehr 44* (assault rifle), the very weapon after which the Russian Kalashnikov 47 was modeled, hung within plain sight of everyone on the corner of our wooden fence facing the main road. Knowing how trigger happy the Americans were, and having read the threats in their proclamations to the German population, I couldn't afford to touch the thing.

The restrictions and demands that were imposed on us by the Allies were far worse than the restrictions, for instance, the Frenchmen, the Hungarians and the Belgians had had to deal with under the German occupation. (I am mentioning only these because I had personal knowledge regarding these countries.) There was, for instance, the order, given with the warning of severe punishment if disobeyed, of turning in all radios, cameras, weapons (including museum pieces from Napoleonic times and before), and gold and silver. Certainly, it was promised that these things were going to be returned to their rightful owners once martial laws were lifted, but to the best of my knowledge, nobody ever got anything back once it was turned in to the occupiers. Particularly bothersome were the severe hours of curfew, coupled with the threat of being shot if caught outside of the designated (short) hours, and, among many others things, the order that any kitchen knife longer than 9" (15cm) was considered a weapon, the ownership of which might lead to execution. (I doubt that such an execution was ever carried out but it shows to what extraordinary lengths the Allies went to avoid that which they themselves had inflicted on Germany during the war, namely, unrestricted partisan warfare ("unrestricted terror warfare"!). The law about the kitchen knives was part of the occupation statutes of Berlin until the city was reunited after the fall of the Berlin Wall in 1990.

In their proclamations to us, the Allies threatened to shoot far more German hostages than were allowed under the then generally accepted Laws of War, should one of their soldiers come to harm at the hands of German underground fighters. The Americans went as high as 25 German hostages to be shot if a GI was killed by a German partisan movement, while in my archives I have a French order to the effect that 50 Germans would be executed for every French soldier killed. This latter order is especially galling (no pun intended) because just about that time a French General allowed the greatest mass rape to occur on the Western front when he permitted his soldiers to rape the women of Stuttgart. It may well be that German men were supposed to be made helpless and defenseless while their wives and daughters were ravished.

There is also the story of the death in a combat zone of the American Maj. Gen. Maurice Rose, ("the son of a rabbi",) a divisional commander, who was killed in northwest Germany in early April of 1945. It seems that German civilians had hung white flags of surrender out of their windows without consulting with the scattering of German troops still fighting in the area. Rose, thinking that the town was secured, ventured too far out, and was killed. The result was that well over a hundred Germans, including prisoners of war, lost their lives in revenge shootings by American troops.

In touching on the matter of the execution of hostages, I must mention the current (2001) incarceration in Italy of the former

Waffen-SS Captain Erich Priebke (now age 88) who was with the German security forces in Rome when Communist Italian partisans murdered approximately 40 German soldiers during a terrorist attack. As a result, 335 Italian hostages were executed at the ratio of 1:10 on direct orders from Hitler. Priebke himself shot two of them. The execution was legal under the *international* laws of war then existing, but fifty years after the incident Captain Priebke was illegally taken from Argentina, where he and his family lived, to Italy, where at first he was acquitted by a military court but then, due to Jewish pressure (there had been seventeen Jewish underground fighters among the executed hostages), he was sentenced to life-imprisonment. The executed hostages had been taken from Rome jails. Most or all were *not* innocent bystanders of the great war conflagration then affecting every sphere of life. During the time the Priebke trial was held, an older Jewish woman in Rome lamented publicly that as a result of the execution of the hostages the anti-German partisan movement in the Italian capital was left without leadership, never to recover from this devastation.

While I enjoyed being home and at the same time anticipating the return of the rest our family to Luisenthal, my comrades from the *Leibstandarte* did not fare so well. Just as the Waffen-SS was generally separated from the other "ordinary" German POWs, so were the soldiers of the LAH separated from the other Waffen-SS POWs, and at first brought to the former concentration camp of Dachau where the U.S. Army had a preliminary team investigating the so-called "Malmedy Massacre". At the time I had obviously not the slightest inkling about these happenings since the Allies were very careful that the German people were kept in the dark about their criminal activities. For this reason I also did not know of the extent of the *Vertreibung*, namely, the expulsion from their ancestral homes in the true East Germany and in Eastern European countries of up to 18 million Germans, about 3 million who lost their lives in the process, until I arrived in the United States in 1949. To this day no one has been called to account for this greatest "ethnic cleansing" in history.

The fact that the Americans had almost everywhere replaced the regular and able German administrators with Communists just returning from the concentration camps proved of benefit to me. You may remember my assurance given the Americans in Bamberg that I was going to work in the coal mines, and I believe a notice to that effect was attached to the papers that the GIs had with them when we entered the Saarbrücken City Hall on the 7th of June. For a week or two I was actually expecting to hear from the new German rulers, the former concentration camp inmates and returned emigrants now presiding over the Saarland, but nothing happened. I assume most of these guys were so busy feathering their own nest that they forgot to do what was really necessary in order to get things moving again.

Most Communists I have met in my life were not well educated, and the Marxist dogmas had probably clouded their minds. Real work, including that in an office, was usually not their forte. Invariably, the first German administrators placed in charge of the cities by the U.S. forces did not stay long in office. Corruption and thievery was rampant among these people, many ended up being incarcerated again. Perhaps the best-known of these types of crooks was a Bavarian Commissioner named Auerbach, a Jewish war survivor (the word "holocaust" had not yet been appropriated for its present usage,) who was the person responsible for having the sign with "238,000 people murdered here" placed at the Dachau concentration camp. The sign remained for about 15 years after the war, and its message was not to be questioned under penalties of law.) Auerbach enriched himself with millions of marks that did not belong to him and he subsequently ended up in jail again. It was in context with such occurrences that General Patton preferred efficient, well trained German administrators, even if most of them had been "Nazis", to remain at their posts. Unfortunately, this wise and natural decision by this American General is still being held against him to this day. Patton's actions obviously ran counter to the long-term plans for Germany that emanated from New York, Washington, London, and later, Tel Aviv.)

It was truly amazing that I had managed to get home from the war so soon. Luisenthal and the surrounding area was still empty of most of its population, and in the first few weeks I did not meet anybody whom I knew who had been a German soldier and was now discharged. I might have been the first returned soldier in our town.

As mentioned before, exactly a month after my return Richard suddenly stood before me; haggard and hungry, but healthy. He did not seem surprised to see me home already. I kidded him a lot that he had needed a month longer than I to cover the same 600 mile stretch from Austria to the Saarland. By nature being much more cautious than I am, Richard had avoided all contacts with Allied soldiers until he was in Luisenthal. As a result, he needed French POW discharge papers when they replaced the Americans as occupation soldiers of the Saar area in Mid-July, and thus he had to go to work in the coal mine for some time against his will. But first, we both continued working together in making the house livable again, and we also saw to it that some fresh food, for instance potatoes, vegetables and fruits, were in the house when the rest of the family got home.

We did not have to wait long. Perhaps two weeks after Richard's arrival, and soon after the railroad had resumed operation, I was just standing in the kitchen when Manfred, my then eight-year-old brother, came running into the room. He was almost out of breath running all the way from the railroad station where, he told me, our mother and sister were just loading their possession on a hand wagon they had with them. I almost didn't recognize Manfred, and soon the others also: from sitting on an open railroad car right behind the soot-spewing steam engine for part of their long trip the entire family, including the baby Siegfried, looked as if they were refugees from Africa, they were that black. It had taken my mother, my sister and the three boys two weeks to get back home, using any sort of transportation that was available. I was glad that I had been able to scrounge some nice-smelling soap from GIs, and with that we got everybody clean again. Little Harald told me that near Frankfurt kindly black soldiers of the U.S. Army had given them bananas to eat, a fruit the boys hardly remembered.

A week after Richard's arrival the Americans had quietly left the Saarland and other areas, for instance Central Germany, which they had conquered but which according to the Yalta and Potsdam agreements now became part of the French, respectively Russian zones. I looked with misgivings at the arrival of the French. Because they had been beaten so decisively by the Germans in 1940, it was to be expected that they were going to play the victorious conquerors this time around, even if they wore, as a rule, American uniforms and drove American tanks and other vehicles. In the following two years I should not be disappointed.

While the Americans were still in Luisenthal and surroundings, all able-bodied men had to do one day a week of unpaid "*Pflichtarbeit*", work for the victors. It consisted of doing almost any chores the Americans didn't want to do themselves or which they thought was too dangerous for them. Once they had a few of us clear our weapons and ammunition from the many *Westwall* bunkers (pill boxes) dotting the area. I remember taking an undamaged MG-42 out of a bunker and throwing it on a truck full of other war material, but leaving all explosives in the little fortress just in case it was needed some time in the future. I knew the American soldiers supervising us would be afraid to go inside the bunkers for inspection since they feared everything was booby-trapped. Another time I discovered a mountain of Third Reich uniforms (from the Armed Forces, Party, Hitler Youth and other organizations) being readied for destruction by burning in an American military warehouse in Völklingen. I regretted not having had the opportunity to remove the Iron Crosses and other decorations from these uniforms before the flames reached them. I assume the GIs of this unit had already enough of these things, or they were more interested in the beautiful private weapons, cameras and fine silverware and cutlery the population had also been ordered to turn in under threat of severe punishment for disobeyance.

The German occupation soldiers that were in Norway, among them my father, struck their colors at the beginning of May with the rest of the *Wehrmacht.* My father thus became a captive of the British. It was obviously the intention of the victors to punish the entire German people by not permitting normal conditions to return too fast. This might have been the major reason for leaving millions of German POWs sitting around in prison camps and doing nothing while their families suffered from their continued absence.

Somebody among the Allies must have gotten the idea that the German POWs held in Norway could be used as slave laborers in France because they were presumably in good physical shape, having done "nothing" since 1940. The fact that the stipulations of the Geneva Conventions prohibited the transfer of POWs from one country to another for purposes of slave labor did not stop the victors.

In early August of 1945, a train carrying my father and more than a thousand other German POWs who had been stationed in Northern Europe traveled through the Saarland in the direction of coal mines of Northern France. Less than twenty miles from Luisenthal the steam engine of the train broke down, and since the Allies of East and West (but in this case not the Americans) had in the meantime stolen most of the rolling stock of the German railways, no replacement engine could be arranged for a few days. As a result, those POWs living within 50km of the stopped train received their discharge papers, and were allowed to go home. My father was one of them.

When our father, then 43 years of age, entered the house, he was only skin and bones. Three months on a starvation diet had taken its toll. I am certain that he would not have survived the (then) horrible conditions of a French POW camp.

With Saarbrücken and its suburbs having been largely (65%) destroyed, dwellings were needed for the returning evacuees and former soldiers. By law people were forced to move together, or create their own living quarters, something that was very difficilt since th French had requsitioned all buildings materials. I remember visiting a former buddy of mine from the Labor Service who lived near the slightly damaged Burbach steel works. He and his family had moved into the stables behind the ruin of their house. There they had formerly they had kept a couple of goats to supply milk during the wartime shortage. I was wondering how this family could stand the pungent smell of their new dwelling but since it was built out of bricks, it was obviously better than a difficult-to-heat wooden shack.

In Luisenthal there was not one family that did not have to provide one or more rooms to those that had been bombed-out of their homes. The Schmidt mansion that in better times habored only our family and their servants in 27 rooms, was split and and quartered, and changed inside to the point where according to my estimates 10 families were forced to live in it for a number of years after the war. This close proximity and the daily deprivations, especially of food, led to unnecessary albeit often serious frictions, even among relatives.

As the Allied administration had really begun to execute its long-range criminal aims for Germany, including, under the spurious claim of "de-Nazification," the most intensive and relentless brainwashing[33] a modern nation had ever undergone, it came to pass that every German over the age of 18 years had to fill out a questionnaire of 131 points about the individual's life, that in its insidiousness and extent puts even the long form of the annual United States IRS income tax return to shame. Without a properly executed, signed and sworn-to questionnaire that had been turned in to the "authorities," it was not possible to obtain work and receive food ration coupons. No pleading of any "Fifth Amendment" was permitted. I still remember my father slaving over the document, trying to figure out, for instance, on what date in 1938 he had taken part in a rally of the NSDAP, or what rank in one of the various NS organizations some of his cousins had been holding. Not to forget: By Allied law one also had to describe all

---

[33] The unabated brainwashing of the Germans continues to this day. Now (in 2001!) so-called laws are still in place that prohibit Germans, under severe penalty, from doubting much of the victor's depiction of history. The "Auschwitz cudgel" is used daily, without fail, by the government, the media and the educational system to convince Germans of their collective guilt for the crimes their grandfathers had allegedly committed. Tragically, young Germans, born many decades after the war, feel guilt and shame for things they cannot understand and have no way to judge.

As this is being written, plans are afoot to erect on the most important and most expensive piece of real estate in the heart of Berlin, right next to the Brandenburg gate, a huge, so-called Holocaust memorial consisting of 2,700 (!) concrete steles that are supposed to depict Jewish grave stones. Underneath the memorial, large chambers for this or that subject are planned which the visitors (German school children!) can only enter with bowed heads due to the purposely low entrances. This is to show "forever" that the Germans should feel ashamed and do penance for the mythical "Six Million" Jews who allegedly lost their lives in the war.

For Americans to understand the vicious insanity of such a brow-beating of the people of an entire nation one would have to compare it to a huge "Monument to the Genocide of the American Indians" being built at the mall in Washington on orders of the enemies of America, right between the Washington Monument and the Capitol, and if the main feature of this monument were to consist of 2,700 concrete tee-pees of various sizes that would encompass the entire area.

I realize that this Berlin Holocaust memorial will not stand for long after its completion (it will undoubtedly become a focal point of so-called anti-Semitic acts for people of many nationalities) but the fact that the construction of this monstrosity goes forth as planned proves the point I want to make.

possessions and properties, and whether one still owned precious metals like gold and silver which, naturally, had to be delivered to the victors.

MILITARY GOVERNMENT OF GERMANY

MG / PS / G / 9a
(Rev. 15 May 45)

Fragebogen

WARNING: Read the entire Fragebogen carefully before you start to fill it out. The English language will prevail if discrepancies exist between it and the German translation. Answers must be typewritten or printed clearly in block letters. Every question must be answered precisely and conscientiously and no space is to be left blank. If a question is to be answered by either "yes" or "no", print the word "yes" or "no" in the appropriate space. If the question is inapplicable, so indicate by some appropriate word or phrase such as "none" or "not applicable". Add supplementary sheets if there is not enough space in the questionaire. Omissions or false or incomplete statements are offenses against Military Government and will result in prosecution and punishment.

WARNUNG: Vor Beantwortung ist der gesamte Fragebogen sorgfältig durchzulesen. In Zweifelsfällen ist die englische Fassung maßgebend. Die Antworten müssen mit der Schreibmaschine oder in klaren Blockbuchstaben geschrieben werden. Jede Frage ist genau und gewissenhaft zu beantworten und keine Frage darf unbeantwortet gelassen werden. Das Wort „Ja" oder „Nein" ist an der jeweilig vorgesehene Stelle unbedingt einzusetzen. Falls die Frage durch „Ja" oder „Nein" nicht zu beantworten ist, so ist eine entsprechenden Antwort wie z. B. „keine" oder „nicht betreffend" zu geben. In Ermangelung von ausreichendem Platz in dem Fragebogen können Bogen angeheftet werden. Auslassungen sowie falsche oder unvollständige Angaben stellen Vergehen gegen die Verordnungen der Militärregierung dar und werden dementsprechend geahndet.

A. PERSONAL / A. Persönliche Angaben

1. List position for which you are under consideration (include agency or firm). — 2. Name (Surname). (Fore Names.) — 3. Other names which you have used or by which you have been known. — 4. Date of birth. — 5. Place of birth. — 6. Height. — 7. Weight. — 8. Color of hair. — 9. Color of eyes. — 10. Scars, marks or deformities. — 11. Present address (City, street and house number). — 12. Permanent residence (City, street and house number). — 13. Identity card type and number. — 14. Wehrpass No. — 15. Passport No. — 16. Citizenship. — 17. If a naturalized citizen, give date and place of naturalization. — 18. List any titles of nobility ever held by you or your wife or by the parents or grandparents of either of you. — 19. Religion. — 20. With what church are you affiliated? — 21. Have you ever severed your connection with any church, officially or unofficially? — 22. If so, give particulars and reason. — 23. What religious preference did you give in the census of 1939? — 24. List any crimes of which you have been convicted, giving dates, locations and nature of the crimes. —

1. Für Sie in Frage kommende Stellung: ________

2. Name ________ Zu- (Familien-) name ________ Vor- (Tauf-) name 3. Andere von Ihnen benutzte Namen oder solche, unter welchen Sie bekannt sind ________

4. Geburtsdatum ______ 5. Geburtsort ________

6. Größe ______ 7. Gewicht ______ 8. Haarfarbe ______ 9. Farbe der Augen ______

10. Narben, Geburtsmale oder Entstellungen ________

11. Gegenwärtige Anschrift ________ (Stadt, Straße und Hausnummer)

12. Ständiger Wohnsitz ________ (Stadt, Straße und Hausnummer)

13. Art der Ausweiskarte ______ Nr. ______ 14. Wehrpaß-Nr. ______ 15. Reisepaß-Nr. ______

16. Staatsangehörigkeit ______ 17. Falls naturalisierter Bürger, geben Sie Datum und Einbürgerungsort an ________

18. Aufzählung aller Ihrerseits oder seitens Ihrer Ehefrau oder ihrer beiden Großeltern innegehabten Adelstitel ________

19. Religion ______ 20. Welcher Kirche gehören Sie an? ______ 21. Haben Sie je offiziell oder inoffiziell Ihre Verbindung mit einer Kirche aufgelöst? ______ 22. Falls ja, geben Sie Einzelheiten und Gründe an ________ 23. Welche Religionsangehörigkeit haben Sie bei der Volkszählung 1939 angegeben? ______ 24. Führen Sie alle Vergehen, Übertretungen oder Verbrechen an, für welche Sie je verurteilt worden sind, mit Angaben des Datums, des Orts und der Art ________

B. SECONDARY AND HIGHER EDUCATION / B. Grundschul- und höhere Bildung

Name and Type of School (If a special Nazi school or military academy, so specify) Name und Art der Schule (Im Fall einer besonderen NS oder Militärakademie geben Sie dies an)	Location Ort	Dates of Attendance Wann besucht?	Certificate Diploma or Degree Zeugnis, Diplom oder akademischer Grad	Did Abitur permit University matriculation? Berechtigt Abitur oder Reifezeugnis zur Universitätsimmatrikulation?	Date Datum

25. List any German University Student Corps to which you have ever belonged. — 26. List (giving location and dates) any Napola, Adolph Hitler School, Nazi Leaders College or military academy in which you have ever been a teacher. — 27. Have your children ever attended any of such schools? Which ones, where and when? — 28. List (giving location and dates) any school in which you have ever been a Vertrauenslehrer (formerly) Jugendwalter).

25. Welchen deutschen Universitäts-Studentenburschenschaften haben Sie je angehört? ________

26. In welchen Napola, Adolf-Hitler-, NS-Führerschulen oder Militärakademien waren Sie Lehrer? Anzugeben mit genauer Orts-

I did not trouble myself much with the questionnaire, taking the matter rather lightly. For instance, while I did mention my service in the Hitler Youth, I saw no reason to bother the French and their new German stooges with my Waffen-SS history, since I had American discharge papers declaring me an Army private. This enabled me to resume my apprenticeship in October of 1945, and finishing this phase of my education, after passing a stringent test, in the following year.

In the spring of 1947 "the criminality" (their words, not mine!) of my Waffen-SS service did catch up with me.[34] Probably because too many of their German POW-slave laborers had died through hunger, neglect and outright murder, the French Government suddenly was in need of more Germans whom to press into unpaid labor in the coal mines in Northwestern France. One night friends with knowledge of French plans informed me surreptitiously that the French military was re-arresting all former Waffen-SS members, whether properly discharged by other Allies or not, to ship them to the Lille area for slave labor. My name was on this list! I had no choice but to immediately make good a plan which I had formed in mind for some time because I saw no chance to have a decent future in destroyed Germany: I was going to leave the Saarland and then try from a more hospitable place to emigrate overseas. At the time the Allies were still removing manufacturing machinery from Germany, and they were also still dynamiting large factories that could become a competition to their own economy in the future. The Cold War had then not yet begun, and the Germans were not yet needed as a bulwark against Communism.

I had never regretted that fate brought me to the United States. During my 52-year residence in this nation I had a rich and full life, and later events proved that my innate free spirit had a much better chance to develop here than would have been possible in still occupied Germany. Tragically, I have to state that the main impetus for keeping the German people in chains, and the legitimate German Reich impotent, came from the United States. It took me a long time to realize it, but it is that thin veneer of a ruling clique on the American "East Coast" that sees the suppression of everything

---

34 It is likely that the French military government was informed of my former Waffen-SS service by a Luisenthal mother whose son was still being held in a French POW camp so long after the cessation of the hostilities. She might have gone there with a complaint about the continuing imprisonment of her son, at the same time perhaps inadvertently blurting out that someone like Hans Schmidt, "who had been in the SS", had already been home since 1945. Can one be angry with such a woman? I can't.

When I write of the dismal treatment German POWs (and others) received from the French, I do not want to imply that all or most French bear any responsibility for these transgressions against helpless human beings. I am certain that most Frenchmen and women were not even aware of the crimes that were being committed in their name. The same holds true for Americans.

German necessary for the retention of its own inordinate power and, ultimately perhaps, for its own survival. **That is the reason why to this day World War II has not officially ended, and why so far no valid peace treaty has been signed between Germany and the United Sates**. Until such a treaty has been signed no real peace is possible either for America or for Europe, all talk about "democracy" and "human rights" notwithstanding.

In May of 1946 the French Government made the first attempt to draw the Saarlanders to its side. After having purposely starved the population into submission for a year (using all 'democractic' methods in the process), a series of French Cultural Days was announced in Saarlouis, a famous fortress city about 25 kilometers downriver from my home town. In order to get the Saarlanders to attend and make a show for the foreign press, the French Military Government arranged for special trains to bring in the visitors, and everyone who came was promised a pack of cigarettes and a free *Bratwurst* sandwich. Hearing of this, my brother Richard and I immediately got into an argument. I opted for going to Saarlouis and get the *very valuable* cigarettes and the sandwich, while he considered an attendance at the French festivities treason. I was of the opinion that, for years anyway, the Allies were going to do with Germany anyway what they wanted, whether we liked it or not. At the festivities either General De Gaulle or General Koenig spoke, and as a strong wind came up several of the French flags, badly fastened, came crashing from their poles to the ground which led to applause by the starving Germans. In later years my brother agreed with me that it was wise to get the French goodies (which they had taken from the Germans in the first place). At that time obstinacy didn't do much good.

Appendix

This is an excerpt of the report by a British historian of the terror attack on the city of Darmstadt, 11 September 1944

When the time came on 11th September for No.5 Group to mount an attack on Darmstadt, Germany, a still further improvement in the technique of 'offset bombing' had been affected, The line attack developed by Air Vice-Marshal Cochrane was specifically related to the attack on Darmstadt. In the western outskirts of the town was a large and prominent rectangular Exhibition Ground, built on a chalky subsoil, which emerged conspicuously white on reconnaissance photographs. It was this area which served as the marking point for the attack. No. 627 Squadron, who had distinguished themselves by their low-level visual marking attacks since Munich, had provided 14 pathfinder Mosquitoes both for the visual marking and for dive-bombing attacks.

At 10.25 the sirens sounded the public air-raid warning. The "Drahtfunk" service signaled "Heavy enemy bomber formations approaching from Oppenheim and Heidelberg, acute danger for Darmstadt." At 11.25 p.m. the "Fliegeralarm" was sounded. By 11.45 the first bombs were already failing. The fire-watching posts reported that there appeared to be no definite center of the attack. They were correct: The 240 Lancasters had been briefed to approach the clearly marked Exhibition Ground on two different bearings, not only was the force thus divided into two sections, but each squadron had been ordered to bomb on a different over-shoot over the marking point. The intended result was that two wide lines of attack would extend across the city in a V shape from the western marking point, taking in the whole area. In this way sticks of bombs *were* calculated to saturate the town's residential areas. Of the 240 Lancasters dispatched 234 attacked, dropping 872 tons of bombs within forty minutes, including 236,000 thermite fire bombs. and nearly two hundred 4,000 pound blockbusters. Although the left-hand line went partly astray, the operation was considered a major success and It was clear that Bomber Command would never need to return to Darmstadt.

The post-raid report drawn up *by* the town's Police President provides a documentary description of the attack: 'The raid on the night of 11th -12th September was recorded as massed and concentrated bombing. The firestorm which emerged after about one hour embraced the entire Inner City, even igniting buildings damaged only slightly by explosives. Immediate rescue operations were out of the question as the streets and squares were inaccessible. Even the external fire brigades trying to penetrate to the city center were forced back by the lack of water and by the unbearably fierce heat radiation which threatened both the men and their vehicles. The doors and windows which had been broken by explosions and decompression waves now gave access to the fires on every floor and buildings were gutted not only from the roof downwards, but from the ground floor as well.

By about 2.00 am. the fire-typhoon in the streets had exceeded hurricane force 10 or 12 and any kind of movement in the open was out of the question. The typhoon subsided only slowly towards 4.00 a.m. In consequence, the inhabitants of this area were unable to save themselves. The whole Inner City was destroyed. The devastation reached 78 percent. The British Bombing Survey estimated from photographs that 68 percent of the total built-up area was destroyed, 516 acres of a total of 745. In the old city only five buildings had escaped destruction: the prison in Rundeturm-Strasse; a tavern called "The Crown", a butcher's shop next to it; an architect's house a little further away; and the rear buildings of St. Ludwig's Catholic church. As Darmstadt had been only a second degree zone (L.S.-Ort 2. Ordnung) no expenditure was made by the Reich an air-raid bunkers. The unprotected citizens, accordingly, suffered more severely than their counterparts in Kassel, and later Brunswick. The dead were unidentifiable because of total incineration. Events had shown that whole families with all their members had been killed, whose disappearance as a result was never reported. The cause of death was in 90 per cent of the cases asphyxiation or burning.

For the first four days after the attack the recovery of the dead presented considerable difficulties, as there were no vehicles left within the town for their removal. Only with the arrival of a Transport Unit of the Speer Organization was the situation alleviated. The same scenes which had greeted the rescue troops penetrating the gutted streets of the fire-storm areas of Hamburg and Kassel now met the eyes of the rescue gangs in Darmstadt, The streets were strewn with naked, brilliantly hued corpses, or charred objects some three feet long, which looked like logs, but which had been human beings. On 24th September the Roman Catholic Bishop of Mainz celebrated a Requiem Mass for the Darmstadt citizens who had lost their lives in the forty-minute No. 5 Group attack on the town.

PS: The U.S. public was informed, a day or two later, that the British had successfully completed a major air raid on German *industrial* facilities in and near Darmstadt. No mentioning of "collateral damage" was made.
Note that the Darmstadt air raid occurred exactly 57 years to the day before the destruction of the World Trade Center in New York.

Oradour-sur-Glane

Considering the post-World War II allied propaganda (lasting to this day and camouflaged as Holocaust studies in American schools), which portrays both the concentration camp system and the "black" SS as major expressions of absolute evil, it was clear that the reputation of the Waffen-SS had to be besmirched also. Rather than explain the real reason for the fact that nearly a million young Europeans, most of them volunteers, had donned the uniform with the two lightning-bolt runes on their collar and were willing to sacrifice their lives for a higher cause, it was much easier to paint everything that had to do with the SS as criminal, and stick to this fallacy come hell or high water.

Note the following from a book jacket printed in 1988:

"On June 10, 1944, four days after the invasion of Normandy, an SS company rounded up all the men, women and children of Oradour, a remote village in southwestern France, and brutally murdered all but a handful of its almost seven hundred inhabitants."

This text is from the jacket of a book titled "Massacre at Oradour" by the English writer Robin Mackness. (Random House, N.Y., 1988)

However, another Englishman, James Lucas, wrote the following in his book "Das Reich, the military role of the 2nd SS Division" (Arms and Armour, London, 1991) about the same incident:

"It was during the Division's march to Normandy that punitive action was taken against the village of Oradour-sur-Glane. It is not my intention to discuss the actions of the French resistance in this matter nor the counteractions of the Das Reich Division. The Allies saw the men and women of the Maquis as resistance fighters determined to liberate France. Front-line soldiers see such people in a different light, as franc tireurs who commit murder and who deserve no mercy. I intend to say no more on this matter other than that a murderous attack was carried out near Oradour-sur-Glane and that this resulted in savage reprisals being taken by some units of the Division against the civil population of that village."

Not having much proof regarding real war crimes which to pin on the Waffen-SS, the enemies of Germany were desperate to find something - anything - that would enhance their past claims of SS murderous behavior. In the light of the revelations of the Katyn murders of tens of thousands of Polish officers by the Soviets (America's allies!), and the discovery, in German archives, of Stalin's 1941 order that the Soviet Secret Police should attack Ukrainian villages dressed in SS uniforms and massacre most of the inhabitants so that the population would rise against the German occupiers, anti-SS claims emanating from Moscow could not be used. This was the real reasons for the exaggerated propaganda surrounding the Malmedy and Oradour incidents.

Perhaps the most striking fact concerning the Oradour deaths is the knowledge that a French court has sealed the records of the "Oradour trial" until way into the Twenty-first Century. This trial of the mostly young SS-soldiers, many of them, by the way, French citizens from Alsace, had been held in Bordeaux in the early 1950s. It ended with long prison sentences for some of the accused, all of whom were released a long time ago. To this day all German efforts to have access to these Bordeaux files have failed, and we can be certain that the French refusal to open the documents is not based upon the desire to spare the Germans from embarrassment.

Personally, I believe what one of the former soldiers of *Das Reich* told me.

In 1944 he was in the vicinity of Oradour and was well acquainted with the details of the incident:

From April to June 1944, *Das Reich* had been stationed for rest, recuperation and replenishment in the Toulouse area north of the Pyrenees mountains in Southern France. Up to the beginning of 1944 France had been one of the safest areas in Europe to do occupation duty, but this situation drastically changed soon after the start of that year, the likely cause being orders from abroad (London!) for the French underground to become more active.

In France, as in all occupied territories, most German soldiers did not heed Hitler's orders to always carry weapons when leaving their barracks or their posts even for the most innocent foray. As the result of this naiveté, which derived from the fact that German soldiers usually got along very well with the locals, about one hundred soldiers of *Das Reich* had been murdered or kidnapped by the "heroes" of the Maquis (terrorists!) before the division embarked, by road and train, on the difficult trip to the Normandy. In doing so, *Das Reich* had to traverse the mountainous area in the surroundings of the city of Limoges where partisans were especially active.

While the division was on route to the Normandy area, the Maquis managed to ambush a German staff car in which one of the best-known battalion commanders of *Das Reich*, *Ritterkreuzträger* Major (Sturmbannführer) Helmut Kämpfe had been riding. Immediately after this beloved officer was reported missing, search parties went out but while his destroyed vehicle was discovered, there was no trace of either Kämpfe or his driver. (Their bodies were never found.) Kämpfe's men, however, discovered also a burned-out German ambulance that had been set afire, with the partisans/terrorists having made certain that both the driver of the ambulance as well as the wounded soldiers inside were burned to death: The driver had been tied to the steering wheel of his vehicle with wire.

For the Germans, all indications pointed to Oradour as a hotbed of the Maquis. Reprisals were in order. In spite of later French claims to the contrary, weapons were found hidden in houses of the village.[35] Following Hitler's orders, the men of the town were to be executed and all the houses leveled. (This sounds awfully brutal today but we can judge the entire matter only in the context of the times: In June of 1944 the Allies killed tens of thousands of *innocent* French civilians in their bombing raids on railroad junctions in their cities and other important targets, and during the previous years many German cities had been destroyed, each with civilian victims in the thousands.)

While the reprisals were being carried out, the women and children of the village had been ordered into the village church for their own safekeeping. Then the unthinkable happened: The church caught fire, and 'somehow' an inferno developed that would cost most of the women and children their lives. Young SS-soldiers tried desperately to help the people trapped in the church but not many could be saved.

The French underground maintained that the Germans had deliberately killed the women and children in the church. The soldiers of "Das Reich", on the other hand, were certain that the Maquis had hidden armaments and explosives underneath the roof and elsewhere in the church, and that it was this material that had caused the catastrophe. Knowing how German soldiers were careful not to infringe on religion, and thereby on the churches in occupied territories, it would make sense that a church would be

---

35 * Almost every French village in the Limoges area claimed after the war to have been a hotbed of resistance against the German occupiers. It was so nice to play the heroes after four years of submission. Alas, according to postwar French reports, of all the villages in the vicinity Oradour-sur-Glane was allegedly totally innocent of anti-German terrorist activities. It just shows how dumb the Germans are, always picking on the innocent.

considered a safe hiding place for contraband. Reading books about the resistance, it is noticeable how often the former members of the Maquis are boasting of having outwitted the 'stupid' Germans by hiding weapons and explosives (and escaped allied Airmen) in cloisters, churches and other religious institutions. Furthermore, if the soldiers of the division *Das Reich* were intent on killing *all* the inhabitants of Oradour, why herd the women and children inside the church in the first place? An all-out assault on the surrounded village with the intention of destroying all houses, and without permitting anybody to escape would have been simpler.

The Oradour incident has *to this day* tragic consequences in the person of Heinz Barth, a former lieutenant and platoon leader in the 3rd Company, *Panzergrenadierregiment 4,* of the *Das Reich* Division. It was his company which had received orders to search for their battalion commander in Oradour.

Toward the end of the war Barth was badly wounded and had a leg amputated. After spending some time as a prisoner of war, he returned to his home in Central Germany which in the meantime had become the East German Communist republic "DDR". There he lived under his name unmolested for 35 years until 1981 when the DDR Communist regime needed some publicity to get in good graces with the Western news media and certain behind-the-scenes powers in New York. Barth was arrested and in Communist fashion "interrogated" because of his involvement in the Oradour reprisals. After two years he was ready to confess anything, and thus the outcome of his trial in 1983 war a foregone conclusion: The German Bolshevists gave him a life sentence. Former Waffen-SS soldiers read Barth's confessions with wonderment: he had admitted to deeds that, under the circumstances and according to his rank and position, simply could not have happened.

Everyone hoped that Heinz Barth, like tens of thousands of other political prisoners in the "German Democratic Republic" would be freed immediately after the reunification of Germany in 1990. Alas, this was not to be. Instead of freeing the invalid, the rulers of the new Germany added five years to Barth's sentence, and kept him in prison.

Finally, in 1997, after 16 years of imprisonment, Barth, now nearly 80 years of age, was permitted to go home but not before the "authorities" had, as a result of international Jewish pressure, canceled the small pension which was due him because of the serious injuries he had sustained during the war. It is said that Barth was only freed after former German soldiers went to bat for him, and there are also indications that the Paris government acted in his behalf: all French legal actions concerning Oradour had ended twenty years before Barth's arrest by the Communists. His name had never come up during the 1953 trial in Bordeaux.

A Bridge too far

Perhaps the best and, oddly enough, least known example of the true chivalrous spirit of the Waffen-SS was the local armistice that permitted the evacuation of thousands of Allied wounded soldiers during operation Market Garden, part of which was the assault on the bridge at Arnhem in Holland ("A bridge too far"). This happened in September of 1944.

The following is an excerpt from the large pictorial "*Wenn alle Brüder schweigen*" - (When all brothers remain silent.) that was published by Waffen-SS veterans in 1973:

"*The situation of the encircled Allied soldiers near Arnhem was desperate, and the British commander, General Urquhart, informed his superiors in London of this fact by radio telephone. In the meantime, the Germans had broken the Allied code, and were listening in. Thus the higher SS-officers in charge, among them the commander of the 9th SS-Panzerdivision Hohenstaufen, Colonel Harzer, discovered that several thousand wounded British soldiers were without proper care and medicine. Thereupon Dr. Egon Skalka, the chief medical officer of the "Hohenstaufen", was ordered by Col. Harzer to contact the British medical corps, and offer his assistance.*

On the enemy side of the front, the chief medical officer of the British forces, Col. Warrack, was expecting Dr. Skalka as the latter arrived in a captured Jeep that flew the Red Cross flag. The wounded Allied soldiers were operated on at the Tafelsberg Hotel. The British Chief surgeon made the decision which of his severely wounded men he was going to turn over to the Waffen-SS for better treatment. For several days, hundreds of badly wounded Allied soldiers were thus turned over to the medical corps of the Hohenstaufen division for further medical attention.

During these battles 'for the bridge too far', altogether about 2,000 wounded Allied soldiers were given into the care of the Waffen-SS doctors and medics. In addition, the Waffen-SS sent British wounded who did not want to remain in German captivity back into the encirclement to their comrades whenever a load of bandages and other medicinal needs was taken to the British doctors.

Eventually, after seven days of hard fighting, all the British forces in this sector of the front had to capitulate."

Wounded British paratroopers of *Operation Market Garden* standing next to a Waffen-SS *Sturmgeschütz III* . Note the relaxed atmosphere even though this is still in the combat area. How would American soldiers act now under similar circumstances with - perhaps - Taliban POWs nearby?

In the book "Steel Inferno" (Sarpedon, New York, 1997) about the summer 1944 battles of the First SS Panzer Corps, namely, the LAH and the *Hitlerjugend* divisions, in the Normandy, written by the British General Michael Reynolds, I found the following paragraphs:

"The officers and men of the Leibstandarte and Hitlerjugend Divisions were indeed extraordinary men - considered heroes and revered by some, judged as criminals and reviled by others. Not all of them acted bravely - there were plenty of examples of terrified youngsters surrendering to Allied soldiers. But they can as a whole be equated to the men of Caesar's finest Legions and to

Napoleon's Old Guard. They have also been compared to Ghengis Kahn's scourging hordes and Attila's invading Huns! But whatever else they were, they were remarkable soldiers - the like of which we may never see again."

And, *"The willingness of the members of the Waffen-SS to go on fighting when it was clear that the war was lost can only be a source of wonder to today's generation. However, their experiences in the East undoubtedly added to their resolve to protect their homeland for as long as possible and at whatever cost.*

"The fact that these men were part of the elite organization which was stamped with their charismatic leader's own name was an important influence on their outlook. But attractive uniforms, fine weapons, abundant quantities of meaningful medals worn even in battle to single out the proven brave, a string emphasis on comradeship - these were all factors which played a part in making these men unique. Perhaps, though, the most significant thing which singled out the men of these Divisions was their obvious pride in being soldiers. It is strange that in postwar years the former Allies have spent so much time criticizing each other's performances in WWII but admiring that of their enemy - particularly the Waffen-SS. At the end of the day it has to be said that the soldiers of the First SS Panzer Corps excelled in what is still, in some circles, called The Art of War."

In retrospect I can only state I am proud to have served in the Waffen-SS during World War II. Like most of my comrades I had to suffer because of it, once the shooting had stopped. In the final analysis, however, I have to agree with Rudolf Hess, a true martyr for the German cause, who said that if he had to live his life over again, there was little he would do differently.

To those of the "now' generation who would like to hear regrets, or "mea culpas" from me, I can only say that I may be wrong and that surely I will not toe the current line of political correctness, but as a human being I have a right to defend both the country of my birth and the ideals for which we had fought. Only the future will prove whether the cause of the victors or that of the vanquished was the right one.

EISENHOWER'S DEATH CAMPS, again

These are personal experiences of a friend of mine, a former German soldier who was held at the Remagen POW camp and elsewhere, at the time of the German defeat in the spring of 1945. A man for whose honesty and integrity I can vouch:

by Walter M.

"I was a soldier in the German 338th Infantry Division doing occupation duty in France from January 1942 to the Summer of 1944. For most of this time we were stationed at Arles, in the South of France, where we had an excellent rapport with the population, and where there was very little partisan activity. Since our division had been stationed in one place for a long time, our transport equipment was very limited, consisting mainly of horse-drawn wagons and captured vehicles. It took the 11th Panzer Division to guide us through the partisan-infested mountains near Grenoble and Lyon, when, after the invasion, Southern France had to be abandoned by the German Armed Forces. Only once, when we crossed the river Drome (a tributary of the Rhone), did we come under fire from American artillery. Eventually, we went across the Rhine near Freiburg, and from there we were transported by rail to Düsseldorf in the Ruhr area. Arriving at our destination, our train was attacked by Allied fighter bombers, resulting in the loss of most of our equipment.

"By April 4, 1945, the German Army Group B, to which we belonged, was trapped in the Ruhr pocket. The chief of our battery (I was with the field artillery) thereupon told us that we had the choice of either trying to get home, or go into American captivity. Since my home town in the Eastern part of the Reich was by then within range of the Red Army, I chose the latter. Although the war was going to last for another month, we disarmed ourselves by smashing our rifles, discarding other weaponry, and surrendered to the first Americans we saw. After some confusion as the result of the unclear battle situation, we were taken to a factory, where we spent the first night in captivity. The next morning an American soldier spoke to us in German from atop a vehicle,

explaining that all weapons, including pocket knives, had to be turned in, or else we were subject to execution.

"The same day we were loaded aboard trucks and driven across the Rhine, where on the so-called Rheinwiesen (the Rhine meadows) near Remagen there was a huge barbed wire enclosure holding thousands upon thousands of German prisoners like cattle, ie. absolutely without any provisions for their personal needs. Incidentally, when we crossed the Rhine river, young German women and girls on the other side showered us with flowers. At the Remagen camp we had no shelter of any kind, in spite of the cold spring weather, and hardly any food and water for many months. Since we had no equipment like spades, we dug holes into the ground with our spoons. But soon it started to rain, and the grounds of the camp became one huge quagmire. Among the prisoners were amputees, very old men and many young boys. Officers were separated from their soldiers (resulting in a loss of discipline). For weeks it rained. The starvation diet reduced most of us to skeletons. The death toll rose accordingly. German civilians from nearby towns were not allowed to aid us.

"Near the camp entrance there was a large tent, the sick bay, from which every day a number of corpses were taken away. Also, daily some push carts went through the masses of prisoners to pick up the dead of the previous night. In their desperation many of the POWs ate grass and insects. Some of the GI guards did a brisk business bartering watches and rings from the prisoners. Most of the Americans looked like us, except for the different uniforms, and we felt no animosity toward them, believing that the lack of food and shelter was the result of the huge numbers of POWs in the camp. I remember listening to a Waffen-SS soldier from the Leibstandarte who told of being brutally interrogated by "inquisitors" who knocked out many of his teeth. The most cruel interrogations were done in a group of small tents by Americans that did not seem to belong to the unit guarding us. One of them, who had no insignia of rank on his uniform, was named Cohen, and spoke fluent German. He acted as the interpreter for American officers. Cohen (and others like him) had surrounded themselves with young, good-looking German boys who received special favors, and were allowed to treat us with disdain.

"Since I was fairly fluent in English, I was soon able to apply for the job as an interpreter, and had the opportunity to get out of the camp working on a construction job. As a rule, the individual GIs with whom I came in contact were fair and treated us well. This was also true of the American soldiers at another camp to which I was eventually transferred. In the middle of July 1945, the American, British, French and Russian armies moved to their permanent occupation zones. The camp I was in became part of the French zone, and soon we were guarded by French troops, although I personally was still assigned to the Americans. One day a French guard told us that if one of us ran away, two others would be shot. The US sergeant thereupon told me to tell the French that HE would then shoot four Frenchmen in return. Eventually, we were moved to a camp near Andernach, walking on foot. German civilians threw slices of bread to us, and many women cried when they saw us in our emaciated shape, and how sometimes five prisoners fought amongst each other for a single piece of bread.

"One day, at Andernach, we saw a column of tall skeletons marching toward us. They were a group of emaciated young Waffen-SS soldiers who in mock fashion had to carry some kind of banner, like an SS flag, in front of them, as if they were on parade. They were guarded, every two yards, by short Frenchmen carrying rubber truncheons. In the town all windows were closed, and nobody was allowed on the street. Behind the column drove several trucks loaded with corpses of dead POWs.

"Once the Russians had occupied "their" part of Germany, all discharges to that area were stopped. That meant I could not return home. As a result, most of us were shipped to France for slave labor. The transport took place in open-top freight wagons. Inside France people threw rocks at us from overpasses. I also heard that they emptied their chamber pots (human waste) on inmates of other trains. When we arrived in Epinal, we were again frisked, and everything of value "removed". I still had a raw potato, and ate it before someone took it. Our final destination was a camp near Luneville. There we heard that soldiers of the Waffen-SS had been forced to work in the icy river until veterans of the French Army protested and were able to put a stop to this cruelty.

"At Luneville the starvation diet continued. Our daily meal consisted of a bowl of watery soup and one slice of bread. Every day someone died. We were so weak that it took six men to carry an emaciated corpse in a wooden box. In addition, an extra one or two teams went along to relieve the others when they couldn't carry on. Soon well-nourished and well-clothed German POWs who had been held in camps in the United States arrived at Luneville (and other camps in France, HS). For months they lay around doing nothing except starving, until they were reduced to our level.

"As time went by, our treatment in France improved. Most of us eventually were sent to work on French farms or in the coal mines, obviously without any payment to speak of. In 1947 we had the opportunity to sign a voluntary labor contract whereby one could exchange the POW status for one additional work-year in France under much improved conditions. I took this chance. Afterward, I never did move back to my home city of Dresden, emigrating first to Canada and finally to the United States instead."

It must be noted that Walter M. had surrendered to American troops, and that it was against the rules of the Geneva Conventions to turn him and hundreds of thousands others over to the French. It is known that great numbers of German soldiers who were taken prisoner by the Americans (mainly in North Africa), and who subsequently spent some time in camps in the continental United States, where they were generally well treated, eventually died in French captivity after having been "sold" to the Paris government by Dwight D. Eisenhower. Those who survived, and whom I could interview in France in 1948 and 1949, told of being stripped of everything (including the fairly good clothing they had brought from America), and then purposely starved, probably to break their will. Later, when the survivors were released, they were turned over to the Adenauer government which promptly confiscated the hard-earned U.S. dollars the German POWs had made by picking cotton or harvesting peanuts for pennies a day, and exchanged them at a very disadvantageous rate for (then) far less valuable German marks.

With myself having been able to get out of one of Eisenhower's stockades for illegally named "Disarmed Enemy Forces", instead of POWs, as which we would have been under the supervision of the International Red Cross, it behooves me to make a short reference to the Rules of War that had been in force in 1945, and which the United States had signed also:

- The First Geneva Convention (1864) governs the treatment of sick and wounded soldiers. The party holding them must protect and care for them. Medical personnel are to be protected.
- The Second Geneva Convention (1906) extends protection to wounded, sick and ship-wrecked combatants at sea. Hospital ships are to be protected.
- The Third Geneva Convention (1929) governs the treatment of prisoners of war. **POWs must have adequate housing, food, clothing and medical care,** and must be protected against acts of violence, insults and 'public curiosity'. POWs may not be tortured, and are required only to tell captors their name, rank and service number. This information must be transmitted to the Red Cross so that relatives of the POWs may be informed. All the signatories agree to allow Red Cross inspections of camps and other facilities. Inspections must be permitted without prior notification. In addition, the signatories assure the delivery of Red Cross packages that include certain food stuffs, toiletries and reading material.

There is no doubt that the U.S. Army transgressed, on Eisenhower's orders, against all these treaties after 1944. The excuse told by the U.S. Government that because so many Germans were captured no adequate provisions for the feeding and housing of such a large number could be made, is unacceptable. The war was over. The Germans were beaten and disarmed. Why not do what Hitler did *during the war* and shortly after the campaign in the West in 1940, when almost all Dutch and Belgian, and at least half of the French POWs, millions of men, were sent home immediately after capture?

Ninety-nine percent of the German soldiers who became POWs of the Western nations in 1945 went into captivity voluntarily, and they had no interest in fighting on. If true peace really had been a major aim of the Americans, the French and the British, they would have sent most of these former German soldiers home to their families. Unfortunately though, all Allied governments and whoever was part of them wanted to exact revenge on the defeated enemy who had held almost the entire world at bay for six long years. It is no coincidence that the most vengeful of the Allied officers were those, like Dwight D. Eisenhower, who had never really seen and experienced combat duty.

I realize that there are many defenders of Eisenhower who will ascribe this or that measure he ordered as being necessary, and, under the general circumstances prevailing at the time, even unavoidable. (This includes the capture of Berlin denied to the U.S. Army as a whole.) As someone who suffered due to Eisenhower's wrongdoing, however little, I think it best to list the chronology of the worst transgressions against human decency that prove "Ike's" guilt:

1944: General Dwight D. Eisenhower talks to the British ambassador to the United States during a visit to the American capital and it is stated that he ventured the opinion that 3,500 officers of the German General staff should be "exterminated." He also suggested that perhaps as many as 100,000 prominent Germans should be killed. To his wife Mamie he wrote: "God, I hate the Germans."

On March 10, 1945, Eisenhower sent a message to the Allied Combined Chiefs of Staff recommending a new class of prisoners called Disarmed Enemy Forces (DEFs). This policy is implemented within days of the German surrender in the first week of May. It stipulates that the German POWs thus designated do not fall under the auspices of the International Red Cross. While American POWs that fell in German hands during the war were at all times under Red Cross supervision, millions of German POWs were now at the mercy of hateful Eisenhower subordinates.

In May of 1945, the International Red Cross had over 100,000 tons of food stockpiled in Switzerland. Red Cross attempts to ship these goods to starving German POWs in camps on German soil and in France failed. The American Military Government sent trains loaded with foodstuffs back to Switzerland on Eisenhower's orders. Some of these IRC efforts are described in the book "Dunant's Dream" by Caroline Moorehead (Carroll & Graf, New York, 1999).

In 1992, two history professors at the University of New Orleans, the German-born Günter Bischof and the aforementioned Stephen E. Ambrose, felt it necessary to defend Dwight D. Eisenhower against James Baque's accusations that appeared in the book *Other Losses.* Their work *Eisenhower and the German POWs* (Louisian State Press) makes interesting reading but it does not answer the questions why, for instance, GIs like Corporal John Shoemaker were forbidden to even give opened, half-consumed cans of food to starving German POWs, and whatever happened to the bodies of *most of the* German prisoners that died in U.S. camps.

In July of 1945, after the Potsdam Conference, General Eisenhower became the military governor of the American zone of Germany. He continued to refuse entry into Germany to Red Cross assistance to the starving Germans (both POWs and the civilian population).

On July 26, 1945, almost three months after the end of the hostilities, the International Red Cross suggested the restoration of mail service to German POWs so that they could inform their families of their survival. Eisenhower, who did not want the outside world to know what was occurring in the camps under his command, refused this request, allegedly on orders from the War Department. Most families of Waffen-SS soldiers in American captivity did not find out whether their loved ones were still alive until the end of 1945, when postcards with "I am alive!" notices are finally permitted to be sent for the first time.

This should suffice to prove Dwight D. Eisenhower's culpability. The question I personally have is this: How can a man of Eisenhower's undoubted intelligence have stooped so low as to seek revenge among the ordinary soldiers of the enemy nation? Did he fall for all the propaganda nonsense his own soldiers were fed in the late years of the war? Did he not, for instance, know that the more than 1,200 dead concentration camp inmates that were so neatly laid out in the open and presented as proof of German brutality at the Nordhausen *Mittelwerk* complex had in fact been killed in an Allied air raid a few days earlier? And who had really killed those dead Jews that were still on a "death train" at the Dachau concentration camp siding when the first American soldiers entered this camp? Was their train not machine-gunned by American fighter bombers before it arrived at the camp? How many

Americans realize that the famous Eisenhower quote* that is now chiseled in stone at the U.S. Holocaust Museum in Washington, DC, had actually been written by "Ike's" press officer Colonel Bernstein, and that it was Bernstein who did not permit - for about a week - the burial of dead concentration camp inmates at the Ohrdruf camp until he had arranged a photo opportunity showing Eisenhower and Patton together in front of bloated corpses.

> * **"THE THINGS I SAW BEGGAR DESCRIPTION... THE VISUAL EVIDENCE AND THE VERBAL TESTIMONY OF STARVATION, CRUELTY AND BESTIALITY WERE SO OVERPOWERING... I MADE THE VISIT DELIBERATELY, IN ORDER TO BE IN A POSITION TO GIVE FIRST-HAND EVIDENCE OF THESE THINGS IF EVER, IN THE FUTURE, THERE DEVELOPS A TENDENCY TO CHARGE THESE ALLEGATIONS TO PROPAGANDA.**
>
> **Gen. Dwight D. Eisenhower**
> **Supreme Commander of the Allied Forces**
> **Ohrdruf Concentration Camp, April 15, 1945**

(There is a certain irony connected with this statement: How did both Bernstein and Eisenhower know that years later historical revisionists would voice their opinion that that which allegedly happened in the German realm during WWII really did not happen *as told*. Does it not look as if Bernstein and Eisenhower - and others - knew in advance that their <u>lies</u> would someday come under scrutiny? Is this also the reason why one cannot find the word "Holocaust", the gas chambers claim and the "Six million" figure in the memoirs of Eisenhower, Truman, Churchill, De Gaulle and other famous World War II leaders?)

The horrible hypocrisy of Eisenhower's statement can be proven by reading again, on page 382, the story of Walter M., the former German soldier and ex-POW who suffered in Eisenhower's death camps in the Rhineland and France. Alas, "Ike" never visited these living examples of *his* kind of "humanity".

Could Eisenhower's hate have derived from the realization that the Germans really bested him, even in defeat? Was it the envy of not belonging, and the acknowledgment that in the German *Wehrmacht* of World War II, "Ike" would never have risen above the rank of a Colonel in charge of supplies? Patton and MacArthur - - and there were others - - were both true generals that in body and spirit would have easily fitted with Rommel, Jodl, Kesselring, Model, Von Manstein and, yes, Sepp Dietrich. But "Ike"? A hero he wasn't.

In its November 1989-issue, the Canadian magazine *Saturday Night* published an article about Eisenhower's Death Camps from which the following excerpt is taken:

" Wolfgang Iff, who was imprisoned at Rheinberg and still lives in Germany, reports that in his subsection of perhaps 10,000 prisoners, thirty or forty bodies were dragged out every day. A member of the burial work party, Iff says he helped haul the dead from his cage out to the gate of the camp, where the bodies were carried by wheelbarrow to several big steel garages. There Iff and his team stripped the corpses of clothing, snapped off half of each aluminum dog tag,[36] *spread the bodies in layers of fifteen to twenty, with ten shovelfuls of quicklime over each layer till they were stacked a meter high, placed the personal effects in a bag for the American, then left. (Some of the POWs...) had grown too weak to cling to the log flung across the ditch for a latrine, and had fallen off and drowned."*

Also:

"General Patton's Third Army was the only army in the whole European theater to free significant numbers of captives (including myself, HS) *during May and June, saving many of them from possible death. Both Generals Bradley and Lee, ordered the release of prisoners within a week of war's end, but SHAFF orders signed by Eisenhower countermanded them on May 15."*

Personally I also remember when Dwight D.Eisenhower, as the President of the United States, did not permit free elections in Vietnam in or about 1954, because most of the Vietnamese would have elected Ho Chi Min, a self-acknowledged Communist, as their leader. The result was the Vietnam war that cost so many Vietnamese and American lives unnecessarily.

The great interest in the exploits of the Waffen-SS by many citizens of the victor nations shows the way into the future. While

---

[36] By international agreement the U.S. Army was supposed to keep track of the names, rank and last place of domicile of dead POWs, and to turn the dog tag halves along with this information over to the International Red Cross. That this often was not done can be discovered in the farm fields near Bad Kreuznach where the owners of these properties are to this day finding batches of dog tag halves that had been surreptitiously discarded.

at this time in history the rulers everywhere would stamp out a re-establishment of the SS or Waffen-SS with a vengeance, it bears remembering that the same happened to the Catholic Jesuits. Soon after the founding of this order in 1534 by Ignatius of Loyola, it became both the envy and the bane of its enemies, and there were many times when in some countries it was prohibited from being active for hundreds of years. However, there is no denying that even today, after nearly 500 years, the Jesuits still play an important religious, social and political function in all the countries where they are permitted. Of all the various Catholic orders it is undoubtedly the most important one. Heinrich Himmler, a Catholic, had studied the history of the Jesuits well, and undoubtedly he emulated what he had learned in 'his' SS. I would not be surprised if Himmler eventually turns out to have been the German (Aryan) Ignatius of Loyola.

As I was writing these memoirs, and made parts of them available to a wider circle of friends, the question was often asked, how is it possible for someone to have so many details imprinted in one's mind after the passage of more than half a century.

The best explanation is simply that war, and especially combat, proves a unique experience. Particularly the infantryman is often for days, and 24 hours a day, both the hunter and the hunted, and he has to develop an awareness that can be rarely found in civilian life. Perhaps the best example would be to ask a "normal" person, years after he or she had survived a horrific accident in a car or plane crash, how it was "then," and it is surprising to note how detailed the person's description can be. Well, the experiences of war often force a soldier to be in that state of ultra-awareness, often combined with fear, for days on end, and therefore details are being imprinted in his mind that would under normal circumstances vanish in the deep recesses of memory.

However, it is also true that a healthy mind has the mechanism to wipe out, so to say, occurrences that were simply too horrific for retention. Thus, for instance, no matter how hard I tried there is very little memory left of a week of close combat in Austria toward the end of the war. Even in retrospect is obvious, looking at the known dates, that I could not have slept through the entire engagement.

In our daily lives one thought leads to another. This is also true for our war reminiscences. Once we begin delving into our memory, things come back to life that we hadn't thought about for years or decades. In my own case it helps that already as a small child I seemed to have had a memory that was better than that of my play- and school mates. When I was about nine years old, for instance, someone could ask me not only the place but also the exact dates when and where I was three years earlier, when I was just six and sent to what Americans would call summer camp. Having possessed this aptitude probably through my genetic inheritance, I never gave it a thought, but years later, as a teenager, I was surprised to discover that not everybody was like that.

Also, besides having an excellent memory, I have always been an inveterate collector of things, and keeper of both documents and even hastily written notes. Things that came in handy as I embarked on the writing of these wartime memoirs. Whenever and wherever necessary, I checked my statements in the great number of books pertaining to World War II that can be found in my personal library.

Finally it deserves mentioning that in postwar Germany an unusually high percentage of former Waffen-SS soldiers (officers and enlistend men) rose to the tops of their professions. In my opinion, this was undoubtedly the result of the excellent training in the Waffen-SS, whereby private initiative, integrity and personal responsibility - - and not any sort of "hate" - - had been promoted.

Index